Migration Processes and Patterns

Volume 2

Migration Processes and Patterns

Volume 2

Population Redistribution in the United Kingdom

Edited by

John Stillwell, Philip Rees and Peter Boden

Belhaven Press
London and New York

© Editors and contributors, 1992

First published in Great Britain in 1992 by
Belhaven Press (a division of Pinter Publishers Limited)
25 Floral Street, London WC2E 9DS

British Library Cataloguing in Publication Data

A CIP catalogue record for this book is available from the
British Library

ISBN 1 85293 194 9

For enquiries in North America please contact
PO Box 197, Irvington, NY 10533

Library of Congress Cataloging in Publication Data

Migration processes and patterns.
  p. cm.
  Includes bibliographical references and indexes.
  Contents: v. 1. Research progress and prospects/edited by Tony
Champion and Tony Fielding – v. 2. Population redistribution in the
United Kingdom/edited by John Stillwell, Philip Rees, and Peter
Boden.
  ISBN 1–85293–193–0 (v. 1: hardback): –
ISBN 1–85293–194–9 (v. 2: hardback):
  1. Migration. Internal – Great Britain. 2. Great Britain – Economic
conditions – 1945–   . – Regional disparities.   I. Champion, A.G.
(Anthony Gerard)
HB2043.M555   1992
304.8′0941–dc20   91–34230
                                                                CIP

Typeset by Mayhew Typesetting, Rhayader, Powys
Printed and bound in Great Britain by Biddles Ltd, Guildford and King's Lynn

Contents

List of figures

List of tables

LIST OF TABLES

List of contributors

Peter Boden is currently General Operations Manager of GMAP Ltd, a commercial subsidiary of the University of Leeds. He is also Honorary Research Fellow in the University's School of Geography. He has maintained an active research interest in internal migration in the UK following on from his PhD which examined the value of the Census and National Health Service Central Register as alternative sources of information for migration analysis and population projection.

Paul Boyle has recently completed his postgraduate study in the Geography Department at Lancaster University. He is now Lecturer in the Department of Geography at the University College of Swansea. His PhD focused on studying human migration processes at the local level using quantitative modelling techniques. He also has interests in the field of geographical information systems, with particular emphasis on methods of representing and estimating populations.

Tony Champion is Senior Lecturer in Geography at the University of Newcastle upon Tyne. His current research interests lie principally in population and social geography, particularly in the redistribution of population between larger cities and more rural areas. He acted as chairman of the IBG Working Party on Migration in Britain. Recent publications include *Contemporary Britain: A Geographical Perspective* (co-authored with Alan Townsend) and *People in the Countryside: Studies in Social Change in Rural Britain* (co-edited with Charles Watkins).

Martin Charlton is Senior Research Associate in the North East Regional Research Laboratory, part of the Centre for Urban and Regional Development Studies at the University of Newcastle upon Tyne. He has been a member of CURDS' spatial analysis team since 1983. His research interests include spatial data structures, the analysis of large spatially referenced data sets, and geographical information systems.

Paul Compton is Professor of Geography and Director of the School of Geosciences at Queen's University, Belfast. He has written extensively on the demography of Northern Ireland, including *Fertility and Family Planning in Northern Ireland* (with the late John Coward) and *Northern Ireland: Demographic Trends*. He is currently engaged on a survey of Northern Ireland emigration/out-migration funded by the Northern

Ireland Government. His other principle research interest concerns the demography and population geography of Hungary.

Peter Congdon is Principal Researcher and Leader of the Population Projections and Statistics Team at the London Research Centre. He is responsible for demographic analysis and modelling relating to the London boroughs and beyond. His interests include statistical demography, migration, social indicator analysis and areas classification. He has published widely in official reports, books and journals.

Mike Coombes is Principal Research Associate in the Centre for Urban and Regional Development Studies at the University of Newcastle upon Tyne. He has been a core researcher in CURDS' spatial analysis and local labour market team since 1977 and is currently the North East Regional Research Laboratory Coordinator. One of his major research interests is the analysis of spatial interaction flows in the construction of functional regionalizations.

Tony Fielding is Lecturer in the School of Social Sciences at the University of Sussex. His research interests include patterns and trends of migration in Western Europe and the relationship between social and geographical mobility. He is currently engaged in a study of migration flows affecting London and South East England. Recent publications include *Patterns and Processes of Urban Change in the UK* (HMSO, 1990).

Robin Flowerdew is Lecturer in Geography at Lancaster University and is on the Management Team of the North West Regional Research Laboratory. He has been interested in many aspects of migration since his PhD (from Northwestern University), including behavioural studies of migration decision-making and quantitative migration modelling as well as the substantive issues discussed in this book.

Anne Green is Senior Research Fellow at the Institute for Employment Research, University of Warwick. She is a geographer with particular interests in spatial aspects of economic, social and demographic change; local labour market issues; and urban and regional development. She has contributed to numerous research projects for a wide range of government, other public sector and private sector sponsors.

John Jenkins is the Head of Research and Information in Northamptonshire County Council's Corporate Headquarters Department. He has worked in local government for the last twelve years, previously with Cambridgeshire County Council, and has a wide experience in interpreting and modelling population trends for policy and service planning purposes.

Huw Jones is Senior Lecturer and Head of the Department of

Geography at the University of Dundee. His research interests have focused on contemporary demographic analysis in a variety of environments and his textbook on *Population Geography* was published in 1990. He has studied aspects of Scottish, Welsh, Canadian and Maltese migration and is currently involved in a study of crime and fear of crime in Dundee.

David Owen is Research Associate at the Department of City and Regional Planning, University of Wales College of Cardiff. He has research interests in the analysis of small-area census and other socio-economic data sets, and in investigating the relationships between migration patterns and local economic change in Britain.

Philip Rees is Professor of Population Geography at the University of Leeds. His recent research has centred on applying population projection methods to small area forecasting for local government, to the elderly and to student populations and on supervising postgraduate research into migration trends, organic farming, and microsimulation, with contributions to edited collections in all these subjects.

Vaughan Robinson is Senior Lecturer in Geography at University College, Swansea, having previously been a Prize Research Fellow at Nuffield College, Oxford. His research interests centre upon ethnic relations, migration and refugee studies. He is the author or editor of four books, including *Transients, Settlers and Refugees: Asians in Britain* and *The International Refugee crisis: British and Canadian Responses*.

John Stillwell is Lecturer in the School of Geography at the University of Leeds. He has carried out research on patterns of internal migration in Britain and has particular interests in migration modelling and projection methods. Recent publications include *Contemporary Research in Population Geography* (co-edited with Henk Scholten) and *Migration Models: Macro and Micro Approaches* (co-edited with Peter Congdon). He also has research interests in regional economic development in Yorkshire and Humberside.

Tony Warnes is Reader at Kings College London and Senior Research Associate at the Age Concern Institute of Gerontology. His interests in population and housing issues associated with elderly people have developed since the early 1970s through several social surveys, analyses of national data sets and numerous publications. He has recently contributed to a United Nations Population Division international workshop on 'Ageing in the context of the family', has edited a multi-disciplinary text in gerontology, *Human Ageing and Later Life*, and is currently involved in an EC study of the potential of new information technologies to assist older drivers.

Preface

Throughout history, the geographical distribution and demographic structure of the population of the UK has been shaped by the movement of individuals between dwelling places. Different combinations of motivation and control have stimulated a complex matrix of internal flows, the dynamic character of which reflects the processes of economic and social development taking place. Rural depopulation and extensive movement to the nation's industrial heartland were the dominant migration phenomena of the nineteenth century, followed by the pre-war drift to the South East and the post-war growth in shorter-distance suburbanisation moves. In more recent years, metropolitan depopulation or counterurbanisation processes have been the focus of much research attention and debate. Aggregate streams such as these, together with the myriad of movement patterns associated with various population sub-groups, make migration a vital component of sub-national population change requiring continual monitoring and interpretation.

This volume of *Migration Processes and Patterns* therefore has as its aim the empirical analysis of the migration component of population redistribution between and within the regions, counties and districts of the UK. It draws on evidence from a variety of different information sources to provide an account of the dynamics of migration during the 1980s and in some instances, where more recent data is unavailable, of changes in migration occurring during the previous decade. The companion volume, entitled *Research Progress and Prospects*, provides a 'state of the art' review of progress made by recent migration research and identifies the main opportunities and challenges which the academic community and its funding sponsors should be addressing over the next few years.

Together, the two books present a statement about the importance of migration as a component of population change and its significance as an agent of demographic, economic and social change in a 'post-industrial' society. They show that there have been major alterations in migration patterns over the past decade and that contemporary trends in the economy and society are leading to further change. They clearly demonstrate that these developments raise both theoretical and policy issues and chart out the main aspects of migration which need more detailed attention.

The focus on migration within the UK derives from the way in which the studies brought together in these two volumes were initiated. They constitute the primary outcome of the Working Party on 'Internal

Migration' which was set up in 1988 under the aegis of the Institute of British Geographers (IBG), following the successful completion of the work of the IBG Limited Life Working Party on 'Skilled International Migration' (Findlay and Gould, 1989, and the Special Issue of *Geoforum* 19, 4, 1988). The IBG recognised that the patterns and processes of migration within Britain, particularly flows between regional and local labour market areas, were constituting an issue of major policy concern in late 1980s Britain, with questions being raised concerning the apparent lack of individual mobility in the search for jobs as well as over the emergence of marked changes in migration patterns which had important implications for the provision of housing and related services and for the social complexion of individual communities. Yet, as the IBG also acknowledged, these developments had attracted relatively little research activity, noting that – with a few honourable exceptions – the pioneering work of Johnson et al. (1974) on housing and labour migration had not been built on subsequently. The case for a review of migration was reinforced when the Economic and Social Research Council (ESRC) and the Joseph Rowntree Memorial Trust (now the Joseph Rowntree Foundation (JRF)) both agreed to act as co-sponsors of the Working Party.

The activities of the Working Party took two principal directions, as reflected in the contents of the two books. Tony Champion convened a series of meetings designed to identify the key areas of existing or potential research on the causes and consequences of migration and, with Tony Fielding, co-ordinated the preparation of review papers on these topics. John Stillwell, Philip Rees and Peter Boden undertook the commissioning of studies on migration patterns, including the task of processing key data sets provided by the Office of Population Censuses and Surveys (OPCS). Computer files containing mid-year population estimates and quarterly information on patient re-registrations from the National Health Service Central Register were acquired, aggregated into a consistent time series at Leeds and disseminated to authors for use in preparing their chapters. The support and assistance from colleagues at St Catherine's House was much appreciated in this data gathering and distribution exercise.

The preliminary results of these two lines of approach were presented to an academic audience at a one-day meeting arranged as part of the IBG's Annual Conference programme at Sheffield University in January 1991, and the Working Party's Final Report launched at a public meeting held at the London School of Economics in September 1991. These activities have served to alert various interested parties (including research-funding bodies, central and local government, and the private and voluntary sectors) to the significance of migration as a force in societal change and have also helped to weld together a coherent group of active migration researchers ready to take up the challenge of plugging gaps in our current knowledge of this field.

These two volumes form an essential part of this process of stimulating greater interest in migration and increased involvement in migration research. They are aimed at the academic community, particularly at postgraduate level but also students on second- and third-year under-graduate lecture courses. The principal readership is obviously considered to be in the field of population studies, but this nowadays embraces a variety of disciplinary perspectives besides demography, including geography, economics, sociology, anthropology, planning and social policy. The books are designed to provide essential background informa-tion on related topics such as housing, employment, environmental studies, and urban and regional development; indeed, the consideration of migration in these subjects provides one of the most fruitful routes for a better understanding of migration and its significance. At the same time, the aim has been for the books to be written in a style which makes them both interesting and intelligible to relevant professionals in govern-ment and business, for whom some of the books' messages are intended. As mentioned above, the primary focus is on the UK, but, where appropriate, reference is made to migration trends and related research in other countries and it is hoped that two books will provide a useful basis for initiating comparative analyses across the developed world.

Even more than usual with edited collections such as these, the two sets of editors have cause to be grateful to their authors. Not only have the contributors to both volumes been prepared to follow the sets of guidelines laid down by the editors, but most of them have also been involved in the various meetings which have shaped the recommendations of the Working Party and thus helped to determine the contents of the volumes. In this connection, thanks go to John Salt for hosting the Working Party's initial one-day meeting at University College, London, in May 1989, and to Ray Forrest for acting as local organiser for two subsequent residential meetings at the School of Advanced Urban Studies at Bristol in December 1989 and July 1990. The Working Party is indebted to the IBG for its support in giving formal recognition to the Working Party and in providing pump-priming funds, and to the ESRC and JRF for sharing the main costs of its activities (ESRC Grant No. W100261034). The editors of Volume 2 also wish to acknowledge the cartographic support provided by Tim Hadwin and Alison Barclay in the School of Geography at the University of Leeds. Individual contributors have added their own acknowledgements as appropriate, but the editors' primary gratitude is to Iain Stevenson and his colleagues at Belhaven Press for agreeing to publish this double-volume set and for seeing the venture through its production stages so efficiently.

For the editors and hopefully for the contributors, however, these books are not seen as an end in themselves, but rather – paraphrasing Winston Churchill's comments at the conclusion of the Battle of Britain in 1940 – merely the end of the beginning. The success of the two volumes and of the Working Party from which they stem, should be measured as much in terms of what happens from here on as in terms of the work that has been carried out so far. The primary aims have been to generate a heightened awareness of migration as a phenomenon and to instil a degree of interest in migration research which will continue and indeed grow over the next few years. There are many

positive omens including the opportunities provided by new data from
the 1991 Census, the British Household Panel Study, the Department of
Employment's Working Lives Survey and a mooted OPCS survey of
household formation and dissolution. There is also a wide range of
academic and political issues that are not likely to get any less salient,
including new patterns of population movement within the UK, the
migration effects of the Single European Market '1992' and the far-
reaching challenges in Eastern Europe, and the implications of increasing
pressures from refugees, asylum seekers and economic migrants from less
developed countries. The evidence of these two books is that, partly as
a result of the efforts which went into the activities of this Working
Party and those of its predecessor, British academics are well prepared
to play a leading role in the development of the next stages of international research on migration.

John Stillwell, Philip Rees and Peter Boden
Leeds, July 1991

1 Internal migration in the 1980s

Philip Rees, John Stillwell and Peter Boden

1.1 Why study 1980s migration trends in 1991?

The first question that must be asked is: why have we chosen to study the migration component of population redistribution in the UK during the 1980s at a time very close to the administration in April 1991 of the Census of Population whose results, when published, will enable us to assess the changes that have occurred over the 10 years since the previous Census of 1981? The principal answer to this question is that migration trends are too important and too volatile to be studied for just one year in every ten. It is essential to monitor trends in migration levels, patterns and processes in the intervening, inter-censal years. It would be hard, for example, to envisage a science of economics that did not pay close attention to the way economies evolved month by month, quarter by quarter, and year by year. Similarly, demographic science focuses interest on the way in which fertility and mortality levels have fluctuated in the past and attempts to predict how these components of population change will vary in the future, as an essential input to national population projection.

For anyone interested in the way the populations of sub-national areas change over time, however, it is insufficient to have information about the level of births and deaths alone. It is also necessary to develop knowledge of the way migration levels and directions fluctuate over time in sub-national areas. It is also insufficient to analyse migration trends over time for areas in isolation because migration, by definition, connects origins with destinations. What happens in origin areas as well as destination areas affects the process of migrational redistribution of the population.

Investigation of trends in internal migration in the UK has been a neglected field of investigation in the past. The principal difficulty has been the long intervals between national censuses (normally ten years). This volume seeks to rectify the situation by focusing primarily on a relatively underused data set which provides migration information for a continuous time series throughout the 1980s.

1.2 The migration data generated from the NHSCR

Over the past 20 years the Office of Population Censuses and Surveys

(OPCS), the General Register Office, Scotland and the Government of Northern Ireland have developed systems for reporting the re-registrations of patients between the areas used to administer the general practitioner services of the National Health Service (Devis and Mills, 1986; Devis, 1984). The original data are compiled at the National Health Service Central Register (NHSCR) at Southport (Fox, 1990). These areas were called Family Practitioner Committee (FPC) areas in England and Wales until September 1990, when they were renamed Family Health Service Authorities (FHSAs). In Scotland the areas were known as Area Health Boards (AHBs).

Because a patient must request a re-registration in a new area before being recorded as a migrant, only a fraction of all migrations (defined as changes of usual residence) are captured by the NHSCR data set. Between 2.8 and 4.0 per cent of the population migrate between FPC areas each year compared with the 7 to 11 per cent of individuals who migrate between residences each year.

Data first became available from the NHSCR for the period 1971–72 (Ogilvy, 1980) but a regular time series was not developed until 1975. From mid-1975 until the present, NHSCR migration data have been made available by the Migration Analysis Unit of OPCS on paper, magnetic tape and diskette to OPCS's other divisions, to other government departments and to local government and academic researchers, principally as an aid in producing local population estimates and projections (Rowntree, 1990).

A summary giving recorded movements into and out of Wales, Scotland, Northern Ireland and the standard regions of England was introduced into the statistical tables published quarterly by OPCS in *Population Trends 50*. Articles are published from time to time on the broad trends in internal migration that are occurring (Population Statistics Division OPCS, 1987; Bulusu, 1989, 1990). The migration statistics are published for recent quarters (over the last four years) and otherwise for selected years (1971, 1976, 1981, 1986). The migration data together with the 1985-based projections to 2011 are also made available through the National Online Manpower Information System (NOMIS) at the University of Durham.

It is important to monitor the tables of NHSCR patient transfers on a continual basis to form a correct picture of current migration trends. Figure 1.1 illustrates interaction of spatial patterns and temporal trends for the regions whose migration characteristics are discussed in detail in later chapters. The regional graphs of net migration flows for the eight quarters of 1988–89 (from OPCS, 1990c) show both constant and highly volatile elements. Net inflows to Wales and net outflows from Northern Ireland are the most consistent time series. Sharp temporal changes, however, occur in Scotland between the second and fourth quarters of 1989. The North exhibits a roller-coaster ride of variations between net losses and gains. In the last quarter of 1989 there is a dramatic shift from severe losses to net gains for Greater London. These graphs make the case for studying the behaviour of British internal migrants in the 1980s in depth.

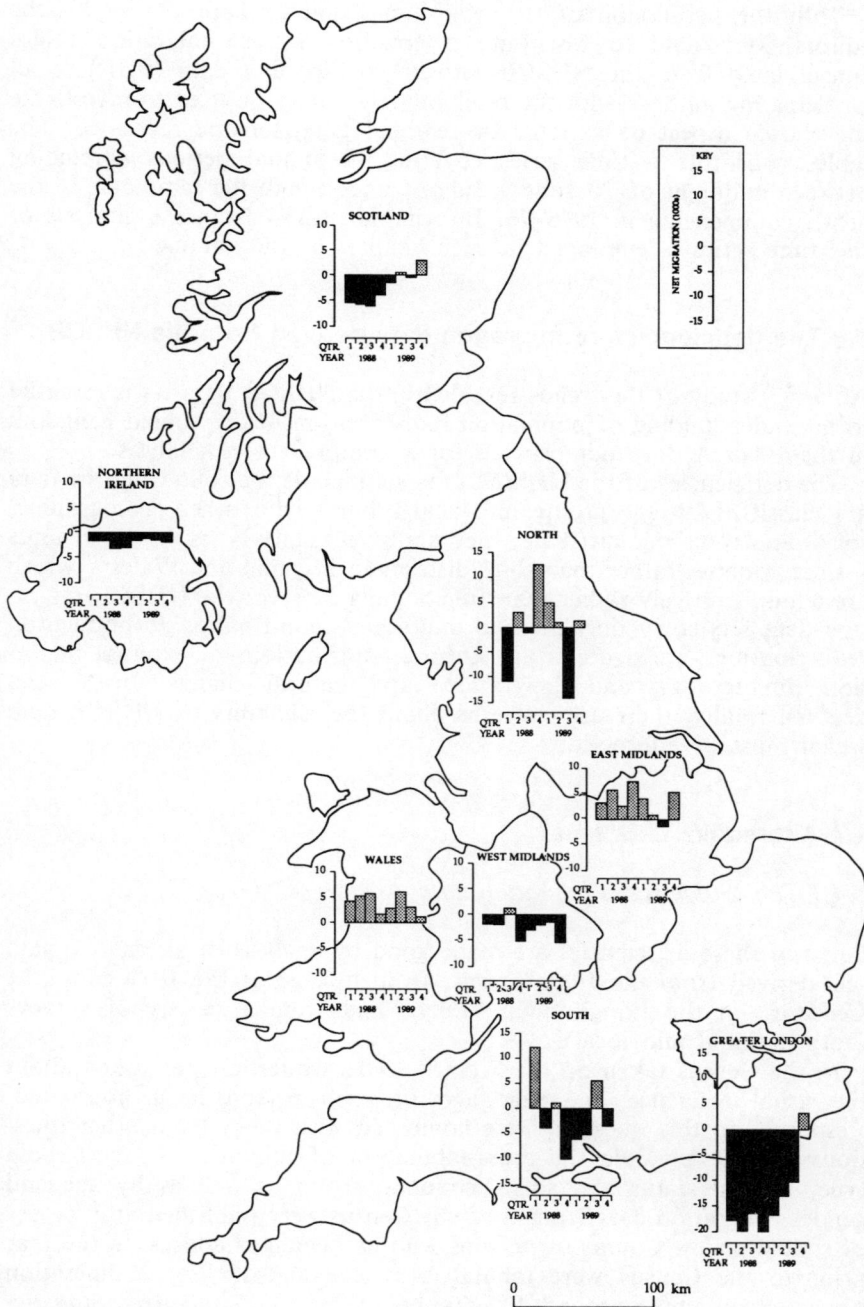

Figure 1.1 Net internal migration for UK regions by quarter, 1988–89
Source: OPCS (1990c, Table 20, p. 59).

With the permission of the Migration Analysis Unit of OPCS, the editors were able to distribute a common set of migration tables consolidated from the NHSCR-derived primary unit data (PUD) to all participating authors with the brief that the tables be used to investigate the chosen aspect of national or regional or systematic relevance. The tables constitute a time series covering 14 annual periods (stretching between midnight on 30 June/1 July of one year to the same date in the next), commencing in 1975–76. Information taken from the analysis of this time series is employed in each chapter of the volume.

1.3 The deficiencies of migration data derived from the NHSCR

Although study of the trends revealed in the NHSCR data set is essential to an understanding of population redistribution in the United Kingdom in the 1980s it does not provide for a comprehensive analysis.

The deficiencies of the NHSCR data set include the following: the data are classified by age group and gender but by no other demographic, social and economic attribute; they apply to relatively large spatial units – shire counties rather than shire districts in England and Wales – which are administratively rather than functionally defined; the NHSCR migration data sets cover only internal migration's contribution to population redistribution – also important are the contributions of external migration (immigration and emigration) and natural change (births and deaths); finally, there are concerns about the reliability of NHSCR data which must be addressed.

1.4 Alternative data sets

1.4.1 The 1981 Census migration data

Some of these deficiencies are made good by analysis of alternative data sets derived from the 1981 Census, from linkage of the 1971 and 1981 Censuses (in the Longitudinal Study), and from a variety of surveys (both national and local).

In the Census taken on the 5 April 1981, a question was asked about the usual residence one year ago of each person in a household. Responses to this question were combined with those from other questions making possible the cross-tabulation of migration by household type, marital status and socio-economic group as well as by age and gender. Migration data from the 1981 Census were published at a variety of spatial scales. Counts of persons who had changed address in the year prior to the Census were tabulated by age and sex for enumeration districts (containing around 400–500 people) in the *Small Area Statistics* (SAS). More detailed tables were available, in theory, for migration between wards in the *Special Migration Statistics* (SMS), Set 1, but unfortunately the procedures for protecting confidentiality imposed made the data highly unreliable (Cole and Squires, 1987; Rees, 1989a). Set two of the SMS does yield inter-ward migration tables, classified by gender, which have proved useful in work on simulating and projecting small-area populations (Duley, 1989; Duley and Rees, 1991; Rees and Rees, 1990) and in studying migration between special areas aggregated from wards such as the local labour market areas used in Chapter 4. Flowerdew and Boyle, in Chapter 7, utilise this data set to explore shorter distance movements within Hereford and Worcester and movements to wards in the county from the adjacent West Midlands conurbation. Most use, however, has been made of the district and county migration statistics made available in the *Regional Migration* volumes (OPCS, 1983a) which provide a variety of cross-classifications for use with migration.

The intention of OPCS (OPCS and GRO(S), 1990) is to publish improved migration tabulations from the Census of 1991, making available a Special Migration Statistics data set for inter-district flows not subject to the cascading problems that beset the SMS1 data set from the 1981 Census. In addition, inter-ward data will be made available disaggregated by age and sex (OPCS, 1990a), so it should be considerably easier to analyse migration patterns for 1990–91 compared with those for 1980–81.

1.4.2 A linked data set: the Longitudinal Study

OPCS has developed over the past decade a sample of linked records from the 1971 and 1981 Censuses in a project known as the Longitudinal Study (OPCS, 1988a). The sample consists of all persons born on each of four birth dates, initially selected from the 1971 Census, but traced forward into the 1981 Census. The sample was topped up by additions of births in the 1971–81 period on those selected birth dates and of immigrants with the same birth dates. The sample lost members through death before the 1981 Census, through emigration prior to 1981 and through matching failures (OPCS, 1988a). Tony Fielding in Chapter 13 of this volume uses this data set to gain an insight into the relationship of migrational relocation and socio-economic transition.

1.4.3 Population estimates and vital statistics

Over the course of the 1980s OPCS, the General Register Office (Scotland) and the Government of Northern Ireland have produced estimates of the population by age and gender of the regions, counties and districts of England, Wales, Scotland and Northern Ireland. These estimates are built forward from the 1981 Census counts using births and deaths counts and net migration figures estimated from a mixture of International Passenger Survey (IPS) migration data, NHSCR migration data and electoral statistics (Rowntree, 1990; Jones and Armitage, 1990;

Armitage, 1989). The estimates are published in the relevant annual volumes (e.g. OPCS, 1990a; General Register Office (Scotland), 1990; Welsh Office/Y Swyddfa Gymreig, 1990; Government of Northern Ireland, 1988) and republished in *Regional Trends* (e.g. Central Statistical Office, 1990). These estimates are used by various authors in Part II of this volume to monitor population redistribution since the 1981 Census.

1.4.4 Survey data sets

OPCS and its sister offices carry out several nationwide, rolling surveys of the social and economic state of the nation's households. The most important of these for migration studies are the *General Household Survey* (GHS) and the *Labour Force Survey* (LFS). The GHS asks a sample of respondents in Great Britain the questions (OPCS, 1990b):

> (Could I just check) how many years
> has . . . lived at this address?,

followed by:

> How many moves has . . . made in the last
> five years, not counting moves between places
> outside Great Britain?

From the first question a table of population distribution by length of residence can be assembled (Table 1.1). The first line of the table provides the equivalent of one-year migration data generated in the Census and shows a sustained rise over the 1980s. In Chapter 3 this rise is placed in the longer-term context of 1960–89 trends using both Census and NHSCR data.

It is possible to cross-tabulate GHS data by standard region but the wording of the questions excludes any possibility of generating information on place-to-place migration. The researcher must turn to the LFS for help in this direction because the LFS contains the question (OPCS, 1988c):

> Where was . . . living one year ago?
> IF IN UK: Town ....   County ....
> IF OUTSIDE UK: Country ....

Chapter 11 by David Owen in this volume makes use of the LFS data to examine the relationship between migration and employment. Direct access to the full data set is necessary for useful work with both these surveys as published tables suffer from the problem revealed in Table 1.1 of excessive rounding which makes it difficult to detect changes over time, except with a long run of years. An additional deficiency of survey

Table 1.1 Length of residence distributions for the GB population, 1980–88

Length of residence of head of household	Year of survey % of valid responses								
	1980	1981	1982	1983	1984	1985	1986	1987	1988
Under 1 year	7	8	8	8	9	10	10	10.6	10.6
1 but under 3	15	14	13	14	15	15	14	15.0	15.5
3 but under 5	12	13	12	11	12	12	12	11.5	11.5
5–10	22	22	22	22	22	22	22	21.4	21.1
11–15	13	13	13	13	12	11	11	10.4	11.1
16–20	9	9	10	9	9	9	10	9.7	8.6
21–30	11	11	12	11	11	11	11	11.7	11.0
31 or more	11	10	11	11	11	10	10	10.0	10.6

Note: The GHS in 1980 suggests that one year movers have been underestimated (OPCS, 1981, Table 3.39, p. 69).
Source: General Household Survey, 1980–88.

data is the large scale of the areas (regions) for which reliable tabulations can be made.

1.5 Plan of this volume

The conclusion we derive from this brief review of the data sources available for the investigation of population redistribution in the 1980s is that eclectic use must be made of all available information since no source provides an ideal picture. Nevertheless at the heart of the analyses reported in this volume are careful investigation and interpretation of the patterns of change revealed by the continuous time series of migration data provided from the NHS Central Register.

The book is divided into three Parts. Part I: National Perspectives, contains three chapters whose range covers the whole of the national territory, or very large portions of it. Part II contains a set of chapters, which concentrates on migration trends in a particular region of the country. Part III chapters return to a national focus on subgroups of the population.

Part I begins with Chapter 2 (How good are the NHSCR data?) by the editors. In this chapter a careful comparison is carried out of migration data from the 1981 Census with migration information from the NHSCR time series for quarters two, three and four of 1980 and quarter one of 1981. Neither source provides a complete picture but this chapter establishes a high level of confidence in the spatial patterns contained in the NHSCR data, even if the differences in migration level between the two sources are shown to have complex origins.

Chapter 3 (Internal migration trends: an overview) by the editors, establishes the general picture of migration trends in the UK in the 1980s by using both coarse (North/South) and fine (FPC areas) spatial scales and by reorganising the flow data using alternative classifications such as metropolitan/non-metropolitan or population density categories. Interesting departures from the all-age patterns and trends are evident in the age-disaggregated analyses of the chapter.

In Chapter 4 (Flows to and from London: a decade of change?) Mike Coombes and Martin Charlton focus on the role of the nation's capital and largest city in the British migration system. A refined description of the way in which interactions fall off with distance from London (controlling for the population distributions) is provided, and the important deviations (particularly for retirement migration) are identified.

The seven chapters of Part II: Regional Perspectives provide detailed analyses of the major sections of the country. The regionalisation of the UK (Figure 1.1) is a product of two factors. The first factor was the desire of the editors to cover the whole of the national territory of the UK and to avoid confining attention merely to England or to Great Britain, as is so often the case. Hence the volume includes chapters on Northern Ireland by Paul Compton, on Scotland by Huw Jones and on Wales by Anne Green. The second factor affecting the regionalisation adopted was the range of regional expertise among the members of the Limited Life Working Party on Migration, which meant that some amalgamation of the UK's standard regions was necessary. This was achieved fairly naturally by amalgamating regions in northern England and southern England which form interconnected migration subsystems.

The Part II chapters are deliberately arranged in periphery-to-core order to counterbalance the tendency to view the country from the seat of national government, particularly as such a view is presented in the last chapter of Part I. Each chapter provides a common analysis of migration trends in the relevant region together with an account of unique aspects of population redistribution in the 1980s. The conscientious student of migration will, of course, read all these chapters. Others will select those of most immediate interest.

Chapter 5 (Northern Ireland) by Paul Compton explores the consistency between data from NHS registers in different countries within the UK and focuses on explanations of the fluctuations in migration flows between the province and other parts of the UK. Chapter 6 (Scotland) by Huw Jones links migration trends within Scotland to the fluctuating fortunes of the North Sea oil industry. Chapter 7 (the North) by the editors includes a provocative classification of inter-area flows as representative of suburbanisation, counter-urbanisation and inter-regional exchange. The soundness of this framework can be tested in the future using the migration data from the 1991 Census. Chapter 8 (Wales) by Anne Green discusses the role of migration in cultural and language change. English migration into Welsh-speaking Wales (the counties of Gwynedd, Dyfed and parts of Clwyd, Powys and West Glamorgan) is seen as a threat to Welsh culture by a section of the native population. Chapter 9 (the West Midlands) by Robin Flowerdew and Paul Boyle draws attention to the suburbanisation–counter-urbanisation debate by examining the extent of migration by commuters into Hereford and Worcester from the West Midlands conurbation. The extension of metropolitan labour catchments is a longstanding process of population redistribution. In Chapter 10 (the East Midlands), John Jenkins identifies London house prices and local economic factors as important factors explaining migration patterns for the East Midlands. Finally, Chapter 11 (the South) by Tony Champion and Peter Congdon reviews the continued process of expansion of the London metropolitan system into the South East and beyond into East Anglia and the South West, a process which overheated in the later 1980s with considerable consequences for the South's net migration balances.

Part III: Systematic Perspectives returns to the national perspectives of Part I but focuses on particular subgroups or classifications of the population. Chapter 12 (Migration and employment) by David Owen investigates the temporal and spatial patterns of job-related migration in the 1980s with the help of data from the 1981, 1984 and 1987 Labour Force Surveys. Chapter 13 (Migration and social change) by Tony Fielding considers the interaction of social mobility (movement between the social classes) and geographical mobility, drawing in particular on the Longitudinal Study data sets for 1971–81. These data, though applying only in small measure to the 1980s, provide a very valuable perspective on migration behaviour. Chapter 14 (Temporal and spatial patterns of elderly migration) by Tony Warnes maps out the patterns of migration effected by the elderly which differ substantially from those of younger ages. Flows that occur around retirement are distinguished from those happening later in a person's life span, for example. The former flows see the more affluent and healthy couples move from residence in large cities to lower-density, higher-amenity locations along Britain's coasts or inland. The latter migrations involve some return to more urbanised locations to be close to offspring or good care facilities after loss of a spouse. The final chapter of the book, Chapter 15 (Move on up: the mobility of Britain's Afro-Caribbean and Asian population) by Vaughan Robinson also uses 1971–81 Longitudinal Study evidence to document the internal (within country) migration experienced by West Indians, Indians and Pakistanis.

1.6 Conclusion

The analyses reported in this volume provide a definitive picture of migration within the UK in the 1980s from a wide variety of perspectives. Internal migration is the most important component of change affecting population redistribution. In any one year only a minority of the population participates (7 to 11 per cent according to Table 1.1) but over a whole decade a majority will have made at least one move (56 to 59 per cent according to Table 1.1).

If there is a single thread that runs through the book, it is that no one pattern of flows or relationships is permanent. Changing economic and social circumstances across the regions of the UK produce concomitant responses in migration flows. Spatial and temporal perspectives must be intimately integrated.

PART I

NATIONAL PERSPECTIVES

2 How good are the NHSCR data?

Peter Boden, John Stillwell and Philip Rees

2.1 Introduction

There are two important sources of geographically detailed data on the migration of the population in Britain. At present the source regarded as most reliable is the Census of Population. Currently undertaken every 10 years, the Census identifies people who had different usual residences one year prior to enumeration. Migrants are classified by area of origin and destination, by age and sex and by socio-economic group. Despite providing comprehensive migration statistics at a fine level of spatial resolution the decennial nature of the Census means that only limited analysis of temporal trends in population redistribution through migration can be undertaken.

The second source of information is the National Health Service Central Register (NHSCR) which is now recognised as an increasingly valuable source of data on population redistribution. Virtually all UK residents are patients registered with a general practitioner employed by the NHS (including most people who carry private health insurance). The Central Register of the NHS at Southport provides OPCS with details of all patient re-registrations which involve the transfer of records from one Family Practitioner Committee (FPC) area to another. The register is continually updated and thus provides a quarterly time series of internal migration within the UK.

But how satisfactory is the NHSCR as an alternative source of migration data? This chapter outlines in detail the main features of data from the NHSCR in comparison with Census migration information. Neither source provides a perfect migration data set, but a careful comparison will usefully reveal their respective advantages and disadvantages and the extent to which the NHSCR may be used to provide an account of migration patterns and trends in Britain in the years between censuses. The chapter draws extensively on work by Devis and Mills (1986) and by Boden et al. (1987b, 1988).

Section 2.2 outlines the diagnostic features of each of the two sources of data in terms of conceptual, population coverage and measurement differences. Section 2.3 examines how the respective levels of migration vary by spatial scale and Section 2.4 illustrates the geographical and age–sex differences that exist. The concluding section summarises and assesses the main features of the NHSCR data and provides some pointers for the

Table 2.1   A comparison of the characteristics of migration data derived
from the NHSCR and the Census

Feature	NHSCR migration data	Census migration data
Target concept	Moves	Transitions
Coverage of 'problem' populations:		
Migrants who die	Yes	No
Infant migrants	Yes	No
Armed forces	Only entries and exits	Yes
Students	Yes, if re-registered at HE institution	No, recorded at parental address
Prisoners & long stay psychiatric patients	No	Yes
Operational measurement problems:		
Sampling fraction	10% 1975–83 100% 1983–89	10% 61, 66, 71 100% 81 Census 100% 91 Census
Attributes not stated	Origin, age & sex	Origin
Age–time plans	Period–age	Period–cohort
Missing or wrong information	Timing of move Skipped moves	Missing migrants Faulty recall
Spatial coverage	Migration between FPC areas or AHB areas	Districts, wards, enumeration districts
Temporal coverage	Quarterly from 1975	1960–61 1965–66 & 1961–66 1970–71 & 1966–71 1980–81 1990–91

use and interpretation of NHSCR statistics in migration analysis.

2.2 Census and NHSCR diagnostic features

Systematically set out in Table 2.1 are the characteristics of the two data
sets in terms of the different concepts of migration involved, the differing populations at risk of migration which are covered by the respective
sources, the operational measurement problems faced in each case, and
the spatial and temporal coverage associated with each type of data. The
following subsections outline the contrasting features of the Census and
the NHSCR under each of these headings.

(a) NHSCR

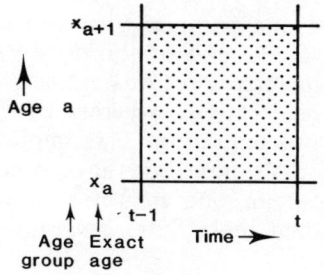

(b) CENSUS

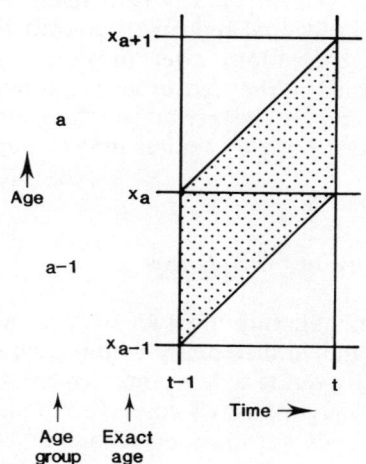

Figure 2.1 Age-time plans for NHSCR and Census migration data

2.2.1 Conceptual differences

The term migration is used to refer to the phenomenon of relocation from one permanent residence to another which involves an event, 'the move', and a participant, 'the migrant'. There are several ways of measuring migration which yield different counts depending on whether the focus is on the events or on the participants, because a migrant can, within any given time interval, make more than one move.

Rees (1977, 1985) identifies the methods of migration measurement adopted by the NHSCR and the Census as 'movement' and 'transition' approaches respectively. The movement approach involves counting the total number of moves that take place in a given time interval with the age of the migrant recorded at the time of the move. Figure 2.1(a) illustrates the age–time framework in which such moves are observed. The transition approach involves counting the number of transitions between locations at one point in time and at another with the age of a migrant recorded at the end of the period of observation (Figure 2.1 (b)). The NHSCR, therefore, records a count of migration events (in the form of patient re-registrations) whereas the Census records a count of the number of persons migrating. This implies that 'since at least some migrants by census definition, will have been involved, by registration definition, in more than one migratory event, counts from registers should normally exceed those from censuses' (Rogers and Castro 1986, p. 158).

So, for example, an individual undertaking several changes of address within a given period of observation will have each move recorded in the NHSCR, provided that a re-registration is made at each new destination, but will only be classed as a single migrant in the 1981 Census if the person's address one year previously is different from that at the time of enumeration. If an individual returns to an initial address before the end of the period of observation, after previous changes of address, the person will be recorded in the Census as a non-migrant, as the address at the beginning and end of the period are the same. In this instance the NHSCR would record both the initial move away and the return movement.

2.2.2 Population coverage differences

Multiple and return migrants are two of a number of population sub-groups which are handled differently within each data source. The movement of students is overlooked by the Census with persons completing Census forms in 1981 instructed to record home address as the usual residence of individuals currently at school or college. In contrast, the NHSCR will record student moves to places of education if re-registration takes place. The extent and timing of re-registration in a new FPC area will vary between educational establishments with some institutions having compulsory registration with a general practitioner or student health service upon arrival and others leaving the timing of registration to the individual. The effect of this difference will be to increase the discrepancy between the level of in-migration recorded by the two sources in FPC areas containing universities, polytechnics or colleges. The recording of moves made by armed forces (AF) personnel and their dependents produces a further discrepancy between the NHSCR and the Census. The Census records recruitments and internal postings while discharges are recorded as civilian migrants provided that the address at enumeration was different from that 12 months earlier. The NHSCR, however, does not record moves within the AF because personnel are registered with the military medical services and although the number of recruitments and discharges are measured, the respective destinations and origins of these moves are not recorded. The effect of the inclusion of AF moves upon the level of NHSCR migration is illustrated in Section 2.3.

Moves by prisoners and long-term psychiatric patients are also included in the Census but excluded from the NHSCR. The 1981 Census specified the usual residence of an inmate as the institution concerned if the person had been in the institution for more than six months, with a person classed as a migrant if the address recorded on Census night was different from that one year previously. The NHSCR excludes all moves to such institutions and all moves between them but will include patient/prisoner discharges on the condition that the person re-registers in a different FPC area from that of the institution.

The methods of measurement adopted by each source and illustrated in the respective age–time plan frameworks (Figure 2.1 (a) and (b)) ensure that the movement of infants (persons aged less than one year) is handled differently within each data set. The NHSCR is a continuous register which records all moves regardless of age. The Census, however, will omit all migrants aged less than 1, since those involved would not have had a usual residence one year prior to enumeration. Furthermore, a person who changes residence but dies before the end of the period will constitute one move in a population register such as the NHSCR but will be ignored by the retrospective Census.

2.2.3 Operational measurement differences

In comparing NHSCR and Census figures there are further operational considerations to be borne in mind in addition to the contrasting methods of migration measurement. Each source suffers from omissions. Devis and Mills (1986) estimate from the Post Enumeration Survey (Britton and Birch, 1985) that approximately 172 thousand migrants remained unrecorded in the 1981 Census because of either non-statement of origin or incorrect completion of forms and misrepresentation of those usually resident on Census night.

The quality of the NHSCR may also be questioned on a number of counts. The NHSCR does not record migrants who do not register with a doctor. Certain groups, particularly young male adults, may not register with a new FPC until they require treatment and may even neglect registration completely. Devis (1984), using household survey statistics suggested that up to 28 per cent of the population never consult a family doctor within a single year. Other subgroups, such as the elderly or mothers with young children, are likely to re-register as soon as a move is made – these groups being the most likely to require frequent medical attention. With the speed of re-registration within the NHSCR dependent upon the age and sex of the migrant involved it has been generally accepted that the 'average' length of time between a move and its accompanying re-registration is approximately three months.

Finally, the respective sampling frameworks adopted for the measurement of migration are also a potential source of discrepancy between the

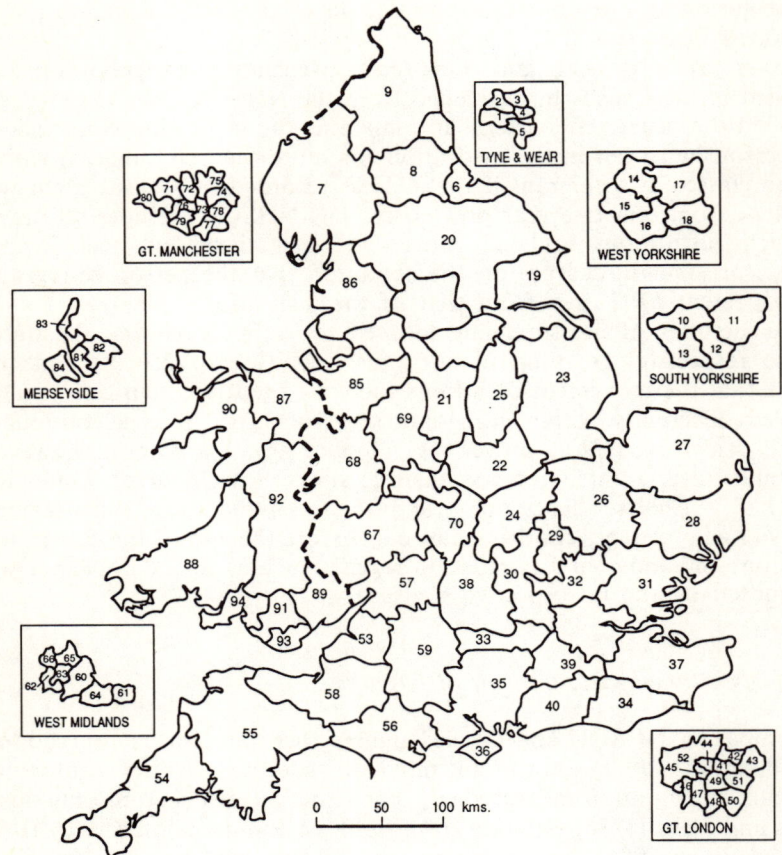

Figure 2.2 Family Practitioner Committee areas in England and Wales

Note: See Table 2.2 for FPC area names.

two data sources. Up to 1983 only a 10 per cent sample of re-registrations were tabulated in the NHSCR. Since April 1984, a 100 per cent count has been taken. The 1981 Census migration question was asked of 100 per cent of the population, but in previous years it had only been asked of a 10 per cent sample.

2.2.4 Spatial coverage

Tabulations of migrants into an area are available at all spatial scales employed in the Census: countries, regions, counties, districts, wards and enumeration districts. Inter-area migrant data are available down to ward scale. The NHSCR has a much more limited spatial coverage and records all moves between FPC areas. The FPC areas in England and Wales are

Table 2.2 Names of Family Practitioner Committee areas in England and Wales

Code FPC area	Code FPC area	Code FPC area
1 Gateshead	36 Isle of Wight	61 Coventry
2 Newcastle	37 Kent	62 Dudley
3 North Tyneside	38 Oxfordshire	63 Sandwell
4 South Tyneside	39 Surrey	64 Solihull
5 Sunderland	40 West Sussex	65 Walsall
6 Cleveland	41 City, Hackney,	66 Wolverhampton
7 Cumbria	Newham & Tower	67 Hereford &
8 Durham	Hamlets	Worcestershire
9 Northumberland	42 Redbridge &	68 Shropshire
10 Barnsley	Waltham Forest	69 Staffordshire
11 Doncaster	43 Barking & Havering	70 Warwickshire
12 Rotherham	44 Camden & Islington	71 Bolton
13 Sheffield	45 Kensington, Chelsea	72 Bury
14 Bradford	& Westminster	73 Manchester
15 Calderdale	46 Richmond &	74 Oldham
16 Kirklees	Kingston	75 Rochdale
17 Leeds	47 Merton, Sutton &	76 Salford
18 Wakefield	Wandsworth	77 Stockport
19 Humberside	48 Croydon	78 Tameside
20 North Yorkshire	49 Lambeth, Southwark	79 Trafford
21 Derbyshire	& Lewisham	80 Wigan
22 Leicestershire	50 Bromley	81 Liverpool
23 Lincolnshire	51 Bexley & Greenwich	82 St Helens &
24 Northamptonshire	52 Middlesex	Knowsley
25 Nottinghamshire	53 Avon	83 Sefton
26 Cambridgeshire	54 Cornwall	84 Wirral
27 Norfolk	55 Devon	85 Cheshire
28 Suffolk	56 Dorset	86 Lancashire
29 Bedfordshire	57 Gloucestershire	87 Clywd
30 Buckinghamshire	58 Somerset	88 Dyfed
31 Essex	59 Wiltshire	89 Gwent
32 Hertfordshire	60 Birmingham	90 Gwynedd
33 Berkshire		91 Mid Glamorgan
34 East Sussex		92 Powys
35 Hampshire		93 South Glamorgan
		94 West Glamorgan

Notes: (i) Middlesex consists of the London boroughs of Barnet, Brent, Harrow, Ealing, Hammersmith, Hounslow, Enfield, Haringey and Hillingden;

(ii) FPC areas became Family Health Service Authorities in 1990;

(iii) After April 1989 Middlesex was subdivided, but for present purposes it is retained as a unit to preserve continuity over the 1975–90 period.

either shire counties, districts within (former) metropolitan counties or aggregations of London boroughs (Figure 2.2 and Table 2.2). A similar system operates within Scotland covering Area Health Boards.

Table 2.3 A comparison of migration levels estimated from the NHSCR and the Census, 1980–81

Migration between:	NHSCR migration (A)	(B)	Census migration (C)	Difference (NHSCR–Census) (A)	(B)	Ratio (NHSCR/Census) (A)	(B)
Standard regions (11)	839	967	630	209	337	1.331	1.536
Metro/non-metro areas (18)	1,149	1,289	882	267	408	1.303	1.462
Metro/non-metro areas, within standard regions	310	322	252	59	70	1.233	1.279
FPC areas within metro/non-metro areas	500	525	443	57	82	1.128	1.185
All flows	1,649	1,814	1,325	324	490	1.245	1.370

Notes: (i) The migration figures are in 1000s, rounded from the original tables.

(ii) In analysis (A) the data refer to civilian re-registrations in which origin, age and sex were all known. In analysis (B) the registrations of recruits to and discharged from the armed forces were allocated to estimated origins and destinations respectively, and the flows with one or more attribute (origin, age, sex) missing were assigned pro rata (see Boden et al., 1988 for details).

Sources: (i) (A), (C): from Boden et al., (1987b, Table 3, p. 23);

(ii) (B): from Boden et al., (1988, Table 3, p. 34).

2.2.5 Temporal coverage

The Census, although providing migration at a fine level of spatial disaggregation, is inadequate in its temporal coverage as at present it is taken only every 10 years. The NHSCR, however, is a continually updated register and provides an excellent time series of migration information, albeit at a fairly aggregate spatial scale.

2.3 A comparison of the levels of migration recorded in the NHSCR and the Census

Table 2.3 sets out migration statistics from the two sources assembled for 12-month periods differing by only a few days, and using the same spatial definitions and age–time plan (see Boden et al., 1988 for a description of age–time plan conversion procedures). Two alternative data sets were prepared from the NHSCR records of individual moves (primary unit data): set (A) comprises those re-registration records for

Table 2.4 An estimated decomposition of migration flows between FPC areas from the NHSCR and the Census, 1980–81

NHSCR component	NHSCR migration flows	Census migration flows	Census component
First moves of non-student survivors who are 1 year of age and whose sex and age are stated	1,301.3	1,131.1	Civilian, non-institutional surviving migrants aged 1 or more
		172.0	Migrants missed in Census
Common component	1,301.3	1,303.1	
Migrants who die	4.7	–	
Infant migrants	17.6	–	
	–	78.6	Armed forces migrants
Moves by students	100.1	–	
		7.4	Prisoners and psychiatric patients
Sampling error	+ or – 7.3	–	
Moves with sex not stated	25.5	–	
Moves with age not stated	3.3	–	
Second and further moves	101.7	–	
Total re-registrations	1,554.2	1,216.6	Total (less missed)

Sources: See Table 2.3.

which origin, destination, age and sex are known; set (B) includes, in addition, estimated re-assignments of records with missing information to specific origin–destination age–sex group flows, the largest number of which involve entry into or exit from the armed forces.

The NHSCR records substantially more moves than the Census records migrants: some 24.5 per cent more if data set (A) is used, and 37.0 per cent when data set (B) is employed in the comparison. Given this result, it is clearly difficult to ascertain the actual level of migration activity. The rate of migration between FPC areas is either 23.5 per 1,000 (Census figures), or 29.3 per 1,000 (NHSCR figures), or 32.2 (adjusted NHSCR figures). The ratio between Census and NHSCR flows increases as the spatial scale becomes more aggregate and the average distance travelled increases, with the largest discrepancy evident for inter-regional migration. The relationship that exists between short- and longer-distance migration is examined in more detail in Section 2.4.

The differences between the migration counts recorded in the NHSCR and the Census (Table 2.3) are clearly the net outcome of the various differences outlined in Section 2.3. A quantitative estimate of these differences is attempted in Table 2.4, drawing on and extending estimates given in Devis and Mills (1986). The table reveals an encouraging closeness of estimates of the conceptual component common to each source: there were around 1.3 million civilian first migrations/migrants between FPC areas in 1980–81. Approximately 122 thousand migrations were recorded in the NHSCR for populations not covered in the Census, and conversely about 86 thousand migrants were recorded in the Census who are outside the NHS registration system. A further 29 thousand moves are recorded in the NHSCR deficient in age or sex label, leaving 102 thousand second or further moves by migrants already subsumed by the Census in the common component.

The differences between the two sources in the level of migration are therefore attributable to undernumeration by the Census, inclusion of multiple and return moves in the NHSCR and the net effect of the inclusion of student moves in the NHSCR and the omission of armed forces from that source. Data set (B) attempts to reassign these missing AF flows in the NHSCR and the following section examines the spatial and age–sex differences that exist between NHSCR and Census migration data and interprets these differences in the light of discrepancies outlined above.

2.4 A comparison of patterns of migration recorded in the NHSCR and the Census

2.4.1 The statistical relationship between NHSCR and Census migration data

Level differences in migration measured using different instruments would not matter overmuch if we could be confident that both instruments were measuring the same pattern of migration; that is, ordering the different spatial units in the same way in terms of their rates of migration activity. The degree of association between the patterns of migration revealed by the two sources at three different spatial scales is illustrated by the scatterplots in Figure 2.3. The correlation is high in each instance with the strongest relationship evident between inflow rates at the standard region scale and weakest for net flows at the level of FPC area. This suggests that the patterns of migration derived from each source are very similar and that although NHSCR levels of movement may be higher than those of the Census the directional flow of migration recorded by the NHSCR is reliably accurate.

The relationship between inter-zonal flows is quantified in the form of goodness-of-fit statistics (Table 2.5), again illustrating a high degree of similarity and correlation at each spatial scale with the strength of

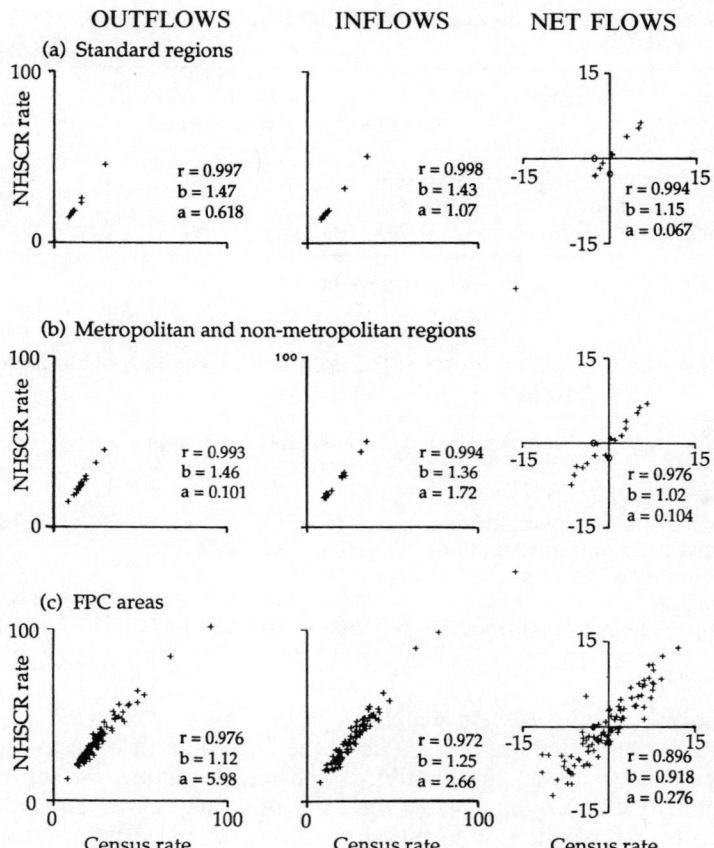

Figure 2.3 Scatterplots for NHSCR and Census outflow, inflow and net flow rates at three spatial scales, 1980–81

Note: The migration rates are expressed as moves or migrants per 1,000 population (from the 1981 Census).

relationship decreasing as the level of spatial disaggregation increases. With such a high degree of association between flow patterns where do the major discrepancies in the level of migration appear?

2.4.2 Spatial differences

Figure 2.4 illustrates the spatial variation in the ratio of NHSCR to Census in-migration and out-migration flows using data set (B). The major feature of the outflow comparison is that the large majority of metropolitan area ratios are below the mean figure. This is also true of inflow ratios but some of the highest ratio values are also found in

Table 2.5 Association between NHSCR and Census migration flows, 1980–81

Goodness-of-fit statistic		Spatial scale	
	Regions	MNM zones	FPC areas
Information gain	0.004	0.009	0.047
Index of dissimilarity	3.3	5.1	11.4
Correlation coefficient	0.997	0.997	0.982

Note: MNM = metropolitan/non-metropolitan zone system.

Table 2.6 Categorisation of inter-FPC area flows by metropolitan status, 1980–81

Type	NHSCR 000	%	Census 000	%	Ratio (NHSCR/Census)
Metropolitan to metropolitan	337.4	19	285.2	22	1.18
Metropolitan to non-metropolitan	376.1	21	277.5	21	1.36
Non-metropolitan to non-metropolitan	808.8	44	572.2	43	1.41
Non-metropolitan to metropolitan	292.1	16	189.9	14	1.54

metropolitan FPC areas. In general it is the 'big-city' FPC areas within each metropolitan county which have the highest inflow ratio values.

How might these metropolitan/non-metropolitan differences be explained? Table 2.6 categorises the inter-FPC area flows from data set (B) into four types depending upon the status of the origin and destination. In percentage terms, the number of Census migrants moving to non-metropolitan FPC areas (rows two and three) is similar to the corresponding number of NHSCR moves. The ratio values for these two types of flow are close to the national average of 1.37. More extreme ratio values are found for flows to metropolitan FPC areas which originate in both non-metropolitan and other metropolitan zones. For inter-metropolitan area flows the level of association between Census and NHSCR migration is high with the percentage of Census flows recorded in this category three points higher than that of the NHSCR. This relatively low figure for the NHSCR may be explained to some extent by the potential under-recording of moves by the more mobile sectors of the population – young adults, particularly males. Boden (1989) has indicated that the NHSCR and the Census will invariably be more consistent for these predominantly shorter-distance, inter-metropolitan flows as the importance of return and multiple moves will not be as great for migration flows which, it is suggested, are dominated by the more permanent relocation of people later in their life course. Furthermore, the shorter the distance travelled by a migrant the less likely that a re-registration will occur.

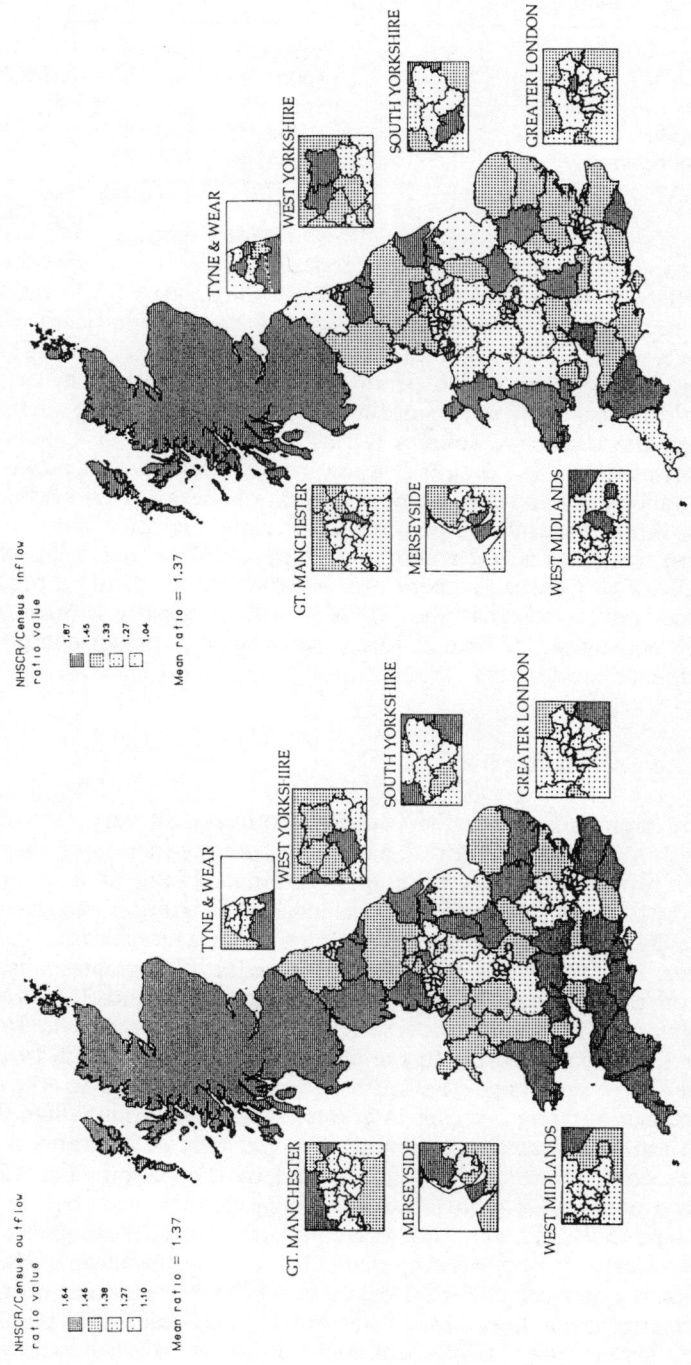

Figure 2.4 Outflow and inflow ratio values at the FPC area scale, 1980–81

Table 2.7 Categorisation of inter-FPC area flows by contiguity status, 1980–81

Type	NHSCR 000	%	Census 000	%	Ratio (NHSCR/Census)
Contiguous	653	36	556	42	1.15
Non-contiguous	1,161	64	768	58	1.54

The fourth row in Table 2.6, flows to metropolitan FPC areas which originate from non-metropolitan zones, illustrates the opposite extreme with NHSCR flows exceeding those from the Census by 54 per cent. The assignment of armed forces discharges will have a significant effect upon the level of NHSCR data in this instance but it is more likely to be student in-migration which produces such large discrepancies.

The differences in the recording of shorter and longer distance flows between the respective sources is further emphasised in Table 2.7 which categorises inter-FPC area migration into contiguous and non-contiguous flows (a contiguous flow being a migration between two adjacent FPC areas). Approximately 42 per cent of Census migration consists of flows between contiguous areas compared to only 36 per cent within the NHSCR. The Census is, therefore, much more adept at recording short-distance moves, whereas the NHSCR will be greatly influenced by the greater percentage of armed forces recruitments and discharges and the inclusion of student moves.

2.4.3 Age–sex differences

The differences between the two data sources will vary considerably by age with the student factor, for example, greatly increasing the NHSCR–Census ratio within only a limited age-range. Using data set (B), Figure 2.5 illustrates the variation in the level of migration recorded by each source by five-year age group and sex. The average ratio value varies between 1.34 for males and 1.46 for females. The greatest discrepancies between the two sources are found in the 15–19 and 75+ age groups. The absence of student moves from the Census data is undoubtedly a major factor contributing to the large ratio value in the 15–19 age-range. In the 75+ age-range the difference is attributable to the increased importance of non-surviving migrants. Devis and Mills (1986, Table 3.8, p. 17) estimate that approximately five per cent of migrants in the 75+ age category do not survive to the end of the period. The Census will not record migrants who move and die within the year before enumeration. The NHSCR will, however, record all such moves as they are always likely to be accompanied by a re-registration. The greatest discrepancy between the sexes exists in the 20–39 age-range with the male ratio being much lower than the female, particularly in the 20–24 age group. Young male adults are more likely to postpone re-registration

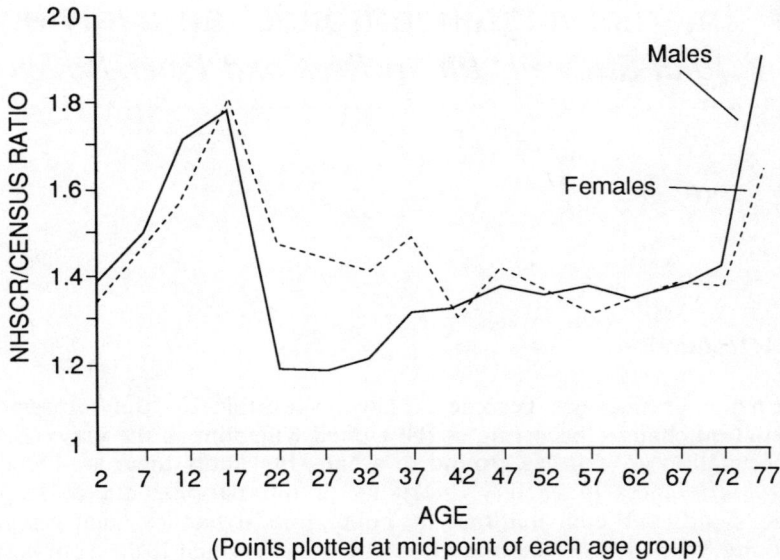

Figure 2.5 Overall NHSCR/Census ratios by age and sex, 1980–81

with the NHS upon moving to a new FPC area unless medical treatment is required and this may not be until subsequent moves have been made. Females are likely to be more prompt in their re-registration.

2.5 Conclusions

This chapter has attempted to address the question posed as its title by clarifying the conceptual, population-at-risk and measurement differences that exist between the NHSCR movement data set and the Census migration data set and by comparing variables from the two sources for a common time-period. However, a strong association between the aggregate patterns of migration recorded by the respective sources has been confirmed. Important differences do emerge between the two data sets when disaggregated spatially and by age and sex. Those who use NHSCR statistics should be particularly aware of certain features including the effect of student flows upon the level of metropolitan in-migration, the potential for inclusion of armed forces moves and the importance of multiple moves especially in longer-distance migration streams. In general terms the user may now be more confident of the credibility of the NHSCR data as a means of monitoring changing levels and patterns of internal population redistribution in Britain between Censuses. We look forward to the opportunity of repeating this comparative analysis using data from the two sources for 1990–91.

3 Internal migration trends: an overview
John Stillwell, Philip Rees and Peter Boden

3.1 Introduction

Internal migration has become largely responsible for the sub-regional population changes occurring in the United Kingdom as the national rate of population growth has ground to a halt. Inevitably there are localities where differences in fertility, mortality or international migration have made significant contributions to population dynamics, but generally speaking, it is the internal migration component which is determining the changing geography of the nation's zero-growth population (Champion, 1989b).

This chapter outlines the major trends in migration activity during the 1980s, drawing on a time series of National Health Service (NHS) patient re-registration statistics commencing in 1975–76. Studies of internal migration in the UK based on this type of data were initially undertaken in the 1950s (Newton and Jeffery, 1951; Rowntree, 1957), but most analysis has been focused on the 1970s and early 1980s (including Ogilvy, 1979, 1982; Devis, 1984, Stillwell, 1985, Stillwell et al., 1990, for example). The NHS Central Register (NHSCR) has been recognised by the Office of Population Censuses and Surveys (OPCS) and the Department of the Environment (DoE) as a source of very useful information. In particular, the data are being used for updating Census migration figures in the procedures for generating the net migration assumptions employed in the sub-national population projection model (reviewed in Boden et al., 1991).

The problems and limitations of the NHSCR data such as the omission of short-distance moves where no re-registration takes place, or the undercounting of young adult males, are now well documented (Ogilvy, 1980; Devis and Mills, 1986; Bulusu, 1988; Boden, 1989). Doubts about the reliability of the data have stimulated comparative studies with 1981 Census data (Devis and Mills, 1986; Boden et al., 1987b, 1988) and the conclusions from this work which have been summarised in Chapter 2 of this volume suggest that the data does have credibility as an indicator of inter-area population redistribution, although clearly its interpretation must be handled with due regard to the features that distinguish it from transition data.

The time series has been compiled from computer summaries of a 10 per cent sample of re-registrations from 1975 to 1983 and from 100 per cent primary unit data (PUD) for subsequent years, made available on a quarter-year basis by OPCS. A detailed explanation of the extraction of NHSCR data from magnetic tape and the construction of the data files is available in Boden (1989).

This chapter begins with an examination of the fluctuating trends in migration activity at the national level over the last three decades, based on both Census and NHSCR information. Trends in the geographical redistribution of the population through migration are described in Sections 3.3 and 3.4, using a hierarchy of selected spatial frameworks which begin with the division of the country into two parts (North and South) and end with a much larger system of 97 zones (including the 94 Family Practitioner Committee (FPC) areas in England and Wales shown in Figure 2.2). At different scales, the analysis considers aggregate net migration exchanges, gross migration outflows or inflows, or origin–destination interactions. Some insights into age variation in the propensity to migrate are provided and in Section 3.4 a classification is proposed which groups FPC areas on the basis of the characteristics of their in-migration rate profiles. The final section of the chapter contains some concluding comments.

3.2 Variations in the national migration level

The propensity to migrate within Britain has fluctuated appreciably over the last 30 years. Transition data from the 1981 Census of Population indicates that nearly 8.5 per cent of the population were migrants in the year preceding the Census. This level of migration is lower than that occurring in the equivalent period prior to the Census 10 years previously, when 10.5 per cent of the population changed address. At that time, the internal migration rate was well below comparable rates in the USA, Canada and Australia, and above rates in France, the Netherlands and Japan (Long and Boertlein, 1975). Census evidence shows substantial variation over time in the migration rates at all spatial scales. Total female migration between the British standard regions, for example, declined by 28 per cent whereas male intra-district migration fell by 14 per cent between 1970–71 and 1980–81. Overall, the level of internal migration activity in the country fell by 21.2 per cent during the 1970s after having increased by 9 per cent during the 1960s (Stillwell and Boden, 1986, 1989).

The gross migraproduction rate (gmr), which measures the number of migrations that a person makes over a lifetime if exposed to observed age-specific migration rates, provides a more refined measure of migration which avoids the age structure bias inherent in aggregate migration rates. The gmr computed on the basis of transitions in the year before the 1981 Census indicates that males and females both move around 6.5 times during a lifetime; four of these transitions occur over relatively short distances within local authority districts in Great Britain and the remaining moves are equally distributed between transitions between

Table 3.1 Yearly movement totals and rates, 1975–89

Period	Inter-FPC area		Inter-region	
	Total (000)	Rate (/000)	Total (000)	Rate (/000)
1975–76	1,914	34.4	1,175	20.9
1976–77	1,789	31.8	1,088	19.4
1977–78	1,879	33.4	1,151	20.5
1978–79	1,762	31.3	1,091	19.4
1979–80	1,633	29.0	1,018	18.1
1980–81	1,691	30.0	1,048	18.6
1981–82	1,595	28.3	984	17.5
1982–83	1,658	29.4	1,030	18.3
1983–84	1,677	29.7	1,038	18.4
1984–85	1,725	30.5	1,066	18.9
1985–86	1,806	33.9	1,124	21.1
1986–87	1,900	37.9	1,183	23.6
1987–88	2,049	40.7	1,295	25.7
1988–89	1,949	38.7	1,231	24.4
1989–90	–	–	1,076	21.2

Notes: (i) The FPC area set includes 94 FPC areas in England and Wales, plus Northern Ireland, Isle of Man and Scotland as single units.
(ii) The region set includes Greater London, Rest of the South East, plus the remaining UK regions.
(iii) Rates computed using mid-year population estimates for England and Wales.
Source: Computer summaries and PUD supplied by OPCS.

districts in the same county (or region in the case of Scotland), between counties in the same region, or between regions. The gmr in 1980–81 had declined from nearly eight transitions per lifetime in 1970–71 (Rees and Stillwell, 1990). However, these Census-based migration figures are likely underestimates since they do not allow for underenumeration, differences in populations at risk, or multiple movements.

The NHSCR data allows a continuous time series of movements to be assembled from mid-year 1975 to mid-year 1989 (Table 3.1). It is clear that the level of movement between FPC areas declined from 1.91 million in 1975–76 to a low of 1.59 million in 1981–82 before rising to 2.05 million in 1987–88. The time series indices plotted in Figure 3.1 illustrate the temporal fluctuations in movements between FPC areas and between regions. Linkage between the NHSCR time series indices and Census figures is achieved by relating values around a common year, 1980–81, where the index value for all data series is set to 100. The time series are most reliable and smoothest from 1983 onwards when annual figures from a 100 per cent count of the NHSCR re-registrations became available.

There seems little doubt that the explanation for the reduced rate of migration activity in the 1970s is to be found in the effects of changes

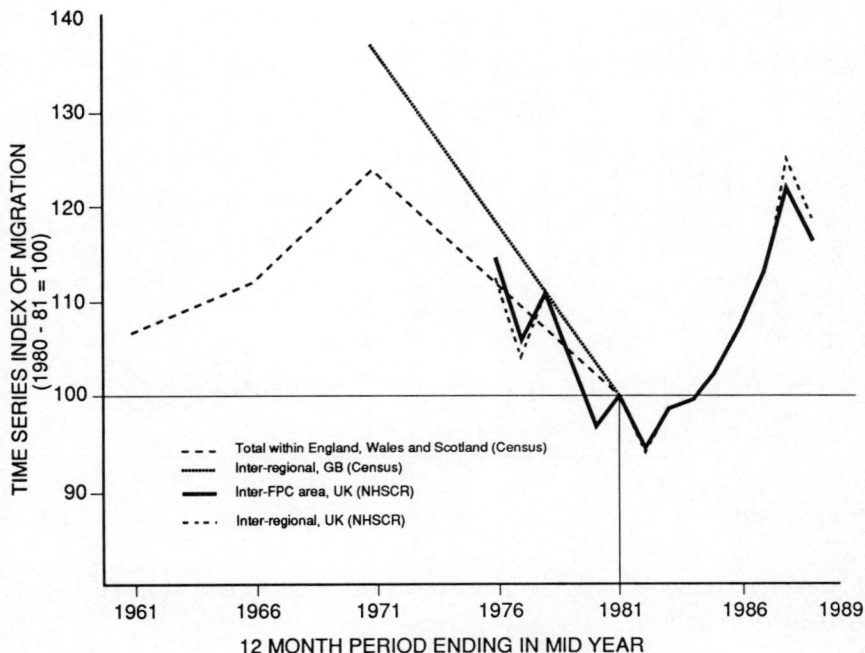

Figure 3.1 The changing level of migration, 1960–89

Sources: (i) Census data from Stillwell and Boden (1986, Tables 1 and 2);
        (ii) NHSCR data from Table 3.1;
        (iii) Adapted from Rees (1989b).

in the economy on employment, incomes and housing. Ogilvy (1979) has identified the turning point from General Household Survey data as taking place in 1973 and it can be argued that the oil crisis and heavy economic recession after 1973 had a dampening influence on internal migration in the UK, in a manner similar to that evident in the Netherlands (Scholten and van de Velde, 1989).

It was during the 1979–83 period that the British economy experienced its severest post-war recession with large increases in unemployment and widespread redundancy. The NHSCR data indicates that migration activity was at its lowest ebb in 1981–82. Since then, total migration has risen steadily up to 1987–88 when it reached a level of over two million before dropping back to around 1.95 million in 1988–89. Thus the 1980s was a decade in which the migration level increased by 28.5 per cent between 1981–82 and 1987–88, a period which also saw the increase in national unemployment decline annually to 1985–86 and be followed by increasing reductions in the unemployment level thereafter.

Migration rates exhibit considerable age variation, reflecting the different stages in life cycle through which individuals pass and at which migration becomes a more or less probable event. The elements of the

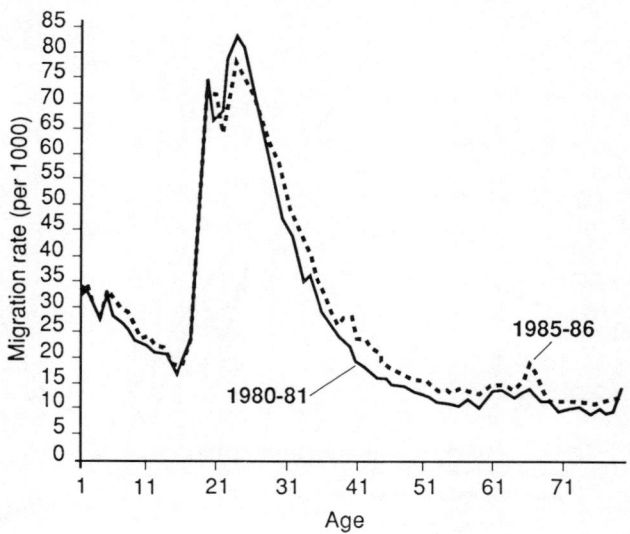

Figure 3.2 National migration rate schedules, 1980–81 and 1985–86
Source: PUD (OPCS).

migration rate schedule which define its familiar shape, described schematically by Rogers and Castro (1981), are evident in the schedules of observed rates for inter-FPC area migration by single year of age (up to age 79) for 1980–81 and 1985–86 (Figure 3.2). The first part of each schedule represents the migration propensities of children, usually dependent on the moves undertaken by their parents. This part of the schedule therefore slopes downwards with a gradient slightly lower than that of the corresponding section of the adult curve. Migration rates in the parental ages are higher because they also contain non-family adults with higher propensities to move in the first place.

The child dependent component of the schedule ends at age 16 and is followed by a steeply rising migration rate which reflects the movement into new households by late adolescents and young adults in the process of entering the labour force or moving to institutions of higher education. One idiosyncratic feature of each of the schedules depicted in Figure 3.2 is the kink in the upward curve of what Rogers et al. (1978) call the labour force component. This feature is likely to be associated with the fact that NHSCR data includes student transfers, with the result that a local peak in the migration rate schedule appears at age 19, followed by a drop for ages 20 and 21. A second peak at a higher level than the first reflects movements between jobs of those already in employment, boosted by moves of students away from higher education and into their first jobs. The NHSCR data for 1987–88 shows that 42 per cent of males and 46 per cent of females re-registering in a different FPC area were aged between 20 and 24, compared with 48 per cent and

Table 3.2 Migration flows across the North–South divide, 1975–89

Period	North to South		South to North		Total flow		Net flow from North	
	No. (000)	Annual	No. (000)	Annual	No. (000)	Annual	No. (000)	Annual
1975–78	714	238	617	206	1,331	444	– 97	– 32
1978–81	708	236	558	186	1,266	422	– 150	– 50
1981–84	689	230	531	177	1,220	407	– 158	– 53
1984–87	779	260	597	199	1,376	459	– 182	– 61
1987–89	548	274	523	262	1,071	536	– 25	– 13

Notes: (i) North contains Northern Ireland, Scotland, North Wales, Yorkshire & Humberside, North West and West Midlands.
(ii) South contains East Midlands, East Anglia, South West and South East.
(iii) Figures are rounded to nearest thousand.
Source: Computer summaries and PUD (OPCS).

51 per cent respectively in 1980–81. The relative decline between 1980–81 and 1985–86 in the migration rates of those with the highest propensities is evident in Figure 3.2. In contrast, the rates of those aged above 25 have increased since 1980–81. A retirement component is apparent in the migration flows occurring at this spatial scale in both 12 month periods and migration activity at age 66 is particularly noticeable in 1985–86. The migrant sex ratio has remained fairly constant during the 1980s with females constituting around 52 per cent of the total movement between FPC areas.

3.3 Spatial variations in migration activity

The geographical analysis of migration can be undertaken at a variety of spatial scales. In the case of NHSCR data, the basic system of spatial units is equivalent to the set of FPC areas in England and Wales which correspond with provincial metropolitan districts, London borough groups and shire counties, together with Scotland and Northern Ireland as single regions (Figure 2.2 and Table 2.2). However, it is convenient to aggregate the data in order to describe the characteristic patterns and important trends occurring in the 1980s. Our spatial analysis therefore begins by dividing the country into two parts, North and South, whose experiences of changing economic fortunes have differed during the decade.

3.3.1 Across the main divides

Aggregate flows between the North and the South of the country are set

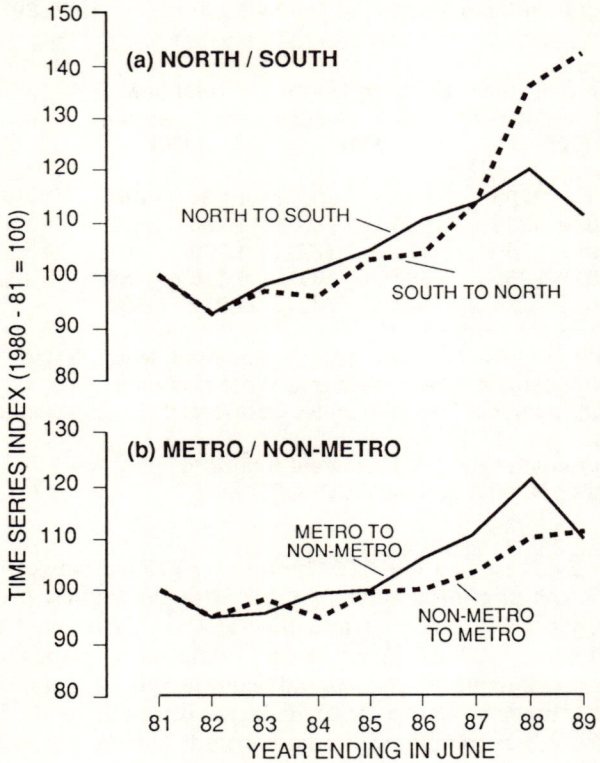

Figure 3.3 The tempo of North/South and metropolitan/non-metropolitan
migration, 1980–89

Source: Computer summaries and PUD (OPCS).

out in Table 3.2 for five time periods: 1975–78 and 1978–81, when the
migration level nationally was falling, 1981–84, when the decline was
reversed, and 1984–87 and 1987–89, when the migration propensity
increased substantially. The annual volume of migration across the
North–South divide declined to 407 thousand per year in the earlier years
before rising to 536 thousand by the end of the decade. The total net loss
from the North to the South increased steadily during the first four
periods, widening the migration 'gap' to over 60 thousand moves per
year in 1984–87. Since then, the net loss from the North has fallen back
to the extent that a net gain of seven thousand was recorded for the final
year, 1988–89. The time series indices of gross flows plotted in Figure
3.3(a) illustrate that whilst the greater job opportunities in the South kept
stimulating increased in-migration in the first half of the decade, the
tempo of movement northwards quickened relative to that in the
opposite direction after 1986. It was only in the final year that out-
movement from the North experienced its first downturn since 1980–81.

Table 3.3 Migration flows across the metropolitan/non-metropolitan divide, 1975–89

Period	Metro to non-metro No. (000)	Annual	Non-metro to metro No. (000)	Annual	Total flow No. (000)	Annual	Net flow from metro No. (000)	Annual
1975–78	1,255	418	864	288	2,119	706	– 391	– 130
1978–81	1,124	375	798	266	1,922	641	– 326	– 109
1981–84	1,047	349	789	263	1,836	612	– 258	– 86
1984–87	1,151	384	830	277	1,981	660	– 321	– 107
1987–89	838	419	607	304	1,445	723	– 231	– 116

Notes: (i) Metro contains Tyne & Wear, West Yorkshire, South Yorkshire, Greater Manchester, Merseyside, West Midlands, Greater London.
    (ii) Non-metro contains Northern Ireland, Scotland, North remainder, Yorkshire & Humberside remainder, North West remainder, West Midlands remainder, Wales, East Midlands, East Anglia, South West, South East remainder.
    (iii) Figures rounded to nearest thousand.
Source: Computer summaries and PUD (OPCS).

Shortages of housing, house-price levels, pressures of congestion and increased commuting distances are all factors likely to be responsible for this dramatic trend reversal, in addition to the effects of the downturn in the economy being felt earlier in the South than in the North.

Rather more significant in the 1971–81 inter-censal period than the North–South divide was the distinctive pattern of net migration losses from each of the old metropolitan counties (containing the big cities) and net gains in the areas outside those cities (containing smaller cities, towns and rural areas) (Rees and Stillwell, 1984). The evidence of migration flows between metropolitan and non-metropolitan areas contained in Table 3.3 suggests that the metropolitan areas have continued to lose migrants in net terms, in numbers that have not been diminishing in the later 1980s, after the reduced losses during the earlier, recession years of the decade. The last two years, 1987–89, saw a net loss of 116 thousand per year from the metropolitan areas. In volume terms, the North/South movements occurring during this latter period account for 27 per cent of all NHSCR inter-FPC area moves, whereas metropolitan/non-metropolitan movements represent 37 per cent of the total. The time series indices in Figure 3.3 (b) confirm that the tempo of movement from metropolitan to non-metropolitan areas has exceeded that in the opposite direction, except in the final year, when a downturn in migration away from the metropolitan areas occurred.

The graphs illustrated in Figure 3.4 summarise the age structure of net migration rates for FPC areas classified into these aggregate spatial divisions. The graphs depict single year of age net migration rates for 1980–81 and 1985–86. The North–South profiles show net losses from the

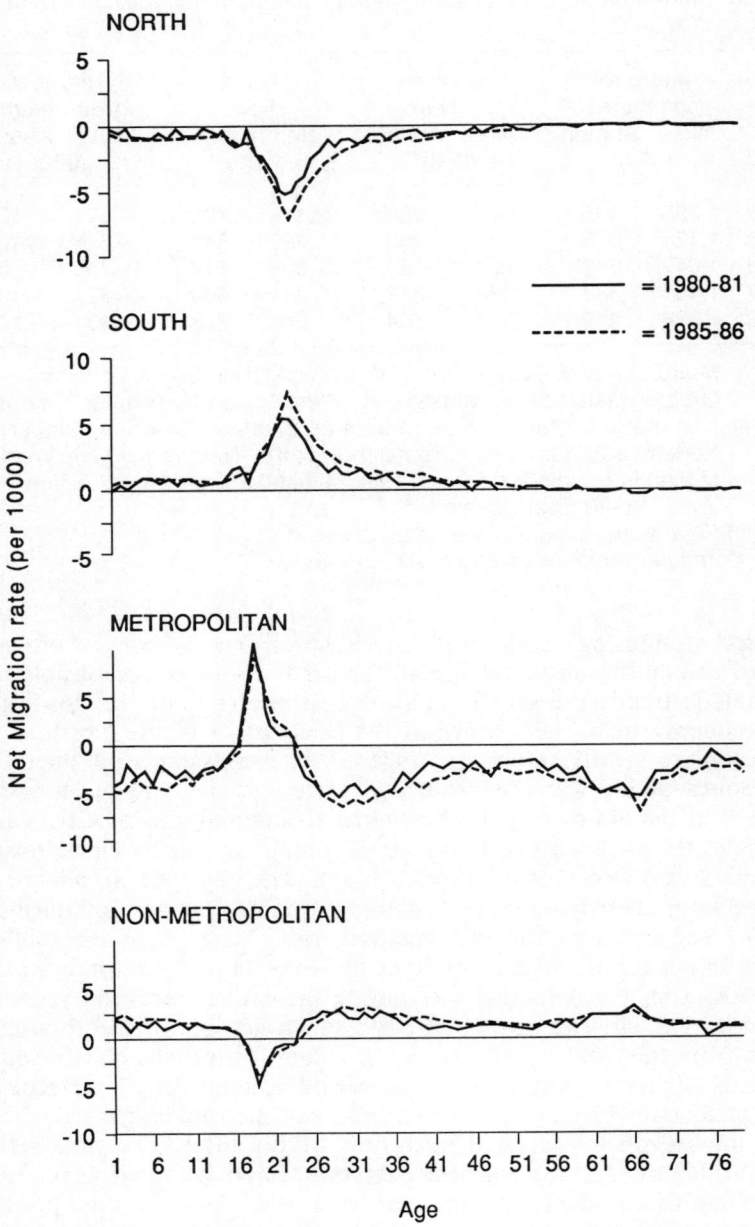

Figure 3.4 Age-specific net migration rates by North/South and
metropolitan/non-metropolitan divisions, 1980–81 and 1985–86

Source: PUD (OPCS).

North of people in all age groups apart from those around retirement age. The peak in the age schedule comes at age 23 in both the 12-month periods selected and the difference between the schedules in 1980–81 and 1985–86 demonstrates the growing attraction of the South to this particular section of the population between these years. The metropolitan/non-metropolitan classification shows that it is only in the age range 17–23 that the metropolitan areas as a whole gain migrants. The peak of these schedules is at age 19, partly reflecting the importance of student movement to higher education establishments as well as movement into and between jobs. The highest rates of migration loss from the metropolitan areas occur in the late twenties/early thirties and also around retirement age. These patterns are mirrored by the non-metropolitan area profiles, although the rates are lower in the case of the latter.

3.3.2 Macro regions and density classes

Trends in the geography of net migration can be investigated using two further aggregate spatial classifications. The first of these divides the country into four macro regions: the periphery (Northern Ireland, Scotland and Wales), the industrial heartland (North, North West, Yorkshire and Humberside, West Midlands), Greater London and the remainder of the South. Figure 3.5 illustrates the importance of the migration system operating within the South, with Greater London losing large numbers of migrants to its surrounding regions. Although the capital city's net loss declined from over 80 thousand in 1975–76 to around 31 thousand in 1982–83, it subsequently increased to exceed 85 thousand in 1987–88.

Migration losses have also been experienced by the periphery and to a greater extent by the industrial heartland during the 1980s, but the last two to three years have seen significant reductions in the negative balances of both these regions, which together with the decline in net losses from Greater London in 1988–89 has resulted in the reversal of the North–South balance also plotted in Figure 3.5.

The second classification allows us to examine whether there are differences in the migration characteristics of metropolitan and non-metropolitan areas in the North of the country compared with the South. Density is considered a proxy for urbanisation and FPC areas have been ranked on the basis of their usually resident populations in 1981. The ranking is divided into quartile groupings of areas labelled as high, medium high, medium low and low density. The net migration schedules for each of these density groupings in the North and South are presented in Figure 3.6. In the South, the low-density FPC areas have experienced a sustained increase in the level of net inmigration from 1980–81 to 1988–89 which is of a similar order of magnitude to the net outflows from London. Counterurbanisation has continued to extend to the most rural areas in the southern half of Britain, whilst the annual volume of net in-

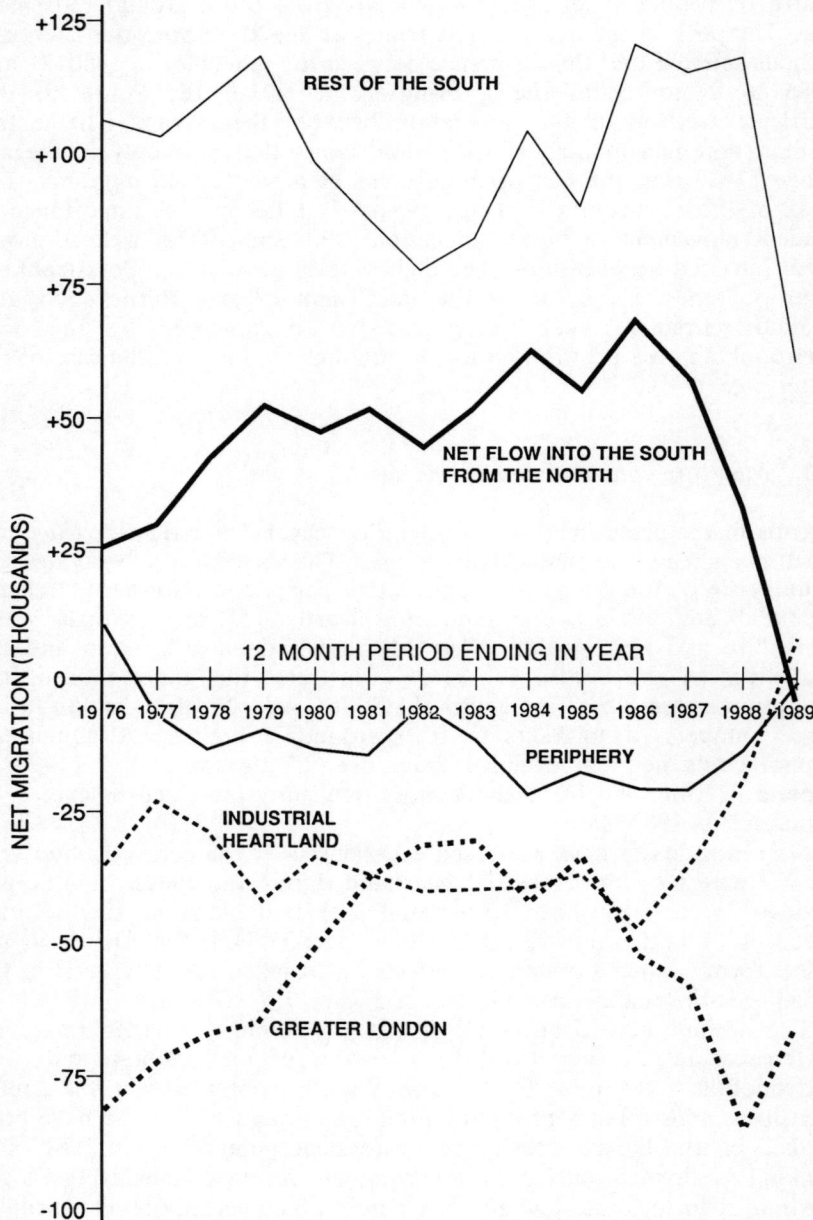

Figure 3.5   Net migration for broad regional divisions, 1975–89
Source: Computer summaries and PUD (OPCS).

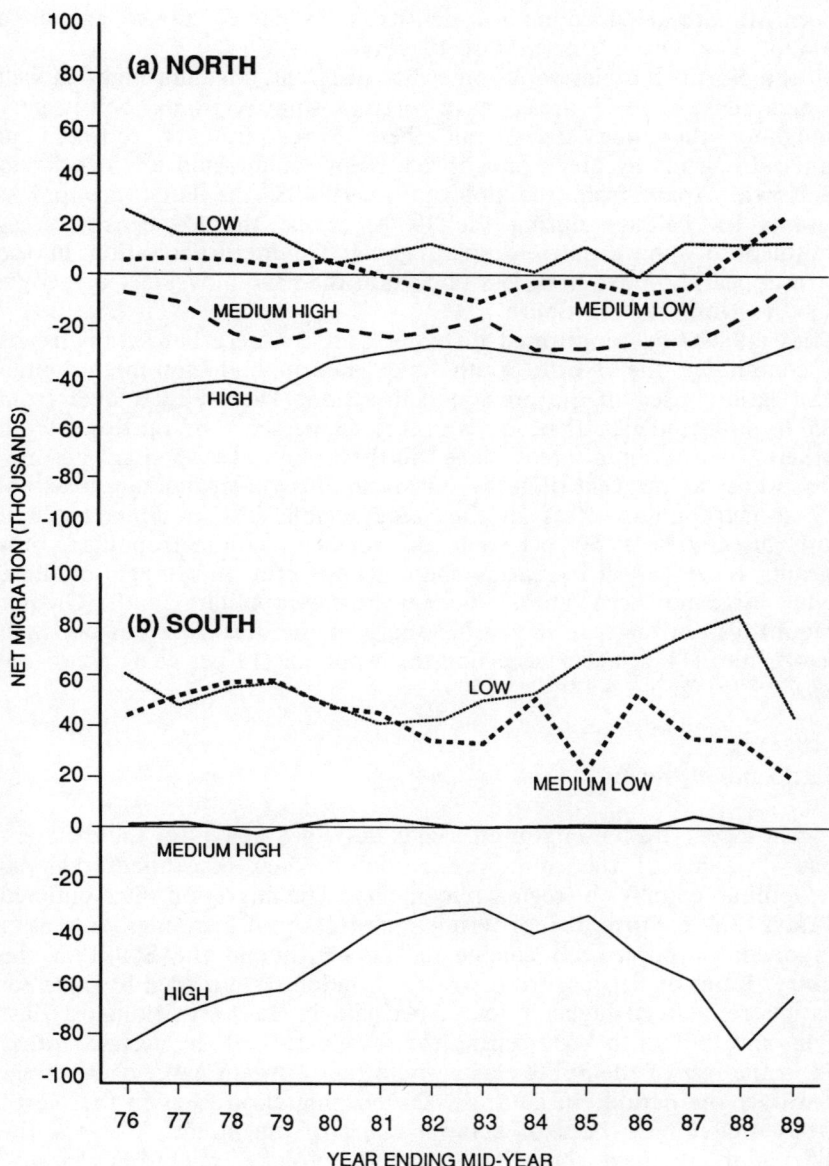

Figure 3.6 Net migration flows for FPC area density categories in the North and the South, 1975–89

Source: Computer summaries and PUD (OPCS).

movement into the medium low-density areas has fluctuated around a mean of 35 thousand in the last 10 years.

In the North, the picture is somewhat different. Medium high- as well as high-density FPC areas have been losing migrants consistently throughout the time series, but these losses are not reflected in comparable gains by areas categorised as low or medium low density in the North. Apart from the upturn in 1987–88, the latter group lost migrants on balance during the 1980s, whilst the low-density areas continued to show relatively small gains. Counterurbanisation in the North appears to have been less important than the movement of people from the North to the South.

Rees (1989b) has confirmed differences in counterurbanisation trends by combining the North/South and metropolitan/non-metropolitan classifications used in the previous subsection. The NHSCR data from 1975 to 1986 indicate that, on average, 55 per cent of outflows from northern metropolitan areas have northern non-metropolitan destinations, whilst 81 per cent of flows out of southern metropolitan areas are to non-metropolitan areas in the same region. The non-metropolitan South also attracts 50 per cent of northern non-metropolitan out-migrants as well as an increasing share (34 per cent on average) of those leaving large northern cities, whereas the metropolitan South (Greater London) also attracts an increasing share of the outflow from northern metropolitan (11 per cent) and non-metropolitan (13 per cent) areas (see Rees, 1989b, Table 6.14).

3.3.3 Regional trends

To what extent are the migration trends described above for the different broad divisions of the country mirrored in their constituent regions, metropolitan counties or region remainders? The migration rates outlined in Table 3.4 confirm the differing importance of net migration as a component of population change in the North and the South of the country. Rates of net loss from Greater London have tended to increase. This has resulted in higher rates of net gain in the East Midlands, East Anglia and the South West during the second half of the decade, rather than in the rest of the South East, where rates of gain have, if anything, fallen over the period. In contrast, the net migration rates in the North of the country have been of a lower order of magnitude. Wales is the only region to have benefited from a positive migration balance throughout the 1980s, with rates increasing substantially in the last two years. The increased attractiveness of the North, Yorkshire and Humberside and the North West is reflected in the shift from negative to positive balances in the last couple of years.

Figure 3.7 presents the net migration rates over the complete time series from 1975 to 1989 for metropolitan counties, region remainders and other regions, grouped by their broad divisions. The first set of graphs in Figure 3.7 are the net migration rates for the metropolitan

Table 3.4 Regional net migration rates, 1980–89

	North	Yorks & Humbs	Northern Regions North West	West Midlands	Wales
1980–81	− 3.3	− 1.1	− 3.0	− 2.2	0.6
1981–82	− 1.8	− 1.1	− 3.3	− 2.5	1.2
1982–83	− 1.4	− 1.1	− 3.1	− 2.7	0.7
1983–84	− 1.9	− 1.7	− 3.1	− 2.2	0.4
1984–85	− 2.8	− 1.6	− 3.5	− 1.4	1.7
1985–86	− 2.3	− 2.0	− 3.2	− 3.2	1.8
1986–87	− 2.9	− 1.6	− 4.0	− 0.2	3.2
1987–88	− 1.8	0.5	− 2.9	− 0.5	6.2
1988–89	0.1	2.1	0.9	− 1.6	5.6

	East Midlands	East Anglia	Southern Regions Greater London	Rest of South East	South West
1980–81	2.0	6.2	− 5.5	4.4	5.7
1981–82	0.4	6.7	− 4.8	4.0	4.9
1982–83	1.2	8.2	− 4.6	3.4	6.3
1983–84	1.5	6.6	− 6.2	4.7	8.1
1984–85	0.9	7.5	− 5.0	2.5	10.0
1985–86	4.0	10.5	− 7.6	4.7	7.7
1986–87	3.2	9.7	− 8.6	3.4	10.4
1987–88	5.7	11.5	− 12.6	2.6	9.8
1988–89	3.5	4.8	− 9.8	1.0	5.5

Source: Computer summaries and PUD (OPCS).

areas in the North, characterised by losses in the majority of cases. Merseyside and the West Midlands have experienced the most severe rates of loss, although in comparing these profiles it is necessary to recognise that the metropolitan district boundaries may not necessarily reflect the functional urban areas in the same way in each case. Greater Manchester has the most stable net rate profile, South Yorkshire the least stable. Reductions in the net losses are evident in each of these conurbation areas in the last two years but are most significant in South Yorkshire, West Yorkshire and Merseyside.

The pattern of net out-migration from FPC areas in Greater London has been commented on already. The remaining graphs are for non-metropolitan areas. The profiles of those areas in the North show much less consistency. Scotland, Northern Ireland and the remainder of the North exhibit negative rates whereas Wales and non-metropolitan Yorkshire and Humberside, the North West and West Midlands are characterised by net in-migration rates, although net losses were recorded in the remainder of the North West in 1983 and 1987. The final set of graphs in Figure 3.7 show how the rates of net migration vary for non-

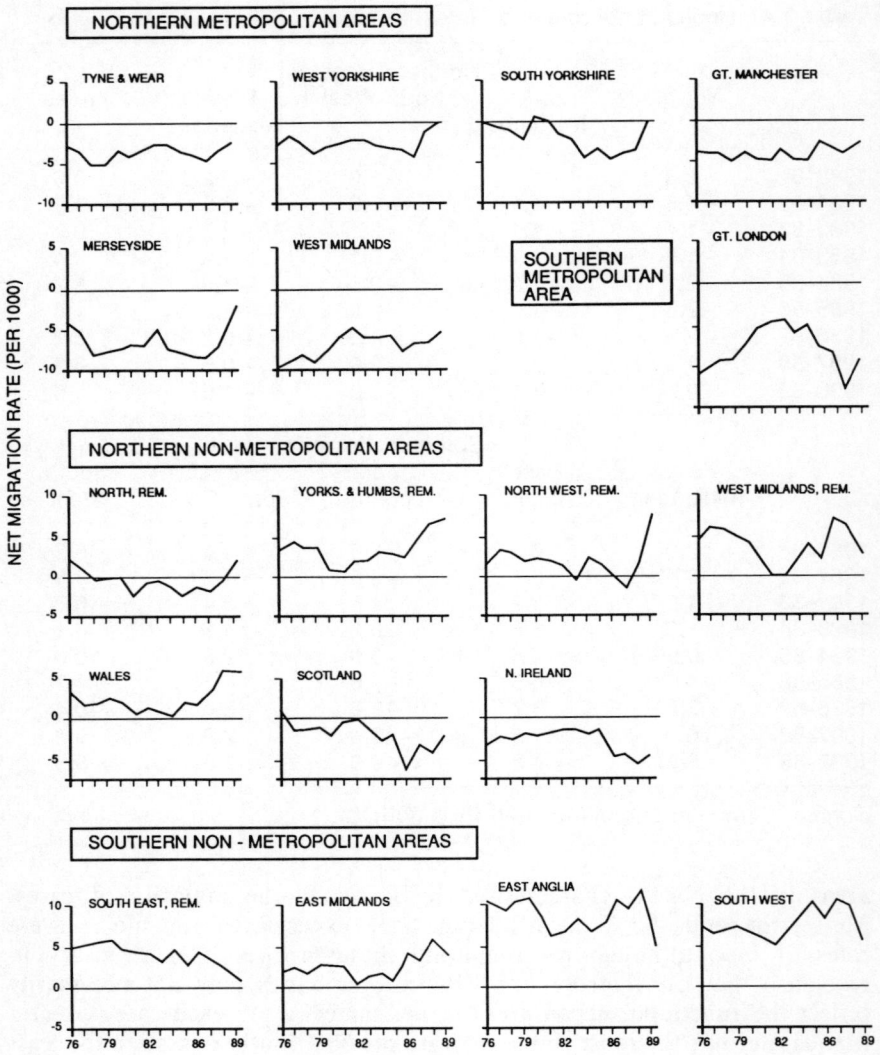

Figure 3.7 Net migration rates for metropolitan and non-metropolitan regions, 1975–89

Source: Computer summaries and PUD (OPCS).

metropolitan regions in the South. East Anglia and the South West continue to have the highest rates although with significant falls taking place in 1988–89. Rates of net gain in the remainder of the South East have declined over time whereas movements into the East Midlands have increased during the decade.

Net migration, of course, only indicates the difference between the gross flows into and out of each area, which themselves vary spatially

Table 3.5 Metropolitan and non-metropolitan gross migration rates, 1981–88

| | 1981–82 | | 1987–88 | | 1982–88 change | |
| | Out | In | Out | In | Out | In |
	(per 1,000)		(per 1,000)		(%)	
Metropolitan regions						
Greater London	27.1	22.3	38.2	25.6	41.0	14.8
Merseyside	22.0	15.0	24.5	17.4	11.4	16.0
Tyne and Wear	20.7	17.3	24.1	20.5	16.4	18.5
West Midlands	20.6	15.6	26.4	19.5	28.2	25.0
Greater Manchester	19.6	14.5	22.7	18.3	15.8	26.2
West Yorkshire	18.8	16.3	22.9	21.7	21.8	33.1
South Yorkshire	17.0	14.9	23.4	19.5	37.6	30.8
Non-metropolitan regions						
North West, remainder	24.4	25.5	27.7	28.8	13.5	12.9
West Midlands, remainder	23.7	23.9	27.9	33.8	17.7	41.4
Yorks & Humbs remainder	22.5	24.3	27.2	33.5	20.9	37.9
East Anglia	21.9	28.6	27.3	38.8	24.7	35.7
South East, remainder	20.6	26.2	27.8	30.4	35.0	16.0
South West	19.7	24.6	24.0	33.7	21.8	37.0
North, remainder	19.0	18.1	23.5	22.8	23.7	26.0
East Midlands	18.8	19.2	22.9	28.5	21.8	48.4
Wales	14.9	16.1	17.8	23.9	19.5	48.4

Note: Regions ordered on the basis of their out-migration rates in 1981–82.
Source: Computer summaries and PUD (OPCS).

(Table 3.5). The most noticeable increases in gross migration rates between the low point in 1981–82 and the high point in 1987–88 are associated with the rates of migration from Greater London, South Yorkshire and the rest of the South East, and rates of migration into the East Midlands, Wales, West Midlands remainder. Yorkshire and Humberside remainder, East Anglia and the South West.

To examine the relationship between changes in outflows and inflows over time, it is convenient to compute time series indices of generation and attraction following Willekens and Baydar (1986). The generation component for zone i can be defined as the proportion of total out-migration which occurs from that zone, whereas the attraction component involves in-migration to that zone expressed as a proportion of total migration. Time series indices of each component are derived by dividing annual figures by the respective component for a base year (1975–76 in Figure 3.8). Thus the indices show changes taking place in the zonal shares of out- and in-migration. The generation component tends to be more stable than the attraction component and consequently fluctuations in net migration tend to follow changes in in-migration shares.

Particular features of the schedules in Figure 3.8 deserve comment.

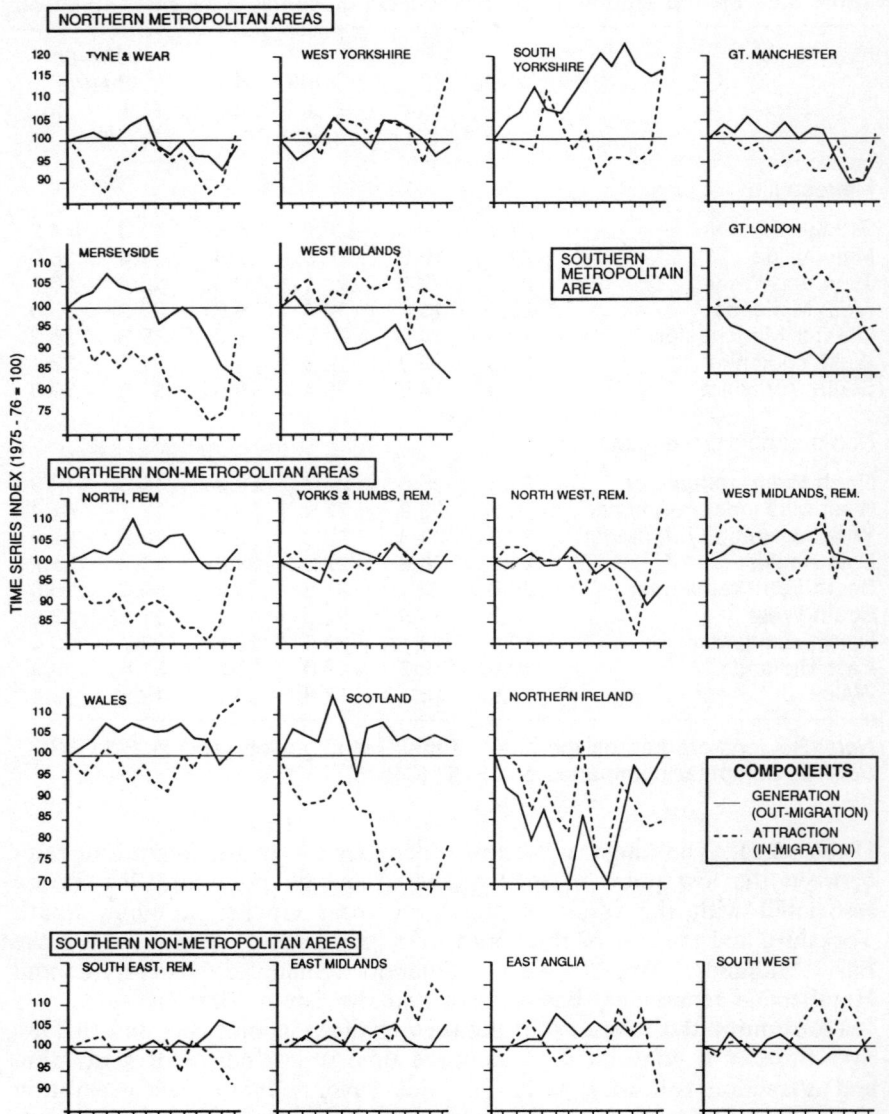

Figure 3.8 The generation and attraction components of migration for metropolitan and non-metropolitan regions, 1975–89

Source: Computer summaries and PUD (OPCS).

Table 3.6 The ordering of metropolitan and non-metropolitan areas by the number of net inflows from other areas, 1980–89

Region	Number of net in-migration flows		
	1980–81	1985–86	1988–89
South West	18	17	10
East Anglia	15	17	7
Greater London	14	14	10
Isle of Man	14	12	17
East Midlands	13	16	11
South East, remainder	13	14	7
Scotland	11	3	2
South Yorkshire	10	6	13
Wales	10	11	14
West Midlands, remainder	8	9	6
North West, remainder	8	10	15
Yorks & Humbs, remainder	7	12	14
Tyne and Wear	6	6	9
Northern Ireland	5	0	0
West Yorkshire	5	7	12
West Midlands	5	2	2
North, remainder	3	7	13
Greater Manchester	2	6	5
Merseyside	2	1	4

Note: The order is based on the number of net in-migration flows during 1980–81.
Source: Computer summaries and PUD (OPCS).

Among the metropolitan regions, Merseyside and the West Midlands exhibit marked declines in their generation components whereas South Yorkshire has increased its share of total out-migration over the period. Merseyside's share of total in-migration declined by 25 per cent between 1975–76 and 1986–87 although it has pulled back closer to the base line in the last two years. Temporal variation in net migration losses from Greater London reflects both declines in the generation component and increases in the attraction component during the first part of the time period. This was followed by a reversal of the trends in both components after 1985. In the so-called non-metropolitan areas, features of significance include: the drop in Scotland's share of total in-migration, the decline also apparent in the attraction component for the remainder of the North up to 1987, the improved attraction components for each of the northern region remainders in the last two or three years of the time series, the unstable nature of both of Northern Ireland's components and the relative similarity and stability of both components in the southern non-metropolitan areas.

Changes in the volume of gross in- and out-migration for any single area are determined by fluctuations in the migration flows taking place between that zone and other origin or destination areas. Detailed analysis

of the interaction flow matrices is not attempted here, but it is possible
to gain some insights into the pattern of directional movements between
the zones in our metropolitan/non-metropolitan system by counting the
number of net migration inflows into each zone from the other zones in
the system. In Table 3.6, the counts for 1980–81 have been used to
arrange the regions in rank order, with the South West at the top of the
hierarchy gaining from all other regions. Merseyside, at the bottom, loses
to all regions bar two. Generally, the ranking represents a hierarchy in
which an individual zone loses migrants to regions above it and gains
from those below it in the league table.

What changes in the regional ranking are evident over the 1980s?
Table 3.6 also contains the numbers of net inflows for each of the
regions in 1985–86 and 1988–89. Between 1980–81 and 1985–86, little
changed at the top of the hierarchy, with the South West and East
Anglia gaining from virtually all regions. The East Midlands improved
its position to third place. Only three of Scotland's net migration
balances with other regions remained positive in 1985–86 so Scotland
moved several places down the ranking. Furthermore, Northern Ireland
registered no net gains in 1985–86 and therefore dropped to occupy
bottom position. Differences in the net inflow counts between 1985–86
and 1988–89 serve to emphasise the emergence of the non-metropolitan
North West and Yorkshire and Humberside, together with the remainder
of the North (and the Isle of Man) as regions gaining in net terms from
at least 13 other regions. Similarly, metropolitan South and West
Yorkshire also registered gains from 13 and 12 other regions respectively
in 1988–89. In contrast, the southern non-metropolitan regions and
Greater London all moved down the hierarchy with East Anglia main-
taining a positive balance with only seven other regions. The pattern of
directional net migration has therefore undergone quite a considerable
transformation in the later years of the 1980s.

3.4 Migration at the FPC area scale

3.4.1 Aggregate patterns

The spatial pattern of aggregate net migration at the FPC area scale in
England and Wales has remained dominated by the losses from metropolitan districts and boroughs and gains by the majority of shire counties. The mid-decade map of net migration balances (Figure 3.9) shows
that positive rate values were recorded for only six metropolitan areas.
The shire counties which experienced net losses included some of those
that are part of the outer metropolitan area surrounding Greater
London; Cleveland and Durham in the North; West Glamorgan, Mid
Glamorgan and Gwent in South Wales; and Humberside, Staffordshire
and Nottinghamshire. All of these northern areas suffered major
manufacturing declines in the 1980s. The counties with the highest rates
of net gain were the rural areas of Powys, Lincolnshire, Norfolk,

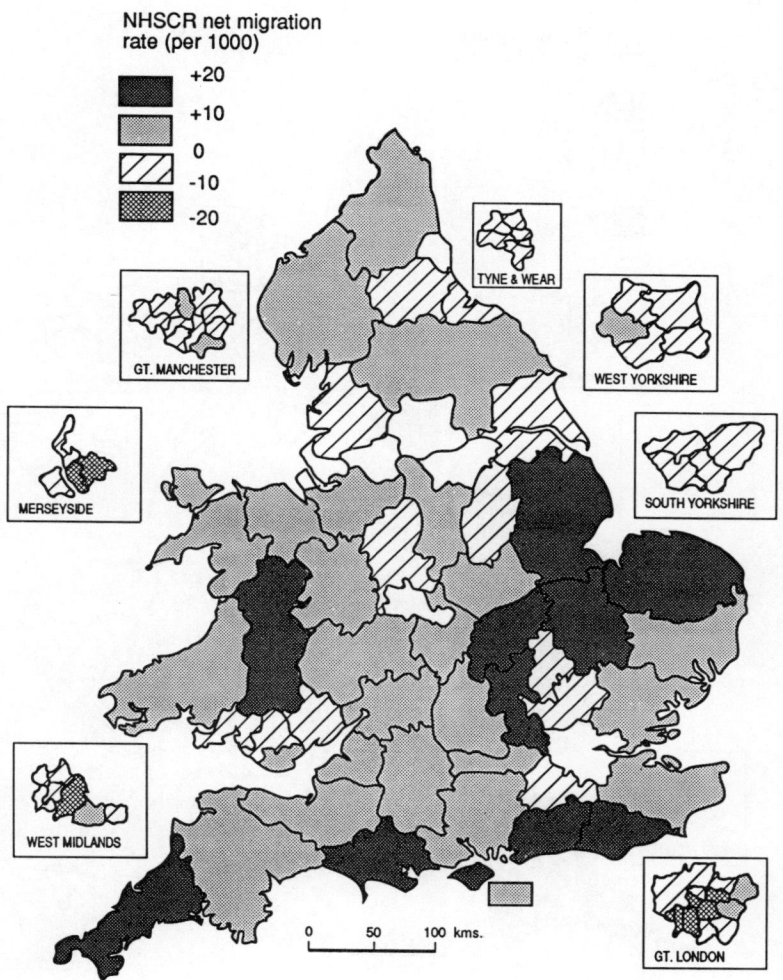

NHSCR net migration
rate (per 1000)

+20
+10
0
-10
-20

Figure 3.9 The spatial pattern of net migration rates by FPC area, 1985–86
Source: PUD (OPCS).

Suffolk, Cambridgeshire and counties on the south coast where retirement in-migration is likely to be particularly important.

By 1988–89 (Figure 3.10), the focus of high net in-migration rates had
shifted to Wales and the West of England, with fewer shire counties
having rates above 20 per thousand. Many more of the districts in
northern metropolitan areas registered positive net migration balances. In

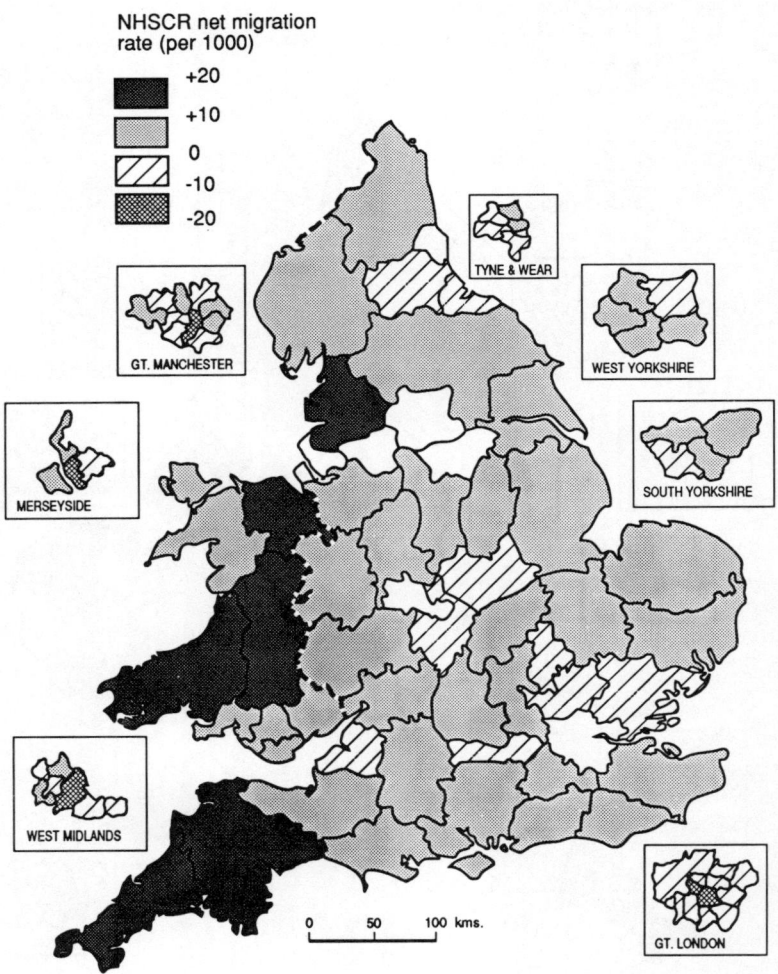

Figure 3.10 The spatial pattern of net migration rates by FPC area, 1988–89

Source: PUD (OPCS).

Greater London, where all the FPC areas recorded negative balances, losses were particularly severe from central areas. Net migration outflows from Greater London are the residual flows resulting from much higher rates of out-migration and in-migration than rates for zones in the rest of the country, as indicated in Figure 3.11 where the gross rates for 1988–89 for each FPC area are plotted against one another.

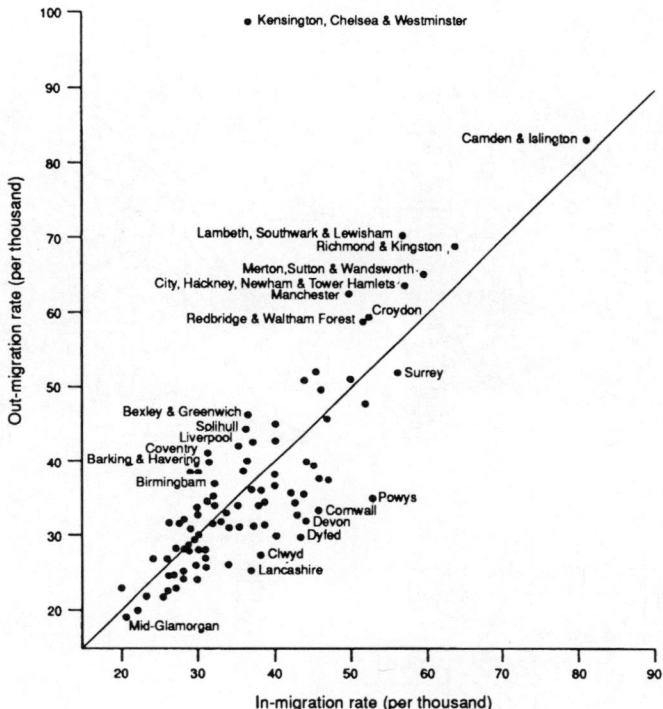

Figure 3.11   The relationship between gross migration rates for FPC areas, 1988–89

Source: PUD (OPCS).

3.4.2 Age group patterns

Inevitably the patterns of age-specific net migration differ appreciably from the aggregate distribution. The 20–24-year age group comprises approximately 20 per cent of total inter-FPC area migration and the changing distribution of this group during the 1980s is indicated in Figure 3.12. Between 1980–81 and 1985–86, the pattern of net gains became more concentrated in the south of the country with the negative balances being recorded in almost all the northern metropolitan and non-metropolitan FPC areas (with the exception of Greater Manchester). Moves undertaken by this most mobile age group became increasingly directed towards the high density areas of the South East at the expense of the rest of the country. Between 1985–86 and 1988–89, the pattern became even more focused on Greater London and the rest of the South East, although certain districts in West and South Yorkshire and in Greater Manchester registered rates of net gain.

It is perhaps not surprising to discover that migrants in this age group are the least affected by the distance over which they have to move. This

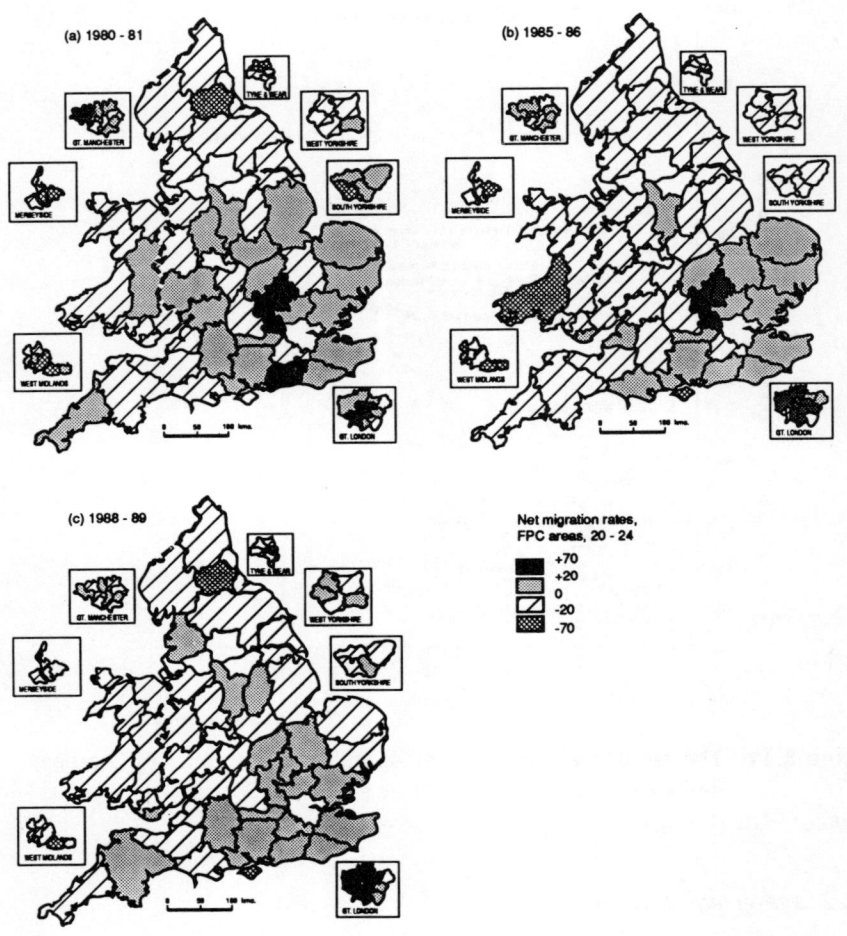

Figure 3.12 The changing pattern of net migration rates for FPC areas by those aged 20–24, 1980–89

Source: Computer summaries and PUD (OPCS).

is demonstrated by the calibration decay parameters associated with doubly constrained spatial interaction models using age-specific data on moves between FPC areas in 1985–86 (Stillwell, 1990a). Mean distances of movement and parameters representing the frictional effect of distance on migration in 16 different age groups (0–4, ... 75+) are illustrated in Figure 3.13. The schedules reflect some of the characteristics of individuals in particular life course groups. In the early age groups (0–14), distance exerts considerable influence on the general propensity to move. The lowest parameters are associated with those in the first part of the labour force age-range. Thereafter, as the parameter value

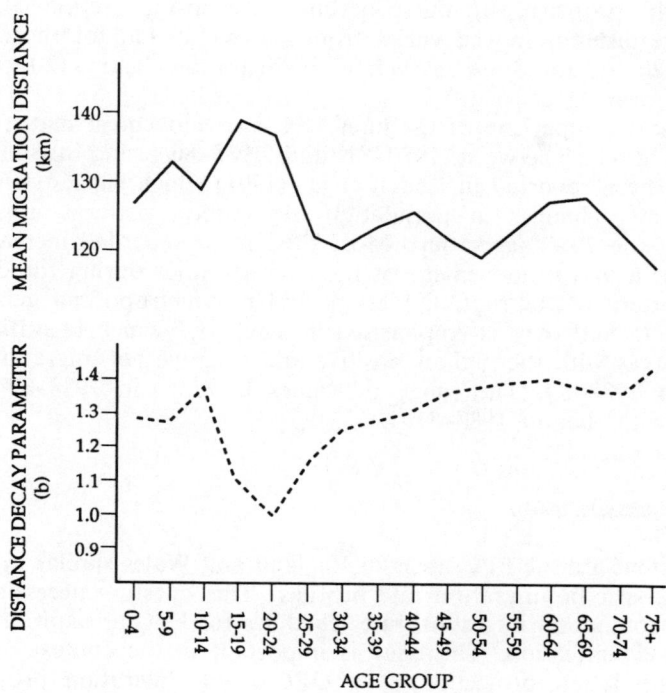

Figure 3.13 Spatial interaction model distance decay parameters and mean movement distances for inter-FPC area migration, 1985–86

Source: Parameters generated using IMP (Stillwell, 1984).

Table 3.7 Highest and lowest net migration rates of 75 + age group, 1980–81 and 1988–89

FPC area	1980–81	1988–89
		(per thousand)
Highest gainers		
Powys	− 2.7	18.6
Hereford & Worcestershire	14.1	11.3
North Yorkshire	2.4	10.7
Northumberland	2.3	10.4
Dyfed	− 1.9	9.0
Highest losers		
Lambeth, Southwark & Lewisham	− 13.1	− 23.2
Kensington, Chelsea & Westminster	− 23.7	− 22.8
City, Hackney, Newham & Tower Hamlets	− 15.7	− 19.8
Manchester	− 10.7	− 18.5
Liverpool	− 5.6	− 17.5

Source: PUD (OPCS).

increases, the propensity to move declines until around retirement age. The average distance moved varies from nearly 140 km for those aged 15–19 to 120 km for those in their early fifties and below 120 km for those aged over 75.

A statistical comparison of the inter-FPC area movement matrices for broad age groups between 1980–81 and 1985–86 using dissimilarity indices has been reported in Boden et al. (1991) which suggests that, in relative terms, changes in population distribution patterns are most marked for the 70+ age group. Most FPC areas recorded increases in out-movement and in-movement of the over-seventies during the decade and the pattern of metropolitan losses and non-metropolitan gains for those aged 75 and over is emphasised in Table 3.7 which identifies the five FPC areas with the highest positive and negative net migration rate balances in 1988–89. The range of values is wider in 1988–89 when compared with that in 1980–81.

3.4.3 Area classification

To what extent are the FPC areas in England and Wales similar in terms of their age-specific migration rate profiles? This question necessitates a method of comparing migration rate schedules for FPC areas in order to generate a classification. The issue is important in the context of sub-national population projection. The OPCS/DoE migration projection model involves the grouping of model migration schedules calibrated for standardised out- and in-migration rate profiles for each FPC area in England based on 1981 Census data (Martin, Voorhees and Bates, 1981; Bracken and Bates, 1983; Bates and Bracken, 1987).

An alternative methodology is employed here which derives groupings of areas on the basis of observed NHSCR single year-of-age movement rates for 1985–86 and fits model schedules to the profiles of the clusters which emerge. The derivation of a classification based on in-migration is used here to exemplify the procedure which is described in more detail in Boden et al. (1991). The initial step in the process is the computation of the squared euclidian distance (SED) between the standardised age-specific rates for two areas:

$$SED_{ij} = \sum_a (m^a_i - m^a_j)^2 \qquad (3.1)$$

where m^a_i and m^a_j are the standardised in-migration rates by age group a for areas i and j. The 'average linkage between groups' method is used where the distance between the clusters I and J, D_{IJ}, is the average distance between all pairs of FPC areas in which one member of the pair is from each cluster:

$$D_{IJ} = \sum_{i \in I} \sum_{j \in J} SED_{ij}/n_I \, n_J \qquad (3.2)$$

where n_I and n_J are the number of areas in clusters I and J.

Table 3.8 FPC area classification based on in-migration rates, 1985–86

Group	Constituent FPC areas
1	Camden & Islington; Kensington, Chelsea & Westminster
2	Redbridge & Waltham Forest; Croydon; Bexley & Greenwich
3	City, Hackney, Newham & Tower Hamlets; Richmond & Kingston; Merton, Sutton & Wandsworth; Lambeth, Southwark & Lewisham; Middlesex
4	Lincolnshire; Suffolk; Isle of Wight; West Sussex; Cornwall; Dorset; Somerset; Hereford; Salop; Clwyd; Powys
5	Humberside; Norfolk; East Sussex; Devon; Lancashire; Dyfed; Gwynedd
6	Cumbria; Northumberland; Rotherham; Calderdale; Wakefield; Derbyshire; Northamptonshire; Buckinghamshire; Essex; Kent; Gloucestershire; Wiltshire; Warwickshire; Bolton; Oldham; Rochdale; Tameside; Sefton; Wirral; Cheshire; Gwent
7	Gateshead; North Tyneside; Barnsley; Bedfordshire; Hertfordshire; Berkshire; Barking & Havering; Bromley; Dudley; Sandwell; Walsall; Bury; Stockport; Trafford; Wigan; St Helens
8	Durham; Leicestershire; Nottinghamshire; Oxfordshire; Avon; Birmingham; Wolverhampton; Manchester; Salford; South Glamorgan
9	Newcastle; Sheffield; Coventry
10	Leeds; Liverpool
11	Sunderland; Cleveland; Bradford; Kirklees; Cambridgeshire; Staffordshire; Mid-Glamorgan
12	Scotland; Doncaster; North Yorkshire; Hampshire
13	South Tyneside
14	Solihull
15	West Glamorgan

A break in the agglomeration schedule produced in the clustering of in-migration profiles indicates that 15 is the optimum number of groups. Fewer groups results in much larger increases in the distance coefficient. The FPC areas which comprise each of the 15 clusters are indicated in Table 3.8 and the observed age-specific rates for each cluster are aggregated to produce a cluster profile. In the final stage of the procedure, model migration schedules are fitted to each of the cluster profiles using a version of the MODEL package developed by Rogers and Planck (1984) and operationalised at Leeds by Stillwell et al. (1987). Figure 3.14 illustrates the model migration schedules superimposed on the observed rates of in-migration for the 15 clusters. Most E values fall below 10.0, indicating satisfactory goodness-of-fit.

The first three clusters contain groups of London FPC areas. Camden and Islington and Kensington, Chelsea and Westminster, with a double peaking in the observed rates, form the first cluster. The model (without a retirement component) smoothes the curve and the shape of the schedule is characterised by a high measure of asymmetry in the labour force component, emphasised by the sharp increase in the rate of in-migration at age 18. The other two groups of London FPC areas have

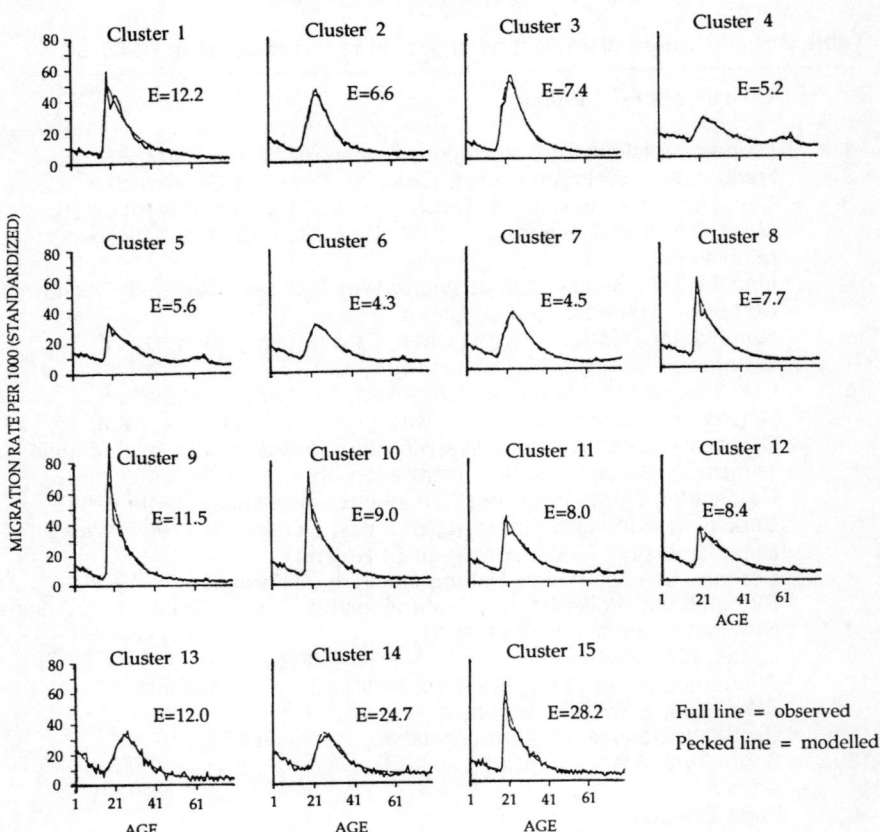

MIGRATION RATE PER 1000 (STANDARDIZED)

Cluster 1 E=12.2
Cluster 2 E=6.6
Cluster 3 E=7.4
Cluster 4 E=5.2
Cluster 5 E=5.6
Cluster 6 E=4.3
Cluster 7 E=4.5
Cluster 8 E=7.7
Cluster 9 E=11.5
Cluster 10 E=9.0
Cluster 11 E=8.0
Cluster 12 E=8.4
Cluster 13 E=12.0
Cluster 14 E=24.7
Cluster 15 E=28.2

Full line = observed
Pecked line = modelled

Note:

$$E = 100 \sum_a | m^a_I (mod) - m^a_I (obs) | / \sum_a m^a_I (obs)$$

where m^a_I (mod) and m^a_I (obs) are the predicted and observed migration rates for single year age group a for cluster I.

Figure 3.14 Observed and modelled in-migration schedules for optimum clustering of FPC areas

Source: Model parameters calibrated using MODEL (Rogers and Planck, 1984).

schedules with a high but later labour force peak. The labour force curves are rather more symmetrical with a less dramatic jump in the rate of in-migration on the upward slope. Schedules of clusters four, five and six are very different in shape in comparison with the previous schedules. Most of the FPC areas are non-metropolitan counties and since all the observed rates show some evidence of retirement, full model schedules (i.e. with retirement components) are constructed. The labour force peaks for these schedules are at a lower level than for the Greater London clusters and, significantly, these clusters exhibit a higher child dependency index. Cluster seven includes several provincial metropolitan districts as well as the remaining London boroughs and four of the counties in the South East. Its schedule, which includes an upward retirement slope, indicates a labour force component less pronounced than in clusters one to three but more so than in clusters four to six.

The schedules of clusters eight, nine and 10 are dominated by very high peaks in their labour force curves at an early age and no retirement component. The dramatic increase in the rate of in-movement around age 18 suggests that the student factor may be important in determining the shape of the schedule for these three groups, which turn out to contain FPC areas that all have major institutions of higher education located within their boundaries. Clusters 11 and 12 contain rather unusual combinations of areas, whilst the only areas failing to combine are South Tyneside, which has a relatively late labour force peak, Solihull and West Glamorgan.

The classification and modelling procedure outlined above provides a summary of the main types of migration schedule evident at the FPC area scale. It would also provide a systematic method of incorporating more up-to-date age-specific information from the NHSCR into the model used by OPCS for projecting sub-national migration.

3.5 Conclusions

Despite shortcomings, migration data from the NHSCR provide a wealth of valuable information on how migration propensities and patterns are changing from year to year. One of the most emphatic changes during the latter years of the 1980s has been the reversal in the pattern of net loss from the North to the South which had been increasing steadily since the mid-1970s. Faster growth in the tempo of migration northwards since 1985–86 has resulted in the North–South aggregate net migration balance turning positive in 1988–89. Migration across the metropolitan/non-metropolitan divide during the 1980s has also gathered pace as rates of loss from Greater London accelerated after 1983.

Since marked shifts have taken place in the distribution as well as in the volume of internal movement, it becomes increasingly important to use up-to-date information such as that available from the NHSCR more effectively to generate improved projections of future migration and population change.

4 Flows to and from London: a decade of change?

Mike Coombes and Martin Charlton

In seventeenth-century England, London was 'the dominant node in the national migratory system and one of overwhelming attractive power' (Pattern, 1973). Since that time the country has industrialised and then begun to de-industrialise. How does London stand now in the national system of migration flows? This chapter considers the experience of Britain's capital city over the last decade or so, but places emphasis on the role that London plays in relation to the rest of the country.

4.1 The importance of London for Britain's migration system: a review

This chapter's emphasis upon the salience of London for areas across the country may seem to be at odds with recent evidence for counterurbanisation in southern England (e.g. Champion, 1989b). Indeed, the proportion of Britain's population that lives within the Greater London county boundary has been declining since the 1930s (Coombes et al., 1989). However, the same period – at least until recently – has been characterised by increasing mobility of the population, so that London could still have been home for an increasing share of the population, if only for an increasingly short period of their lives. This notion of London as the key nodal point in the interlocking mesh of migration streams had been identified in flows between labour markets in 1970–71 by Kennett (1983). Although differing processes have been dominant in shaping migration flows in recent years, each has tended to re-shape rather than undermine 'the special character of London's role in the national pattern of labour migration' (Johnson et al., 1974, p. 89).

The de-industrialisation of London took place a decade earlier than in Britain's other conurbations, alongside the continuing growth of the City's financial services and the capital's remorseless attraction of corporate headquarters and other control functions. The employment associated with these centralised activities is at the upper end of the occupational hierarchy, and inevitably attracts large numbers of well-qualified people from elsewhere in Britain to meet the high level of demand. This demand-side analysis provides a framework for several of the key observations related to migration, and the role of London in particular. For example, the corporate dimension here echoes the importance placed by many commentators upon longer-distance migration by key staff moving between posts in the same multi-site organisation (Green et al., 1986). These internal labour markets in effect shrink distance by easing the obstacles to inter-regional migration – and most major organisations feature London as the key node in their own network. This process is, of course, fuelled by London's role as a world city, experiencing pressures that are not evident elsewhere in Britain. The nearest equivalent would be Paris, which has also seen an apparent loss of population to its rural hinterland regions. However, for white-collar migrants, the attraction of Paris is scarcely dimmed. Indeed, it is probably 'enhanced through the increase in the importance of internal labour markets within large organisations' (White, 1990, p. 105).

Another aspect of migration differentials that has become abundantly evident is the contrast between the two ends of the occupational hierarchy. Despite the Thatcher Government's insistence that national economic growth was being held back by restricted levels of mobility, their White Paper on regional policy accepted that 'it tends to be the young, the more skilled and the more enterprising who are ready to move in search of work' (Department of Trade and Industry, 1983). One twist to London's recurring inflow of higher-skilled workers has come with the recent widening of house price differentials leading to suggestions that the capital has become increasingly inaccessible to the less well-paid occupation groups. This would exacerbate the position in the early 1980s when net flows from North to South were already almost exclusively non-manual workers, despite the greater regional differential in job prospects being for manual workers (Champion and Townsend, 1990). Even within London itself, house prices differentials can be seen to be restricting the mobility of the less well paid, with the effect that 'migration and commuting are alternative equilibrating mechanisms in metropolitan labour sub-markets' (Congdon, 1989, p. 93). The larger-scale consequence has been the explosion of longer-distance commuting at the time of escalating house prices, so that it has become increasingly important to situate the experience of London within a much larger surrounding region that in effect represents the other symbiotic half of London's metropolitan system.

The most specific work on migration and the wider South East region, with a particular focus on the occupational segmentation of the migrant flows, is that reported in Fielding (1989). The analysis centres on evidence from the 1971–81 Longitudinal Study and emphasises the growth of those white-collar groups termed the 'service class' (although the category appears to include large numbers of small shopkeepers, as well as professionals and other highly paid groups). Taking the period as a whole, the South East was in fact a net exporter of service-class workers, but this net loss was far smaller than other key flows such as those moving from education in 1971 to being in the service class 10 years later. This transition was strongly associated with being a migrant

to the South East from other parts of the country. The conclusion from
the large series of disaggregated analyses is that the South East is an
'escalator region' within which promotion occurs much more rapidly.
The small net outflow of service-class workers may be in part due to the
numbers of promoted individuals – now perhaps having reached the level
of their own incompetence (Peter, 1985) – leaving the 'escalator' in order
to consolidate their advancement elsewhere. The South East thus gains
these individuals' most creative and motivated period of work inputs –
over which period they will most likely be in the young adult and early
family age group that also provides the highest per capita consumer
expenditure to that local economy. However, there is also anecdotal
evidence of a very different group of young in-migrants who are largely
destined to join the metropolitan 'underclass' – at worst living on the
streets, but certainly unlikely to move upward and outward from London
as time progresses.

This review has begun to sketch an outline of the relationship between
London and the rest of Britain – but it is hampered by the empirical
evidence upon which the work has had to depend. Many of the interesting hypotheses concern the 'life course' of individuals and the locations
at which they act out key phases of their work histories and family
developments. Unfortunately, these models can only be tested with long-
term monitoring of individuals' movements – data which in Britain
remains conspicuously lacking. The Longitudinal Study as yet covers
only one 10-year period in its information on migration within Britain.
Moreover the geographical perspective that is central to this chapter
requires very large numbers of cases to enable robust observations to
explore how far these generalisations apply predictably across the country, and whether different areas have quite distinct migration linkages
with the capital. For the moment, only aggregate measures can be readily
employed: the aim of the following analyses is to investigate with the
available information how far different parts of the country confirm or
contradict the patterns of linkage with London that have been sketched
so far.

4.2 The characteristics of migrants to and from London

The previous section has stressed the difficulty of investigating
empirically the issues that have been raised so far: available data sources
report the residential location of individuals at two time points only,
when the real need here is for life histories. The migration information
in the Longitudinal Study does not yet cover a sufficiently long period,
while the cohort studies (such as the National Child Development Study)
which have followed individuals over several decades do not cover sufficient numbers to support reliable analyses of relatively small subgroups
(e.g. comparisons of migrants to London from northern conurbations
with those from the rural South). A particular problem in the London
case is the lack of combined information on both migration and

commuting behaviour, which would allow areas' in-migration from London to be compared with the expansion of long-distance commuting to the capital.

4.2.1 The role of London migration in life chances

The 'snapshot' character of the available data shapes the analysis in to the artificial binary categories of 'out-' and 'in-migrants'. These categories clearly do not provide proxies for 'Londoners' and 'outsiders' – even if these latter categories could be defined in a meaningful way. One of the reasons for some apparent discrepancies between alternative migration data sets is the omission from the Census of those separate migration movements that were followed by a second move within the 12 months between the 'before' and 'after' information requested on the Census form (Boden et al., 1987a). This discrepancy is sizeable, showing that among those who do migrate, movements can be quite frequent. Thus a flow of recorded migrants from London is likely to mix 'born and bred' Londoners leaving the capital, together with some (quite recent) in-migrants to London returning to their previous origins, plus some others for whom London had been the fairly recent point of arrival (on a migration from somewhere else, perhaps abroad). However, the emphasis here is more on the role that London plays as the focus for opportunities which become open to people from other parts of the country through migration. In-migration flows from London may be more likely to include the longstanding London residents who are of less interest for this chapter – although evidence elsewhere suggests that migrant streams in general show that the influence of birthplace remains surprisingly pervasive even among more mobile populations (Rogers and Belanger, 1990).

4.2.2 Migration to London from overseas

The oft-repeated assertion that London has long been a focal point for migration can be illustrated by the fact that in 1981 barely 80 per cent of residents in the local labour market area (LLMA) covering the capital had been born in England. Of the other LLMAs (Coombes et al., 1982) in England, only Slough and Corby had higher proportions of residents born outside England. A crucial factor in this context is that nearly one in seven of London residents in 1981 had been born outside the British Isles, a value unmatched by any other British LLMA. This group exemplifies the role of London as a focal point, particularly perhaps for the first and/or longest movement, which may then be followed by other moves. Salt and Kitching (1990) show that by the mid-1980s around one in eight of Greater London's workforce were non-UK citizens, so that London was the home of over one in three of all the international in-migrants in Britain's labour force. The period 1985–88 saw London's share falling slightly, yet of all those non-UK citizens who had moved into Britain within the previous year, over half lived in London. In effect then, London can represent a virtual 'transit camp' that may provide the dramatic attraction that is sufficient to stimulate the initial decision to move from the home location – only to then open up unanticipated further opportunities that lead to a future migration, perhaps to a more rural location not too far from London in the first instance. Salt and Kitching also stress the importance of internal labour markets within multinational firms, showing that almost half of all recent in-migrants to Britain had remained with the same employer while moving internationally. This process will tend to explain some of London's high share of new in-migrants, through the multinationals' practice of short-term posting of key workers in a succession of major international centres such as London. Thus one group of the capital's non-UK workers will experience return migration overseas without moving on from London to other parts of the country.

4.2.3 Migration between London and the Celtic fringe

These generic patterns of movement are likely to find some echoes in the migration flows to London from other parts of Britain. Just as Salt and Kitching (1990) found international migration to be stratified (with the internal labour market being crucial for professional staff, alongside speculative migration by the low skilled seeking London's surplus poorly paid service jobs), so Fielding (1989) had noted the flows into the South East's service class alongside those into its potential underclass. More anecdotal evidence on the experience of migrants from North to South (see Green et al., 1986) stresses the high level of return migration – although this is usually seen to be more the experience of the marginal, opportunistic migrant than of those sheltered within internal labour markets. This leads on to the key concern here, the differences in the 'relationship' between London and different parts of Britain.

The proportions of London's 1981 residents who were born in the other countries of the UK were all quite modest, in being not very much above average for English LLMAs. In contrast, the proportion born in the Irish Republic was the fifth highest among English LLMAs, even though recent decades have effectively allowed equal ease of migration between all parts of the British Isles. However, the fact that there are far fewer Irish in LLMAs such as Guildford (to where people moving 'upward and onward' from London tend to move) suggests that the critical difference is that migrants from the Irish Republic have not been as successful as others in progressing beyond London (Table 4.1). This probably reflects the occupational bias that Salt and Kitching (1990) note in the continuing preponderance of the low skilled among migrants from the Irish Republic. All the 'Celtic fringe' countries have long had severe problems of underemployed low-skilled labour, and also limited local opportunities for the highly skilled (McCormick, 1991). The suggestion

Table 4.1 Share of selected LLMAs' 1981 population born in countries of the British Isles

LLMA	England	Wales	% born in Scotland	N. Ireland	Irish Republic
London	80.0	1.2	1.7	0.6	2.8
Woking & Weybridge	86.2	1.7	2.1	0.6	1.5
Guildford	88.8	1.6	1.9	0.5	1.0
Reigate & Redhill	90.4	1.4	1.6	0.5	1.1
Tunbridge Wells	92.2	1.1	1.5	0.4	0.6
Maidstone	93.5	1.0	1.3	0.4	0.6
Britain	78.1	5.2	9.9	0.5	1.1

Note: Northern Ireland refers here to the rest of UK, i.e. small numbers from elsewhere are also included.

is that Scotland, Wales and Northern Ireland have supplied streams of migrants to the London region that included a higher proportion who reached the 'stockbroker belt' than was the case of the migrant stream from the Irish Republic. If such difference can be observed from coarse regional data, it is unlikely that quite dramatic variations are to be found between localities, in terms of their relative dependence upon London as a focal point for migration flows.

4.2.4 The rate of migration into and out of London

The active involvement of London in the national migratory system can be illustrated with the 1981 Census migration data when aggregated to the LLMA framework. Since the Census definition of migration is a change of address, and most such movements are short distance, then the larger the LLMA the higher the proportion of its in-migrants that tend to be from within the same LLMA. Yet the proportion of London's 1981 residents who had been living in a different LLMA a year before was virtually the same as Birmingham's – a city less than a fifth the size of London. The capital also had a surprisingly high proportion of its 1980 residents who had moved to other LLMAs by 1981 (Table 4.2). Although it is common for areas of high in-migration also to record high out-migration (Stillwell et al., 1988), London is unusual among such 'hyperactive' LLMAs in also experiencing net out-migration (Owen and Green, 1989).

Table 4.2 1981 Census migration rates for England's largest LLMAs

LLMA	Population (,000)	Out-migrant %	In-migrant %	Net migrant %
London	7,593.1	2.0	1.5	− 0.5
Birmingham	1,419.2	2.1	1.5	− 0.6
Manchester	1,138.4	2.5	1.7	− 0.8
Newcastle	926.3	1.8	1.5	− 0.3
Liverpool	926.2	2.1	1.1	− 1.0
Leeds	725.7	2.2	1.8	− 0.4
Bristol	723.3	2.0	2.0	− 0.0
Nottingham	659.5	2.0	1.8	− 0.2
Sheffield	629.8	1.8	1.4	− 0.4

Note: The number of migrants (excluding those moving solely within the LLMA) is expressed as a percentage of the 1981 population.

4.2.5 The effect of distance from London

Turning to the influence of London on other LLMAs, Figure 4.1 expresses the sum of both in-migrants from, and out-migrants to London as a proportion of each LLMA's 1981 population. The location of LLMAs in the three highest septiles shows the strong significance of distance from London. Stillwell (1990a) has recently confirmed the well-established observation that much of the patterning of migration flows can be modelled in terms of the frictional effect of distance. Figure 4.1 demonstrates that, even if some links with London are less deterred by distance, these aggregate patterns still show a clear distance deterrence. The middle septile effectively provides a North–South border, extending in a nearly unbroken chain of LLMAs from the Severn to the Wash. This definition of the North–South divide, which was also confirmed by the cross-sectional analyses of Openshaw et al. (1988), is all the more remarkable in that it is also virtually the same as the outer limit of those LLMAs which experienced net in-migration from London. These LLMAs that gained from the migration exchange with London comprise a contiguous group of LLMAs in southern/eastern England, plus just four outliers – in fact, only six LLMAs north of the Severn–Wash 'chain' of LLMAs shown in Figure 4.1 experienced net in-migration from London. Furthermore, only five LLMAs south of that 'chain' (that is, among those with high levels of interaction with London) were net losers in their exchange with the capital.

In this relationship with London, then, higher aggregate levels of migration are clearly associated with a net inflow, and this pattern is in turn related to the effect of distance. The key here is the strong contrast shown by Stillwell et al. (1988) in the distance deterrence for flows to and from London: moves to the capital from other LLMAs are distinct

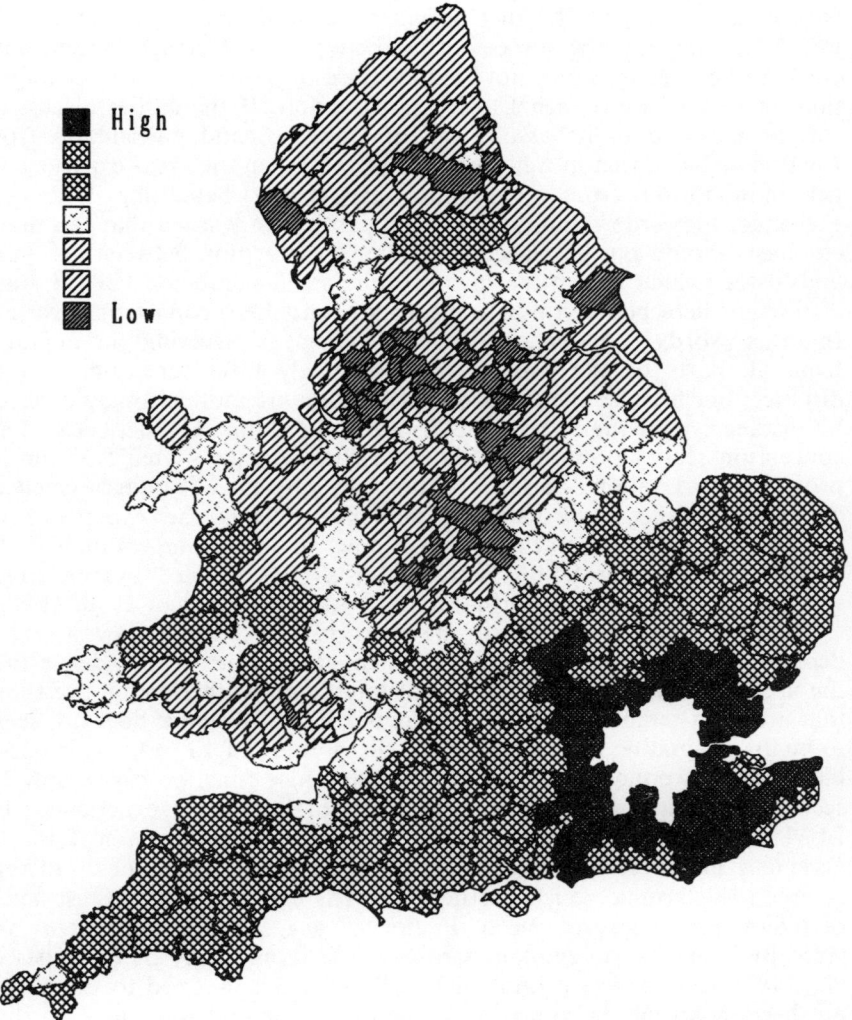

Figure 4.1 LLMAs' migration to and from London, 1980–81

from those leaving London (and the national pattern of migration flows in general) in being much more weakly deterred by distance. This reflects the special attractiveness of the capital which was speculatively interpreted earlier in terms of its propensity to provoke the first movement away from home.

This discussion has begun to highlight the distinctiveness of 'in' and 'out' flows involving London, whereas Figure 4.1 provides a highly aggregate analysis. The aggregate picture remains crucial as the context for more detailed modelling, in that it is the very distance effect which is so evident in Figure 4.1 that provides a central feature of that modelling. None the less, the stark contrast between the North and the South needs to be kept in mind, not least because of its echo in the net migration balance between each LLMA and London. If the earlier discussion was at all valid in its association of flows to, and particularly from London as being rich in well-qualified people, then the areas experiencing net in-migration from the capital are clearly benefiting from the exchange. Flowerdew and Salt (1979, p. 214) have warned that too much emphasis should not be placed on a simple distinction between net gains and losses (which may often involve quite small numbers), but the stark distinction here between north and south must be a robust observation. In other words, London could be envisaged as 'levering' in migrants from all parts of the country with relatively little constraint due to distance; but because the flows out of London are more strongly deterred by distance, then the rest of the South is the ultimate beneficiary. This conception sees the South gaining almost incidentally – that is, from its proximity to London – and not from any inherent advantages (such as climatic or other environmental attributes). Thus the experience of London migration is crucial in explaining an important component of growth in the wider South East, rather as was implied by the cross-sectional analyses of the North–South divide by Openshaw et al. (1988).

The final point here relates to the areas that make up the lowest septile depicted on Figure 4.1 Within the North, there is no real evidence that the areas showing the lowest levels of interaction with London are those that are most remote. Thus the deterrent effect of distance does not seem to be discriminating at this end of the distribution of LLMAs. It is possible that the exponential nature of the deterrence function can simply be seen as only strongly influencing the level of interaction experienced by LLMAs up to a certain distance away from the capital. Even if this is accepted, however, it leaves open the question of what 'local' factors emerge to determine which northern LLMAs experience the lowest levels of interaction. The evidence of Figure 4.1 suggests that these areas are typically 'conurbation subdominants' (in the terminology of Coombes et al., 1982); that is, towns and small cities closely connected to the major northern conurbation centres. A reasonable hypothesis may be that nearby major cities, such as Manchester, provide a competing attraction to London for those residents of towns like Bolton or Rochdale who are seeking the distinctive opportunities of a metropolis and might otherwise migrate to London. The urban dimension can be seen in the net outflow to London from the North's largest cities, and net inflow from London to Britain's smaller towns and settlements (Owen and Green, 1989). The following section seeks to anatomise these general patterns.

4.3 Models of the patterns of migration to and from London

In modelling spatial interaction, one of the components of the model is a deterrence function – representing some variable that is hypothesised

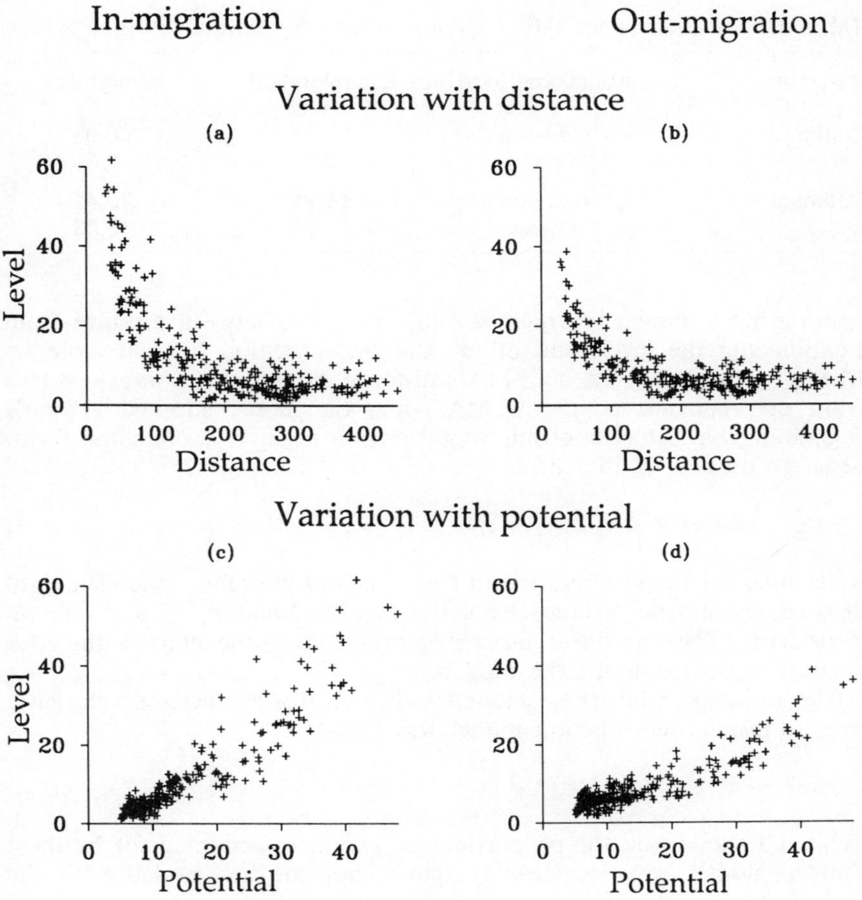

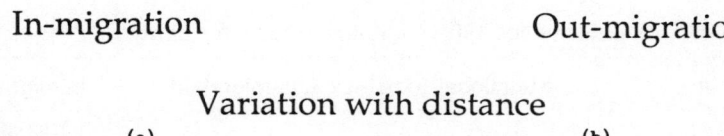

Figure 4.2   Modelling migration links with London, 1980–81

to restrict spatial interaction. The most familiar version is the distance deterrence function, but other alternative variables include travel time or generalised cost (Gleave and Cordey-Hayes, 1977). The form of the function may vary from the simple power or exponential form to more complex functions based on polynominals, or piecewise functions. Wilson (1974, p. 70) suggests that for short-distance applications there are good theoretical reasons for starting with the negative exponential form.

4.3.1 Migration as a function of distance

The first stage in the modelling exercise used migration flows from the 1981 Census, aggregated to LLMAs. The initial models explore the

Table 4.3 F statistics for 1981 migration models for LLMAs

Variable	Functional form	Out-migration	In-migration
Distance	Exponential	6.27	6.98
	Power	10.34	9.39
Potential	Exponential	18.11	12.41
	Power	14.18	15.09

relationship – shown in Figure 4.2 (a) and (b) – between distance from London and the levels and of in- and out-migration (to and from an LLMA respectively). Each LLMA's distance from London was measured from the centroids of the LLMAs, and the model adopted Wilson's suggestion that the relationship might have a negative exponential form. Separate models of the form:

$$\text{rate}_i = b_1 \exp(-b_0 \text{ dist}_{il}) + e_i \tag{4.1}$$

were fitted for the in-migration rate and the out-migration rate. The term dist_{il} represents the distance from the area to London; e_i is a random error term. The non-linear modelling procedure (proc nlin) in the SAS package was used to fit the models.

The residuals from these models indicated distinct heteroscedasticity, so a simple power function model was tried:

$$\text{rate}_i = b_1 \exp (\text{dist}_{il}^{-b_0}) + e_i \tag{4.2}$$

Table 4.3 shows that the proportions of variance accounted for by these simpler models were noticeably higher than for the models with the negative exponential form.

4.3.2 Migration as a function of population potential

The problem with using distance as a regressor is that it accords equal weight to locations equidistant from London. Clearly, this makes a nonsense of the local relationship between, for example, Keighley and Leeds. A possible substitute regressor should try to take this into account and, at the same time, exhibit some variations with distance from London. One measure which has been used in the past to account for intensity of spatial interaction between different locations is that termed 'population potential' (Stewart, 1947). There are a number of different forms of this measure (Rich, 1980, provides several alternatives). In this application, the measure is based on a simple ratio:

$$\text{pot}_i = (\text{pop}_l/\text{dist}_{il}) \, / \, \sum_j (\text{pop}_j/\text{dist}_{ij}) \tag{4.3}$$

where j is any other area than i (including London). The term pop_i is the population of London, so pot_i represents the potential due to interaction with London only, expressing this as a proportion of the total potential for that area.

Again, the centroids of the LLMAs (in actuality, they are the positions where ARC/INFO chooses to place its label points) are used as the locations between which distances are calculated. This assumes that the population is located at a series of some 246 'spikes' around England and Wales. Figure 4.2 (c) and (d) shows the relationship between migration rates and this potential measure. Non-linear models, of both forms above, were used here, the exponential form being:

$$rate_i = b_1 \exp(-b_0 \, pot_i) + e_i \tag{4.4}$$

and the power function form:

$$rate_i = b_1 (pot_i^{-b_0}) + e_i \tag{4.5}$$

where pot_i is as defined in equation 4.3. As shown in Table 4.3, the power function performed better for the in-migration model, but the exponential form accounted for more of the variation in the observed out-migration rates. Given this ambivalent evaluation, the power function model (equation 4.5) is used in the rest of this chapter because it is the simpler form and offers the more consistently high F statistics as a foundation for the later disaggregated modelling. One problem not addressed here is that the potentials of neighbouring zones will be spatially autocorrelerated. This will inflate the goodness-of-fit statistics – for this reason, care is required in their interpretation.

4.3.3 The variation of distance deterrence between age groups

So far, this chapter has solely considered modelling migration patterns in 1981, using information from the 1981 Census of Population. The remaining sections extend the modelling here to consider migration at the Family Practitioner Committee (FPC) area level, and for the 1980–81 flows and the 1985–86 flows. It is important to note that the transition here to the FPC data also shifts the definition of the areas being analysed from the functionally defined LLMAs to a set of administrative areas (Boden et al., 1987a). The LLMA centred on London is, however, only slightly larger than the Greater London county which becomes the object of interest for the remaining analysis.

The inter-FPC data was aggregated to provide measures of in- and out-migration for all ages for both 1980–81 and 1985–86. This permits comparison of the LLMA models for 1980–81 and the FPC-level models for the same time period. By then extending the modelling to the 1985–86 time period, these results can be compared with the results of the

Table 4.4 Distance deterrence parameters for migration streams, 1980–81

Age-group	Out-migration to London	In-migration from London
Total*	1.04	1.44
Total	0.90	1.33
0–14	1.06	1.45
15–24	0.77	1.14
25–39	0.90	1.44
40–54	1.02	1.32
55–69	1.28	1.22[†]
70 +	1.32	1.44

Notes: (i)   The values are the model estimates of b_0 (so that the higher the value, the greater the decline from areas near to London to those further away in the average rate of migration).

    (ii)* Using LLMAs; the remainder of the table refers to FPC–area analyses.

   (iii)[†] The F statistic of this model falls below the level which indicates statistical significance.

1980–81 models. Because of the variability in migration among different age groups, the data were aggregated into the following age classes: 0–14, 15–24, 25–39, 40–54, 55–69, and 70 or over. The regressor in all cases is the proportion of the FPC area's total potential that is due to London (in effect, the relative attractiveness of London for that FPC area). The potentials were computed separately for 1981 and 1986. The way that the potential values are calculated (equation 4.3) allows the critical values in these models to be interpreted as portraying the deterrent effect of distance (as mediated by the relative attraction of London for any area).

The earlier discussion of migration processes speculated that the pattern of migration links between LLMAs would vary substantially according to the stage in the life course that was the subject of analysis. Stillwell et al. (1988, p. 37) show a consistently lower distance deterrence for young adults, from school-leaving through to their late twenties. Those aged over 50 are the most deterred by distance, showing a distinctly shorter mean length of movement in the National Health Service Central Register (NHSCR) data set. The deterrence model (equation 4.5) developed in the previous section can be used to explore the age-specific evidence with regard to links with London – just as it served to confirm the lower deterrent effect for flows to London when compared to those out of the capital. This latter point is reinforced by the total values (for both types of areas) in the top two rows of Table 4.4, which show a distance deterrence value for migration from London almost half as much again as that for flows to the capital. A similar

Table 4.5 Rates of migration to and from London by age group, 1980–81 and 1985–86

Age group	Out-migration to London		In-migration from London	
	1980–81	1985–86	1980–81	1985–86
Total	0.358	0.356	0.448	0.488
0–14	0.198	0.192	0.346	0.399
15–24	0.945	0.912	0.688	0.639
25–39	0.523	0.550	0.702	0.741
40–54	0.139	0.172	0.239	0.340
55–69	0.077	0.071	0.315	0.323
70 +	0.116	0.095	0.283	0.327

Note: Migration rate computed as the number of migrants to/from London as a percentage of the 1981 or 1986 population.

observation of the paramount effect of distance in decentralisation from London was made from 1971 data by Flowerdew and Salt (1979, p. 223).

The age-specific values in the remainder of Table 4.4 confirm that the first post-education age group shows the lowest distance deterrence value for both directions of migration. For out-migration to London, the deterrent effect clearly increases with age in adult life, the childhood value not surprisingly echoing those of the age groups in which most of their parents are to be found. The fact that the children's value is slightly higher than either of the two middle age groups suggests that, given most households migrate together, adults who are parents apparently are more deterred by distance than those who are DINKY (double income, no kids yet) or single. Table 4.5 provides a series of values for the rate of out-migration to London in both 1980–81 and 1985–86. Comparing the data for 1980–81 with the equivalent values in Table 4.4 tends to suggest that as distance deterrence rises then the overall level of migration to London falls. Since the values for the distance deterrent are derived from actual migration flows, then the rising of the deterrent value with age (for out-migration especially) implies that the number of longer-distance migrants diminishes with age faster than does the volume of shorter-distance flows to London. This pattern would be consistent with the notion that the immediate post-education age group is exceptional, after which the process of migration to London resumes a more conventional profile. The most visible element of this exceptional age-specific movement to London is the continuing longer-distance inflow of well-qualified young people such as graduates (Munro, 1991).

The values shown in Tables 4.4 and 4.5 for inflows from London do not make up so clear-cut a story line. The lowest distance deterrence

value is once again for the youngest adult group, but this is not an
exceptionally high value by national standards – providing an echo of
the Labour Force Survey analysis of Molho (1987) which found young
men in London not to be highly mobile. Migration from London shows
a less clear relationship between the deterrence values and age than does
migration to London. The most interesting observation may be that the
model itself fails to perform adequately when attention shifts to the
migration from London of those around retirement age (55–69). The
model's emphasis upon distance fails to reduce adequately the variation
in the observed values for areas' receipt of inflows from London. This
may reflect a high level of selectivity of destination by this age group,
as suggested by the evidence of the Longitudinal Study (OPCS SSRU
1990, p. 4). Those 55–69-year-olds who had moved out of the London
metropolitan area between 1971 and 1981 did show a notable distance
deterrence in their choice of destination, but within this pattern there
remains dramatic variation. For example, 32 migrants had moved to
Thanet, but none to the similarly accessible Bedford; 16 went to
Cornwall, but only six to equally distant Shropshire. This evidence is
particularly interesting given that the origin area is defined to be substantially wider than Greater London alone. As a result, there is much
less probability that longer-distance migration is being understated
through the London data only identifying moves to nearby locations,
when these prove to be only the first part of a longer move. This
question is raised by the evidence of Bolton (1988) that the 10 per cent
of in-migrants to a North Devon study area who came from Greater
London were outnumbered two to one by those from outer parts of the
metropolitan area. Similarly, Cross (1990) found that the peak zone for
net in-migration from London itself was a nearby arc of areas from
Chelmsford to Brighton – that is, much of the outer metropolitan area
itself – whereas the strongest net flows from these areas stretch from
Norfolk to Dorset, plus some parts of Devon. The issue that remains
unresolved, of course, is how far the flows from areas near London are
made up of people who previously had moved out of London itself.
Without life history data these questions remain unresolved, so that the
full effect of London as an influence in the past upon in-migrants to
other parts of Britain may remain understated.

4.4 Change through the 1980s?

The period since 1981 has been one of sporadic economic recovery,
prompting the possibility of increased migration levels during the years
of strong contrast in economic conditions of the North and the South.
Stillwell et al. (1988) show that overall migration levels did indeed
increase over this period – confirming that the 1981 Census was taken
when migration was at a low ebb. Total flows in 1986 were about eight
per cent higher than in 1981, while the South generally has experienced
a growth in net in-migration. However, London's net migration loss of

1981 was already far less than it had been through the late 1970s and there was no further relative improvement during the early 1980s, and then in 1986 the net loss accelerated once again. Stillwell et al. (1988, p. 25) stress that most northern regions 'have experienced significant increases in the proportion of their outmoves which involve Greater London' from 1981–86. As for moves from London, there was some evidence for an increase of in-movement to the West Midlands, but these time series are far less clear-cut than those for migration to London.

There is unfortunately all too little data available to examine the socio-occupational aspect of London's migration trends since 1981. Champion (1989b) echoed the evidence of the Longitudinal Study analyses by finding that the main change between 1971 and 1981 had been the relative increase of in-migrants to London of non-manual workers (who provided recruits for the 'service-class' expansion). Hamnett (1991, p. 201) assesses the changes since 1981 as implying that London 'has become increasingly professionalised' as a generality. If so, then higher-skilled migrants are likely to have continued to have made a substantial contribution to the process.

The modelling of 1980–81 patterns can be repeated on 1985–86 data to identify the major changes that have taken place to the migration relationships between London and the rest of the country. The aggregate models show that the deterrence coefficient is unchanged at 1.33 for movement from London, but that for out-migration to London in 1986 had fallen to 0.82 (compared to the 1981 value of 0.90). Table 4.5 showed clearly that out-migration rates to London had slightly fallen, but in-migration rates from London had risen markedly between 1981 and 1986. The reduction in the distance deterrence for out-migration, then, may not be associated with an increase in migration from the still-depressed northern regions so much as a decline in the flow from southern regions that was noted earlier. The age-specific models show that the most dramatic drop in the distance deterrence was for the child age group, perhaps indicating a reduced resistance of whole families to longer-distance moves. The second steepest decline in deterrence value is for the post-education age group, reinforcing this group's behaviour as being the most willing to migrate over long distances. Figure 4.3 shows the residuals from this model, with the large northern cities all contributing more young in-migrants to London than the model predicts – but otherwise there is no very consistent spatial pattern to the residuals. For the older age groups the main difference is the considerable strengthening of the model's significance, even though Table 4.5 suggested that it was only the 40–54-year-old group that had increased their migration flow to London.

Turning briefly to flows from London, the stability of the aggregate deterrence value is quite closely mirrored in the age-specific models. As with the flows to London, the 1985–86 models tend to show higher levels of significance – with one notable exception. The retirement age group (55–69) was the one model of inflows from London that was not

Standardised
residuals

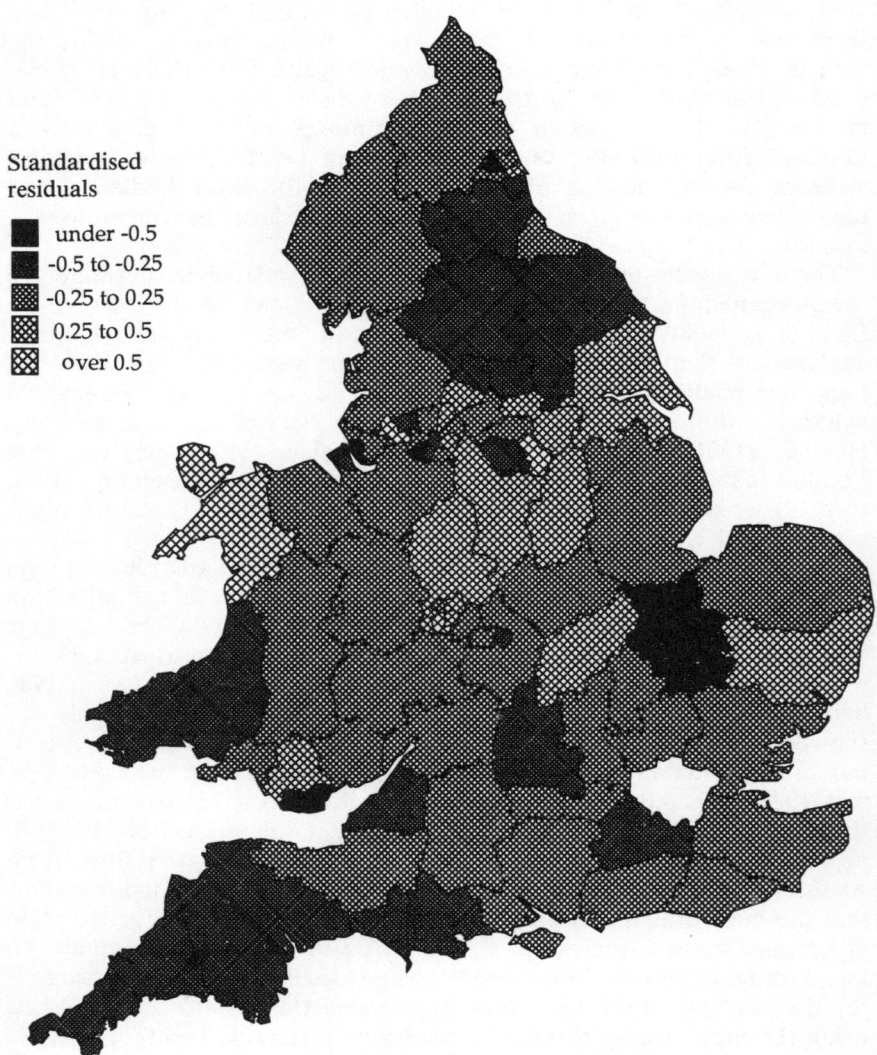

Figure 4.3 Standardised residuals from modelling FPC area outflows to
London of 15–24-year-olds, 1980–81

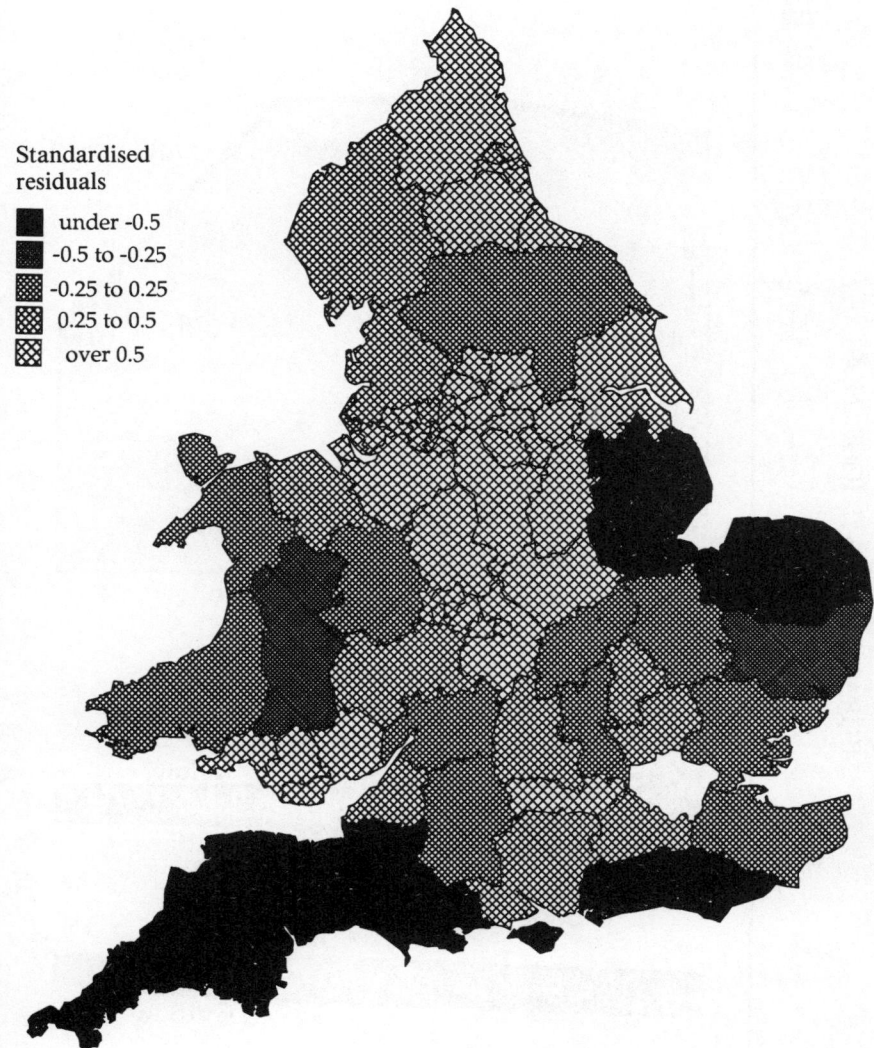

Figure 4.4 Standardised residuals from modelling FPC area inflows from London of 55–69-year-olds, 1985–86

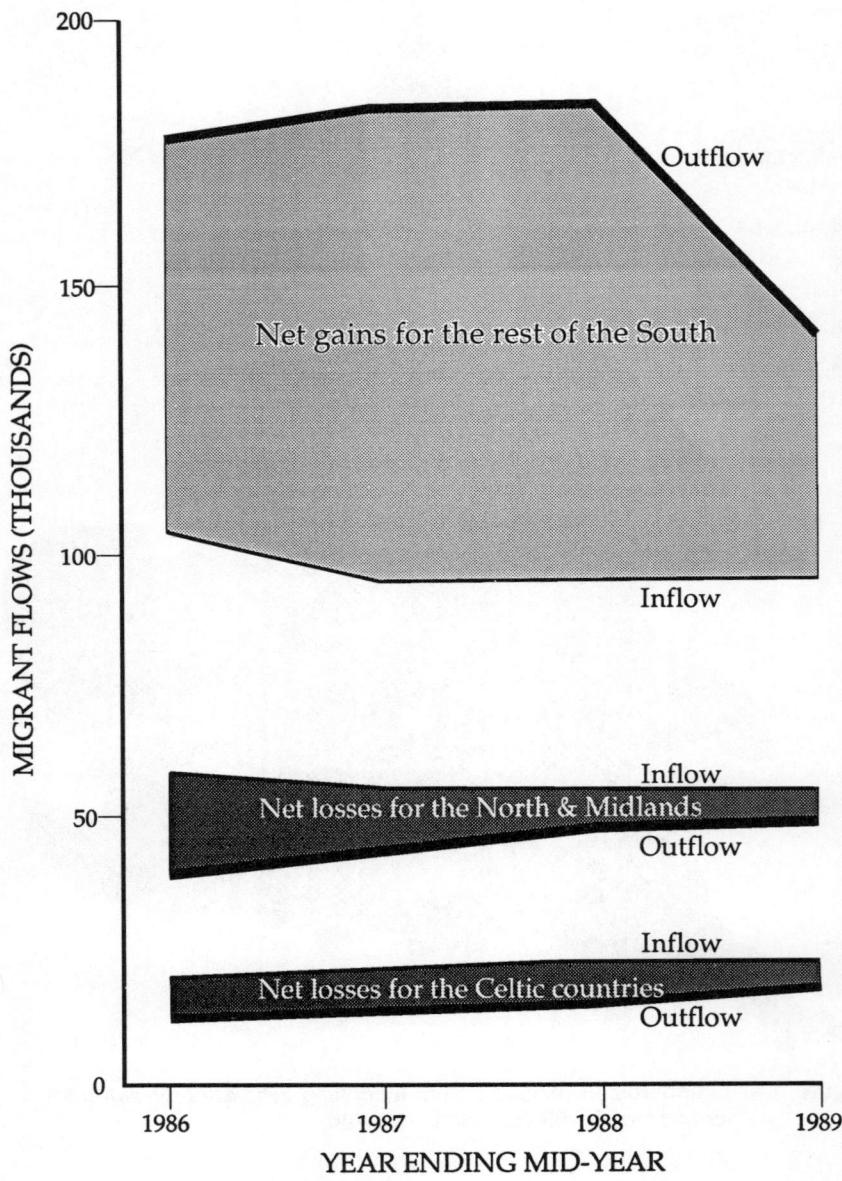

Figure 4.5 Migration links between London and other parts of the UK, 1986–89

significant in 1981, its F value in fact declined further by 1985–86. Figure 4.4 shows the residual values for these flows, illustrating the variation between contiguous areas that proved too diffuse for the distance-based model to estimate. The higher values for familiar resort/ retirement areas, compared to others equidistant from London, illustrates the selectivity of this particular movement pattern.

The modelling work has shown that, to a large extent, the distributional pattern of flows to and from London has been quite stable from 1981 to 1986. Yet the same period was one in which the scale of the flows varied in response to changes in relative regional economic prosperity. The initial surge of economic recovery in London had diffused outwards by 1986, so that the rate of out-migration to London was just slightly less than it had been five years earlier when the recession was still deep. On the other hand, the flow from London was almost 10 per cent higher by 1986 than it had been in 1981. This latter change is primarily related to shorter-distance movement, with economic recovery apparently fuelling further suburbanisation and other moves to southern areas.

The final question is whether these patterns have persisted since 1986. Figure 4.5 shows the trends in flows to and from London for the three broad parts of Britain that have been discussed here. Once again it is clear that any very substantial aggregate change must be based on flows from – and particularly to – other parts of southern England. There is a notable reduction to the net out-migration from northern England, but this is dwarfed by the waxing and (here) waning of migration into the South. The narrowing of the migration 'balance' between London and the Midlands and northern England could reflect the spread of economic recovery beyond the South of England, but it might also relate to house price inflation. The late 1980s saw rapidly widening regional price differentials which only began to close as the 'ripple' of inflation reached the North at the end of the decade (Coombes and Raybould, 1991). However, the evidence of Figure 4.5 clearly highlights the change within the South from 1988 to 1989, a full year after any incentive to move out from London for cheaper houses would have ceased to apply to most of accessible southern England. Therefore the migration time series depicted in Figure 4.5 may well be more closely tied to broader economic trends than to house price relativities.

4.5 Retrospective and prospective

The empirical analyses in this chapter has been restricted, by data availability, to very indirect 'testing' of the key processes that were identified in the early discussion of London's role in the migration system of Britain. Due to this caveat, relatively little weight can be placed upon claims to have demonstrated the validity of any hypothesis. Certainly confirmed is the importance of the young adult age group in the flows of migrants to London; various contextual material supports the interpretation that these flows substantially reduce the numbers of higher-skilled young people in the origin areas. Equally clear is that the flows from London of 'family building' age groups are much more strongly deterred by distance, so that the net effect of these two major migrant streams is a transfer of people from the North, via London, to the South. Whether these flows often include the same individuals, with a time-lag, cannot be known without long-term monitoring data (for example, from the incorporation of 1991 Census data into the Longitudinal Study). The need to use the NHSCR data here provides an ironic echo with the preface of Hollingsworth (1970) whose research 'was begun at a time [1963] when migration statistics in Great Britain were much scarcer than they are now and perhaps it seems to lay undue stress on the National Health Service Register data at the expense of the Census'.

On another methodological point, this chapter has provided encouraging results from its models using measures derived from population potential calculations. In this way, analyses need only data for the flows involving a single origin or destination – two vectors out of the whole movement matrix. Yet the explanatory model is not similarly constrained by effectively assuming that the single destination was the only feasible option: the independent variable derived from a full proportion potential analysis represents the relative attraction of that destination among the system of competing alternative destinations. This model proved flexible and robust, failing only when faced with the highly selective pattern of retirement-age migration out from London.

The notion of a 'transit camp' was put forward at an early stage to dramatise the very high mobility levels of the London population. The unique position of the capital has been illustrated by its role as the main entry point for international migrants – who include both high-level staff of multinational corporations and also low-skilled migrants who may now be taking the jobs that in previous decades attracted surplus labour from peripheral parts of Britain. The transient character of migration to London was portrayed more speculatively in relation to the net flows from the North, which were characterised as being increasingly of well-qualified young people who may well then join the move on to more rural parts of the South.

In this context, a number of changes since 1981 appear to suggest an increasing dependence of some northern areas upon the opportunities afforded by London. Of course, the years since 1986 saw escalating house prices heighten the barrier to migration from the North, but the underlying pressures showed through the increase in other forms of response such as long-distance daily or weekly commuting. These new developments, so far only documented in relation to London, provide another twist to the long-standing uniqueness of the capital's role. Thus the evidence reviewed here has confirmed a key conclusion of the seminal study of Johnson et al. (1974, pp. 77–8): unfortunately, their assertion of the capital's crucial position in British migration patterns was simply inverted by the statement that 'the significance of the London labour market in sustaining national mobility levels is difficult to underestimate' (sic). The evidence in other chapters of this book, in which London is cited as a major feature of the migration experience of particular regions and groups of the population, confirms that this chapter has not over-estimated London's continuing significance.

PART II

REGIONAL PERSPECTIVES

5 Migration trends for Northern Ireland: links with Great Britain

Paul Compton

5.1 Introduction

With an estimated population of 1.6 million in 1990, or 2.75 per cent of the national total, Northern Ireland is the smallest formal region in the UK. For this as well as other reasons, like its geographical separation from the rest of Britain, it is often omitted from national overviews. Yet, population size alone considerably understates its significance within the current UK demographic scene. At the moment, the province accounts for more than 3.5 per cent of UK live births and for almost 10 per cent of natural increase. Furthermore, net migration from Northern Ireland has accounted for over five per cent of actual population growth in Great Britain since the mid-1970s. In effect, it is the only part of the UK where the natural reproduction of the labour force is buoyant, and for this reason Northern Ireland migrants will remain significant within the overall structure of UK internal migration for the foreseeable future, and will continue to play an important role in satisfying the manpower demands of labour-deficient GB regions.

The inclusion of Northern Ireland in a volume about UK internal migration patterns is therefore wholly appropriate. The approach, however, is a little different from that adopted in other chapters. Internal migration within the province is not considered because NHSCR data are lacking on the topic. Instead, the chapter concentrates upon the migrational relationships of Northern Ireland with Great Britain. Recent temporal trends of in-, out- and net migration are treated in some detail and explanations offered. The spatial patterns of the destinations of Northern Ireland migrants in GB and the GB origins of movers to Northern Ireland are also examined at different spatial scales. The chapter begins, however, with a brief review of migration data sources and procedures in the province. The primary purpose here is to take advantage of the fact that independent NHSCRs exist in Belfast and Edinburgh to explore the internal consistency of NHSCR transfers as estimators of migration.

5.2 Migration data for Northern Ireland

Migration statistics for Northern Ireland are derived in essentially the same way as for Great Britain. The Census of Population is the main source of information about internal mobility. Inward migration is also picked up in the process although the failure to distinguish between civilian mobility and movements of the armed forces makes these data difficult to interpret. Otherwise, inter-censal estimates of flows into and out of the province are based on the transfer of NHS records. In this respect, Northern Ireland is like Scotland in having its own NHSCR maintained by the Central Services Agency (CSA) in Belfast. As a consequence of this arrangement two parallel sets of migration estimates for Northern Ireland are available – those based on CSA registrations and those derived from the corresponding data recorded by Southport and Edinburgh (a CSA de-registration should appear as a re-registration in Southport or Edinburgh and vice versa).

In one important respect the CSA is managed differently from the other NHSCRs. The transfer of patient records within Northern Ireland is not available by geographical area and estimates of migration internal to the province cannot be derived from the Belfast NHSCR, although it would only require a relatively small administrative change in the way the system is currently operated to overcome this limitation. The province is divided into four Area Health Boards (AHB), analogous to the Family Practitioner Committee areas of England and Wales and the Area Health Boards in Scotland, and there is no reason why statistics of transfers between these areas should not be made available by the CSA. A drawback, however, would be in interpreting what such transfers would imply about internal migration. In a small territory like Northern Ireland, it cannot be assumed that transfers between doctors in different AHBs will always imply a migration since transfers may take place without a change of residence. The potential for drawing false inferences from such data would be particularly acute in the Belfast urban area which falls into two AHBs.

Migration between Northern Ireland and non-UK places is estimated in the following way. Immigration to the province is derived from new NHS registrations by country of origin. As regards emigration, movements to Southern Ireland are derived from the Republic's Labour Force Survey, whereas migration to the rest of the world is estimated from either CSA de-registrations, grossed up on the assumption that 40 per cent of emigrants return their medical cards, or from the International Passenger Survey, whichever source gives the larger estimate.

5.3 Consistency of NHSCR data

Reference has already been made to the fact that separate NHSCR-based estimates of Northern Ireland migration with Great Britain are available. In an ideal 'statistical' world, the two would tally, e.g. transfers to

Table 5.1   A comparison of estimated movements between Northern Ireland and England and Wales and Scotland, 1983 and 1989

| | | Based on NHSCR in: | | |
	Belfast	Edinburgh	Southport	Discrepancy
		1983 figures		
To NI from Scotland	1,142	598	–	544
From NI to Scotland	1,491	1,279	–	212
NI balance	– 349	– 681	–	332
To NI from E & W	8,454	–	6,067	2,387
From NI to E & W	8,300	–	8,543	243
NI balance	154	–	– 2,476	2,630
Overall NI balance	– 195	–	– 3,157	2,962
		1989 figures		
To NI from Scotland	1,494	1,039	–	455
From NI to Scotland	1,875	1,633	–	242
NI balance	– 381	– 594	–	213
To NI from E & W	9,154	–	8,873	281
From NI to E & W	13,935	–	14,148	213
NI balance	– 4,781	–	– 5,275	494
Overall NI balance	– 5,162	–	– 5,869	707

Scotland (England and Wales) would produce the same number of re-registrations in Edinburgh (Southport) as de-registrations in Belfast and so on. But this is not the case as the estimates for 1983 and 1989, for example, illustrate (Table 5.1). The lack of consistency is particularly apparent in the data for 1983 when there were large discrepancies in the estimates of outflow from Northern Ireland. But it was in the determination of the migration balance that the problem was most serious – Belfast suggesting a small net gain at the expense of England and Wales against Southport's substantial net loss, while the Edinburgh figures suggest a net loss to Scotland roughly double the Belfast estimate. In 1989, although the Belfast and Southport estimates of the gross flows between the two areas are quite close, because Belfast recorded a higher level of movement to Northern Ireland and Southport a higher estimate of migration to England, the discrepancy between the net migration estimates still amounted to 10 per cent. The discrepancy was even larger in the case of the estimated net flow to Scotland.

Two explanations have been advanced to explain such discrepancies. The first concerns the wide variation in the interval between moves and subsequent re-registrations – an average interval of three months' delay is assumed. But while this might account for small random discrepancies, it cannot explain consistent errors, e.g. why the receiving NHSCR should generally record the larger number of transfers. The other explanation is that the Southport transfers were obtained from a 10 per cent sample

Table 5.2 Northern Ireland population change, mid-1975 to mid-1989

Period	Natural change	Net migration with: England	Scotland	Wales	Other places	Total	Actual change
		Numbers in 00s					
Mid-1975–81	61,4	− 20,6	− 1,6	− 1,1	− 19,2	− 42,5	18,9
Mid-1981–88	94,0	− 32,2	− 1,9	− 1,1	− 10,6	− 45,8	48,2
		Annual rates per 1,000 Northern Ireland population					
1975–81	6.7	− 2.3	− 0.2	− 0.1	− 2.1	− 4.7	2.1
1981–88	7.6	− 2.6	− 0.2	− 0.1	− 0.9	− 3.7	3.9

before 1985 whereas the Belfast and Edinburgh transfers have always been based on full counts. This may well account for the large discrepancies between the Southport and Belfast figures in 1983 but would also imply that the Belfast data are the more reliable estimators of movement between England and Wales and Northern Ireland before 1985. The close agreement between the Southport and Belfast figures in 1989, when both were full counts, would seem to support this. In this sense, it is therefore a little unfortunate that this study relies on Southport data throughout. Neither explanation accounts for the large, consistent discrepancies between Belfast and Edinburgh.

However, it would be wrong to be unduly critical of NHSCR transfers as estimators of migration. Clearly, the estimates of flows between major areas are of the right order of magnitude and have been shown to be broadly consistent with census-based estimates. They would seem also faithfully to reflect the main temporal trends. But against that there are good reasons to believe that net migration estimates, in particular, may suffer from quite serious inaccuracies because errors are compounded in the process of differencing migration flows. As for which are the preferred migration values to be used for the population estimates, the current procedure is to accept the transfers recorded by the receiving NHSCR as the more reliable estimate of population movements.

5.4 Net migration and population growth in Northern Ireland

Reliable net migration estimates for the area of Northern Ireland go back to 1861. Since then the province has lost around three-quarters of its natural increase through net out-migration, which translates into a net outflow of around 850–900,000 people up to the present. Moreover, at no time during this period did the province grow in population as a result of migration. In recent years the bulk of the net loss has been to Great Britain rather than overseas, but even over this relatively short period significant changes are apparent (Table 5.2). Thus the proportion of the net outflow going to England has risen substantially, from just under half the net loss in the 1970s to more than 70 per cent during the 1980s. Moreover, the actual rate of net loss to England has also increased. As a result of this shift, the loss to places outside the UK was well down in the 1980s, mainly due to a change in the pattern of movement with the Irish Republic – a sizeable loss to the Republic during the second half of the 1970s (probably in excess of 10,000) being converted into a small net gain during the 1980s.

Yet, unlike other UK regions, the migration balance is less important than natural increase in determining actual population change. The preservation of comparatively high fertility has ensured a birth rate well above the UK average (17.5 against 13.5 per 1,000 being typical of the 1980s), which in turn has generated an age structure containing relatively few elderly people by national standards. As a result the crude death-rate is relatively low and natural increase is some three times higher than the UK mean. Furthermore, in only three regions - East Anglia, the South West and the East Midlands – is the actual rate of growth higher than in Northern Ireland, notwithstanding the fact that the province continues to lose at least half its natural increase through net out-migration.

5.5 Migration trends between Northern Ireland and Great Britain

The migration trends between Northern Ireland and Great Britain covering the 15-year period 1975 to 1990 are presented in Figure 5.1 and lead to the following observations. First, the volume of movement between Northern Ireland and Great Britain, i.e. the sum of the inflows and outflows, is substantial but fluctuates over time. It fell sharply between 1975 and 1981 but had fully recovered by the late 1980s, although the most recent figures suggest that the latest peak has now passed and that we are at the beginning of another downturn. Secondly, the gross outflows and inflows are strongly correlated with the volume of migration ($r = 0.96$ and 0.93 respectively) and are also moderately correlated with each other ($r = 0.81$), i.e. when out-migration rises, in-migration also tends to rise and vice versa. Thirdly, net migration from Northern Ireland is positively related to overall mobility, i.e. during phases of low mobility the net loss of population from the province is also likely to be relatively low and vice versa. Fourthly, given points two and three above, not only is the net outflow from Northern Ireland positively related to gross out-migration ($r = 0.91$), it is also positively related to gross in-migration ($r = 0.49$), i.e. as net out-migration grows, so too, somewhat paradoxically, does the influx of people to the province. Fifthly, although it is understandable that studies of Northern Ireland migration should focus on 'emigration', the occurrence of a high level of in-migration to the province should not be overlooked. Over the period in question, the influx has typically fallen in the range of 65 and 75 per cent of the gross outflow and constitutes a clear example of Ravenstein's 'law' – that dominant migration streams generate counterflows in the

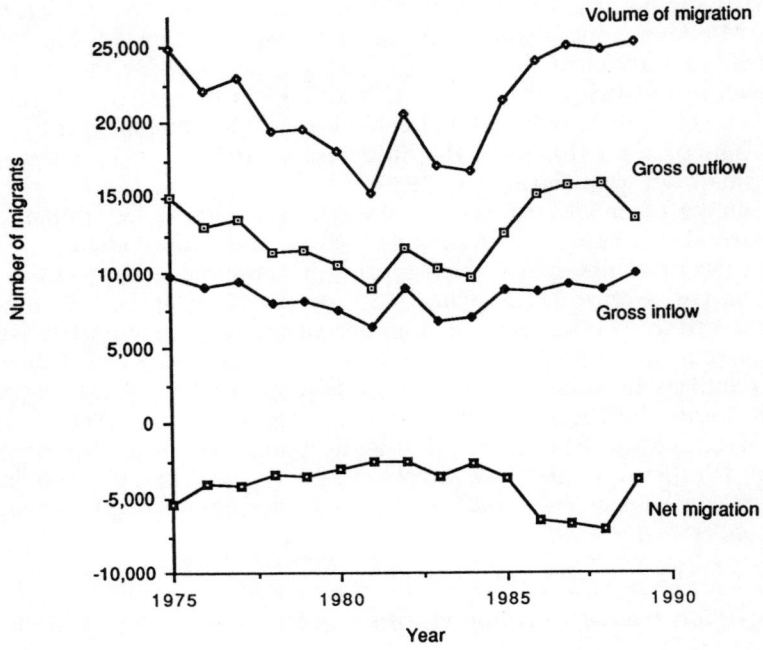

Figure 5.1   Migration trends for Northern Ireland, 1975–89

reverse direction, no matter how unattractive the area originating the dominant stream may seem.

Survey results suggest that the bulk of movement between Northern Ireland and Britain is job-related, i.e. it comprises migrants active in the labour market and their dependants (Compton and Power, 1991). It may also be assumed that a substantial part of the inflow to the province is of people with Northern Ireland connections, and does not consist of what may be termed 'primary' movers from Great Britain. The rather low proportion of Great Britain-born residents in Northern Ireland would bear this out (Department of Health and Social Services, 1983). Given these circumstances, one might expect the observed patterns to be driven mainly by economic factors, notwithstanding the existence of other significant categories of migrant, like students going on to higher education in Britain and retirement movers. It is easy to see that political instability may well deter some primary movement to the province, but otherwise the effect of the 'troubles' on migration is now relatively inconsequential.

The economic mechanisms underlying the trends picked out in Figure 5.1 operate at two separate levels. At the more basic level, there are the circumstances that explain why the dominant direction of movement is towards Great Britain. These are largely connected with the state of the local labour market. But in addition to this, there is a second subsidiary level made up of factors that govern the temporal variability in mobility between the two areas. These, by and large, are associated with the level of economic activity in the UK. Let us briefly examine each in turn. Over the long term, the supply of labour in Northern Ireland has consistently outstripped demand. This is caused not so much by a low rate of new job creation, where the long-run performance of the province has approximated the UK average, but by rapid labour force growth brought about by the high rate of natural increase. It is thus essentially a demographically induced process which generates the movement to Britain. It manifests itself as an imbalance between labour force entrants and leavers. The outcome is twofold – high unemployment within Northern Ireland and substantial out-migration. According to classical economic theory, migration should smooth out regional disparities in unemployment rates. The fact that unemployment in the province has persistently stayed at more than twice the national average should therefore be seen as a measure of the institutional constraints on labour mobility between Northern Ireland and Britain, as manifested, for example, in the workings of the housing market and the system of social security.

Regarding the temporal trends, conventional ideas might lead one to presume that the level of outflow would move in sympathy with the local rate of unemployment, i.e. as unemployment in the province rises, so should the rate of migration to Britain and vice versa. In fact there was no relationship between the Northern Ireland unemployment rate and gross out-migration to Great Britain in the period between 1975 and 1990 ($r = 0.08$) and only a weak relationship with net out migration ($r = 0.27$) although it was in the expected direction. However, theory tells us that for migration to occur, areas should be complementary (Ullman, 1956). Hence, the presence of surplus labour in Northern Ireland is not a sufficient condition to stimulate movement from Northern Ireland; contemporaneously, opportunities must also be available in Great Britain. Herein lies the reason why Northern Ireland migration does not apparently respond to local unemployment; as part of the same economy, periods of high unemployment at home invariably coincide with high unemployment and therefore lack of opportunity in Britain. Hence, during an economic downturn conditions in the two areas will tend to duplicate each other and thereby progressively depress the level of mobility. This was clearly the case during the recession of the early 1980s. It also explains why the loss of population to Great Britain was lowest in 1981 at the very bottom of the recession.

Economic recovery produces a radically different migration scenario. Unlike Britain, where recovery quickly generates opportunities in the more buoyant sectors, recovery in Northern Ireland is never sufficiently strong to soak up the available labour supply. Economic resurgence is therefore accompanied by a re-establishment of complementarity and the outflow of Northern Ireland migrants to labour deficient regions in Great Britain picks up again. The surge in mobility that coincided with the economic recovery of the 1980s, especially after 1984, should be seen in this way.

One way of conceptualising migration between Northern Ireland and Great Britain would therefore be to postulate a 'natural' level of mobility that reflects the normal interaction and connectivity between the two areas and which is relatively constant over time. The inflow to the province, which has been relatively flat over the years, is probably a good approximation of this. On top of this, however, there is a variable component which is responsive to the fluctuating level of opportunities in Britain. The fact that GB vacancies after 1975 are positively related to both the gross outflow (r = 0.60) and the net outflow (r = 0.70) – even stronger correlations pertain post-1980 (r = 0.87 and 0.88 respectively) – supports the notion.

In addition, the gross and net outflows are also strongly and positively correlated with vacancies in the province (r = 0.88 and 0.84). At first sight this would appear another somewhat paradoxical relationship, but it is consistent with the notion that out-migration releases vacancies in Northern Ireland. It also fits the observation that the bulk of Northern Ireland migrants are in work, rather than unemployed, at the time of leaving the province. This would suggest that unemployment in the province is not so much affected by the direct out-migration of the unemployed but by the fact that the unemployed can fill vacancies created by migrants. But at the same time there is a disturbing overtone for the long-term economic health of the province, namely that increased economic activity in the province is accompanied by an accelerating rate of net population loss. It indicates that the relative de-skilling of the province's workforce caused by the outflow of trained workers occurs at the very time when such labour is most needed at home.

5.6 Age and sex differentials in migration between Northern Ireland and Great Britain

Migration between Northern Ireland and Great Britain is no different from elsewhere in being highly selective by age group; it is also gender-specific (Table 5.3). Young adults in the 15 to 29 age-range are the most mobile section of the population and constituted 46 per cent of all movers between 1975 and 1989, but only a quarter of the population at large. Within this group, those aged 20–24 showed the highest propensity to migrate. Otherwise, the number of migrants under the age of 15, presumably dependants moving within family groups, is roughly in line with the general population (26 per cent of movers against a quarter of the population). At all other ages migrants are underrepresented. More subtle variations may be observed, however, according to direction of movement. Hence, young adults are more prominent among migrants leaving Northern Ireland for Britain with the result that the inflow to the province is weighted more towards the other age groups.

Yet the fact that the age pattern should vary in this way is not surprising. The outflow not only contains young adults seeking work but also a large student element, which will never return to the province. In view

Table 5.3 Age and sex composition of migrants between Northern Ireland and GB, 1975–89

Age group	All migrants %	Sex ratio	In-migrants %	Sex ratio	Out-migrants %	Sex ratio	Net migrants %	Sex ratio
Under 15	26.3	947	28.5	994	24.9	959	17.4	850
15–29	45.8	1,507	40.7	1,910	49.3	1,329	67.0	864
30–44	16.9	1,137	18.2	1,284	16.0	1,036	11.4	500
45–64	7.4	1,022	8.4	1,032	6.7	1,014	3.1	924
65 plus	3.6	1,489	4.2	1,352	3.2	1,625	1.1	29,400
All	100.0	1,242	100.0	1,371	100.0	1,163	100.0	832

of this, it is reasonably safe to infer that young single adults constitute a substantial component of the outflow whereas families are a more important element of the inflow to the province. This is consistent with the observation that the average age of adult in-migrants was some three years higher than of adult out-migrants (33.2 as against 30.4 years) over the period under review.

However, the vital factor as far as the demographic structure of the Northern Ireland population is concerned is the age breakdown of net migration. In this regard, its effect is even more strongly focused with over two-thirds of the net loss coming from the 15 to 29 age group, and a further 17 per cent from those under the age of 15 (Table 5.3). When the 30 to 44 age group is added to this, it is apparent that at least 95 per cent of net movement to Great Britain since 1975 – that is, around 58,000 out of a total loss of 60,000 – has come from the population under the age of 45. As we have already argued, a consequence of this has been reduced pressure on the Northern Ireland labour market. But this haemorrhage has also had important demographic implications particularly for the birth-rate. Suffice it to say, that rough calculations suggest that the number of live births in recent years would have been between 2,500 and 3,500 per annum higher – that is, up to 12 per cent more than the number actually registered – had it not been for migration.

Although the discussion has so far focused on aggregate patterns, it is also clear that migrant age composition has changed in a number of important ways since 1975 (Figure 5.2). For example, contrary to the trends in overall mobility and after allowance is made for the size of parental group, the number of young migrants under the age of 15 has tended to decline in line with changes in the overall size of the cohort brought about by recent movements in the birth rate. The pattern among the over 65s has also been different; the outflow has stayed relatively stable, but the inflow has moved sharply upwards. As a result, the province's balance for retirement migration has shifted from an overall loss before 1985 to a net gain in more recent years. One explanation of this turnaround would be that Northern Ireland 'emigres' have been

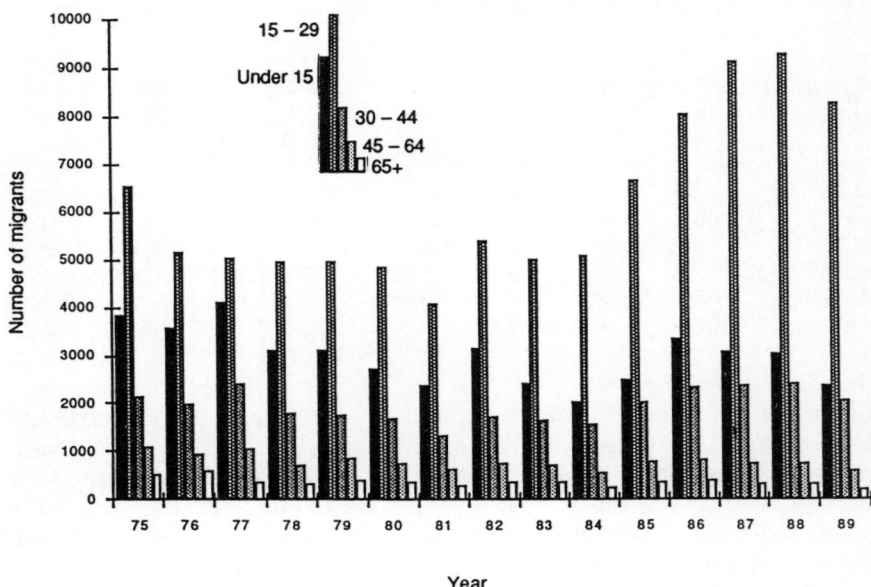

Figure 5.2   Distribution of out-migrants from Northern Ireland by major age
group, 1975–89

cashing in the equity of high-value mainland property and moving to
cheaper housing in the province on retirement. This is a process,
moreover, that shows signs of shifting down the age pyramid into the
active population, with the 45 to 64 age group also recording a small net
gain in 1989–90, the last year for which information is available. The
latter is probably a manifestation of the latest economic downturn; but
it is also worth noting that long-distance commuting by air to the South
East is now perfectly feasible for highly remunerated businessmen and
professionals and may well become a significant factor in the future.

In sharp contrast, the mobility of adults of prime working age, in
being the main component of migration, has closely shadowed the
aggregate trends during the period under question. However, as has
already been pointed out, the situation differs with direction of movement. The trend in the migration of this group to Northern Ireland has
been rather flat throughout the period whereas the outflow has been
much more responsive to the economic cycle. Hence, the number of
leavers fell as the last recession deepened, particularly those aged 30 to
44, but recovered very strongly during the 1980s. The recovery was
particularly sharp in the 15–29 age group and we may well also be seeing
here the effects of the mid-1960s baby boom feeding through to the
number of migrants as well as the segmentation of the labour market.
Indeed, it is clear that this group is the most sensitive to changing opportunities in Great Britain, corroborated by the strong positive relationship

between the outflow and vacancies in Britain (r = 0.82). The growth of the Northern Ireland student population in Great Britain has also contributed to the outflow of 15 to 29-year-olds, and is perhaps one reason why the downward trend of the overall number of young adult leavers was less than might otherwise have been expected in the late 1970s. One last point, given the relatively constant level of in-migration, the temporal variability in the net loss of adults of prime working age is attributable to the fluctuating rate of outflow. As it turns out, the net losses from the group have risen sharply from around 2–2,500 per annum in the mid-1970s to upwards of 5,500 in the late 1980s. Accordingly, the prime adult contribution to total migration loss has doubled from around two-fifths to four-fifths in the same period.

The sex ratio of the migrants is equally distinctive. Females have been substantially more mobile than males since 1975 (1,242 female migrants per 1,000 males) continuing a trend that was first established sometime in the last century. But again the overall picture masks important variations by direction of movement and also by age group. Hence, specific to each flow, females are relatively more likely to move to the province than leave (the sex ratios of the gross inflow and gross outflow were 1,371 and 1,163 respectively). Or to express it another way, there are about 30 per cent more females in the in-migration stream and 12 per cent more in the out-migration stream than one would expect from the sex ratio of the population at large.

The variability by age group is equally distinctive. The excess of female leavers in the outflow comes from two age groups – those aged 15 to 34 and those over the age of 55 – but is particularly marked among young women under the age of 25. At other ages, more males than females leave the province. As regards migrants under the age of 15, the male excess is in line with the male excess in the general population and is therefore unexceptional. The excess within the 35 to 54 age group, however, represents a true male surplus among leavers. The sex ratio of in-migrants is configured in a similar manner and young women again account for much of the overall excess. Indeed, more than twice as many females aged 15 to 29 migrated to the province as would be expected from the general sex ratio of the age group. One interesting point of difference relates to the surplus of males among migrants aged 65 to 69, mirrored by a large female surplus in the 60 to 64 age group; presumably this is some function of retirement in-migration, i.e. older husbands accompanied by their slightly younger wives.

An explanatory model of migrant sex ratios might be something along the following lines. The surplus of young women leaving Northern Ireland is presumably related to the segmentation of the labour market, i.e. young single women leave the province for employment in the public sector and other service industries of Great Britain. This, however, does not necessarily lead to permanent settlement and after an appropriate time many return to the province. Indeed, one may envisage this cycle being repeated to produce a form of circular migration between Northern Ireland and Britain by young women. It is this high rate of turnover among female migrants, coupled with an assumption that the male leavers are more likely to become permanent settlers, i.e. men are more likely to be core as opposed to peripheral workers, that we would advance to explain the female excess among migrants to the province. However, the situation changes after the age of 35 and as female participation in the labour force falls away, male dominance within the outflow is asserted. The re-emergence of a female surplus beyond 55 may presumably be attributed to migration connected with the occurrence of widowhood.

Two last points are significant. First, because males are less likely to return to Northern Ireland, the province loses on balance more men than women to Great Britain. However, there is again an age dimension; up to the age of 55 more men are lost, particularly between the ages of 25 and 44, but thereafter women become an increasingly large part of the net outflow (perhaps widows migrating to be closer to friends and relatives in Britain). Secondly, the sex ratios of migrants have remained reasonably stable over the period under review with two exceptions: the first is that females have constituted a progressively higher proportion of the elderly outflow in recent years; the second is that the excess of young female leavers may vary with the cycle of economic activity – declining during an economic upturn and rising with the onset of recession. This is because the active male outflow is more responsive to economic conditions in Britain and would again seem to be connected with the way the labour market is segmented.

5.7 Spatial patterns

This section is devoted to an examination of the geographical patterns of Northern Ireland migration by British destinations and origins. Two scales of analysis have been selected – FPC areas for England and Wales which provide the finest spatial detail and a broader regional scale for covering the whole of Britain – standard regions plus Scotland and Wales. The analyses are complementary; the FPC-area analysis is based on absolute numbers and stresses spatial pattern whereas the regional investigation is based on rates and emphasises temporal change.

5.7.1 Patterns by FPC areas in England and Wales

The first thing to strike the observer is that the different FPC areas of England and Wales receive migrants from Northern Ireland in more or less the same proportions as they send migrants to the province. As a result the geographical patterns of origins and destinations within England and Wales are virtually identical ($r = 0.99$). To avoid excessive repetition, therefore, the emphasis here is on destinations only.

Two main areas of destination may be discerned from Figure 5.3 (a) – London and the southern counties of Kent, Essex, Surrey, Berkshire

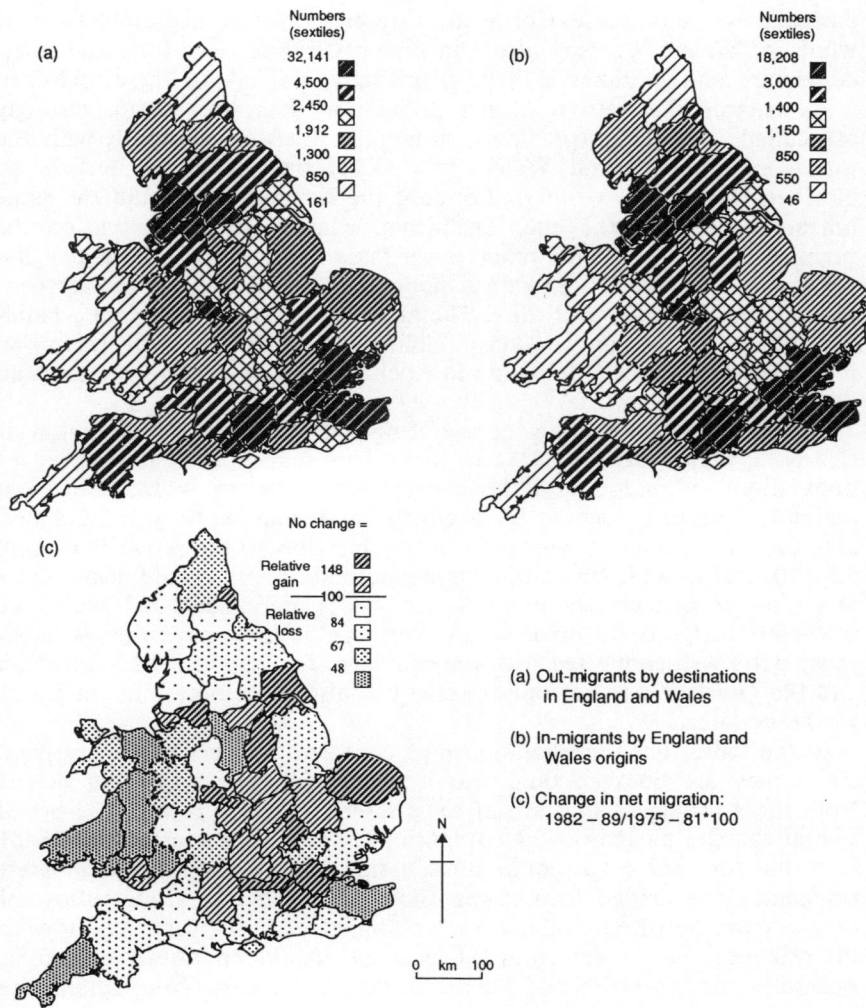

Figure 5.3   Migration between Northern Ireland and England and Wales,
1975–89

and Hampshire, and a swathe of territory across the southern portion of
northern England (North and West Yorkshire, Lancashire, Greater
Manchester, Cheshire and Merseyside). Within the capital itself, destinations have been widely dispersed although there has been some tendency
towards concentration in north and west London (Middlesex, Camden
and Islington). In addition to these, the Birmingham area, Tyne and
Wear, Devon, Wiltshire and Cambridgeshire have been other areas to
attract significant inflows from Northern Ireland. The peripheries of
Britain, by contrast, have attracted fewest migrants and into this

category we may place Cornwall, Cumbria, Northumberland and the whole of Wales. We may also add Gloucestershire, Hereford and Worcestershire and, perhaps a little surprisingly, Suffolk to these areas.

As regards the pattern of net population gain, this too is strongly associated with the gross flows, although somewhat more so with the inflow to England and Wales (r = 0.97) than with the outflow to Northern Ireland (r = 0.93). London, the home counties and the same northern areas are the main recipients, whereas the net gains on the peripheries have been on a much lower scale. It should also be noted that practically every FPC area gained population at the expense of Northern Ireland between 1975 and 1989. The only exceptions to this were a handful of areas in the conurbations – Solihull, Walsall and Wolverhampton in the West Midlands, Oldham and Rochdale in Greater Manchester, and St Helens in Merseyside.

The general distribution of the England and Wales population is clearly a major determinant of these patterns. The main centres of population – London and the metropolitan counties – have all been major recipients of people from Northern Ireland, both gross and net, and also the main contributors to the counterflow to the province (Figure 5.3 (b)). But in addition to this, an accessibility factor would also appear to be involved; hence the more isolated areas of England and Wales are the least likely to be involved in Northern Ireland migration whereas those parts well connected with the province, for instance the South East and the North West, not only receive but also contribute most migrants to the counterflow.

In the sense that these relationships conform with broad gravity principles they are unexceptional and it is therefore the areas that depart from these principles that are of most interest. In this regard, the broad spatial changes picked out by comparing the average pattern for 1975–81 with that for 1982–89 are quite illuminating (Figure 5.3 (c)). The greatest net gains have tended to occur in those areas where a rising inflow of people from Northern Ireland has combined with decreased outflow to the province. Prominent among such areas are the counties of Norfolk, Berkshire, Bedfordshire and Surrey in the South East, Nottinghamshire in the East Midlands, Humberside, and South and Mid Glamorgan in Wales.

Although it is difficult to be specific about the factors behind these changes, one presumes they are mainly economic. But equally the effects of other factors, like student mobility and the movement of army personnel, cannot be discounted. In addition, the strong performance of a county like Norfolk would appear to suggest that the general factors behind counterurbanisation have also informed Northern Ireland migrants about destinations, although the fact that the pull of Greater London grew substantially in the second period would point to a more complex interpretation. Hence, it is clear that the sharp rise in migration to London was mainly of young adults, whereas counterurbanising influences carry more weight with older people.

Areas where the comparative gains were substantially less in 1982–89 than 1975–81 form the mirror image of the above. Two mechanisms were responsible. In Cornwall, West Glamorgan, Powys, Derbyshire and Cleveland the influx from Northern Ireland declined between the two periods, whereas the outflow increased. In Clwyd, Shropshire and Kent, on the other hand, the inflow increased but at a slower rate than the counterflow to the province. Regardless of the specific circumstances, however, the result was a sharp fall off in the net gain from Northern Ireland. As before, the explanations are not easy to discern. The cases of Cornwall, West Glamorgan, Powys and to a lesser extent Clwyd may well be linked with peripherality. Otherwise the explanation is to be found in the specific circumstances of each area. The decline in the attractiveness of the extreme south east corner of England, encompassing Kent, Essex and Sussex, should also be noted and may well be linked with the excessive cost of housing.

Lastly in this section, we shall briefly consider the residuals from the simple regression models of in-, out- and net migration covering the whole period, 1975–89. In showing the deviations from some average relationship, residuals also identify atypical areas. Those areas, where the net gain was less than commensurate with the gross inflow from Northern Ireland because the counterflow to the province was greater than expected, are particularly interesting. The Greater Manchester, West Midlands, Merseyside and West Yorkshire conurbations fall into this category, plus Essex, Hampshire and Kent. Each of these areas acts as a powerful magnet to Northern Ireland migrants; but the forces of 'repulsion' are also strong and many migrants to these areas do not apparently settle long-term. Moreover, one would suspect that the patterns are differentiated by age and that the relatively large flows back to Northern Ireland are biased towards older migrants. They may also be the areas involved in the circular migration of young women postulated in the previous section. But whatever the explanations, the processes are clearly complex and deserve fuller investigation than is possible here.

Greater London, North Yorkshire, Cheshire, Norfolk, Cambridge, Surrey and Avon stand in sharp contrast as the areas where the net gain was greater than the gross inflow would suggest. The case of Greater London has already been discussed; otherwise, these areas may be conceptualised as losing fewer than expected in the counterflows to Northern Ireland due to their intrinsic attractiveness. Cheshire and North Yorkshire, like Norfolk, would seem to fit a counterurbanising explanation. On the other hand, in the case of Surrey, Cambridge and Avon it is economic buoyancy that we would point to.

5.7.2 Regional scale – standard regions, Scotland and Wales

Migration flows can be normalised against population size at the regional scale. This complements the FPC-area analysis in that the comparative standing of the different parts of Britain *vis-à-vis* Northern Ireland migration can now be established with greater confidence. Moreover,

changes in comparative standing can be charted by calendar year inte.
vals. Although a similar analysis is possible for FPC areas, the reliability
of the findings at this more detailed scale is subject to uncertainties
resulting from a greater chance of error in FPC-area population
estimates and migration flow data. The method of analysis is straight-
forward and involves two steps. The flows are normalised by size of
region; the normalised data are then equated with the average British rate
and expressed as indices against a base of 100. The term 'migration
intensities' is used to describe these indices. Regions with values over 100
are areas where migration intensity with Northern Ireland is above the
British average and vice versa for regions with values less than 100.

Before reporting these findings, however, it is appropriate to outline
the main characteristics of Northern Ireland at this scale. Although there
is a good deal of variability from region to region, the rates of inflow
have generally described an asymmetrical U-shaped curve since 1975 with
the low points in each region occurring sometime between 1980 and 1983.
Furthermore, although the subsequent recovery was generally strong, the
inflows of recent years have generally not attained the peak levels
associated with the earlier phase. The notable exceptions are Greater
London and the rest of the South East where the post-1981 upturn was
exceptionally marked and Scotland, Merseyside, Tyne and Wear and the
non-metropolitan parts of the North West where little if any recovery
occurred. On balance, each region gained substantial numbers of people
at the expense of Northern Ireland after 1975 although there were a few
exceptional years when this did not happen. For instance, the West
Midlands conurbation lost over 200 people net in 1975 which is probably
explained by a temporary upsurge of anti-Irish feeling in the aftermath
of the Birmingham pub bombings. Most of the other instances of net
loss happened around the bottom of the last recession; Greater Manchester, Tyne and Wear, East Anglia and non-metropolitan Yorkshire
and Humberside lost population to the province in at least one year
between 1979 and 1981. Each case of loss was connected with an upsurge
in the counterflow to Northern Ireland, i.e. with a heightened level of
return migration.

The migration intensity values are summarised in Table 5.4 as
aggregate values for the whole period 1975–89; these, in turn, are broken
down into the sub-periods 1975–76, 1981–82 and 1988–89 to convey a
sense of temporal change. Taking the aggregate picture first, the most
favoured destinations were Greater London, non-metropolitan North
West, non-metropolitan Yorkshire and Humberside, Scotland and the
rest of the South East, while South Yorkshire, Wales, the non-
metropolitan North, Tyne and Wear and the East Midlands were least
favoured. However, careful inspection of Table 5.4 illustrates how the
comparative attractiveness of the various regions changed during the
period. For instance, the pull of Greater London, although strong
throughout, increased markedly after 1983. As a result, the capital now
absorbs more than twice as many Northern Ireland migrants as the
national average. By contrast, the intensity of movement to Scotland and

Table 5.4 Migration intensity indices by region, 1975–89

Region	GB destinations (from NI)				Region	GB origins (to NI)			
	Aggregate	1975–76	1981–82	1988–89		Aggregate	1975–76	1981–82	1988–89
Greater London	144	121	123	215	Scotland	138	154	138	122
North West, remainder	134	147	121	96	North West, remainder	133	114	122	107
Yorks & Humbs, remainder	123	121	113	113	Greater London	125	103	127	137
Scotland	115	122	137	86	Greater Manchester	124	151	101	115
South East, remainder	101	105	104	97	Yorks & Humbs, remainder	104	103	89	85
Merseyside	91	110	87	83	South East, remainder	104	115	125	112
South West	91	85	100	72	Merseyside	96	104	110	92
East Anglia	86	76	88	74	West Midlands, remainder	86	69	96	97
Greater Manchester	84	101	75	65	West Yorkshire	83	65	64	70
West Midlands	83	79	80	78	South West	82	82	87	84
West Midlands, remainder	83	104	84	81	East Anglia	72	65	63	61
West Yorkshire	81	82	75	77	North, remainder	71	59	57	69
East Midlands	78	79	87	69	East Midlands	70	78	63	66
Tyne & Wear	75	74	72	65	Tyne & Wear	67	75	58	61
North, remainder	72	85	71	66	Wales	59	55	51	65
Wales	63	69	59	58	West Midlands	55	60	63	51
South Yorkshire	49	43	55	57	South Yorkshire	44	30	28	47

the whole of the North West has fallen sharply. It should be noted, however, that the indices are interconnected statistically and the sharp rise in the rate of movement to London has tended to depress the scores of other regions. Hence, although migration intensity to the South East has hovered around the national average throughout, the region has nevertheless become relatively more attractive as a destination when compared with other areas, as have East Anglia, West Yorkshire and the West Midlands conurbation.

Little has intentionally been said about migration intensity to Northern Ireland because the patterns broadly mirror the above. Yet it is still worthwhile noting some of the more significant differences. For instance, the rest of the South East, Merseyside, Greater Manchester and Scotland all contribute relatively more migrants to Northern Ireland than they receive. East Anglia, Greater London, the West Midlands conurbation and non-metropolitan Yorkshire and Humberside, on the other hand, receive relatively more than they contribute.

How then may we interpret the spatio-temporal patterns of regional movements between Northern Ireland and Great Britain? The single most important factor would seem to be the North–South disparity in economic performance. This explains the reduction in the intensity of migration to the traditional destinations of Scotland and the North West and the upsurge in movement to Greater London, the rest of the South East and to a lesser extent East Anglia. It also accounts for the low level of movement throughout the period to depressed areas like South Yorkshire and Tyne and Wear. Yet this is not the whole story. For instance, the non-metropolitan parts of Yorkshire and Humberside continue to be more favoured by Northern Ireland migrants than the rest of the South East. It is also clear that the pattern of destinations of Northern Ireland migrants conflicts in some important respects with the distributional change in the British population at large. The most obvious case in Greater London which, despite continued migration loss (Bulusu, 1990), is now the destination of around 30 per cent of all individuals moving to Great Britain. It also accounts for almost half the net population gain at the expense of the province. It is as though migrants from Northern Ireland are acting as a replacement population in the tradition of the earlier migrations from the New Commonwealth. In similar vein, Northern Ireland movers are far less likely to move to Wales and, to a lesser extent, the South West, than the British population at large. These deviations strongly suggest that the composition of the factors determining the destinations of Northern Ireland migrants differ from those of British migrants in general. They are certainly worthy of further study.

5.8 Conclusions

One is left with the overwhelming impression that the main determinants of Northern Ireland migration to Britain are economic. The fluctuations in the gross and net outflows are largely governed by the UK cycle of economic activity. These rates are low when the economy is depressed but recover strongly during an economic upturn. The response to economic change has been swift in recent years and the latest slowdown has produced an immediate reduction in outflow. This leads to the rather paradoxical situation that both the numbers leaving the province as well as the rate of net loss rise in line with economic recovery in Northern Ireland. Equally, when the economy would most benefit from some increase in out-migration as during an economic downturn, the rate of outflow actually decreases. In addition to this, the geographical pattern of destinations in Britain is also largely economically determined and is a reaction to variations in the spatial economy and the segmentation of the labour market. It is this that accounts for the decisive shift away from the traditional destinations of Scotland and North West England in the 1970s and the current focus on the South East and Greater London. Labour market segmentation is also important in understanding the distinctive gender patterns of migrants.

Of late, geographers have placed much significance on company-induced mobility, or migration channels as it is sometimes called, when conceptualising the migration process (Salt, 1990; Findlay and Garrick, 1990). This is certainly a factor generating mobility between Northern Ireland and Britain, perhaps more so in the case of mature than younger migrants, but its importance should not be overplayed. For instance, over two-fifths of movers to Britain in recent years have been aged 15 to 29 and most of these have been young women. It seems unlikely to us that many of these would fall into the category of channelled migrants. The different scenarios surrounding migration are quite varied. A proportion of migrants are unemployed when they leave the province. Yet more leave as students and then find permanent work in Britain after completing their studies. Others move immediately on finishing school. For the majority, however, the pattern is to vacate a job in Northern Ireland and move to new work in Britain. Some of these moves happen within the framework of firms and in that sense are contractual but most occur informally and may, in fact, be quite speculative (Silvers, 1977). Whatever the proportionate breakdown of these categories, however, the motivations of migrants are complex and there is still much research to be carried out before Northern Ireland migration is better understood.

6 Migration trends for Scotland: central losses and peripheral gains

Huw Jones

6.1 Introduction

One historical factor and one intrinsically geographical factor make Scotland's migration linkages distinctive among the major regions of Great Britain. First, there is a tradition of overseas emigration stemming from the late eighteenth and early nineteenth centuries, when rapid population growth and revolutionary transformation of the agrarian economy created what Samuel Johnson described as 'an epidemical fury of emigration'. Secondly, the peripheral and peninsular nature of Scotland, accentuated by low population densities along the Anglo-Scottish border, ensures that flows between Scotland and adjacent regions of England are relatively modest. Consequently, Scotland's migration pattern can be expected to be dominated by internal and long-distance external flows. Since the overseas or emigration component of external flows has long been an important and integral part of Scotland's migration pattern – more so than any other part of Britain – it needs to be discussed as a preface to analysis of migration flows within the UK.

6.2 Overseas migration

Overseas migration has played an important role in recent Scottish population trends. Continuing a pattern established in the mid-1960s (excepting only 1979–80), net outflow overseas exceeded that to the rest of the UK until 1983–84 (Figure 6.1). Subsequently the roles have reversed, but the overall net outflow continues to exceed appreciably the modest natural increase, reducing the total population by some 0.25 per cent per year.

The continuous net outflow overseas from Scotland in the 1980s is in marked contrast to England and Wales, which recorded net gains from overseas during 1983–87. The bulk of these gains were concentrated in Greater London, yet no region of England and Wales can approach the Scottish level of net outflow overseas: 15 per 1,000 of the regional population for the 1980s decade, almost twice that of the highest ranking

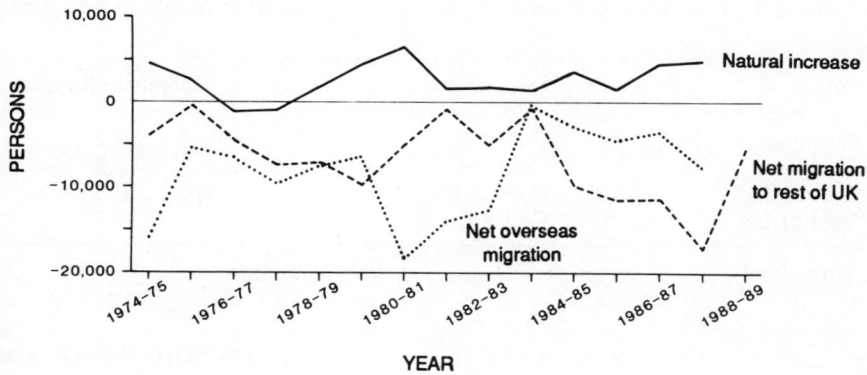

Figure 6.1 Components of Scottish population change, 1974–75 to 1988–89
Source: Registrar General Scotland, Annual Reports.

English region, the North (based on International Passenger Survey data reported in OPCS, 1988b, Table 2.9). The appreciable negative balance for Scotland is derived partly from a relatively high rate of gross emigration, but especially from a very low rate of gross immigration. In particular, Scottish cities have never attracted levels of immigration from the Indian sub-continent and the Caribbean comparable to English cities; in 1981 only 0.8 per cent of Scotland's population recorded a New Commonwealth birthplace, compared with 2.8 per cent of Great Britain's population.

It is difficult to interpret fluctuations in Scottish emigration and immigration, since these are determined by a host of economic and political considerations in a large number of overseas countries as well as in Scotland itself. But the particularly high levels of gross and net emigration from Scotland in the early 1980s are likely to be related to the functional coincidence of appreciable domestic unemployment with booming construction and engineering activity in the Gulf states induced by then surging oil prices. This is symptomatic of the 1980s trend in British overseas migration away from settler migration towards transient skilled migration (Findlay, 1988). In the case of Scotland, a recruitment emphasis on 'bachelor status' managerial and especially technical manpower for overseas construction and engineering projects (Findlay and Garrick, 1989) seems to underlie a sex ratio of 1,182 males per 1,000 females among emigrants from Scotland during 1981–88, as indicated by the International Passenger Survey data from OPCS International Migration (Series MN) annual reports.

6.3 Migration between Scotland and the rest of the UK

NHSCR data indicate that during the 1980s Scotland continued to exhibit

Table 6.1 Coefficients of variation for annual gross movements to and from Scotland, 1975–89

Origin	Destination	Coefficient (%)
Scotland	Overseas	20.2
Overseas	Scotland	16.8
Scotland	Rest of UK	8.6
Rest of UK	Scotland	8.7

Note: Coefficient of variation = (standard deviation/mean) 100.

its traditional pattern of modest net inflow from Northern Ireland and substantial net outflow to England and Wales. Neither gross nor net movements between Scotland and the rest of the UK are as volatile as overseas movements (Figure 6.1 and Table 6.1), yet they are more suited to analysis and interpretation because determining conditions do not have to embrace several countries and there are no political restrictions on movement.

There has been some successful causal modelling of the aggregate migration time series for the 1950s, 1960s and 1970s, with the major explanatory variables in the regression analyses being labour market conditions (Scottish Economic Planning Board, 1970; Markland, 1975; Adams, 1980). The Scotland/UK difference in male unemployment rate has proved to be the most important single variable, alone accounting for 90 per cent of the variation in net migration from Scotland to the rest of the UK, 1954–68, with a one-year lag applied to the data to embrace learning, decision and action lags (Scottish Economic Planning Board, 1970). Unemployment is here almost certainly acting as a proxy for other economic influences, since the unemployed themselves are generally among the more immobile elements in a population.

Attempts by the author to model more recent time series have been rather less successful. For 1975–89, the highest level of 'explanation' ($r^2 = 0.60$) is of one-year lagged gross out-migration from Scotland to the rest of the UK by notified job vacancies and unemployment (both independent variables measured as Scotland relative to England). Similar attempts to model gross in-migration in terms of labour market variables have failed (highest $r^2 = 0.23$), doubtless reflecting the important role in this migration stream of return migration (Bell and Kirwan, 1979) and perhaps quality-of-life considerations.

These findings are consistent with the age structures of the two aggregate migration streams during the 1980s (Table 6.2). The normal overrepresentation among young adults and underrepresentation in the over-45 age groups are particularly evident in the outflow from Scotland, indicative of the relative roles of labour migration and return or retirement migration in the two streams.

Figures 6.2 and 6.3 indicate that the spatial patterns within England and Wales of gross and net migration from Scotland are determined

Table 6.2 Percentage distribution by age of migration streams between
Scotland and the rest of the UK, 1980–81 to 1988–89

Age group	To Scotland	From Scotland	Population of Scotland 1981
0–14	22.1	20.7	21.4
15–24	24.7	29.0	16.7
25–44	37.5	38.5	25.6
45–59	8.2	6.4	17.2
60 +	7.5	5.4	19.1

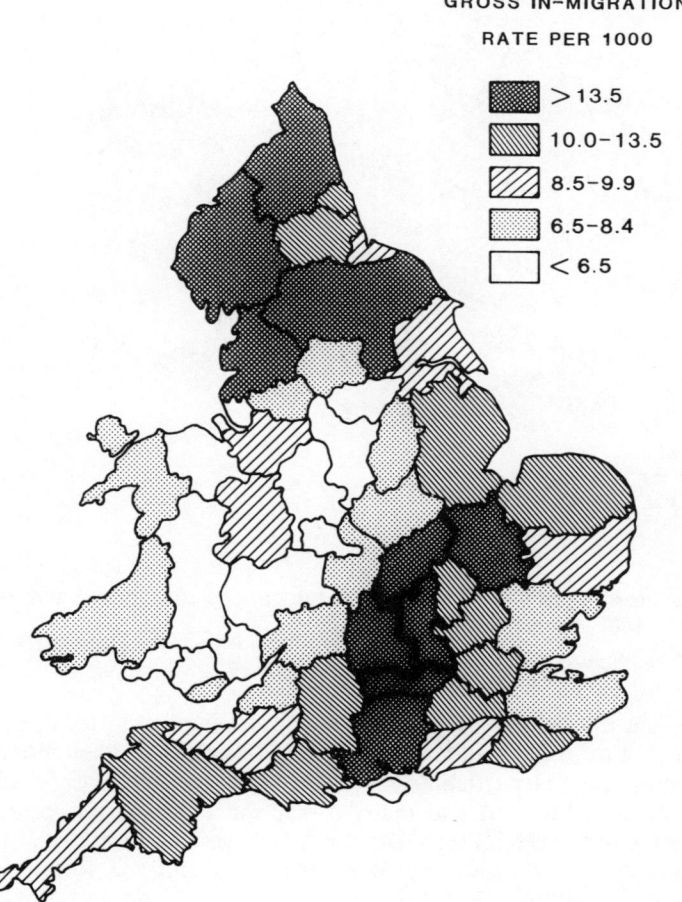

GROSS IN-MIGRATION

RATE PER 1000

> 13.5

10.0–13.5

8.5–9.9

6.5–8.4

< 6.5

Figure 6.2 Gross migration from Scotland to counties of England and
Wales, 1980–81 to 1988–89

Source: Unpublished NHSCR data (OPCS).

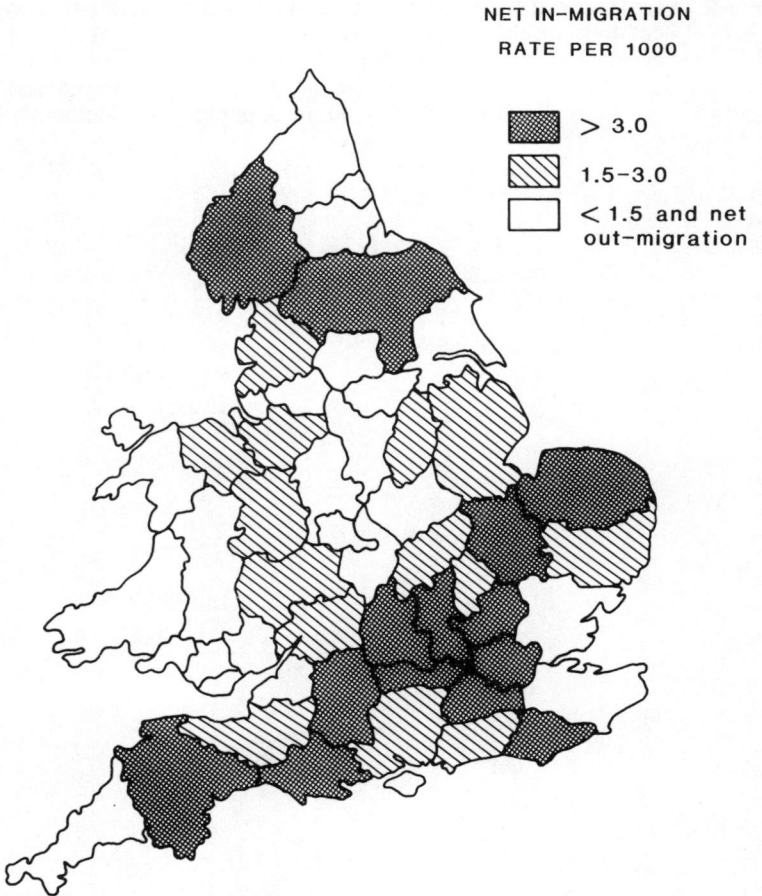

NET IN−MIGRATION
RATE PER 1000

> 3.0

1.5−3.0

< 1.5 and net
out−migration

Figure 6.3   Net migration from Scotland to counties of England and Wales,
1980–81 to 1988–89

Source: Unpublished NHSCR data (OPCS).

largely by the interaction of distance and economic opportunities. Gross
migration (Figure 6.2), standardised for 1981 usually resident population
size at destination, is particularly high in two types of region: adjacent
parts of northern England and many of the more prosperous counties of
southern England, especially to the north and west of London. Unattractive destinations are Wales, the West Midlands and the former metropolitan counties apart from Greater London and Tyne and Wear.

For net migration (Figure 6.3) the role of distance is reduced considerably since it can be expected to have a similar influence on inward
and outward streams. Accordingly, the highest net migration gains from
Scotland are concentrated in Greater London, wide parts of southern

Table 6.3 Net migration by Scottish region, 1980–89

Region	Net migration with rest of UK		Net migration with rest of Scotland	
	Number	Rate per 1,000	Number	Rate per 1,000
Southern Scotland				
Borders	1,565	15.5	4,256	42.3
Dumfries & Galloway	4,234	29.1	1,272	8.8
Central Scotland				
Lothian	– 17,142	– 23.2	4,984	6.8
Tayside	– 2,373	– 6.1	3,083	7.9
Central	– 2,547	– 9.4	2,830	10.4
Fife	– 605	– 1.8	3,559	10.6
Strathclyde	– 71,742	– 29.7	– 38,462	– 15.9
Northern Scotland				
Grampian	6,680	14.0	16,747	35.2
Highland	5,437	28.0	3,054	15.7
Orkney	993	52.1	– 490	– 25.7
Shetland	83	3.5	– 551	– 23.5
Western Isles	460	14.5	– 461	– 14.6

England and only two counties in northern England. There are some interesting differences from the 1960s pattern (Jones, 1970). Then the highest net migration rates from Scotland were to the East and West Midlands (outside the conurbation) – a response to their then buoyant economies, to locations not so distant as southern England, and to vigorous labour recruitment campaigns in Scotland by Midlands' mining and metallurgical industries. By the 1980s, Greater London and the South East had come to dominate the pattern, reflecting structural economic changes, associated swings in regional prosperity, and possibly a reduced role for distance as a deterrent to migration.

Scotland's regional pattern of aggregated net out-migration during the 1980s to, in effect, England is dominated by high levels and rates of net outflow from the Glasgow-based Strathclyde region (Table 6.3; for location of regions, see Figure 6.6). There is also appreciable net exodus from Edinburgh-based Lothian, while the other regions in urban–industrial, central Scotland (Tayside, Fife, Central) show more modest net losses.

The more rural regions in northern and southern Scotland all show net in-migration from the rest of the UK, doubtless reflecting the pull of oil-related employment in Highland and especially Aberdeen-based Grampian, as well as the more geographically pervasive role of peripheral counterurbanisation based on residential preference shifts in an anti-urban, pro-rural direction. Such shifts appear to stem from growing dissatisfaction with the work structure and normative lifestyles associated with metropolitan economies. The trade-off that people make between

Table 6.4 Regional unemployment rates and employees in manufacturing, Scotland, 1980–87

Region	Unemployment rates (% of June workforce)			% employees in manufacturing
	1980	1984	1988	1987
Borders	4.0	8.6	7.2	33.5
Dumfries & Galloway	9.1	12.6	11.0	22.3
Lothian	7.6	11.9	10.4	17.5
Tayside	9.0	14.3	12.0	21.1
Central	8.5	16.1	13.2	29.4
Fife	9.5	13.5	13.7	23.8
Strathclyde	12.1	18.2	15.6	23.8
Grampian	5.1	6.8	7.5	16.2
Highland	8.6	13.0	12.3	12.5
Orkney	6.6	10.2	11.2	11.7
Shetland	3.0	6.6	6.4	11.0
Western Isles	13.5	17.7	20.2	13.5

Source: Scottish Office (1989, Tables 9.3 and 9.10).

material enrichment and quality-of-life/environmental considerations seems to have shifted significantly towards the latter in post-industrial societies. Consequently, the deterioration in job status, earnings and material living standards that long-distance counterurban migration often entails can sometimes be tolerated by the adoption of a 'satisficing' approach to work and lifestyle.

Community-based studies have revealed the growth in the 1970s and early 1980s of such counterurban migration from England to parts of northern Scotland, particularly Orkney (Forsythe, 1980; Lumb, 1980) and Mull, Syke and Wester Ross (Jones et al., 1986). However, the often demographically revitalising but culturally divisive effect of such migration on local communities should not be regarded as typical of rural Scotland. The traditional pattern of population decline and population ageing through selective migration persists in most of the truly rural areas, especially in southern Scotland (Jones, 1988). The positive demographic impact of long-distance in-migration of the counterurban or 'green-wave' type tends to be concentrated in a limited number of small, sparsely peopled areas with special scenic and image appeal.

6.4 Migration within Scotland

The regional pattern of aggregate net migration within Scotland during the 1980s is also shown in Table 6.3. There are substantial losses from Strathclyde with its depressed industrial economy (Table 6.4), and even higher net outflow rates from the three peripheral island groups; in the latter case it seems that population gains by counterurban processes are

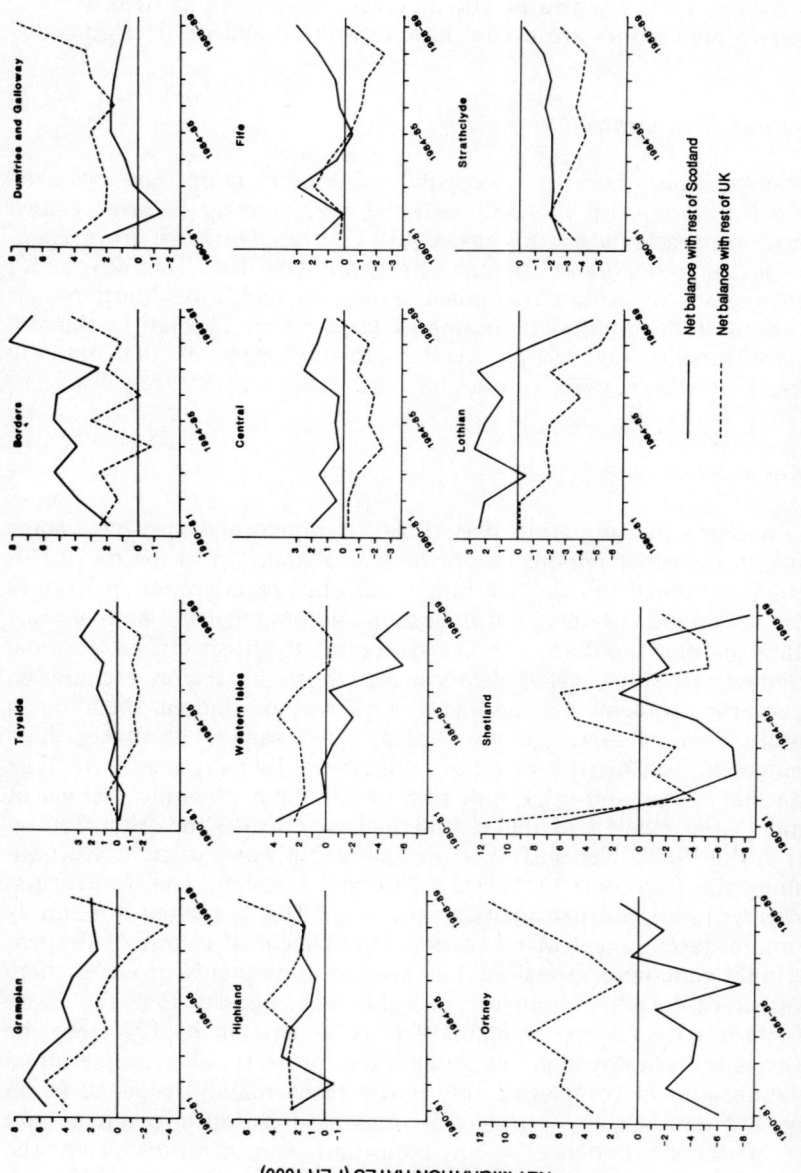

Figure 6.4 Net migration rates for Scottish regions, 1980–81 to 1988–89
Source: Unpublished NHSCR data (OPCS).

Net balance with rest of Scotland

Net balance with rest of UK

exclusively from English origins. The most substantial absolute gain of population is in oil-boosted Grampian, but the highest rate of gain is in the Borders region, reflecting low unemployment in its small-town, textile-based economy (Table 6.4) and a location facilitating commuting to Edinburgh.

More detailed migration information is provided by Figure 6.4. For each region, it depicts fluctuations in rates of net migration both with the rest of Scotland and the rest of UK. Several influences may be discerned, but the two major ones are urban deconcentration and oil developments.

6.4.1 Urban deconcentration

The overwhelming bulk of Glasgow's deconcentration has occurred within Strathclyde, and the only external region likely to have gained population appreciably by this process is Central. Dispersal from Edinburgh, on the other hand, is more likely to have led to spillover into adjacent regions enjoying environmental amenity and lower house prices. There seems little doubt that the major losses from Lothian in the late 1980s are functionally related to the growing gains at that time in Borders, Fife and Tayside (presumably its Perth and Kinross district).

6.4.2 Oil developments

These dominate the migration pattern of Grampian and also have some influence in the other regions of northern Scotland. Up to the mid-1970s Grampian continued to exhibit a long-established demographic pattern in northern Scotland of net out-migration accompanying, and usually exceeding, natural increase. The Gaskin report (Scottish Office Regional Development Division, 1969) demonstrated how the region exemplified the structural problems of peripheral rural regions: labour shedding in agriculture, low female activity rates, low wages, relatively high unemployment and high rates of out-migration. In fact, the North East had the highest net out-migration rate of the eight planning regions of Scotland in the 1950s and the second highest rate (to the West-Central region) in the 1960s. Net outflow from the region was particularly prominent along the east coast to Tayside, Fife and Lothian. The transformation of this traditional pattern from the mid-1970s is related not simply to the rapid development of oil-related employment at a time of deepening national economic recession, but also to Grampian's growing share of Scottish oil-related employment. Table 6.5 suggests that the share grew from less than 50 per cent in 1976 to 80 per cent by 1986, but the table excludes employment in temporary projects like oil terminal construction and in companies only partly (even mainly) engaged in oil activity. The data are also arranged by regional location of company and not of workers' residence – an important consideration given the normative 'fortnight on–fortnight off' nature of off-shore shiftwork

Table 6.5 Regional employment in companies wholly related to North Sea oil, Scotland, 1976–88

Region	Employment (in thousands)						
	1976	1978	1980	1982	1984	1986	1988
Central and Lothian	0.69	0.55	0.86	1.15	0.98	0.39	0.63
Fife	2.03	1.38	0.81	1.25	1.41	1.71	1.68
Grampian	11.54	22.89	32.32	40.02	49.51	48.34	44.16
Highland	6.78	6.00	4.35	7.38	4.44	4.02	2.35
Strathclyde	4.23	0.50	2.73	3.80	3.38	3.10	1.32
Tayside	1.44	2.05	1.81	2.50	2.33	1.80	1.19
Islands	0.40	0.63	3.47	2.23	2.00	2.09	2.35

Note: Onshore and offshore employment, but excluding temporary oil-related projects.
Source: Scottish Office (1989).

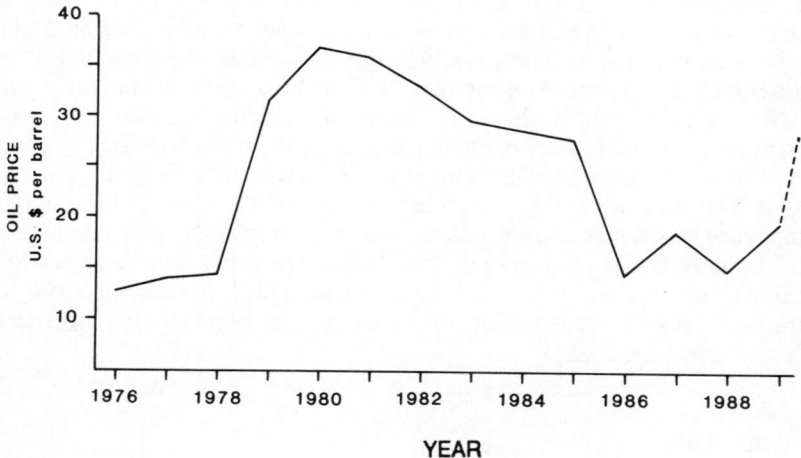

Figure 6.5 Spot prices for Forties-Brent crude oil, 1976–89
Source: BP (1990).

which allows workers to retain their residence in various parts of Britain and travel fortnightly to and from Aberdeen. Only a small minority of the circa 23,000 offshore workers in the UK sector of the northern North Sea in 1988 (McVittie and Birse, 1989) are thought to reside in the Grampian region itself.

A supplementary, although indirect, measure of oil activity and employment is the price of North Sea crude oil – mainly through its effect on exploration and development rather than production. There is a very close relationship between the oil-price series (Figure 6.5) and the Grampian migration rates (Figure 6.4). One immediate implication is that the hike in prices to over $30 per barrel during the 1990 Gulf crisis can be expected to accelerate net migration flows to Grampian in 1990–91, particularly if this is associated with national economic recession.

The migrational effects of oil developments can also be discerned elsewhere in northern Scotland. In the Western Isles, the deterioration in migration performance from the mid-1980s must be related to the rundown and closure of the platform fabrication yard at Stornoway which had employed several hundred men in the early 1980s. In Shetland, 1980–81 continued the pattern established in the 1970s of appreciable net in-migration from the rest of Scotland and from England associated with Shetland's role as a major transit point both for crude oil and oil workers moving between North Sea platforms and the British mainland. There were two major types of incomer: temporary construction workers, unaccompanied by families, especially at the huge Sullom Voe oil terminal (Philip et al., 1982), and operational and servicing personnel, often with families, especially at Sumburgh airport, which was employing over 500 people in the late 1970s (Byron and MacFarlane, 1982). But during the 1980s an appreciable reduction in activity has led to net out-migration. Construction at Sullom Voe, involving some 3,000 workers, was completed in the early 1980s, although the great majority of itinerant, camp-based construction workers are excluded from NHSCR data, as indeed they are from the Census 'usually resident' population; such workers normally retain medical registration in their home area, and if they need treatment during their 'travelling' they make use of private health services provided by employers or local GPs under a temporary residence dispensation. More importantly for residential migration as opposed to itinerant 'travelling', there has been a reduction of activity at Sumburgh airport consequent upon the completion of Sullom Voe and the centralising of helicopter services for the northern North Sea on Aberdeen.

6.4.3 Inter-regional flows

The largest (26 out of 105) rates of net migration between Health Board areas (i.e. net flows standardised for population size at origin and destination) are shown in Figure 6.6 for 1980–82 and 1987–89 respectively. In the early 1980s the pattern is dominated by deconcentration from Greater Glasgow and by the attraction of major oil developments then taking place in Grampian, Shetland and Highland as crude oil prices surged (Figure 6.5). In the late 1980s deconcentration was continuing from Glasgow and was now being developed from Lothian. Reduced oil prices and related activity had diminished the population 'pull' of northern areas, so much so that Shetland was now experiencing high rates of net out-migration to several parts of Scotland.

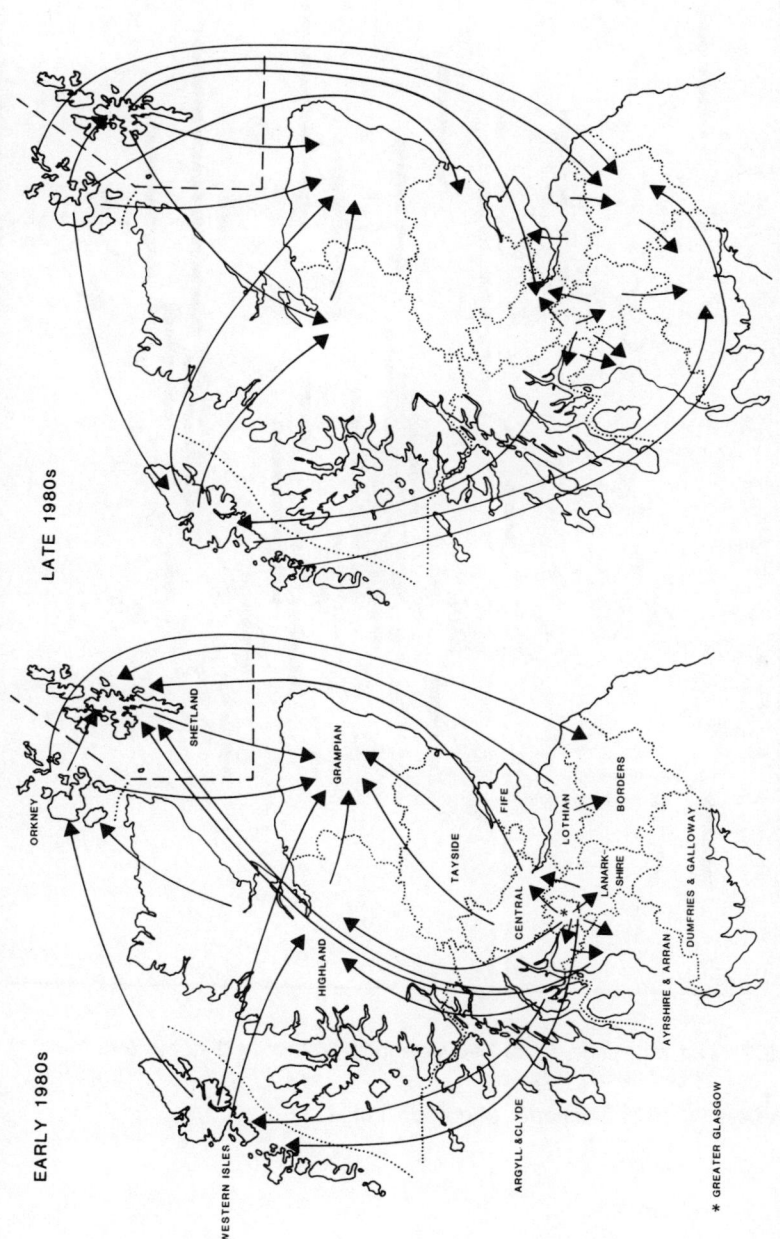

EARLY 1980s

WESTERN ISLES

ORKNEY

SHETLAND

GRAMPIAN

HIGHLAND

TAYSIDE

FIFE

ARGYLL & CLYDE

CENTRAL

LOTHIAN

LANARKSHIRE

BORDERS

AYRSHIRE & ARRAN

DUMFRIES & GALLOWAY

* GREATER GLASGOW

LATE 1980s

Figure 6.6 The largest net migration rates between Scottish Health Board areas, mid-1980 to mid-1982 and mid-1987 to mid-1989

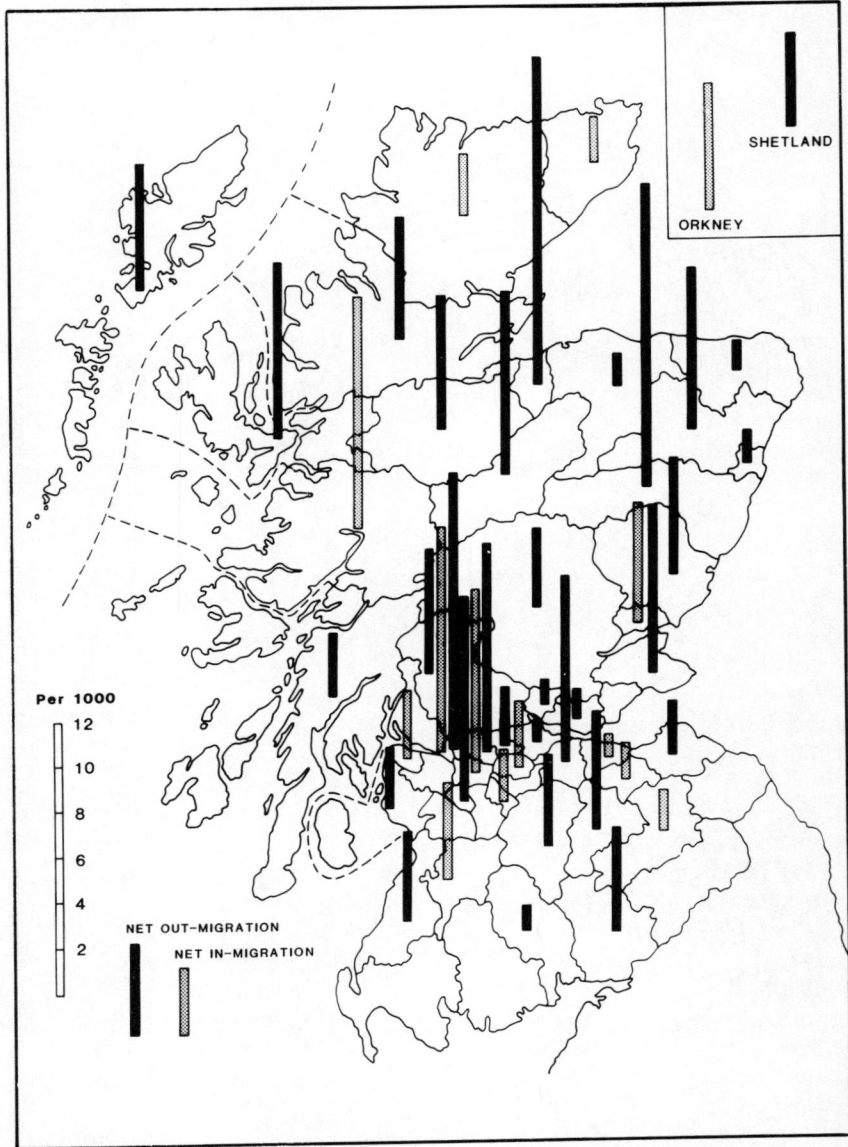

Figure 6.7 Net migration rates between local authority districts and the rest
of Scotland, 1980–81

Source: Census 1981 Scotland, Migration Vol. 1.

Table 6.6 Regional net migration rates by age group, Scotland, 1980–89

Region	Net migration rates (per 1,000) by age				
	0–14	15–24	25–44	45–59	60+
Borders	58	− 55	98	82	74
Dumfries & Galloway	49	− 144	74	80	79
Strathclyde	− 36	− 100	− 62	− 15	− 19
Lothian	− 34	54	− 57	− 11	− 13
Central	27	− 76	3	9	26
Fife	17	− 54	20	23	37
Tayside	25	− 74	− 13	27	32
Grampian	45	89	64	31	22
Highland	36	− 93	95	68	77
Shetland	− 52	− 45	− 9	− 28	18
Orkney	50	− 187	90	57	36
Western Isles	32	− 333	82	48	36

6.4.4 District migration

The most spatially detailed migration data are those provided by the decennial Census for local authority districts, although the data only embrace the 12-month period before Census day. The overall pattern for 1980–81 (Figure 6.7) reveals population deconcentration in three of the most populous regions, as net out-migration from the cities of Glasgow, Edinburgh and Dundee is complemented by appreciable net in-migration in immediately surrounding areas. Heavy industrial and mining areas like Clydebank, the Ayrshire coalfield, Greenock and Hamilton have migration losses, while the oil-servicing economy of Aberdeen stimulated gains in all districts of Grampian, especially in the two districts which incorporate the modern suburban expansion of the city.

The importance of intra-regional variation in migration is shown clearly in the Highland region. There are migration gains associated with: oil-platform fabrication yards in the inner Moray Firth; skiing and other major tourist developments on Speyside; concentration of regional administrative and commercial functions at Inverness; and retirement/counterurban migration to Skye. But those parts of the Highland region away from these place-specific developments continued to reveal the traditional rural pattern of net out-migration, accentuated in Lochaber by the closure of the Fort William pulp mill in 1980 and by the difficulty in Caithness of providing second-generation employment for families attracted in the late 1950s by the Dounreay development.

6.4.5 Migration by age

Within regions, migration is further differentiated by age. Table 6.6 indicates that only in two regions do all five age groups exhibit the same migration trends: Strathclyde (negative) and Grampian (positive).

For most regions, net out-migration is concentrated heavily in the 15–24 group, with particularly high rates in Dumfries and Galloway, Orkney and, above all, the Western Isles, reflecting the traditional exodus of school-leavers from rural regions for further education and employment training within and without Scotland. It is significant that the only two regions with net inflow in this age group are Lothian and Grampian, with their major centres of further and higher education at Edinburgh and Aberdeen; this is confirmed by their concentration of inflow in the 15–19 group.

A remarkably consistent feature of Table 6.6 is that eight of the 12 regions have net inflows in all age groups other than 15–24, the four exceptions reflecting metropolitan processes in Strathclyde and Lothian and oil in Grampian and Shetland.

6.5 Conclusion

The 1980s have witnessed the continuation of well-established migration trends – in particular, the selective net out-migration and population decline in rural areas, large cities and older industrial areas, balanced only in part by population gains in commuting hinterlands. Novel features of the modern period are place-specific oil developments and peripheral counterurbanisation. The impact of oil has been particularly prominent because it coincided chronologically with deepening national economic recession and has been concentrated in sparsely peopled northern regions. Oil has also stimulated distinctive forms of labour recruitment and migration through the harnessing of an industrial reserve army in depressed West-Central Scotland and elsewhere for offshore placement and short-term construction work at fabrication yards and landfall terminals in a form of circulatory migration reminiscent of the hey-day of unbridled nineteenth-century capitalism.

7 Migration trends for the North: patterns identified and processes distinguished

Philip Rees, John Stillwell and Peter Boden

7.1 Introduction

This chapter is concerned with describing population redistribution in northern England, a macro region containing the standard regions of the North, Yorkshire and Humberside and the North West. The chapter focuses in particular on the role of migration in effecting that redistribution. Northern England houses one-quarter of the UK's population, numbering 14.4 million at mid-1989. The population of the area has been in slow decline (0.1 per cent per annum) since the early 1970s when it numbered 14.7 million and constituted 26 per cent of the UK population. However, as the chapter reveals, there are very wide variations from this trend within northern England: some parts of the region have experienced growth rates around 2 per cent per annum in the 1980s (Richmondshire and Selby districts of North Yorkshire) while others have suffered declines of over 1 per cent per annum (Hull, Scunthorpe, Knowsley, Liverpool and Burnley).

It is important to study trends in migration in a macro region for several reasons. Migration plays a crucial role in population redistribution. An empirical description is a crucial preliminary to formulating an explanation for the complex processes involved. Because so little investigation has to date been carried out on the way migration patterns fluctuate over time, we are still at the stage of hypothesis generation. The ultimate aim of research into migration trends should be to help in the construction of integrated, predictive models of the population and economy at fine spatial scales. The current description represents a small step towards that goal.

In the next section, the contribution of migration to population redistribution in northern England is assessed via an analysis of net migration and natural increase at region and county scale. This is followed by a detailed investigation of the migration flows occurring at a middle scale, that of the metropolitan districts and shire counties which make up the Family Practitioner Committee (FPC) areas of the National Health Service, the Central Register (NHSCR) of which provides details of patient re-registrations that cross FPC area boundaries for some 14 mid-year to mid-year periods. In the final section, the description

Table 7.1 Natural change and net migration for regions of northern England, 1981–87 and 1987–88

Region	1981–87			1987–88		
	Natural change (1)	Net migration		Natural change (4)	Net migration	
		Total (2)	Internal (3)		Total (5)	Internal (6)
Numbers (1,000s)						
North	8.7	−49.4	−40.7	2.8	−8.5	−5.5
Yorkshire & Humberside	25.3	−43.5	−44.3	10.0	2.6	2.7
North West	34.8	−123.8	−129.6	13.4	−19.9	−18.4
Northern England	68.8	−216.7	−214.6	26.2	−25.8	−21.2
England & Wales	394.9	213.6	85.5	119.7	30.7	26.0
Annual rates (per 1,000 population)						
North	0.47	−2.66	−2.19	0.91	−2.77	−1.79
Yorkshire & Humberside	0.86	−1.48	−1.50	2.04	0.53	0.55
North West	0.90	−3.22	−3.37	2.10	−3.13	−2.89
Northern England	0.80	−2.50	−2.48	1.83	−1.79	−1.48
England & Wales	1.32	0.71	0.29	2.38	0.61	0.52

Sources: (i) Columns (1), (2), (4) & (5) – OPCS (1990d, Table 3.1);
       (ii) Columns (3) & (6) – NHSCR migration statistics.

descends to the finer scale of metropolitan and non-metropolitan district, using official estimates of population change. New insights are revealed as we delve deeper into the spatial hierarchy.

7.2 The role of migration in population redistribution

It is usually taken for granted that the most important component of regional and local population change is net internal migration, but such an assumption must be checked. Table 7.1 sets out the components of change for the period 1981–88. At the national scale, net in-migration contributes 213.6 thousand in 1981–87 and 30.7 thousand in 1987–88 to the addition of just over three-quarters of a million to the population of England and Wales over the whole period, 1981–88. The net migration figure is just under 50 per cent of the natural increase number. For northern England the two components act in opposite directions (except in Yorkshire and Humberside in 1987–88) but the absolute value of the net migration component is just over 250 per cent of the natural increase component.

If the total net migration column is compared with that for internal (within UK) migration for northern England and for its constituent regions, net internal migration is seen to be almost completely dominant. Net external migration subtracts small numbers from the North and North West regional populations but adds people to Yorkshire and

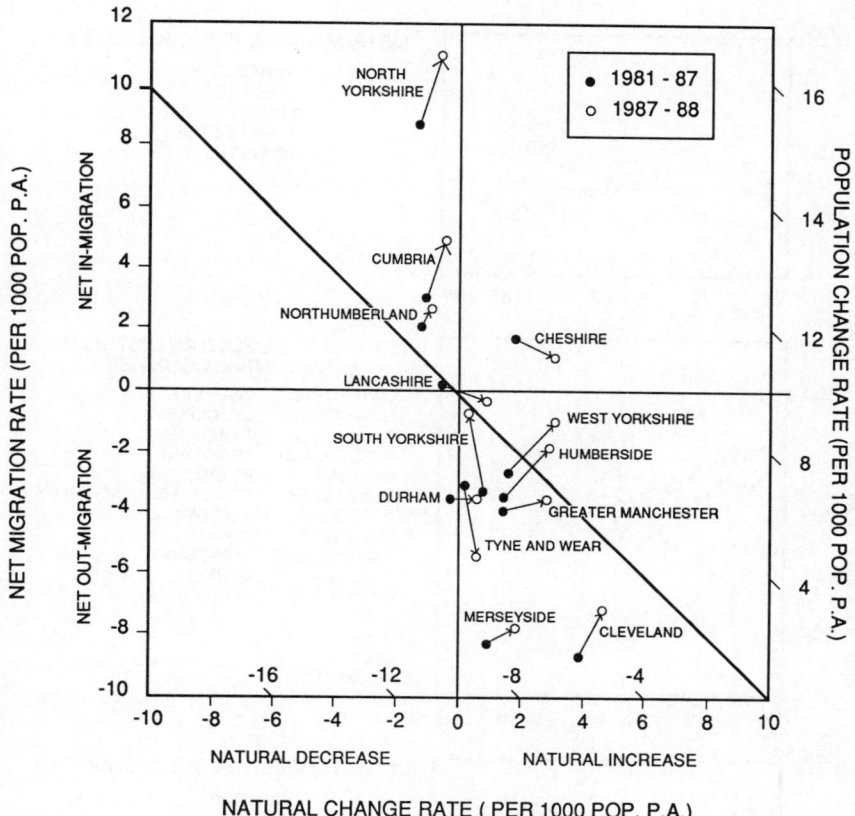

Figure 7.1 Growth regimes for northern counties, 1981–87 and 1987–88

Humberside. The bottom panel of Table 7.1 provides annual rates of natural and migrational change. These point to a contrast between Yorkshire and Humberside on the one hand and the North and North West on the other. Net migration rates in the former region are less negative in both 1981–87 and 1987–88 than in the latter pair. In 1987–88, Yorkshire and Humberside experiences positive net inflows.

The regional averages of natural change and net migration rates conceal interesting variation at the county scale. Figure 7.1 plots such rates for both 1981–87 and 1987–88 on a graph, the diagonal line through which represents equal total population change. It is clear that there is a moderately strong negative association between the natural change and net migration rates: the correlation coefficient is −0.72 for 1981–87 and −0.53 for 1987–88. This is not a chance association; it says something about the nature of the populations of places from which people are migrating and to which they move, on balance. Those areas of high in-migration (North Yorkshire, Cumbria, Northumberland)

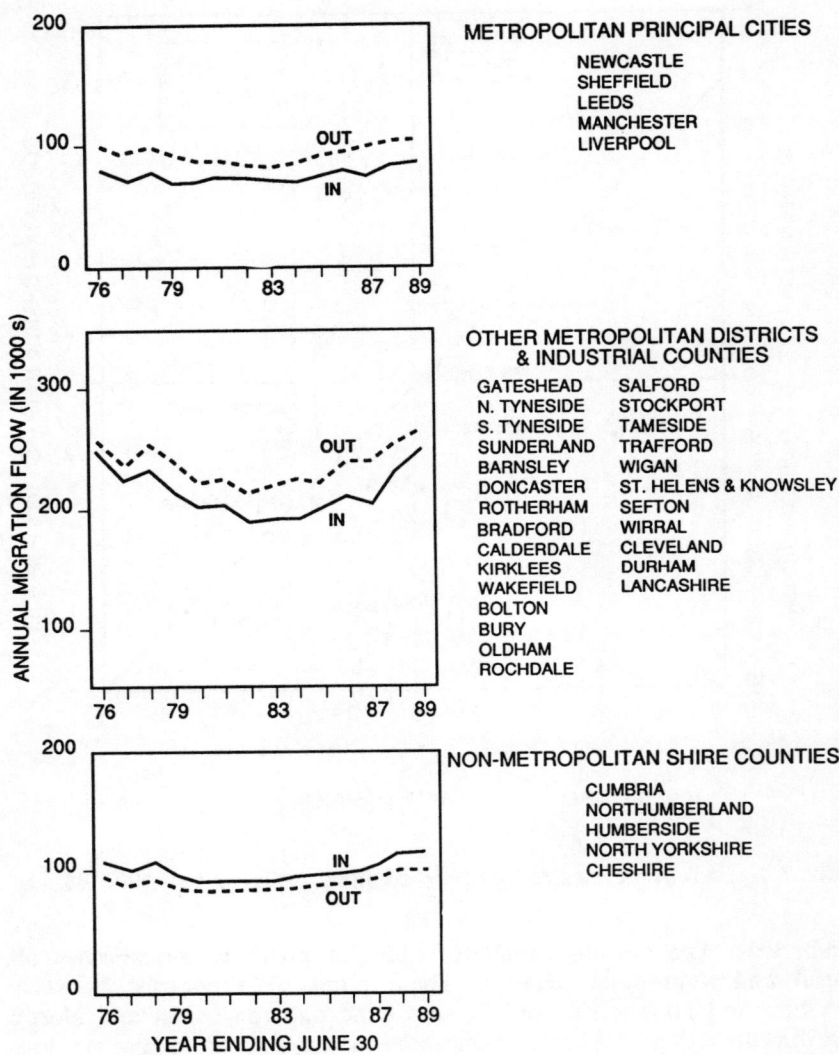

Figure 7.2 Trends in migration for area types, northern England, 1975–89

contain places favoured by the elderly for retirement. The result is a more elderly population and consequently these areas have lower crude birth-rates and higher crude death-rates. The areas of higher out-migration (Cleveland, Merseyside) have high concentrations of younger working-class and unemployed populations and thus have higher than average crude birth-rates and lower than average crude death-rates.

Only one county, Cheshire, falls in the net in-migration and natural increase quadrant of Figure 7.1. Cheshire contains both the southern dormitory suburbs and towns of Greater Manchester and Merseyside but also the new towns of Runcorn and Warrington, all with greater than average population in the family building ages.

7.3 Migration trends between area types

Extensive detailed information on the migration flows between areas is now available. For example, the NHSCR provides tables of migration classified by age and gender between 97 origins and 97 destinations for England and Wales for 14 annual periods between mid-1975 and mid-1989. The general features of this data set have been discussed in Chapters 2 and 3. Here the focus is on the 36 FPC areas falling within northern England.

To aid the analysis, the FPC areas have been classified into three simple types (based loosely on OPCS's equivalent classification of districts used later in the chapter): (a) principal cities within former metropolitan counties; (b) other districts within former metropolitan counties together with non-metropolitan counties of a mainly industrial character; and (c) non-metropolitan counties containing a mixture of medium-sized and small towns together with low-density rural areas. Figure 7.2 lists the members of each type and plots the volume of inflows and outflows over 14 annual intervals (mid-year to mid-year) from 1975–76 to 1988–89. Net migration levels can be deduced by comparing the in- and out-migration profiles.

The graphs in Figure 7.2 shows a clear distinction in migration levels and pattern between four periods. In the 1975–79 period, migration levels were falling; during 1979–83 they reached a nadir; from 1983 to 1987 there was a moderate recovery; in 1987–89 sharp increases occurred in inflows to other metropolitan districts and industrial counties. These periods correspond to the stagflation of the later 1970s, the sharp recession of the early 1980s, the recovery period from recession during 1983–87 and the Lawson boom years of 1987–89. Migration is intimately linked to developments in labour markets (job losses and gains) and in the housing market (increasingly linked to the prevailing interest rate).

Since 1989 the economy has re-entered a period of falling growth in many respects similar to that of 1979–83. Migration inflows to northern England have fallen and outflows have risen (Table 7.2), resulting in a reversal of the net gains of 1988–89 (mid-year to mid-year) in the second half of 1989 (Stillwell, 1990b).

Figure 7.2's graphs also reveal distinctive spatial patterns in migration over the 1975–89 period. Throughout these years the principal cities saw greater outflows than inflows, with a total net loss between 1975 and 1989 of 235 thousand people, constituting 9 per cent of their 1975 population. The other metropolitan districts and industrial counties sustained net losses. These losses totalled 278 thousand but made up only 3 per cent of the 1975 populations of the districts and counties. By contrast the five other non-metropolitan counties experienced net inflows

Table 7.2 Migration inflows and outflows for northern England and
constituent regions, 1988–90

Region	September and December quarters, 1988	September and December quarters, 1989	March and June quarters 1990
North			
Inflow	30.6	29.1	19.7
Outflow	30.4	29.5	20.3
Balance	0.2	− 0.4	− 0.6
Yorkshire & Humberside			
Inflow	57.8	53.0	31.4
Outflow	48.6	49.2	34.1
Balance	9.2	3.8	− 2.7
North West			
Inflow	59.5	53.0	35.7
Outflow	57.6	58.5	39.2
Balance	1.9	− 5.5	− 3.5
Northern England			
Inflow	147.9	135.1	86.8
Outflow	136.6	137.2	93.6
Balance	11.3	− 2.1	− 6.8

Note: Migration inflows, outflows and balances are in 1,000s.
Source: OPCS (1990c, Table 20, p. 59).

throughout the period, totalling 135 thousand and representing a gain of 4 per cent on their 1975 populations.

Figure 7.2 establishes that spatial redistribution of the population from the densely populated metropolitan cores to surrounding areas of lower population is occurring but does not enable us to identify the processes at work. Three processes suggest themselves as candidates: suburbanisation, counterurbanisation and inter-regional exchanges.

By suburbanisation is meant the decanting of population from densely settled urban cores into the immediately surrounding areas, where housing is built. Some workers in suburbanising households continue to be employed in the urban core, but over time other activities (and associated employment) also move out into the suburban hinterland. Increasing car ownership and improved road networks stimulate the process in northern England as elsewhere, and planning policies have attempted in the past to restrain such decentralisation.

Counterurbanisation can be defined as the shift of population from larger, more densely inhabited cities to smaller, less-crowded cities and towns and to the countryside. The workers in migrating households move their job locations as well as their residence locations. Counterurbanisation is driven by employment shifts to smaller places, which, with improved communications and infrastructure, are able to compete in economic markets. However, one important stream of counterurban migrants consists of the more affluent retired, released from the constraint of an urban core workplace and able to satisfy their residential aspirations by choosing smaller, quieter, safer places to spend their post-retirement years.

By inter-regional exchange is meant the flows into and out of the North of England, which on balance involved net losses in all except the last year in the time series. Inter-regional exchange may be combined with either of the first two processes.

Table 7.3 is an attempt to show how the 97 by 97 matrix of migration flows available in the NHSCR data set can be reduced to six by six matrix in which each cell can be interpreted, albeit roughly, as contributing to the processes discussed above. Migration from metropolitan principal cities to other metropolitan districts and industrial counties is interpreted as contributing to suburbanisation. The reverse stream contributes to urban centralisation. Similarly, the migration streams from both metropolitan principal cities and other metropolitan districts or industrial counties to non-metropolitan counties (urban/rural mix) can be interpreted as linked to counterurbanisation. The reverse flows contribute to urbanisation. The diagonal cells labelled exchange migration involve migration flows between FPC areas of a similar type (not including intra-FPC migration which is not recorded in the NHSCR).

The top left and bottom right quadrants of Table 7.3 classify these flows for migration within the North of England and within the rest of the UK respectively. The top right and bottom left quadrants identify the same set of flows which are involved in inter-regional exchanges. The top right quadrant contains outflows from the North of England while the bottom left quadrant contains inflows to the North of England.

Table 7.4 assembles the migration statistics in this framework for the four periods identified from the graphs in Figure 7.2, while Table 7.5 reports the net balances from the migration streams and counterstreams that contribute to the migration accounts for area types in northern England.

The *principal cities* of northern England suffer migration losses through suburbanisation and counterurbanisation within the region and through inter-regional exchange for all periods. These inner cores of metropolitan regions are experiencing decentralisation of all kinds, although we can anticipate from the lower than average losses in 1979–83 that 1989–93 will also see reductions from the 1987–89 tempo.

The *other metropolitan districts and industrial counties* of northern England also experienced large migration losses primarily as a result of movements to the rest of the UK, although they gained consistently through suburbanisation from the principal cities of the North. Note that the losses to principal cities in the rest of the UK represent net urbanisation and are mainly made up of flows to Greater London, particularly in the 1983–87 recovery period. For these areas the two years 1987–89 stand out as very different from prior periods, with net migration loss virtually wiped out both within the North of England and with the rest of the country. These areas were the main beneficiaries of the employment growth of the

Table 7.3 A schema for analysing inter-area flows, northern England and the rest of the UK

	North of England			Rest of the UK		
	Principal cities	Other metro districts	Non-metro shire counties	Principal cities	Other metro districts	Non-metro shire counties
North of England						
Principal cities	Exchange migration	Suburbanisation	Counter-urbanisation	Outflow exchange migration	Outflow suburbanisation	Outflow counter-urbanisation
Other metro districts	Centralisation	Exchange migration	Counter-urbanisation	Outflow centralisation	Outflow exchange migration	Outflow counter-urbanisation
Non-metro shire counties	Urbanisation	Urbanisation	Exchange migration	Outflow urbanisation	Outflow urbanisation	Outflow exchange migration
Rest of the UK						
Principal cities	Inflow exchange migration	Inflow suburbanisation	Inflow counter-urbanisation	Exchange migration	Suburbanisation	Counter-urbanisation
Other metro districts	Inflow centralisation	Inflow exchange migration	Inflow counter-urbanisation	Centralisation	Exchange migration	Counter-urbanisation
Non-metro shire counties	Inflow urbanisation	Inflow urbanisation	Inflow exchange migration	Urbanisation	Urbanisation	Exchange migration

Table 7.4 Inter-area flows for northern England and the rest of the UK, 1975–89

Region	Area type		North PC	North OM	North SC	Rest of UK PC	Rest of UK OM	Rest of UK SC
					1975–79			
North	Principal cities	(PC)	13.7	173.6	57.7	32.1	44.4	69.8
	Other metro	(OM)	133.4	352.8	135.1	59.0	101.6	201.9
	Shire counties	(SC)	38.9	98.7	33.8	23.5	49.8	117.9
Rest of UK	Principal cities	(PC)	24.2	49.6	23.8	729.7	144.0	817.5
	Other metro	(OM)	39.4	95.3	53.4	137.5	252.9	431.3
	Shire counties	(SC)	61.3	155.1	105.9	469.3	362.5	1,669.2
					1979–83			
North	Principal cities	(PC)	13.8	147.9	48.8	32.0	40.2	65.7
	Other metro	(OM)	121.9	298.9	121.3	62.2	94.6	188.0
	Shire counties	(SC)	37.3	89.6	30.3	25.4	48.1	107.5
Rest of UK	Principal cities	(PC)	23.9	42.5	19.5	629.3	123.4	675.7
	Other metro	(OM)	38.5	82.6	48.4	133.5	218.7	386.8
	Shire counties	(SC)	59.3	132.5	91.3	445.3	330.5	1,521.5
					1983–87			
North	Principal cities	(PC)	14.6	153.4	50.5	37.7	40.1	75.1
	Other metro	(OM)	132.1	305.1	129.3	69.1	92.4	208.7
	Shire counties	(SC)	37.2	90.8	33.2	27.5	48.2	119.0
Rest of UK	Principal cities	(PC)	23.8	44.1	22.0	682.0	129.9	736.2
	Other metro	(OM)	38.1	81.0	53.5	145.5	241.8	425.8
	Shire counties	(SC)	60.4	138.3	102.8	452.5	348.5	1,718.3
					1987–89			
North	Principal cities	(PC)	8.1	91.2	26.2	21.6	21.6	39.6
	Other metro	(OM)	70.6	173.6	68.1	37.5	47.7	107.7
	Shire counties	(SC)	21.0	55.7	19.6	14.7	26.7	62.3
Rest of UK	Principal cities	(PC)	14.9	30.9	14.9	363.6	78.6	415.3
	Other metro	(OM)	21.5	49.1	30.5	80.0	139.0	228.0
	Shire counties	(SC)	37.1	101.9	72.4	230.5	215.7	959.2

Note: The migration flows are in 1,000s.
Source: Computed from NHSCR data sets supplied by OPCS.

Table 7.5 Migration balances for northern England areas, 1975–89

Type of balance		1975–79	1979–83	1983–87	1987–89
		Principal cities			
Total balance		– 80.4	– 53.7	– 65.2	– 35.1
Balance within region		– 59.0	– 37.5	– 34.6	– 25.8
Due to suburbanisation		– 40.2	– 26.0	– 21.3	– 20.6
Due to counterurbanisation		– 18.8	– 11.5	– 13.3	– 5.2
Balance between regions		– 21.4	– 16.2	– 30.6	– 9.3
Due to exchange flows		– 7.9	– 8.1	– 13.9	– 6.7
Due to suburbanisation		– 5.0	– 1.7	– 2.0	– 0.1
Due to counterurbanisation		– 8.5	– 6.4	– 14.7	– 2.5
		Other metro districts			
Total balance		– 58.7	– 92.9	– 124.0	– 2.8
Balance within region		3.8	– 5.7	– 17.2	8.2
Due to suburbanisation		40.2	26.0	21.3	20.6
Due to counterurbanisation		– 36.4	– 31.7	– 38.5	– 12.4
Balance between regions		– 62.5	– 87.2	– 106.8	– 11.0
Due to urbanisation		– 9.4	– 19.7	– 25.0	– 6.6
Due to exchange flows		– 6.3	– 12.0	– 11.4	1.4
Due to counterurbanisation		– 46.8	– 55.5	– 70.4	– 5.8
		Shire counties			
Total balance		47.1	21.4	35.4	31.7
Balance within region		55.2	43.2	51.8	17.6
Due to counterurbanisation	(PC)	18.8	11.5	13.3	5.2
Due to counterurbanisation	(OM)	36.4	31.7	38.5	12.4
Balance between regions		– 8.1	– 21.8	– 16.4	14.1
Due to counterurbanisation	(PC)	0.3	– 5.9	– 5.5	0.2
Due to counterurbanisation	(OM)	3.6	0.3	5.3	3.8
Due to exchange flows		– 12.0	– 16.2	– 16.2	10.1

Source: Computed from Table 7.4.

boom period through counterurbanisation within the region through all four periods, though these gains are lower in the final period. This shift is counteracted by a shift from a position of net loss to the rest of the UK between 1975 and 1987 to a position of net gain in 1987–89 from all types in the rest of the country.

Within the *rest of the UK* (dominated by the Southern and Midlands regions), the dominant net flow is from principal cities to shire counties in all periods. This net flow, which dwarfs all those in Table 7.5, has been analysed in detail in Chapter 3 of this volume.

7.4 Population redistribution across northern districts

The FPC areas provide a rather crude spatial framework for the analysis of spatial trends in migration, but inter-district migration data for 1990–91 should become available with the publication of the Special Migration Statistics of the 1991 Census in 1993. In the meantime, it is useful to examine the population changes estimated by OPCS for the 92 districts of northern England.

Figure 7.3 plots the average annual rate of change in population for the districts of northern England between mid-year 1981 and mid-year 1988. Figure 7.3 also depicts the classification of districts adopted in OPCS (1990d), which captures their degree of urbanisation. Table 7.6 provides the average rates of growth in eight district types and for a related classification of districts by density.

The highest rates of loss (more than 0.5 per cent per annum) characterise selected principal cities (Liverpool, Manchester, Sheffield, though not Leeds or Newcastle), and selected metropolitan districts and other cities in the North West (Burnley, Salford, Blackburn, Knowsley), in Yorkshire and Humberside (Scunthorpe, Hull, Greater Grimsby) and the North East (Wansbeck, South Tyneside, Easington, Sedgefield, Hartlepool, Langbaurgh and Middlesbrough). All these areas have local economies struggling to combat the decline of their principal traditional industry. The other districts exhibiting rates of population loss cover much of South East Lancashire and Merseyside, West Cumbria and the North East conurbation.

Outside of these areas, districts gain in population. The highest gainers are to be found in Yorkshire and Humberside in a broad swath from the Craven district in the Yorkshire Dales round to Glanford district in southern Humberside, and in the interstices between the major cities in the North West. Part of the population gain in these areas, accessible to nearby major urban centres, must be due to migration of the suburbanising variety (e.g. Bradford or Leeds workers moving residence to Upper Wharfedale) but part is probably attributable to the growth of successful enterprises in these regions. The remoter rural districts do also gain population but less strongly, along with the resort and retirement areas, where elderly mortality makes for natural decrease and where competition from foreign resorts has dampened employment growth in the areas' principal activity. Some districts with new towns are gainers (Halton containing Runcorn, Warrington containing the new town of the same name, West Lancashire containing Skelmersdale) but others are losers (Easington which houses Peterlee, Sedgefield which contains Newton Aycliffe). The concentration of employment in new towns in the manufacturing sector can mean job losses in times of economic downturn.

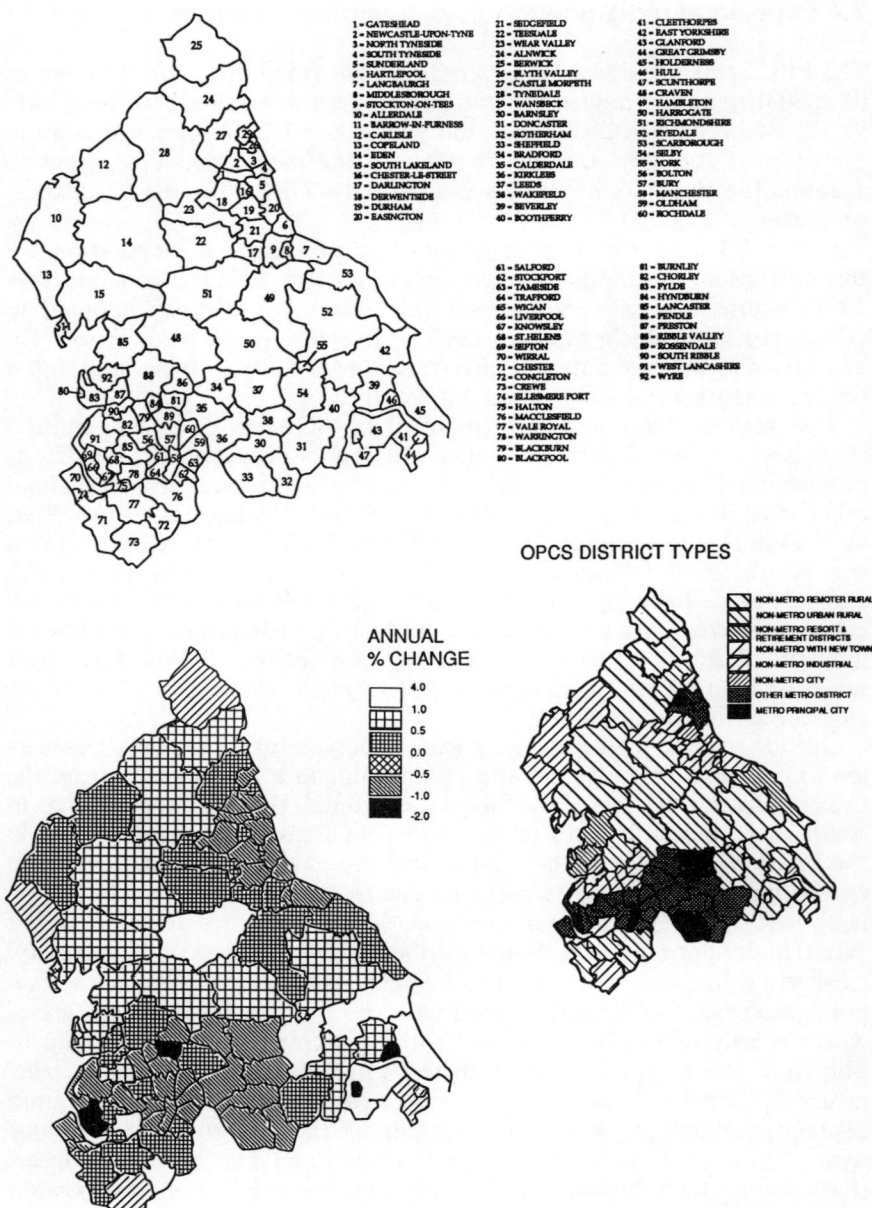

Figure 7.3 Annual percentage change in population, districts of northern England, 1981–88

Table 7.6 Population change rates for districts of northern England, 1981–88

Classification	1981–88	1981–87	1987–88
District type (after OPCS)			
Metro principal city	− 0.56	− 0.53	− 0.70
Other metro district	− 0.18	− 0.22	0.02
Non-metro city	− 0.72	− 0.71	− 0.80
Non-metro industrial	− 0.28	− 0.28	− 0.28
Non-metro with new town	0.12	0.08	0.34
Non-metro resort & retirement	0.30	0.27	0.52
Non-metro urban, rural	0.67	0.64	0.80
Non-metro remoter rural	0.84	0.66	1.92
Density class (quartile)			
1,550 per sq. km. and over	− 0.46	− 0.46	− 0.46
700–1,549 per sq. km.	− 0.16	− 0.19	− 0.01
200–699 per sq. km.	0.04	0.02	0.20
less than 200 per sq. km.	0.68	0.58	1.25

Source: Computed from data in OPCS (1990d, Table 4.2).

7.5 Interpretation

At the start of the chapter we saw the investigation of historical trends in population redistribution as an important input to models of future population change. So what has been learnt from the analyses of this chapter that might be useful to a model builder?

It is clear that population redistribution is the outcome of complex processes occurring at the interface of the region's demographic and economic systems. Any predictive population and development model must incorporate: (a) a model of the shifts in employment within and between areas; (b) a decomposition of migration streams into those associated with continued commuting to current workplace and those associated with workplace relocation; and (c) predictions of non-economic migration (to places of higher education or training, military establishments or to areas attractive to retirees). The detailed information about migration behaviour required to incorporate such processes cannot be provided by a simple time series such as the NHSCR inter-FPC migration data set; reinvestigation of population redistribution using the 1991 Census is strongly indicated.

However, the time series perspective adopted in the chapter points up the need to embed any model of a regional economic–demographic system in a national context and to avoid using the immediate past as a guide to the near-term future. Migration is an activity strongly influenced by economic cycles in both labour and housing markets. These economic cycles exhibit time lags between regions. Thus, the turnaround in net migration flows in northern England is probably the dying outwash of a southern-led boom in economic activity and house buying and selling which was already over in the quarter following the end of the migration time series (to mid-year 1989) used in this volume.

Improving on the descriptive analyses of this chapter and building an integrated model of the population and economy of northern England provide a fruitful agenda for the 1990s.

8 Migration trends for Wales: rural revival?

Anne Green

8.1 Introduction

In this chapter recent migration trends in Wales are outlined. The bulk of the analyses draw upon annual National Health Service Central Register (NHSCR) data at the county scale. However, use is also made of OPCS population data at the local authority district scale, in order to gain an insight into migration at a finer level of spatial disaggregation. In the first substantive section of the chapter patterns and trends in net migration over the period from 1975–76 to 1988–89 are considered – first at the aggregate scale, and secondly disaggregated by age and sex. In the second section the focus of attention shifts to gross migration flows in and out of counties; once again a description of aggregate flows is followed by a consideration of disaggregated flows. Patterns of, and trends in, inter-area flows, both within Wales and to and from the rest of the UK, are discussed in the third section. The labour market, housing market and cultural context for the patterns and trends in net and gross flows described in previous sections are addressed in greater detail in the fourth section of the chapter. An assessment of the contribution of migration change to overall population change is made in the final section of the chapter, and future prospects for, and trends in, migration are outlined.

One of the key themes identified in this chapter which continually re-emerges is the urban–rural shift of population – with continuing out-migration from the older industrial areas and in-migration to the more rural areas. Clearly, this general shift of population from urban to rural areas is not unique to Wales, but the Welsh language and culture provides an additional dimension to debates surrounding the disadvantages and advantages of an influx of population into rural communities. While it is clear that during the 1970s and 1980s in-migration has led to a reversal of long-term population decline in many parts of rural Wales, whether this represents a 'revival' of rural areas is debatable. Do in-migrants from urban areas in Wales and from the rest of the UK destroy the communities they seek by bidding up house prices, opposing new developments – in employment and housing, and diluting the Welsh culture? Use is made of survey data to supplement the migration flow data in an attempt to answer these questions.

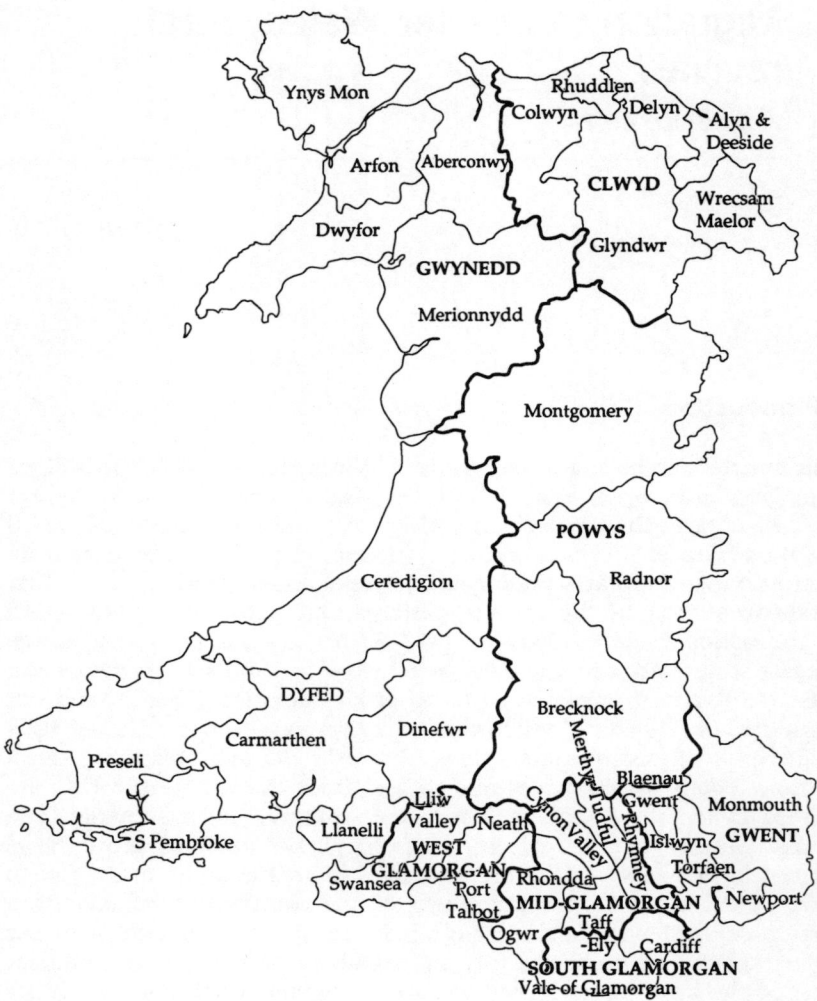

Figure 8.1   Counties and local authority districts in Wales

8.2 Net migration

8.2.1 Aggregate patterns and trends

The NHSCR data is available at the county scale in Wales. There are eight counties: Clwyd, Dyfed, Gwent, Gwynedd, Mid Glamorgan, Powys, South Glamorgan and West Glamorgan (see Figure 8.1). Four counties – all from north, west and mid Wales, and sharing a largely rural complexion – experienced aggregate net in-migration each year from 1975–76 to 1988–89. Mid Glamorgan recorded net out-migration in

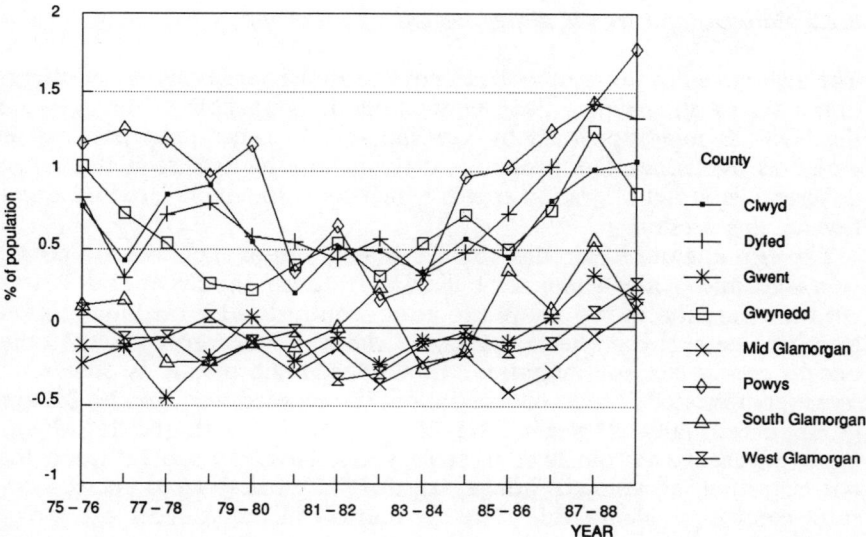

Figure 8.2   Net migration rates for Welsh counties, 1975–89

Source: National Health Service Central Register data (via OPCS).

each year during the period except for 1988–89, while West Glamorgan
and Gwent experienced net out-migration in more years than they experienced net in-migration. There was aggregate net out-migration from
South Glamorgan from 1977–78 to 1981–82 and from 1983–84 to 1984–
85. Hence, at this broad scale net migration trends would appear to
favour rural areas in north, west and mid Wales at the expense of more
urban areas in the south. However, it is notable that for the first time
during the period in question, there was net in-migration into all counties
in Wales in 1988–89; albeit with considerably lower net migration rates
in the cases of South Glamorgan, Mid Glamorgan, Gwent and West
Glamorgan, than in Powys, Dyfed, Clwyd and Gwynedd (see Figure 8.2).

This urban–rural shift is more clearly evident at the local authority
district scale (see Figure 8.1 for location of districts). Analysis of the
migration component derived from the OPCS estimates of mid-year
population for the period 1981–89 reveals that all districts in Powys and
Gwynedd shared in the overall net in-migration, while in the other counties recording net inflows in all years, Alyn & Deeside and Delyn (the
most 'urban' districts in Clwyd) and Llanelli (Dyfed) were the only
districts not registering net inflows over the period from 1981–89. In Mid
Glamorgan, Ogwr was the only district to register a net migration inflow
in the period 1981–89, as was Lliw Valley in West Glamorgan, while in
Gwent strong net outflows from Newport contrasted with strong net
inflows to Monmouth, and in South Glamorgan there were net inflows
to the Vale of Glamorgan and net outflows from Cardiff (further
underlining the general urban–rural trend).

8.2.2 Patterns and trends disaggregated by subgroup

The aggregate net flows described above subsume variations in net migration rates by subgroups of the population. It is possible to disaggregate the NHSCR migration data by age and sex. In general the patterns of variation by sex are less pronounced than those by age, so it is the age differentials in net migration trends which form the main focus of attention in this section.

The net migration profiles for the mainly 'rural' counties of north, west and mid Wales share some similar features. In Clwyd and Powys net out-migration in the 15–19 age group contrasts with net in-migration in other age groups, whereas in Dyfed the 20–29 age group is the only one to record net out-migration. In Gwynedd the picture is somewhat more complicated – net out-migration is recorded for the 20–29 age group in virtually all years 1975–76 to 1988–89, with the 15–19 age group recording net outflows in some years. Hence, a general trend for out-migration of younger adults (aged 15–29 years) from these more rural counties is identifiable. The net outflow in the younger age group (15–19) from Powys and Clwyd may be due, at least in part, to the movement of young people to higher educational institutions outside the area, and this same factor may go some way to 'explaining' net inflows in this younger age group, and outflows in the 20–29 age group for Dyfed (which incorporates Colleges of the University of Wales at Aberystwyth and Lampeter). In all four counties older people (aged over 55) registered among the highest net in-migration rates of any age group by 1988–89, with an increase in the net in-migration rate discernible for this age group in all counties during the 1980s. A clear tendency towards an increase in net in-migration in the 45–54 and 30–44 age groups is also apparent from the mid-1980s.

By contrast, net out-migration is the norm for virtually all age-groups, with the exception of the over-55-year-olds, in Mid Glamorgan throughout much of the period. However, in 1988–89 net out-migration was confined to the 15–19 and 20–29 age groups – with only a marginal net outflow in the latter, and for the first time during the period in question the country experienced aggregate net in-migration, in stark contrast with net outflows in 1985–86; a situation no doubt explained in part by the rundown of the South Wales coalfield and associated industries, followed by net in-migration in the late 1980s as advantage was taken of relatively low house prices in the area while house prices were booming in Cardiff. South Glamorgan and West Glamorgan share in a pattern of highest net in-migration rates for the 15–19-year-olds, and highest net out-migration rates for 20–29-year-olds – illustrating the role of large cities such as Cardiff and Swansea (with their higher education institutions) in 'drawing in' young adults and then 'divulging' them at a later date. In Gwent, net migration rates are fairly small throughout the period in most age groups, with the exception of the 15–19 age group which is characterised by net outflows throughout the period.

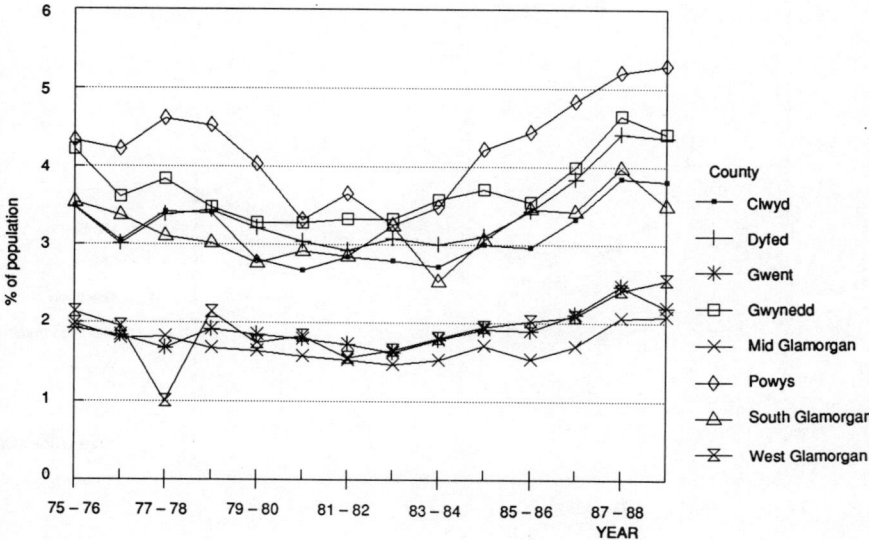

Figure 8.3 Gross in-migration rates to Welsh counties, 1975–89
Source: National Health Service Central Register data (via OPCS).

8.3 Gross flows

8.3.1 Aggregate patterns and trends

The net flows outlined above represent the difference between much larger gross flows. All areas in Wales followed the same general temporal trend, with a decline in gross flows during the late 1970s to a trough in the early 1980s, followed by a subsequent increase in flows from the mid-1980s, so that by 1988–89, gross in-migration rates were slightly above those recorded in 1975–76 in most counties, while gross out-migration rates had returned to the levels recorded in 1975–76. This trend indicates that depressed economic conditions in the recession of the early 1980s served to reduced migration flows, while gross migration rates increased as economic conditions improved.

At the county scale high gross in-migration rates tend to be associated with high gross out-migration rates, and similarly lower gross in-migration rates are usually associated with lower gross out-migration rates. It is those counties experiencing net in-migration which display the highest gross migration rates, while conversely, those recording net out-migration tend to register relatively low gross migration rates, in accordance with established tendencies (Owen and Green, 1989). Hence, Powys, Dyfed and Gwynedd display the highest gross in-migration rates (see Figure 8.3) – not falling below 3 per cent even during the depths of recession, and rising to over 5 per cent in Powys in 1987–88 and 1988–89. Clwyd and South Glamorgan display similar gross in-migration rate

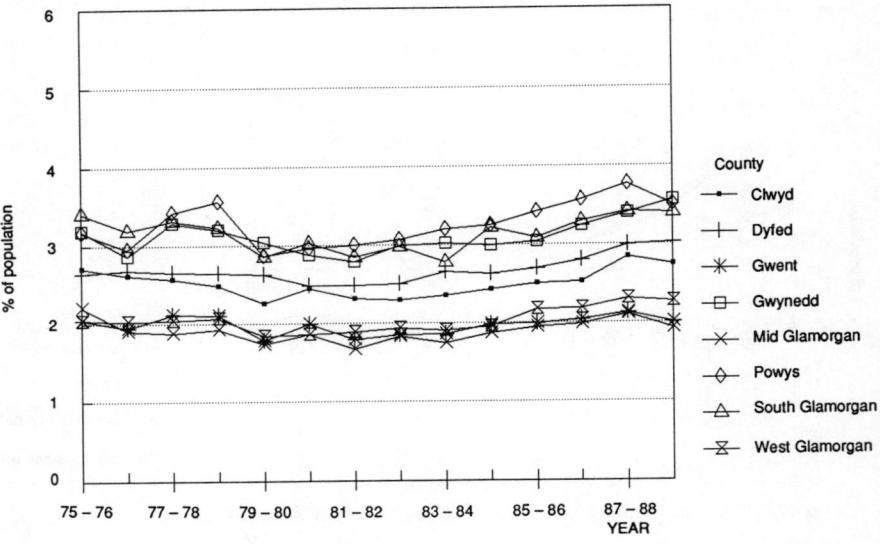

Figure 8.3 Gross out-migration rates from Welsh counties, 1975–89
Source: National Health Service Central Register data (via OPCS).

profiles to these three counties. By contrast, in Mid Glamorgan, Gwent and West Glamorgan the gross in-migration rate rarely rises above 2 per cent during the period.

Somewhat less spatial and temporal variation is evident in gross out-migration rates (see Figure 8.4) than in gross in-migration rates. Highest gross out-migration rates are recorded by Powys, Gwynedd and South Glamorgan (with rates of around 3 per cent throughout the period). The next highest gross out-migration rates are recorded by Dyfed and Clwyd, while once again the lowest gross out-migration rates are exhibited by Mid Glamorgan, West Glamorgan and Gwent (at around 2 per cent).

While Powys displays high scores on gross migration rates, the absolute flows involved in the case of this sparsely populated county are smaller than for all the other more populous counties. In absolute terms, South Glamorgan, Clwyd and Dyfed dominate the gross inflows, while South Glamorgan, Mid Glamorgan and Dyfed dominate gross outflows.

8.3.2 Gross flows disaggregated by subgroup

In general, younger people tend to display a greater propensity to migrate than older people, and hence a disproportionate share of gross flows are accounted for by younger people. In all counties the 20–29 and 15–19 age groups display the highest gross inflow and gross outflow rates, while the 45–54 and 55 plus age groups exhibit the lowest rates of gross flows. In some of the more rural counties – notably Gwynedd, there is some evidence for convergence in gross in-migration rates by age group over the period, with particularly marked increases in the gross in-migration rate in the 30–44 age group during the 1980s, as well as in the 45–54 and over-55 age groups. Dyfed shares with Gwynedd an increase in rates of gross in-migration in the family-forming age groups. In Powys, rates or gross in-migration increased markedly during the 1980s from 1982–83 for all age groups. By contrast, in those counties characterised by lower rates of gross flows the differentials by age in gross inflow and outflow rates remain more constant over time.

8.4 Inter-area flows

The NHSCR data may be used to analyse flows between counties; intra-county flows are not captured in the data and hence it is not possible to capture many of the very short-distance flows involved in suburbanisation. Moreover, it is not possible to identify the impacts of in-migration and out-migration on specific settlements – the scale at which many of those most vociferous about the detrimental impacts of migration have focused.

Considering inflows first, at least one-half of all inflows to counties in Wales – in all age groups and in all years – originate from outside Wales. Clwyd – with its close links to Cheshire and both the Merseyside and Manchester conurbations – displays the highest proportion of in-migrants from outside Wales: over 80 per cent in all age groups. After Clwyd, Gwynedd – where the Welsh language and culture is strongest – has the next highest proportion of in-migrants from outside Wales. Here it is in the over-45 age groups that in-migrants from the rest of the UK are found in the largest proportions (approximately 85 per cent of in-migrants in these age groups in 1985–86 were from outside Wales, compared with just over three-quarters in all other age groups). Similarly in Powys, it is in the over-55 age group that in-migrants from outside Wales are found in the highest proportions. There appear to be few clear temporal trends in the shares of in-migrants from different origins, although there appears to be some evidence for an increase in in-migrants to Dyfed from outside Wales over the period in question.

Mid Glamorgan, West Glamorgan and South Glamorgan record the fewest in-migrants from outside Wales in proportionate terms, with between one-half and two-thirds of in-migrants originating from the rest of the UK. In South Glamorgan, migrants from outside Wales are most prevalent in the working age groups, by contrast with the situation in the more rural counties of north, west and mid Wales where they are over-represented in the older age groups to the greatest degree. Indeed, analysis of the age profiles of in-migrants to the counties of Wales from the rest of the UK (see Figure 8.5) shows that the 20–29-year age group (with their relatively high propensity to migrate) account for over one-third of all such in-migrants, compared with approximately one-quarter

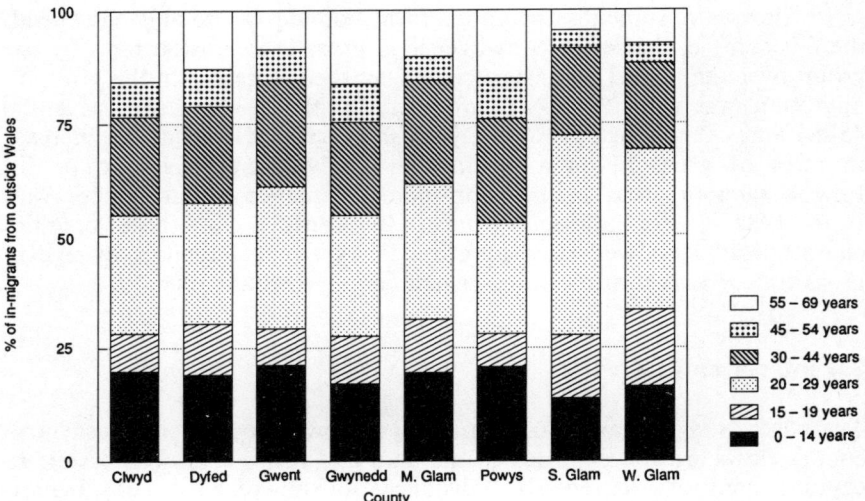

Figure 8.5 Age profile of in-migrants from origins outside Wales, 1985–86
Source: NHSCR data (via OPCS).

in the case of other counties. By contrast, in 1985–86 one-quarter of all in-migrants from outside Wales to Gwynedd, Powys and Clwyd were aged over 45, compared with under 10 per cent in South Glamorgan. With the ageing of the population, the over-55s have come to account for a greater proportion of all migrants over the period.

As over one-half of all inflows to the counties of Wales are from the rest of the UK, so at least one-half of all outflows from the counties of Wales are to be destinations outside Wales. Powys, Clwyd and Gwynedd (with among the highest proportions of in-migrants from outside Wales) consistently record the largest proportions of outflows to the rest of the UK – across all age groups. Mid Glamorgan registers fewer outflows to the rest of the UK than any other county in Wales; there are large net outflows from Mid Glamorgan to South Glamorgan, West Glamorgan and Gwent. After Mid Glamorgan, West Glamorgan and South Glamorgan have the lowest proportion of total outflows to the rest of the UK. Age differentials in outflows to the rest of the UK are not particularly marked. Analyses of the age profiles of out-migrants from the counties of Wales to the rest of the UK (see Figure 8.6) show that Wales loses proportionately more people in the under-30 age groups to the rest of the UK than it gains from outside Wales. The proportion of out-migrants to the rest of the UK accounted for by the over-45 age groups is considerably less than the comparable share of in-migrants from outside Wales accounted for by these older age groups – particularly in the case of the more rural counties of north, west and mid Wales.

Within Wales, the main inter-county flows involve neighbouring areas.

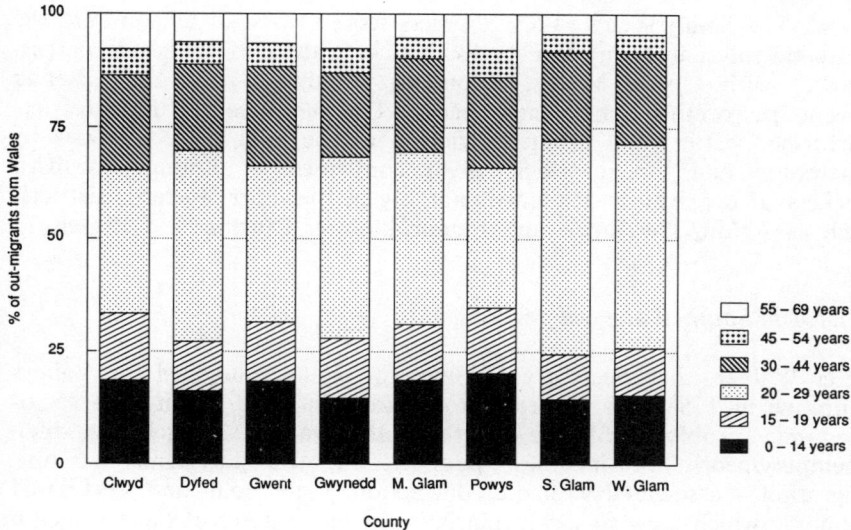

Figure 8.6 Age profile of out-migrants to destinations outside Wales, 1985–86

Source: NHSCR data (via OPCS).

Hence, there are relatively large flows between Gwynedd and Clwyd; between West Glamorgan, Mid Glamorgan and Dyfed; and from Gwent to Mid Glamorgan and South Glamorgan. The flows to and from Powys involve all other counties in Wales, with no single area predominating.

8.5 The labour market, housing market and cultural context

Wales has traditionally been considered as a poorly performing region in the broad national context. As the analyses of net and gross migration flows indicate, and as labour market indicators illustrate even more clearly, there are stark divides between different areas in Wales at the local scale. In studies concerned with the ranking of 280 towns in Britain on a combined index synthesising 10 separate indicators of local economic prosperity, 173 places separated the highest-ranked town (Aberystwyth) and the lowest-ranked town (Holyhead) in an analysis based on the recession period of the early 1980s (Champion and Green, 1988), while 207 places separated the highest- (Carmarthen) and lowest- (Llanelli) ranked towns in a similar analysis focusing on local economic fortunes in the second part of the 1980s (Champion and Green, 1990).

In a study adopting a similar methodology, but confined to the 37 districts in Wales, Morris and Wilkinson (1989) pointed to a marked East–West divide within Wales, with groups of districts labelled 'South East Urban', 'South East Rural' and 'North East Urban' performing considerably better than the 'Urban South West' and 'Rural South

West'. The South Wales valleys districts scored worst of all, on both the synthetic index and on many individual indicators of economic performance, with Cynon Valley, Rhondda, Merthyr Tydfil and Blaenau Gwent performing particularly badly. On the whole, rural districts performed better than urban districts – as the nationwide analyses by Champion and Green (1988, 1990) confirmed – although localised pockets of deprivation remained, notably in the more westerly districts, such as Arfon, Dwyfor, South Pembrokeshire, Dinefwr and Preseli.

8.5.1 The South Wales valleys

Peter Walker, then Secretary of State for Wales, launched the Valleys Initiative in 1988 in an attempt to address in their totality the socio-economic problems of the South Wales valleys – including high unemployment, low incomes, poor health, transport and net out-migration – associated with the contraction of the coal- and steel-based economy which grew so spectacularly in the last quarter of the nineteenth century and in the early years of the twentieth century. Over the subsequent years, many of these communities lost some of the most enterprising and highly skilled members of their populations to other parts of the UK and overseas in the face of a lack of employment openings and relatively poor economic prospects in Wales. In the wake of policies to develop a local enterprise culture in Wales, the success of efforts to promote inward investment (almost 25 per cent of total Japanese investment in Britain is directed into Wales), the benefits South Wales (particularly the coastal strip) has gained from relocations as a result of overheating of the economy of South East England, transport improvements, and an emphasis on improving the image, attractiveness and quality of life in the Valleys, Walker hoped for a 'change in attitudes':

> Once, if a boy went to grammar school, that was his passport out of the valleys and out of Wales. Now more exciting things are happening and there is reason to stay. (Simpson, 1988)

Despite an improvement in the unemployment situation, severe job shortfalls remain in the South Wales valleys (Green and Owen, 1990).

8.5.2 The rural areas of Mid, North and West Wales

These areas have also historically been characterised by net out-migration. Since 1957 the Mid Wales Industrial Development Association and its successor – the Development Board for Rural Wales – have been active in attempting to improve the social and economic well-being of Mid Wales (defined as the area covered by the districts of Montgomery, Radnor, Brecknock, Meirionnydd and Ceredigion (see Figure 8.1)). This area – one of the most sparsely populated in Britain – suffered continual decline in population from 1891 to 1971. During the 1970s and 1980s this trend was reversed, and the population increased through net in-migration (as outlined above) and the economic base, formerly character-ised by overrepresentation in agriculture and most service industries compared with the rest of Wales, was diversified through the attraction of manufacturing (as detailed in a case study of Powys by Champion and Townsend, 1990, pp. 249–52). However, with continued out-migration of young people, and a larger than average proportion of older people – many of them in-migrants – self-sustaining growth of population has not been achieved (as highlighted in the final section of this chapter).

The in-migration of people into rural Wales, many of them from outside Wales (as indicated above), and the impact of such in-migrants on the destination areas, has attracted particular attention in the mid and late 1980s. Hence, it seems appropriate in the remainder of this section to concentrate specifically on the problems and opportunities posed by such in-migration.

In Gwynedd, factors underlying the growing concern at the increasing number of in-migrants into the county and the effects of this influx on the social and cultural life of local communities, and particularly on the state of the Welsh language, were highlighted in the preparation of a memorandum by local councils to the Secretary of State for Wales on the relationship between planning and housing policies and the state of the Welsh language in Gwynedd (Gwynedd County Council, 1988). In this memorandum three main aspects of the in-migration to Gwynedd were emphasised: second homes, permanent in-migration and commuting. These aspects are considered in turn below.

Second homes accounted for 9 per cent of the total housing stock in Gwynedd in 1986, an increase from 7 per cent in 1981, causing a reduc-tion in the proportion of the total housing stock available to local people, and in particular leading to an increase in the price of the types of houses which would appeal to young first-time buyers. In 1979, Meibion Glyndwr (Sons of Glendower – a group named after the fifteenth-century Welsh prince who waged a guerrilla war against the English) began a fire-raising campaign, targeted at this stage on unoc-cupied second homes (Roe, 1989). Gwynedd has had a flourishing market in second homes for some time and surveys have indicated that approx-imately 50 per cent of second home-owners intend to live in their second homes permanently on retirement – adding to the prevailing imbalance in the age structure characterised by a large proportion of elderly people.

The substantial increase in permanent in-migration to Gwynedd and other parts of rural Wales during the 1980s (as outlined in the foregoing sections) is seen by many as a greater threat to the Welsh culture than second home-owners and holiday-makers. The Meibion Glyndwr campaign against 'chequebook colonialism' was broadened in the 1980s to include 'white settlers' (shorthand for the English in general), as well as holiday homes (Heath, 1989). It is acknowledged that at the scale of individual settlements the position varies from area to area and from year to year, but in some areas in-migration has radically changed the character of particular places within a very short period of time. The specific cultural and linguistic heritage of Gwynedd comes under particular threat when in-migration is on such a scale and at such a rate that local communities cannot cope and assimilate in-migrants. In one six-month period in 1988 (at the height of the recent house price boom) a survey in Gwynedd discovered that almost one in three house sales were to people from England; and while it is acknowledged that this is not unique to rural Wales, the consequences may be more destructive:

> Many parts of Britain – East Anglia, for instance – have suffered an influx of southerners with property money to burn, but, say the Welsh, there is a difference: East Anglia has no national identity, no separate language. (Roe 1989)

House prices in rural Wales rose markedly in the late 1980s, as they did elsewhere in Britain, but the large differential between the South East and other areas has remained, such that rural Wales is a 'cheap' area for many in-migrants. The position is compounded by the fact that earnings in rural Wales are considerably lower than the Great Britain average: in 1988 Powys, Dyfed and Gwynedd occupied second, third and fourth positions, respectively, after Cornwall on a county league table of low-pay areas. The majority of the population of rural Wales believe in-migrants get the best homes and the best jobs (Institute of Welsh Affairs, 1988), while the locals find it increasingly difficult to compete.

In linguistic terms, in-migration is such that in many village schools in Gwynedd (where all schools are officially bilingual) only a minority of the pupils now come from Welsh-speaking homes; the language of the playground has changed from Welsh to English, and the new cultural minority is made up of natives. In Dyfed, where 47 per cent of the population speak Welsh, and virtually everyone speaks English, the local education authority's recently instituted language policy in which in two-thirds of primary school lessons are taught almost wholly in Welsh has generated great controversy, with accusations that the council is more concerned with social engineering than in providing a well-rounded education (Heath, 1990).

More recently, commuting has been identified as having particular implications for planning and housing polices. With the increasing tendency to travel further and further to work, transport improvements (notably the up-grading of the A55 along the North Wales coast to the Menai Straits – making the area increasingly accessible from, and to, North West England) and the emergence and growing importance of quality-of-life' factors in decision-making, Gwynedd has become increasingly attractive as a residential area for those working further afield. In the past, the English have been deterred from moving into some of the more isolated areas, such as the Lleyn peninsula, but such areas are more accessible now than ever before. In the face of 'Y Mewnlifiad' (the inflow of English people to Welsh-speaking areas), some militant nationalists favour the imposition of immigration controls on the English

– in the words of a local councillor:

The Foreign Secretary says Britain can't absorb three million Hong Kong Chinese because it would cause social problems. But the equivalent is happening in Wales every year with 70,000 English immigrants. (Linton, 1989)

Hence, in some parts of rural Wales there are tensions between in-movers and longer-established residents, between Welsh and English people, and between Welsh speakers and non-Welsh speakers (Institute of Welsh Affairs, 1988). These tensions vary in intensity from area to area, and in many Welsh-speaking and English-speaking parts of Wales there are few, if any, discernible tensions between the groups. While in quantitative terms the population of rural Wales has by and large been revived, it may be argued that this 'revival' has the potential to destroy – and is indeed destroying – the linguistic and cultural traditions of rural Wales.

8.6 The role of migration in population change and future perspectives

In the context of a relatively stable population (as in the case of Wales in the 1970s and 1980s), migration is often the most important component of population change. As indicated in the preceding sections, migration is significant not only quantitatively, but also qualitatively, in terms of who migrates and where the migration streams originate and terminate.

Of the counties in Wales, components of change calculated from OPCS mid-year population estimate data reveal that overall population loss during the period 1981–89 was confined to Mid Glamorgan and West Glamorgan. In both these areas a negative out-migration component score more than offset population increase through natural change. In the case of Gwent, a positive score on the natural change component outweighed a small negative score on the migration component. South Glamorgan was the only county where both in-migration and natural increase contributed to overall population increase. In the more rural counties of Powys, Gwynedd, Dyfed and Clwyd population gains through migration more than outweighed losses through natural change.

At the district scale many of the rural areas recorded population gains through migration but losses through natural change: Colwyn, Glyndwr and Rhuddlan (in Clwyd); Carmarthen, Ceredigion and Dinefwr (in Dyfed), Aberconwy, Dwyfor and Meirionydd (in Gwynedd); and Brecknock, Montgomeryshire and Radnorshire (in Powys) (see Figure 8.7). Hence, although the long-established trend of population loss and net out-migration has been reversed in these areas in the 1970s and 1980s, the population is not 'self-sustaining'. Approximately one-quarter of the 37 districts registered population gains through migration and natural change: Wrexham Maelor (Clwyd), Preseli and South

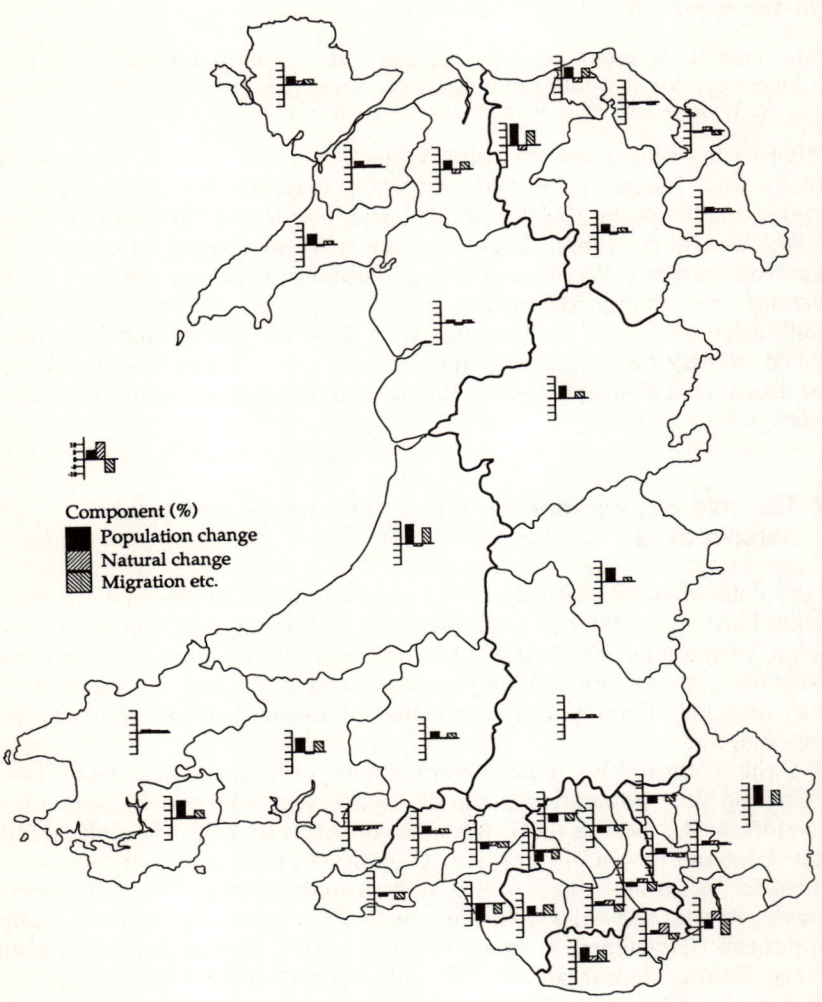

Figure 8.7 Components of Welsh population change by district, 1981–89

Pembrokeshire (Dyfed), Islwyn (Gwent), Arfon and Ynys Mon (Gwynedd), Vale of Glamorgan (South Glamorgan) and Lliw Valley (West Glamorgan).

Looking forward in the short- and medium-term to 2006, the Welsh Office (1989) 1987-based population projections for the counties of Wales show that all counties with the exception of West Glamorgan, and after 1996 Mid Glamorgan, are projected to contribute to an increase in the population of Wales. Of those counties in which population is projected to grow more rapidly than in Wales as a whole – Clwyd, Dyfed, Gwynedd, Powys and South Glamorgan, it is only in South

Glamorgan that natural increase, rather than net in-migration, accounts for the population increase. A lower level of inward migration is assumed in the 1990s compared with that in the late 1980s, and given the fact that births are expected to decrease in number after 1993, it is not surprising that lower population growth rates are projected in the late 1990s and from 2001 to 2006. After 2001 only South Glamorgan, Mid Glamorgan and Gwent are expected, on the assumptions used, to experience natural increase, and in all other counties there are projected to be more deaths than births. However, levels of in-migration are anticipated to be such that population growth will be maintained, albeit at a slower rate than previously in these areas.

Regional economic forecasts indicate relatively favourable prospects for Wales to the year 2000, compared with many of areas of the 'periphery' with which Wales was associated in the late 1970s and early 1980s (Cambridge Econometrics and Northern Ireland Economic Research Centre, 1990). In the late 1980s, much of Wales, along with the Midlands, shared in the spread of the economic recovery from the Greater South East, such that in the second part of the 1980s Wales displayed among the most spectacular increases in economic fortunes of any of the standard economic planning regions (Champion and Green, 1990). Within Wales, however, there remain clear disparities in economic fortunes at the local scale. Much of the inward investment has been attracted to south-east Wales; the same area that has benefited most from private sector relocations from London and from the increasingly congested centres further to the east along the M4 corridor. By contrast, many of the more rural areas in north-west and west Wales retain problems of peripherality and relatively narrow economic bases. Despite major economic initiatives the South Wales valleys emerge as among the poorest areas in Wales – and Great Britain – on many socio-economic indicators.

The urban–rural shift so apparent in the 1970s and 1980s is forecast to continue. Powys is ranked ninth out of 64 in a league table of counties in Great Britain on employment growth forecasts for the period from 1989 to 2000, with a projected rate of increase of 0.9 per cent per annum (Hirst et al., 1990). Clwyd and Gwynedd are also forecast to experience employment growth, while West Glamorgan (ranked sixty-third above Merseyside) is projected to suffer job losses at a rate of 1.7 per cent per annum. Powys, Clwyd, Dyfed and Gwynedd display at least average scores on a league table of county population forecasts over the same period, while Mid Glamorgan and West Glamorgan appear in the bottom quarter of the rankings. In the interim, results from the 1991 Census of Population will provide a useful demographic, social and economic snapshot of the people of Wales.

9 Migration trends for the West Midlands: suburbanisation, counterurbanisation or rural depopulation?

Robin Flowerdew and Paul Boyle

9.1 Introduction

Numerous studies have explored the nature of population migration at various scales, and in relation to different explanatory variables. Of central concern to much of this research is an attempt to gain a more complete understanding of recent trends in population movement. In this study, NHSCR movement data are used to explore the migration trends in the West Midlands over a period of 14 years from 1975 to 1989, and this analysis is complemented by the use of 1981 Census Special Migration Statistics series II (SMS II) to investigate ward-to-ward flows. It is argued that analysis of local-level movement offers insights into the migration process which are hidden by aggregate data and these insights have important implications for the current debate on urban decentralisation. The chapter begins with a short geographical description of the West Midlands regions, followed by a discussion of relevant migration processes at work in contemporary Britain. There is then a systematic analysis of the net and gross migration flows in the region using NHSCR data. These flows are discussed in general, and then disaggregated by age and sex. External migration links are examined by identifying the main origins and destinations of inter-regional moves involving the West Midlands. Disaggregated data for Hereford and Worcester county are used to illuminate ward-level migration. In the light of this local-level analysis, the three processes of suburbanisation, counterurbanisation and rural depopulation are evaluated for their applicability to the contemporary West Midlands.

9.2 The geography of the West Midlands

The West Midlands region is located in the central lowlands of Britain. Only the higher reaches of the western border of the region and parts of the Peak District in north Staffordshire are substantial obstacles to

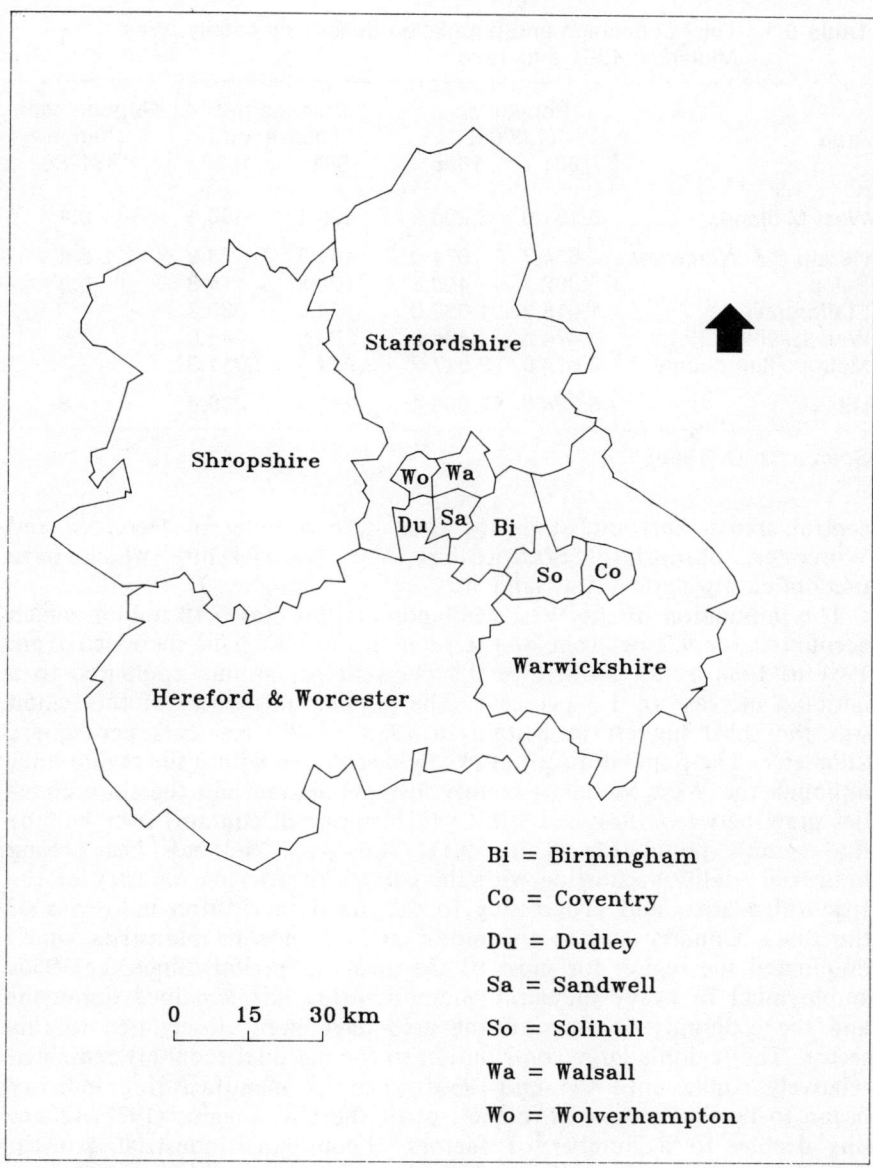

Figure 9.1 FPC areas in the West Midlands

agricultural or industrial development. Figure 9.1 shows the location of the component counties and metropolitan districts of the West Midlands region; these are also the FPC areas used in the NHSCR. The region is centred on the West Midlands conurbation, the seven metropolitan districts which constituted the West Midlands county before abolition; the majority of industrial activity and employment is located here. This

Table 9.1 Total population and population density by county, West Midlands, 1981 and 1988

Area	Population (1,000s)		Persons per square km		% population change
	1981	1988	1981	1988	1981–88
West Midlands	5,181.0	5,206.5	398.1	400.1	0.4
Hereford & Worcester	634.7	671.0	161.7	170.9	5.4
Salop	382.1	400.8	109.5	114.8	5.3
Staffordshire	1,015.7	1,032.9	374.0	380.3	1.3
Warwickshire	474.5	484.6	239.5	244.6	1.6
Metropolitan county	2,674.0	2,617.2	2,974.4	2,911.3	– 2.1
UK	56,224.3	57,065.4	231.9	235.4	1.3

Source: CSO (1989).

central area is surrounded by the four shire counties of Hereford and Worcester, Shropshire, Staffordshire and Warwickshire which have predominantly agricultural land use.

The population of the West Midlands in 1981 was 5.18 million which accounted for 9.2 per cent of the total in the UK. This increased from 1981 to 1988 by an average of 0.4 per cent per annum compared to a national increase of 1.3 per cent. The population density of the region was the third highest in Britain in 1988 at 400 residents per square kilometre. The population is not evenly distributed within the region and, although the West Midlands county lost population and the shire counties grew between 1981 and 1988, the former still contains over half of the region's population (Table 9.1). The West Midlands has a long industrial tradition, starting with the early iron-working industry of the Ironbridge area, and progressing to the metal fabrication industries of the Black Country and to the motor and engineering industries which dominated the region for most of the post-war period. Since the 1950s employment in heavy industrial manufacturing has remained dominant and the economic fortunes of the area have been closely tied to this sector. The region's large contribution to the national economy remained relatively stable until the mid-1960s when its manufacturing industry began to decline compared to the rest of the UK. Liggins (1977) relates this decline to a number of factors discouraging industrial growth, including the conurbation's land shortage problem, which was exacerbated when the 'green belt' surrounding the conurbation was designated in 1975 (Gregory, 1977). A second reason was the growth in union membership in the region and the resulting high labour costs. Perhaps the most important explanation for the region's weakening industrial performance, however, was the reliance upon a few large-scale specialised industries; 'the new science-based industries did not even gain a foothold' (Sutcliffe and Smith, 1974, p. 470). This problem was exacerbated by the continuing decline in the importance of manufacturing industry in the

Table 9.2 Regional disparities in per capita output and employment growth, 1971–87

| Region | GDP per capita (UK = 100) | | | | Employment % change | |
	1971	1979	1987	% change 1979–81	1971–79	1979–88
South East	113.7	116.2	118.5	2.7	3.5	8.2
East Anglia	93.6	94.4	99.8	4.1	15.2	26.2
South West	94.8	91.3	94.0	3.4	7.2	10.6
East Midlands	96.6	96.6	95.1	2.3	8.9	7.3
West Midlands	102.8	96.2	91.6	1.4	0.9	0.0
Yorks. & Humbs.	93.3	92.7	92.7	2.0	3.7	−2.6
North West	96.2	96.1	92.8	1.3	0.8	−10.0
North	86.9	90.7	88.9	1.5	3.0	−6.3
Wales	88.3	85.2	82.4	1.7	7.8	−10.2
Scotland	93.0	94.6	94.5	1.8	5.6	−5.2
N. Ireland	74.3	78.2	77.4	2.3	10.9	−7.0

Source: CSO (1989).

British economy as a whole (Taylor, 1990, p. 11). In addition, the regional ranking of the West Midlands in gross domestic product (GDP) per capita fell from second in 1971 to eighth in 1987 (Table 9.2).

The trends outlined above are typical of those which contribute to the so-called North–South divide. However, the West Midlands could be described as something of a 'floating partner' in this respect (Taylor, 1990) in that it at first appeared to share the characteristics of the southern regions, and then to behave more like the northern regions. Indeed, recent data suggest that the region is witnessing a gradual reversal of those trends which made the area seem 'northern' in the early 1980s.

Returning to the figures for GDP, the region's position is certainly poor in 1987, but the four years preceding this showed an improvement in relative GDP per head following the long-term decline until 1983. Also, employment growth in the region declined in the 1970s and 1980s, but Table 9.2 shows that this decline was negligible compared to some regions which actually lost employment. The widening gap between northern and southern unemployment rates in the early 1980s has also begun to close and between 1982 and 1989 the West Midlands experienced a steady decline in unemployment compared to the UK average (Taylor, 1990, p. 3). Finally, the West Midlands region ranked fourth in the percentage growth of new industries, defined as those registering for Value Added Tax between 1980 and 1988. This suggests that the traditional dependence on a limited number of large industries may be ending.

This analysis of regional trends ignores the fact that disparities in economic variables are often much greater within than between regions. The West Midlands ranges from densely populated urban and industrial areas in the conurbation to sparsely populated remote rural areas in the

Table 9.3 Manufacturing and 'other' employment by county, West Midlands, 1981–87

Area	1981 Manu. %	Other %	1984 Manu. %	Other %	1987 Manu. %	Other %
Hereford & Worcester	31.5	56.5	29.0	60.4	28.3	61.4
Shropshire	26.3	59.1	26.1	60.7	27.4	60.1
Staffordshire	39.8	47.5	38.7	49.8	35.4	54.2
Warwickshire	35.7	52.5	31.9	57.9	28.7	62.3
West Midlands	42.6	51.5	38.0	55.9	35.3	58.6

Source: CSO (1989).

western shires and it is important therefore to disaggregate economic information. Table 9.3 displays the level of manufacturing employment in each of the four counties and the conurbation area. In recent years the importance of manufacturing employment in the shire counties (except Shropshire) and the metropolitan centre has declined. In both 1984 and 1987, Staffordshire had a greater percentage of its workforce employed in manufacturing than did the metropolitan districts. Hereford and Worcester and Shropshire had by far the greatest percentage of agricultural employees compared to the remaining three counties.

The economic figures outlined above show that the West Midlands as a whole experienced a lengthy period of decline which continued into the 1980s. However, since the middle of the decade the region's economic performance has improved so that it is now broadly in line with national trends. Within the region the relative economic productivity of each of the counties has changed, although the metropolitan core retains the highest GDP per head. These changes in the West Midlands are important in interpreting migration trends. The following sections of the chapter will show how far the region's decline and subsequent partial recovery are reflected in migration trends.

9.3 Migration processes at work

The processes affecting migration in the West Midlands can be considered at several different scales. Migration into and out of the region as a whole may be motivated by several factors, differentially affecting different population groups. Survey evidence shows that the vast majority of long-distance moves are associated with employment changes (e.g. Owen and Green, 1991, Table 2). Most of these job-related moves are made to take up jobs vacated through the migration, promotion, retirement, resignation or death of the previous holder; these jobs can therefore arise in a region regardless of its economic health. Only a small proportion of jobs are newly created, and it is only these which can be expected to reflect the economic health of the region. The size of inter-regional migration flows can therefore be expected to reflect the size of the regions concerned, with only minor modifications reflecting economic conditions.

As with job-related migration, the pattern of migration flows for family-related reasons is one of roughly equal interchange between regions; moves related to marriage, separation or divorce, or to a wish to be near parents, children or other relatives should be roughly proportionate to regional population. Other types of migration may also lead to little net change; those highly migratory sections of the population, students and military personnel, should not generate much net change for the West Midlands, a region which contains some universities and some military bases, but not a large concentration of either. Environmentally motivated migration and retirement migration, if anything, might be expected to lead to a net outflow from the West Midlands. Some areas, notably the Malvern Hills, are attractive destinations, but the region cannot compete in this respect with the south coast, Devon and Cornwall.

Migration within the region may also reflect several different processes operating at the county or district scale. Some job-related and family reasons for migration are likely to generate a set of balanced flows between places. Changes in economic fortune, however, will be reflected in inter-county and inter-district migration flows, and moves by elderly parents to be near their children are more likely to be out of the urbanised area than into it. Differences in environmental attractiveness are also likely to be reflected in migration at this scale. A further factor here is change in the housing stock; declining densities of housing in the conurbation force net migration to be in an outwards direction, whilst the construction of new housing in the shire counties facilitates in-migration to them. Spatial differentiation in the housing stock also affects migration; people wanting to rent an inexpensive flat are more likely to find one in the city while those wanting to buy a modern detached house have a better chance of finding one in the suburbs. Improvements in transport are also important, making it possible to live in a shire county and work in the middle of Birmingham, and making it easier to take a job at some distance from home without a move being required.

Planning factors are also important. Large migrant streams from Wolverhampton and Birmingham to Telford in Shropshire and Redditch in Hereford and Worcester result largely from the latter places being designated as New Towns and from agreements reached for urban overspill population to be rehoused there. On the other hand, the designation of a 'green belt' around the conurbation and the control of development within it may have reduced migration to the areas affected, displacing migration to areas beyond the green belt.

Some of these migration processes can be observed clearly at the county level, but others can better be studied with greater spatial disaggregation, at the district or even the ward level. In the West Midlands, the phenomenon of population growth in the more rural parts of the region is a good example. One possible explanation of this is the continued spread of suburbanisation; as people increasingly opt for lower densities of development, suburban growth spreads further from the original centre. The existence of the green belt artificially restricts it, forcing normal suburban development into the countryside.

An alternative, and presently more fashionable, explanation for rural population growth of this type is that another process, counterurbanisation, is at work (Fielding, 1982; Perry et al., 1986; Champion, 1989a). Counterurbanisation takes place when people and jobs move into the countryside, independent of the influence of a major city. It is held to be a 'clean break' with the processes of urban growth observed through the whole of modern history, and to represent a new form of post-industrial social organisation.

The relative importance of these processes can only be gauged by looking at data well below the country scale. If suburbanisation is the main process operative, in-migration should be concentrated mainly in districts or wards on the fringes of the conurbation. If counterurbanisation is more important, there should be substantial in-migration to more distant rural areas. Another important distinction concerns the spatial focus of counterurbanisation, if the process is operative at all. Does it affect all rural areas, or only some? If the latter, which ones? Many small towns are growing (Congdon and Shepherd, 1986) and apparent counterurbanisation in rural areas around them may merely be suburban growth relative to these towns.

If counterurbanisation affects only parts of the rural West Midlands, what migration processes are at work in the other parts? For most of this century, rural depopulation has been the norm in the remoter rural areas of Britain; is this still true in parts of the West Midlands? All these questions require answers at the district or ward scale rather than the broad county or regional scale; hence we have used SMS data to supplement what is available from the NHSCR. The West Midlands, with its progression from the metropolis of Birmingham through the heavily urbanised Black Country and the suburban fringe to the deep countryside of the Welsh Marches, presents an excellent study area for examining these issues.

9.4 Migration trends over time

9.4.1 Net migration

Net migration in most areas is only a small proportion of gross movement. Nevertheless, it is useful to distinguish between areas which gain and those which lose population as a result of migration. The West Midlands region as a whole suffered a net loss of migrants throughout the 1975–89 period, but there were annual differences in the net totals. Figure 9.2 shows that net migration out of the region has fluctuated

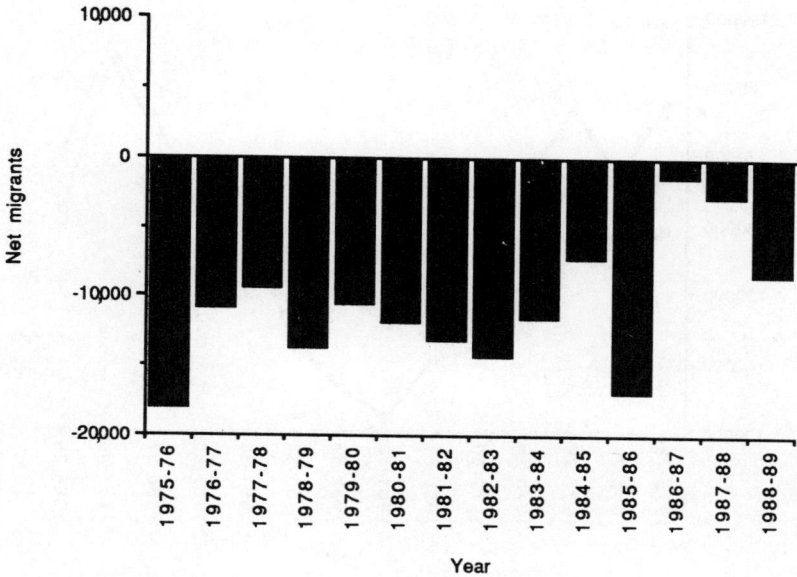

Figure 9.2 Net migrants from the West Midlands, 1975–89

between minus 10 and 20 thousand in most years – the highest totals being recorded in 1975–76 and 1985–86. This net loss of population through migration is a trait which is generally associated with northern regions (Stillwell et al., 1990). However, a significant reduction in net out-migration occurred between 1985–86 and 1986–87, from − 16,813 to only − 1,316, probably as a result of the partial recovery of the West Midlands economy. Even so, it is clear that net out-migration has increased again since then.

Net migration figures at the county scale allow trends to be examined in more detail. Combining the seven metropolitan districts to give net migration totals for the old West Midlands county shows a large net loss in each of the 14 years. The total was largest in 1975–76, when the area lost 26,750 migrants to other FPC areas. The figure steadily declined until 1981–82 when only half as many net out-migrants were recorded (13,550). The total rose again, peaking in 1985–86, and has begun to fall since. The decline in net out-migration at the end of the period may reflect the gradual revitalisation of the West Midlands economy.

There are differences between the metropolitan districts in their net migration experience over the period. The trends in Birmingham (which contains nearly 40 per cent of the conurbation's population) are a good match with the trends for the whole county. Thus net out-migration occurred every year, being highest in 1975–76, peaking again in 1985–86 and declining since. Coventry, Sandwell, Walsall and Wolverhampton show similar, though not identical, patterns to Birmingham, each losing large numbers of migrants every year, but improving their positions in

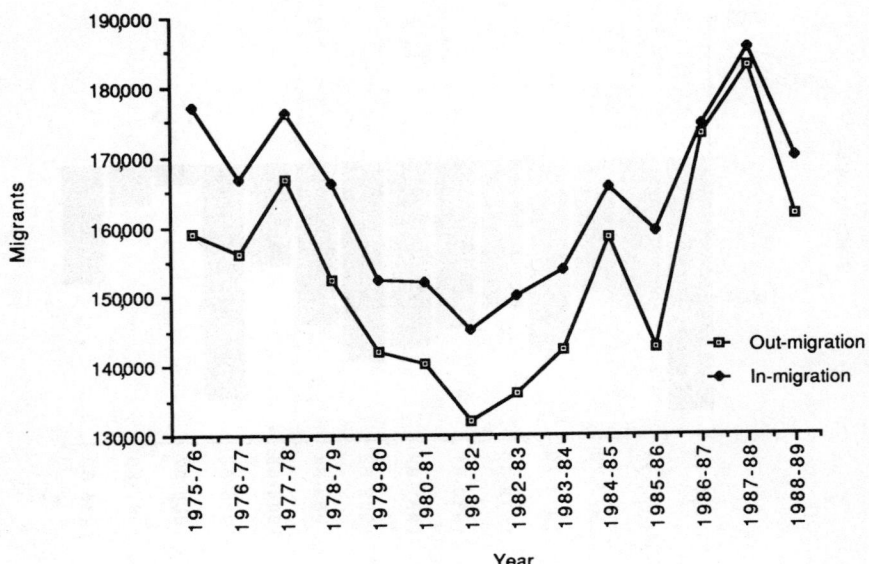

Figure 9.3 In-migrants to and out-migrants from the West Midlands, 1975–89

the last year of the period. Dudley and Solihull, however, have much more erratic net migration trends throughout the period. Solihull, for example, experienced seven years of net in-migration of which the greatest was in 1984–85 (+1,807) and seven years of net out-migration with 1988–89 being the largest (−1,593).

The shire counties within the West Midlands region experienced totally different net migration trends to the metropolitan districts. Hereford and Worcester and Shropshire were both net gainers in each of the 14 years. In both cases the lowest net increases were in the early 1980s when net out-migration from the conurbation districts was lowest (it should be remembered that the early 1980s were characterised by low migration levels nationwide). Indeed, in both Staffordshire and Warwickshire, net out-migration prevailed in the early 1980s. This emphasises the complementarity between out-migration from the metropolitan centre and in-migration to the less densely populated surrounding areas. Similarly, three of the four counties had lower net migration totals in the last year of the period when net out-migration from the conurbation was falling, while Warwickshire witnessed net out-migration after four years of significant net in-migration.

9.4.2 Gross migration

The West Midlands region as a whole has had fluctuations of roughly equal magnitude in both out-migration and in-migration (Figure 9.3). In

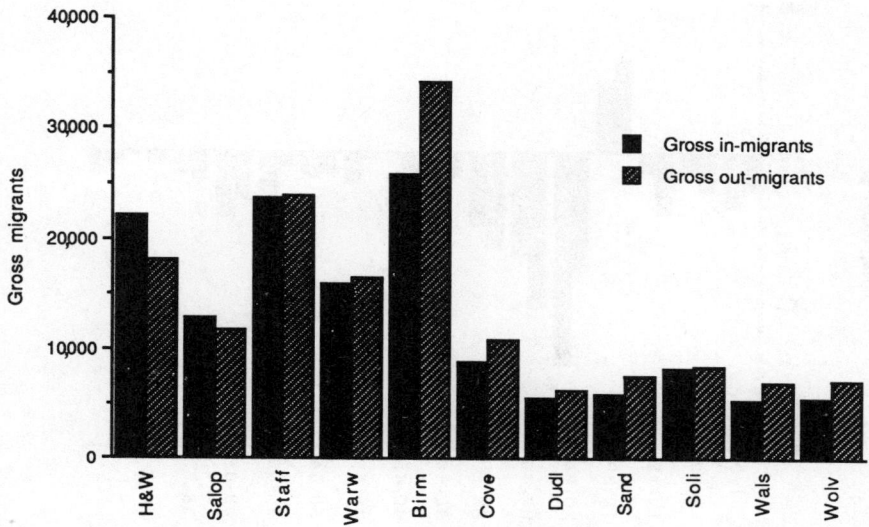

Figure 9.4   In-migrants to and out-migrants from FPC areas in the West Midlands, 1980–81

the middle 1970s, out-migration averaged about 170,000 per year, reducing to 150,000 in the early 1980s and then recovering to the former figure in the later 1980s. Meanwhile, in-migration declined from 160,000 in the middle 1970s to 140,000 in the early 1980s, recovering irregularly to around 170,000 in the later 1980s. In the last years of the period the in- and out-migration totals have converged to a certain degree.

The largest in-migration flows are for Birmingham, followed by the shire counties, followed by the other metropolitan districts. The temporal trends in all areas follow those described for the whole region, and probably have more to do with the ease of moving in terms of job availability and house prices than with differential changes in the desirability of specific places. In fact, each of the 11 separate FPCs experienced peaks in in-migration in 1977–78 (except Walsall) and 1984–85, matched by peaks in out-migration for the same two years. Figure 9.4 shows the relative size of gross inflows and outflows in the Census year of 1980–81. This shows the approximate number of people migrating, and also gives an impression of the imbalance between in-migration and out-migration for the component FPC areas of the region.

9.4.3 Net migration by age and sex

Breaking down the net migration figures by age and sex shows some interesting differences. It is clear from Figure 9.5 that the metropolitan district of Birmingham has negative net migration for all age groups

REGIONAL PERSPECTIVES

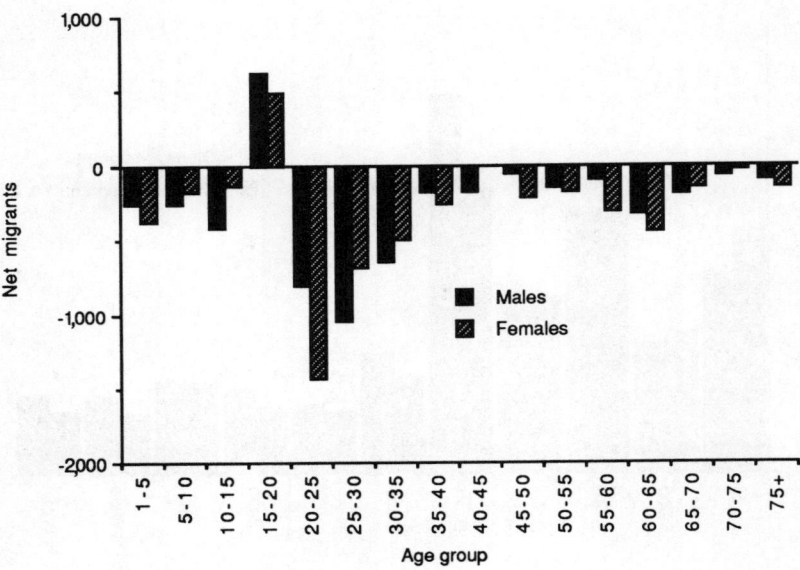

Figure 9.5 Net migrants for Birmingham by age and sex, 1980–81

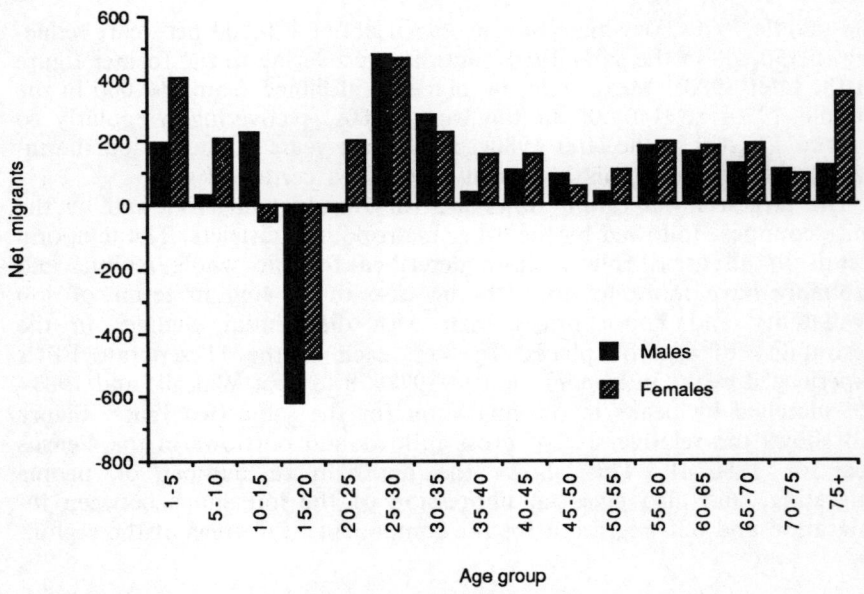

Figure 9.6 Net migrants for Hereford and Worcester by age and sex, 1980–81

except 15–19, where it has a considerable net gain. In 1980–81, there were large net losses of people in their twenties and early thirties, small losses of people in middle age, and rather larger losses of people around retirement age. In 1988–89, the basic features were the same, except that there were fewer differences among middle-aged and older age groups.

The pattern for the shire county of Hereford and Worcester (Figure 9.6) is in complete contrast. Essentially, Hereford and Worcester in 1980–81 had positive net migration for all age groups except 15–19, and a large net loss for that age group. The age groups with the largest net in-movement are children (especially girls), people in their twenties and early thirties, and older age groups from the late fifties onwards.

9.4.4 Gross migration by age and sex

For both Birmingham and Hereford and Worcester, in-migration and out-migration follow the characteristic patterns identified by Bracken and Bates (1983) and others. However, there are important differences. The relative size of the peak for people between 15 and 30 is far higher for Birmingham, which has relatively little in-migration or out-migration of children or of people in old or later middle age. In Hereford and Worcester too, there is a peak for young adults, though the location of the peak is at an older age, especially for in-migrants. However, the relative sizes of migration streams across the age groups are much more even, and there is a clear peak around retirement age. To some extent, there are similarities between in-migration to Birmingham and out-migration from Hereford and Worcester, as opposed to in-migration to Hereford and Worcester and out-migration from Birmingham; the latter two flows tend to include more children, more old people and rather older young adults than the former two flows.

The in-migration and out-migration figures show some interesting differences between male and female migration flows. One of the most striking features is the excess of female over male migrants in the late teens and early twenties in all migration streams. This may reflect greater migration propensities for women of these ages but it is likely to be largely an artefact of the data collection procedure, as women at this age are far more likely then men to consult a doctor, especially if they have children.

9.4.5 Inter-area flows

The relative position of the West Midlands within the overall British migration system can best be examined by looking at the flows linking the West Midlands to the rest of the country. A standard expectation is that flows will be related to the size of the areal units involved, usually measured in terms of population, and to the distance between them. A simple gravity model which included the populations of the origins and destinations, the distance between them and a contiguity factor was used to examine flows between the West Midlands region and the other regions in the UK. The model was defined with a Poisson error distribution (Flowerdew and Aitkin, 1982) and initially it was fitted to NHSCR data for 1980–81. The model fitted very well with a pseudo-R squared value of 91 per cent (broadly comparable with an R squared value in ordinary least squares regression).

The residuals from this model can be inspected to find those flows which were unusually high or low. Compared to the model predictions, high numbers of migrants moved into the region from East Anglia, although these were matched by numbers higher than expected in the opposite direction and may be a result of inadequate specification of the distance term (a straight-line distance between the largest urban areas was used). Significantly low numbers of migrants moved in from Scotland, the North West and London. The movement out of the region to the south of Britain was also unusually high. The South West, South East and East Anglia all attracted more migrants than expected. Relatively few migrants moved across the border into Wales.

To examine change over time, the same model was used on data for 1988–89. This model also accounted for a high proportion of the deviance (93 per cent). The most prominent residuals were those to and from Scotland as the model predicted much larger flows than actually occurred. The numbers moving into the South East and East Anglia from the region were again higher than expected, but not to the same degree as in 1980–81, and more migrants than expected moved into London. Also, much larger numbers moved into the West Midlands from the South East and East Anglia in this period.

It is important that these flows are examined for smaller areal units however, as migration into the region is unlikely to be distributed evenly. For purely spatial reasons, for example, it would be expected that more migrants from the south of Britain would move into the southern half of the region. Also, while we might expect the conurbation area to attract a reasonable number of movers from long distances particularly for employment reasons, the migration trends in the shire counties are likely to be dominated by local movement mainly for residential motives, much of it originating in the conurbation.

Using Birmingham and Hereford and Worcester as examples once more, in- and out-migration in 1988–89 were examined. The largest numbers of in-migrants into Birmingham were from Solihull, Sandwell and Hereford and Worcester respectively. The district lost most migrants to the same three FPCs, but Hereford and Worcester and Sandwell switched places in the rankings. Obviously, migration within the West Midlands has a great influence on Birmingham. Overall, net in-migration was recorded from 23 of the remaining 96 FPCs, and significantly high in-movement, compared to out-movement, came from Scotland and Humberside in the north, Coventry in the West Midlands, and Kent and Kensington, Chelsea and Westminster in the South. Perhaps surprisingly, therefore, Birmingham did attract large numbers of migrants from certain areas in the south.

The position in Hereford and Worcester differed markedly. The county gained net in-migrants from 55 of the FPCs with the highest numbers coming from Birmingham, Gloucestershire and Warwickshire. The largest outflows were to Birmingham, Gloucestershire and Shropshire, again emphasising the importance of intra-regional flows. Significantly, the county gained large numbers from every FPC in the South East except the Isle of Wight, and from the majority of FPCs in London. There was also a small gain from East Anglia, but Hereford and Worcester lost migrants to most of the FPCs in the South West.

Categorising the West Midlands as 'northern' oversimplifies the nature of the migration processes influencing the region. Hereford and Worcester has been a popular destination for many migrants from the South, and even Birmingham attracted migrants from some southern FPCs. Even if the region is not disaggregated into its component counties, it can be seen that it has experienced changing migration patterns throughout the period which may match, to some degree, its improving economy.

9.5 Hereford and Worcester: intra-FPC migration

The descriptions of migration presented above have concentrated on movement between FPC areas using annual NHSCR data. While this data set is regularly updated and offers a useful additional source to the decennial censuses, it does not allow disaggregated migration analysis between smaller areas such as districts or wards. The SMS series II from the 1981 Census, however, allows a matrix of inter- and intra-ward flows to be defined for any region of interest within Britain. Ideas about the relative importance of counterurbanisation and other local-level phenomena can be investigated more adequately with this resource.

As stated above, an important migration process throughout Britain is the decentralisation of population away from the major urban settlements. Distinguishing between the relative importance of counterurbanisation or suburbanisation as an explanation for this process is important both for theoretical and practical planning purposes. One method for doing this is to consider migration and commuting patterns together. We might, for example, distinguish between those out-migrants from a conurbation who continue to commute back into the urban centre for work (suburbanites) and those who have moved their place of residence and their place of employment into more peripheral areas. Unfortunately, data are not available from the Census to link migrants with their place of work, but it is possible to obtain a matrix of commuting flows at the ward level from the Special Workplace Statistics (SWS) for a 10 per cent sample of respondents. Together with inter-ward migration data this information provides a useful insight into the process of metropolitan decentralisation.

Out-movement from the conurbation is extremely important in our case study area. In 1981, Hereford and Worcester experienced a net gain

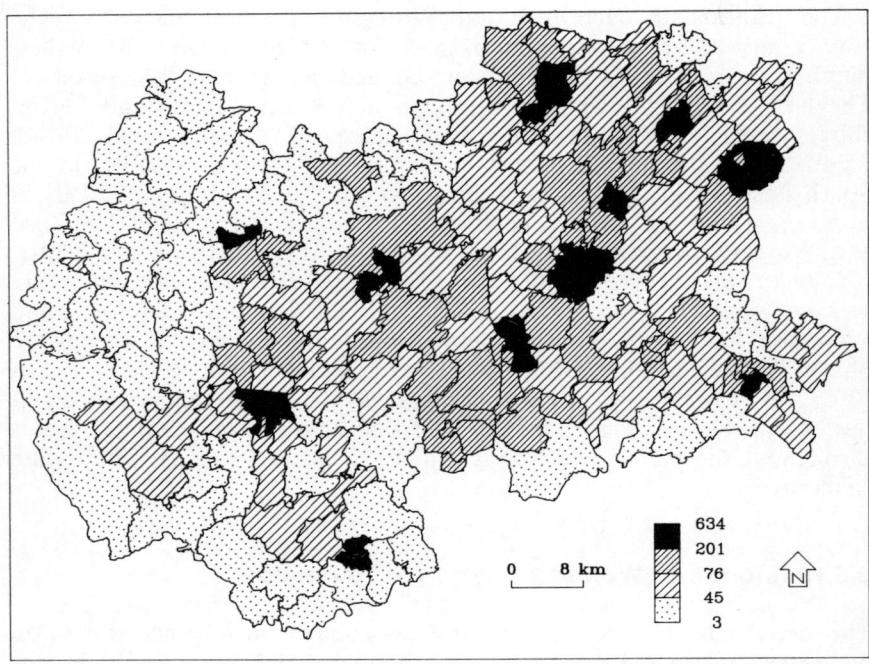

Figure 9.7 Inter-ward migrants within Hereford and Worcester, 1980–81
Source: 1981 Census.

in population through migration of 4,100 according to NHSCR figures. Net in-migration from the conurbation accounted for 2,970, the great majority (2,250) from Birmingham. In most years net in-migration from the conurbation accounted for just over half of the total net growth. This net gain from the metropolitan county was particularly high when compared to the gross flows between the two areas: 6,850 migrants moved into Hereford and Worcester from the conurbation compared to 3,880 in the opposite direction in 1981.

The local distribution of in-migrants can be assessed using Census data. Figure 9.7 shows the number of migrants into each ward who originated within Hereford and Worcester (ignoring migrants within wards) and it is clear that the urban areas attracted the most movers as we would expect. Very few migrants were attracted to the most remote rural areas in the west of the county, although there were a number of wards in the Malvern Hills area which were relatively popular. This diagram can be compared to Figure 9.8 which shows only those migrants who originated in the seven metropolitan districts. The cluster in the north east of the county stands out clearly on this map. The class intervals for the choropleth shading are based on equal quartiles so that three-quarters of the wards received less than 23 migrants from the conurbation. Even

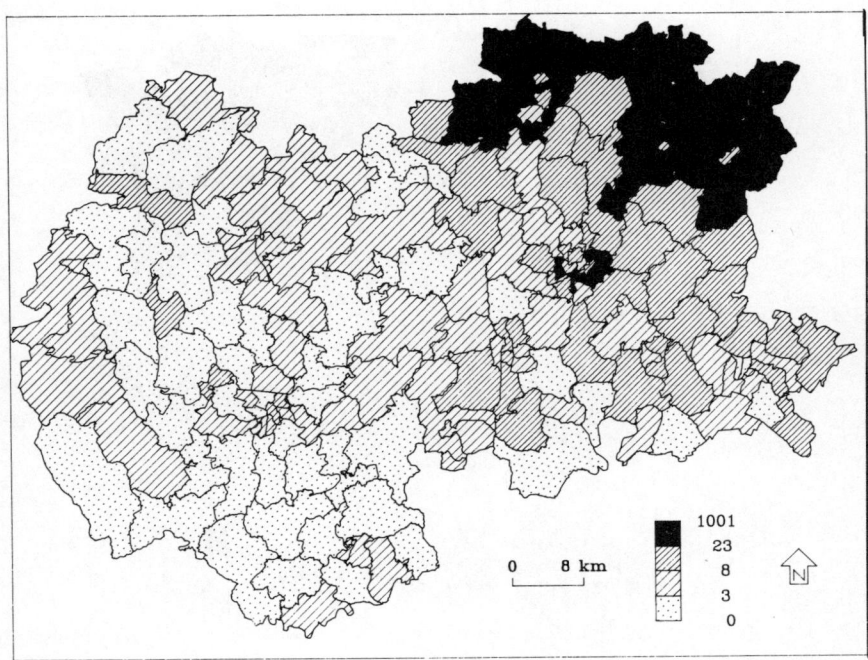

Figure 9.8 Inter-ward migrants from the West Midlands conurbation to
Hereford and Worcester, 1980–81

Source: 1981 Census.

in the city of Hereford, where small firm growth has occurred, the vast
majority of the inter-ward migrants originated within the county.

Fielding (1982) assesses counterurbanisation by correlating net migration with population density (the more negative the correlation value, the
more prominent counterurbanisation is) and for large administrative
areas this gives reasonable results. This measure was computed at the
ward level for Hereford and Worcester. When migration within the
county is considered alone (again ignoring moves within wards) the r
value is -0.036 which suggests little or no relationship. When migrants
originating either within the county or the conurbation area are
considered the r value actually becomes slightly positive at $+0.008$. If the
analysis is restricted to wards in the two most rural districts of
Leominster and South Herefordshire, the relationship between net migration and population density becomes more strongly positive at $+0.626$
suggesting that only the towns in these areas are attracting many
migrants. Analysis at this scale clearly shows little evidence of counterurbanisation in this very rural part of the West Midlands.

The in-migration from the conurbation area can be compared to the
commuting patterns of workers who reside in Hereford and Worcester
but work in the West Midlands county. Figure 9.9 emphasises the

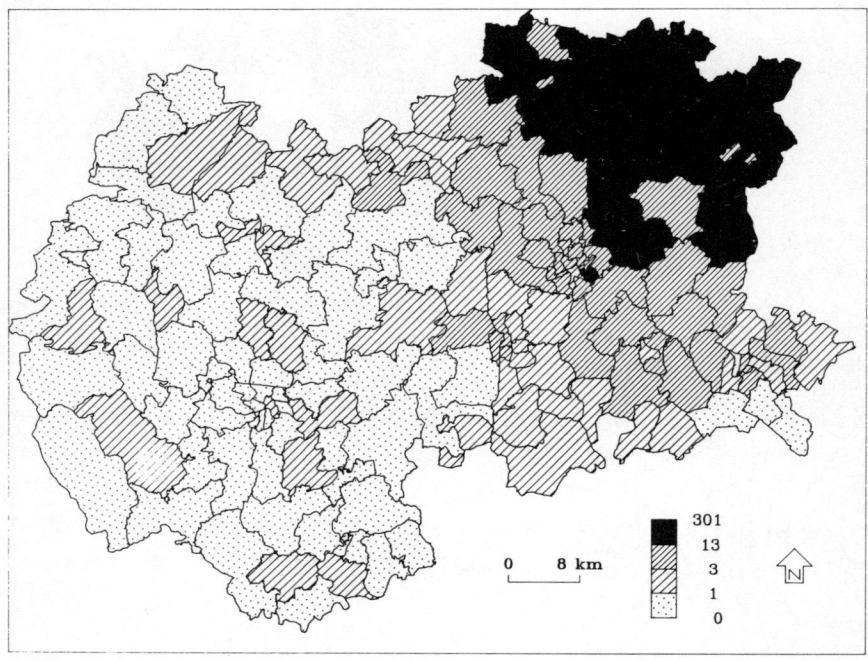

Figure 9.9 Commuters from Hereford and Worcester to the West Midlands
conurbation, 1980–81

Source: 1981 Census.

relationship between the north east of the county and the conurbation.
It is apparent from the maps that those areas which attract large
numbers of migrants from the conurbation are the same as those from
which many residents commute daily into the conurbation. We are reluc-
tant therefore to regard these movers as counterurbanisers rather than
suburbanisers.

Another localised migration process which has been given relatively
little attention recently is rural depopulation. As Weekley (1988) points
out, large-scale patterns of metropolitan decentralisation have suggested
that rural areas are gaining population from migration. However, local-
level analyses show that even in those rural counties or districts which are
growing in population, there are often remote areas which continue to
suffer population losses from migration.

The most remote rural district in Hereford and Worcester is South
Herefordshire. Using district-level migration data from the 1981 Census,
it is apparent that the area experienced a slight decrease in population
through migration to the rest of the county. When broken down by age
a noticeable peak in out-migration occurs between the ages of 15 and 19
with twice as many females moving out of the district than males. In-
migration of males and females for similar ages is lower, but much more

balanced. Importantly, the district loses proportionally more economically active migrants than it gains compared to the total in and out flows.

If migration within this district is considered, it becomes apparent that it is the more urban areas which are attracting migrants – a correlation value of $+0.65$ was found between net migrants and population density. In addition, most migration from the wards with smaller populations took place over relatively short distances. Similar patterns were identified in other more remote wards in the county and although the numbers leaving these areas were often small, they were significant in terms of the total population.

9.6 Conclusion

A number of important findings relating to migration patterns in the West Midlands have been presented here. First, the West Midlands region as a whole has experienced an improving net migration balance in recent years, matching an improvement in the region's economic position. Certainly, net migration in the area has fluctuated through time, with the smallest losses occurring in 1986–87 and 1987–88. Such net migration totals are small compared to the gross inflows and outflows which remained reasonably parallel for most of the 14-year period. In the last three years of the period, however, the inflows and outflows were at their highest for the decade and were much more similar in total. Categorising the region as either northern or southern is difficult, because of temporal instability and the very important intra-regional differences.

Within the region it has been shown that decentralisation away from the metropolitan centre can be explained most satisfactorily by suburbanisation, or the continuing expansion of the densely built-up area, rather than counterurbanisation, where migration would be expected to involve a clean break with the conurbation. Some rural areas within the region have experienced significant in-migration from the metropolitan area, but the vast majority of the migration into the case study area of Hereford and Worcester from the conurbation was over short distances into the north-east of the county. It has also been shown that rural depopulation is still an important process in remote areas of the county. In conclusion, much work is still needed at the local level on movement out of rural areas, the continuing spread of metropolitan areas, and the growth of smaller towns in the periphery. The 1991 Census should offer interesting insights into such recent migration trends.

Acknowledgements
We would like to thank the ESRC Data Archive and the Manchester Computer Centre, especially Keith Cole, for helping us access the 1981 Census data, and Clive Lloyd of Hereford and Worcester County Council for sharing his insights into local migration trends.

10 Migration trends for the East Midlands: the dynamics of a growth region

John Jenkins

10.1 Introduction

This chapter examines migration trends and patterns affecting the East Midlands region over the period from the mid-1970s until the late 1980s. As with most other chapters of this book, the main source of information for this study has been the statistics derived from the National Health Service Central Register (NHSCR) for Family Practitioner Committee (FPC) areas, which in the case of the East Midlands equate with counties. To supplement this source, and to provide a sub-county perspective, use has also been made of the migration elements of the annual OPCS population estimates.

The chapter begins with a brief profile of the East Midlands and shows it as a region of contrasts. On the one hand it has been one of the country's most rapidly growing regions, both in terms of its population and workforce. On the other hand it contains areas suffering from a range of social, economic and environmental problems. Primarily because of its record of growth, the region tends to be classified as part of the South. Section 10.3 reflects upon this classification and concludes that, in demographic terms, the East Midlands might almost be split into two, with Nottinghamshire and Derbyshire more closely related to the North. Section 10.4 reviews population trends in the region more fully and examines the role of migration in its overall demographic change. Section 10.5 uses the NHSCR figures to describe the migration trends and patterns for each of its constituent counties. This confirms the similar experiences of Nottinghamshire and Derbyshire and the contrast with the other counties of the region, although some shifts in patterns are detected in the late 1980s. Section 10.6 considers some key factors behind these trends and patterns, particularly the impact of London house prices and the state of the local economy. Finally Section 10.7 speculates about future trends in migration across the East Midlands.

10.2 A profile of the East Midlands

The East Midlands is made up of five counties – Derbyshire, Leicester-shire, Lincolnshire, Northamptonshire and Nottinghamshire. It has been a rapidly growing region despite facing a range of problems that might have deterred potential migrants from moving in, or might have encouraged residents to leave the area. In the early 1980s, the East Midlands Forum of County Councils summarised these problems as follows:

1. An overreliance on traditional manufacturing industries (such as textiles and clothing; footwear; steel and engineering) and the primary sector (mining and agriculture), coupled with an underdeveloped service sector.
2. High unemployment, particularly affecting localities heavily reliant on declining sectors, as well as the Lincolnshire coast with its generally depressed economic base and seasonal employment.
3. Poor transport infrastructure and services, despite a good strategic national location.
4. Low rural living standards and the burdens of providing uneconomic services in rural areas.
5. Environmental consequences of high concentrations of mining and energy industries (derelict land, waste disposal, etc.).
6. A concentration of social and economic problems in the inner areas of the largest towns (Nottingham, Derby and Leicester).

A decade later many of the themes concerning planners across the region are still the same (East Midlands Regional Planning Forum, 1990, 1991). However the East Midlands also has many positive features likely to have attracted migrants. These include areas of attractive, indeed exceptional, countryside (from rolling rural Northamptonshire to the wilder Peak District National Park), buoyant local economies with areas of unemployment as low as anywhere in the country, at least by the late 1980s, good accessibility, and relatively cheap housing.

While confidence is widely expressed in the area's economic stability and resilience, it has still been recognised, for example, that the East Midlands had the lowest level of growth in the banking, financial, insurance and business services sector in Britain in the 1980s. It also has had a low base and relatively little growth in high technology in recent years. Despite this, the overall growth in the size of the region's workforce between 1983 and 1990 was around 12 per cent (Department of Employment, 1991). Over this period only three other regions experienced higher levels of growth – East Anglia (22 per cent), the South West (21 per cent) and Wales (13 per cent).

10.3 Classifying the East Midlands

The East Midlands is considered in Chapter 2 as part of the South and as an entirely non-metropolitan region, in line with the classification adopted in Champion et al. (1987) and subsequently used in later studies, such as Stillwell et al. (1990).

The broad scale of this spatial classification conceals much intra-regional variation. Consequently, if the East Midlands is broken down into its constituent counties, contrasts between the north and south of the region emerge on a number of key indicators such as population growth, unemployment rates, per capita levels of disposable income and, as later sections will demonstrate, migration rates. In other words, at best the East Midlands sits uneasily within the South, and might even be considered to straddle the North–South divide. Its northern counties of Nottinghamshire and Derbyshire appear to have as much in common with neighbouring areas in the North as with other parts of the East Midlands or the rest of the South.

This conclusion echoes the results of another national classification which uses local authorities as its spatial units (the 'Shaw classification'). This groups areas with similar social/demographic profiles, based primarily on a range of 1981 Census variables. It places Nottinghamshire and Derbyshire together as members of 'family 3', which is characterised by a high incidence of employment in manufacturing and mining, and of households lacking basic amenities (bath and inside WC), and a low incidence, among other items, of migrants. All of the other nine counties in this family are located in the North. By contrast Leicestershire and Northamptonshire lie in 'family 5', which is characterised by high levels of population growth, car ownership and numbers of people aged 25–44. Only 4 of the 15 other counties in this family are in the North. Lincolnshire is placed in 'family 7', along with a number of pre-dominantly rural counties drawn from both sides of the North–South divide.

The region lacks a single major urban centre as a dominant focus and partly as a result of this, lacks a clearly defined image (East Midlands Regional Planning Forum, 1990, p. 9). Consequently, it is tempting to see the East Midlands, because of its non-metropolitan nature, as a residual region falling within the sphere of influence of four major conurbations. Leicestershire and parts of southern Derbyshire are close to Birmingham and the West Midlands. Northern Derbyshire looks to Greater Manchester as well as to Sheffield and South Yorkshire, as does northern Nottinghamshire. In recent years much of southern Northamptonshire has probably come to identify more with London and the South East than with other parts of the East Midlands as a result of both migration and commuting patterns and business links.

Although there are no major metropolitan areas in the East Midlands, there are a number of large urban centres that do exert sub-regional influence. Three urban areas within the region – Leicester, Notting-ham and Derby – are among the largest (non-metropolitan) local authority districts in the country. However, each of these three major urban areas has been losing population through net outward migration in the 1970s and 1980s, according to OPCS estimates (OPCS, 1984; 1990e). This places them on a par with the country's metropolitan areas and suggests that suburbanisation, if not counterurbanisation, is a phenomenon affecting this region, despite its non-metropolitan character. Unfortunately the NHSCR statistics do not relate to areas smaller than the FPC areas. Consequently, it is impossible to explore this issue further using this source.

The sharp contrast between the experience of the major urban centres of the East Midlands and that of its other towns and rural areas indicates the dangers in placing too much emphasis on migration trends at a regional level. Thus the remainder of this chapter relates primarily to FPC areas/counties. However, inevitably figures at any geographical level are no more than an amalgam of more localised patterns, concealing information about a number of contrasting migration streams that may be operating in each locality and changing at different rates over time.

One of the major factors influencing the scale and direction of population redistribution over time is the availability of new housing in an area. Over the course of the 1980s there has been a shift from 'planned' to 'unplanned' (though not necessarily uncontrolled) migration, although 'planned' migration has been a stronger force in some parts of the region than others. Northamptonshire's post-war history, for example, has been characterised by 'planned' population growth schemes, such as the town development schemes at Daventry and Wellingborough in the 1960s and early 1970s. These produced major expansion of the housing stock of both towns (as well as relocation of business in the case of Daventry), and resulted in substantial in-migration from Birmingham and London respectively.

Corby and Northampton were officially designated New Towns in 1950 and 1968 respectively, giving these towns a migration attraction that extended well beyond their immediate locality. Few areas in southern England, for example, can boast, like Corby, having almost 30 per cent of their population born in Scotland.

The shift from 'planned' to 'unplanned' migration is exemplified by the winding-up of the Corby and Northampton Development Corporations in 1980 and 1987 respectively in favour of a greater reliance on market forces to build and fill new houses, although guided by the development control and structure and local planning processes. But it will also be associated with Norman Tebbit's 'advice' to the unemployed to get on their bikes in search of work, thus continuing the shift in emphasis away from policies to encourage firms to move to areas of labour surplus, towards the expectation that individual workers should move to areas of labour demand.

Table 10.1 Components of population change, East Midlands, 1971–89

Area	Period	Change		Components	
		%	Total	Natural change	Migration & other changes
Derbyshire	1971–81	+ 2.8	+ 24,900	+ 6,300	+ 18,600
	1981–89	+ 1.7	+ 15,100	+ 5,000	+ 10,100
Leicestershire	1971–81	+ 6.8	+ 54,400	+ 26,500	+ 27,900
	1981–89	+ 3.8	+ 33,200	+ 23,800	+ 9,400
Lincolnshire	1971–81	+ 8.9	+ 45,000	+ 3,100	+ 41,900
	1981–89	+ 6.2	+ 34,100	− 1,300	+ 35,400
Northamptonshire	1971–81	+ 12.7	+ 60,100	+ 18,200	+ 41,900
	1981–89	+ 8.2	+ 43,600	+ 14,700	+ 28,900
Nottinghamshire	1971–81	+ 1.7	+ 16,400	+ 16,900	− 500
	1981–89	+ 2.1	+ 20,500	+ 14,000	+ 6,500
East Midlands	1971–81	+ 5.5	+ 200,800	+ 71,000	+ 129,800
	1981–89	+ 3.8	+ 146,500	+ 56,300	+ 90,200

Sources: Derived from OPCS population estimates (OPCS, 1984, 1990e).

10.4 Population change and net migration in the East Midlands

It has been suggested in Chapter 3 that internal migration has been the main motor of population change in the past two decades, a period of relative stability at the national level. Between 1971 and 1989, the population of the East Midlands increased by almost 350,000 (or 9.5 per cent), between four and five times the national average. This places it as the third fastest growing region after East Anglia and the South West, the fourth if the rest of the South East is separated from Greater London.

Net inward migration accounts for over 60 per cent of this population growth, suggesting that in the minds of many people the region's positive features outweigh its negative features. However, these aggregate statistics conceal the fact that population growth has taken place in different parts of the region at widely different rates, although above the national average in each county. Table 10.1 illustrates differences within the region in the extent to which migration has dominated growth.

At one extreme, Lincolnshire's growth is almost entirely the result of migration. In fact in the 1980s it experienced negative natural change, albeit small. At the other extreme, Nottinghamshire experienced small net outward migration in the 1970s, but achieved modest overall growth through a positive natural increase. However, in the 1980s, Nottinghamshire's rate of overall population growth has actually increased as a result of increased (indeed net inward) migration. All the other counties in the region underwent lower rates of overall growth in the 1980s than in the 1970s and reduced net inward migration. Only Lincolnshire did not maintain or increase its level of natural population change.

Similar conclusions about the relative levels of overall growth for counties apply to the period for which the NHSCR data are available. Between 1975 and 1989, Northamptonshire's population increased by 13.4 per cent, partly reflecting its New Town schemes. Only six FPC areas in the country experienced greater growth over this period. Lincolnshire is ranked fifteenth with an increase of 10.7 per cent, Leicestershire twenty-seventh (6.9 per cent), Derbyshire thirty-fifth (3.3 per cent) and Nottinghamshire fortieth (2.6 per cent).

The figures in Table 10.1 conceal the fluctuations in growth that have taken place during the last two decades. Apart from Nottinghamshire, whose rate of population growth has increased over the whole period, the East Midlands' counties experienced lower rates of growth in the early 1980s, when Derbyshire's population actually fell according to OPCS estimates. Highest levels of growth were generally in the years around 1986–88, with some reduction in 1988–89 in Lincolnshire and to a lesser extent Northamptonshire, but a sharp increase in Nottinghamshire. Thus recently there has been some evidence of a narrowing in the differential in population growth rates between the more northerly and southerly counties within the region, although it remains to be seen whether this is a short-term feature or a long-term shift.

10.5 Analysis of migration trends at county level

10.5.1 Gross migration rates

The NHSCR-based inward and outward migration rates for Nottinghamshire and for Derbyshire are very similar, as are those for Lincolnshire and for Northamptonshire (Figure 10.1). These similarities relate to both the trends over the period being analysed and to the actual gross migration rates themselves. Leicestershire's experience sits between these two pairs of counties, although by the end of the 1980s its rates had converged with those of Derbyshire and Nottinghamshire.

Derbyshire experienced a small but increasing net inflow in the 1970s, followed by a temporary shift to a net outflow in the early 1980s. By the second half of the 1980s the pattern had reversed and the net inflow had grown well beyond its earliest levels, primarily as a result of increased inward migration. Nottinghamshire's experience was broadly similar except that the second half of the 1970s saw a net outflow gradually shift to a small net inflow. In common with Derbyshire there was a net outflow in the early 1980s, but it was only really towards the end of the decade that any significant net inflow began to be maintained, following a steady and consistent increase in inward migration rates. Leicestershire's migration has been more or less in balance over the whole period from the mid-1970s onward. Annual net migration rates have varied within a very narrow range of around ±1.5 per 1,000.

Both Northamptonshire and Lincolnshire have experienced net inflows

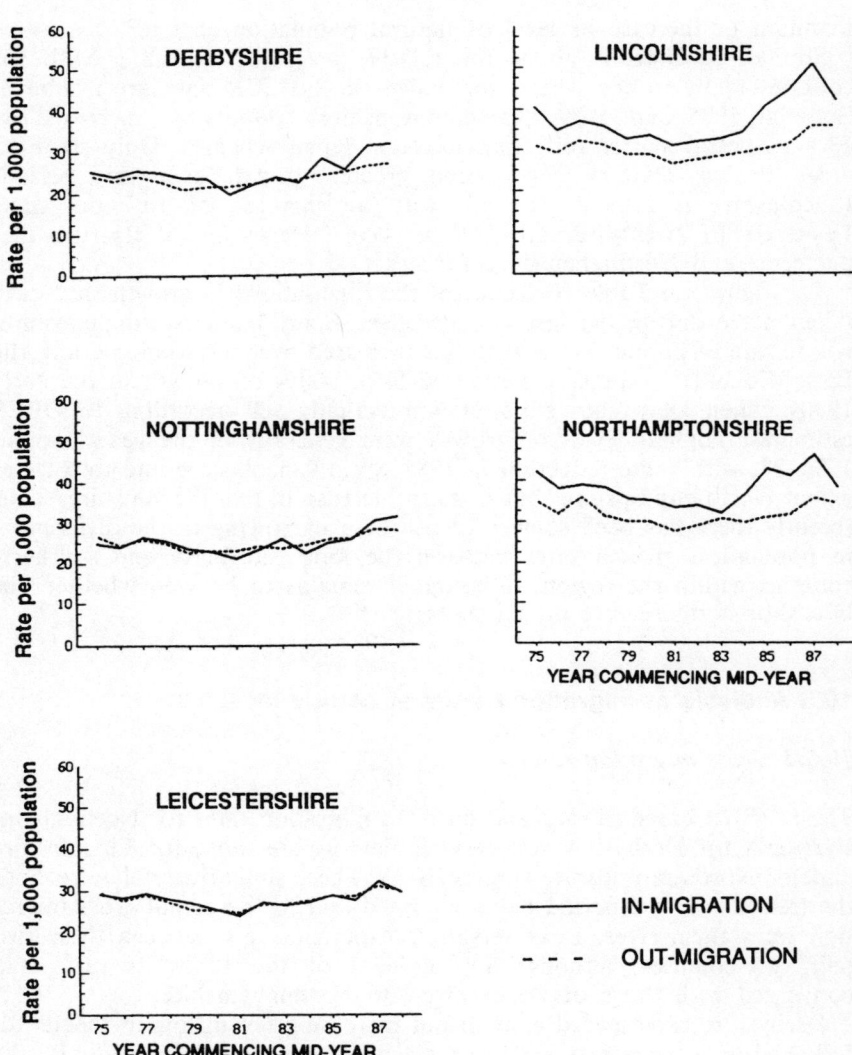

Figure 10.1 County in-migration and out-migration rates, the East Midlands, 1975–89

Source: Derived from NHSCR figures and OPCS population estimates (1984, 1990).

throughout the second half of he 1970s and the 1980s, with broadly similar rates of gross migration, and both at significantly higher levels than the other counties of the region. Both also experienced similar sharp increases in inward migration rates from the mid-1980s onward with similar sharp reductions to earlier levels of net inflow by 1988–89. Northamptonshire's inflows were at a higher rate in the 1970s than

Table 10.2 County gross and net migration rates to and from the North and the South, East Midlands, 1975–89

	Inward migration per 1,000			Outward migration per 1,000			Net migration per 1,000		
	75–76	82–83	88–89	75–76	82–83	88–89	75–76	82–83	88–89
To/from North									
Derbyshire	13.1	11.9	14.4	11.7	10.9	13.1	1.4	1.0	1.3
Leicestershire	12.3	11.7	12.3	11.3	9.2	11.5	1.0	2.5	0.8
Lincolnshire	15.1	13.2	13.3	12.9	10.1	15.8	2.2	3.1	−2.5
Northamptonshire	12.9	10.0	10.7	10.6	8.6	12.1	2.3	1.4	−1.4
Nottinghamshire	10.2	9.9	11.3	9.6	8.8	10.7	0.6	1.1	0.6
To/from South									
Derbyshire	12.1	10.1	16.9	12.7	11.2	13.5	−0.5	−1.1	3.4
Leicestershire	16.8	15.4	17.2	18.2	17.3	18.2	−1.4	−1.9	−1.0
Lincolnshire	25.3	18.5	28.6	18.1	17.1	19.7	7.2	1.4	8.9
Northamptonshire	29.0	23.6	27.3	24.2	20.2	22.0	4.8	3.4	5.3
Nottinghamshire	14.7	11.9	17.3	17.1	15.2	16.9	−2.4	−3.3	0.4

Source: Derived from NHSCR figures and OPCS population estimates.

Lincolnshire's, but reached a lower peak in the second half of the 1980s.

In all five counties in the region inward migration rates have proved more volatile than outward migration rates, and have generally driven the net migration trends. Apart from Leicestershire, the highest levels of net inward migration were in the mid or late 1980s. However, there is much less consistency about when the lowest levels of net inward movement (or highest net outflows) were recorded, although they were most likely to be in the first half of the 1980s.

10.5.2 Origins and destinations of migrants

Three key points emerge in analysing origin and destination-specific flows. First, short-distance (housing-related) moves from neighbouring areas both within the region but also across the regional boundary appear to be an important influence over the course of migration trends, behaving in a cyclical fashion linked to the state of the wider housing market. Secondly, there appears to be a relatively stable undercurrent of long-distance (job-related) moves, reflecting what might be seen as the equally stable 'pecking-order' of regional prosperity and economic structure. Thirdly, the data provides evidence of a shift in trends and patterns in the late 1980s, when compared with the relative stability of the late 1970s and early 1980s.

The migration rates for each county in the East Midlands to and from the North and the South reveal some interesting conclusions. There is much greater variation between the East Midland counties and over time in migration rates to and from the South and the North, although by 1988–89 the differential had become less pronounced (Table 10.2). The southern counties of Lincolnshire and Northamptonshire have experienced net migration from both the North and the South virtually throughout the period. However, by 1987–88 both counties witnessed net out-migration to the non-metropolitan North and the rate in this outflow increased in the following year. In Lincolnshire this was also accompanied by a net outflow to the metropolitan North for the first time. Northamptonshire only just avoided this reversal and in 1988–89 experienced a sharp reduction in the net in-migration rate from the South.

The migration trends for the northern counties of the region were somewhat different. Nottinghamshire, for example, has been a net recipient from both the metropolitan and non-metropolitan North throughout the period. It has also been a consistent net loser to the South, except for the last two years of the series. There was a net inflow from the non-metropolitan South initially in 1987–88 which increased in 1988–89 and was accompanied by net inflows from Greater London. Derbyshire's experience is similar to Nottinghamshire's, although the patterns show less long-term consistency. The main difference to note is that the shift towards a pattern of net inflow from the South began earlier, with a positive balance in three of the four years since 1985–86.

10.5.3 Short- and long-distance migration between neighbouring and non-neighbouring areas

To distinguish between likely shorter-distance housing-related moves and longer-distance job-based moves, migration rates have been calculated for 'neighbouring' and 'non-neighbouring' areas (see Table 10.3). 'Neighbours' are defined as contiguous FPC areas.

Both Northamptonshire and Lincolnshire have consistently gained population from both neighbouring and non-neighbouring areas, although Northamptonshire experienced a short-lived net loss to neighbouring FPC areas (primarily Cambridgeshire, Oxfordshire and Buckinghamshire) in the mid-1970s. Northamptonshire's trends reflect the winding down of its two New Town schemes, and the decline of their influence over migration patterns. In the mid-1970s, when both schemes were still in operation, the county experienced very substantial rates of net inward movement from non-neighbouring areas. These subsequently fell sharply in the late 1970s and early 1980s, although they then recovered with the upturn in housebuilding in the second half of the 1980s. By contrast, rates of gross movement to and from neighbouring areas have remained relatively stable, although the net inward balance gradually widened over the course of the 1980s, only to fall back sharply in 1988–89. Lincolnshire's rate of net migration from non-neighbouring areas increased much more steeply in the second half of the 1980s, before falling back just as sharply in 1988–89, albeit to levels high by comparison even with Northamptonshire.

Table 10.3 County gross and net migration rates to and from neighbouring and non-neighbouring FPC areas, East Midlands, 1975–89

	Inward migration per 1,000			Outward migration per 1,000			Net migration per 1,000		
	75–76	82–83	88–89	75–76	82–83	88–89	75–76	82–83	88–89
To/from neighbouring areas									
Derbyshire	12.4	11.8	15.1	11.1	10.2	12.5	1.4	1.6	2.6
Leicestershire	9.4	8.5	8.5	8.7	8.0	9.2	0.7	0.5	−0.8
Lincolnshire	15.4	11.5	14.2	12.3	11.0	13.7	3.1	0.4	0.4
Northamptonshire	11.0	11.8	12.7	11.3	8.7	10.6	−0.2	3.1	2.1
Nottinghamshire	8.7	8.0	10.4	10.0	8.3	9.9	−1.3	−0.4	0.6
To/from non-neighbouring areas									
Derbyshire	12.9	10.2	16.2	13.4	11.9	14.1	−0.5	−1.7	2.1
Leicestershire	19.6	18.7	21.1	20.9	18.6	20.5	−1.2	0.1	0.5
Lincolnshire	25.0	20.2	27.7	18.7	16.2	21.7	6.4	4.0	6.0
Northamptonshire	30.9	21.8	25.3	23.5	20.1	23.5	7.4	1.7	1.8
Nottinghamshire	16.2	15.3	20.8	16.7	15.7	17.8	−0.5	−0.4	3.0

Source: Derived from NHSCR figures and OPCS population estimates.

Nottinghamshire has typically gained population from non-neighbouring areas (although Table 10.3 happens to give figures for two of the four years when this did not occur), while losing migrants to its neighbours. The shift towards increasing overall net in-migration in the second half of the 1980s has been brought about by rising levels of net in-migration from non-neighbouring areas, such as the Outer South East, which in 1985–86 received a small net outflow (−43), but by 1988–89 supplied a more significant net inflow (+1,568). However, in 1988–89, there was also a net inflow from the rest of the East Midlands, for only the second time since the mid-1970s.

Derbyshire has consistently gained population from its neighbouring FPC areas (including Nottinghamshire), and the trend has been upward. By contrast it has lost migrants to its non-neighbouring areas, except in the late 1970s and late 1980s. Derbyshire stands apart from the other counties in the East Midlands in terms of the ratio in its neighbouring to non-neighbouring area migration rates. In Derbyshire the short-distance and long-distance rates are similar. The other counties all have gross migration rates to and from non-neighbouring areas that are nearer twice those for neighbouring areas (and almost three times in the case of Northamptonshire in the mid-1970s, reflecting its New Town developments). This may be explained by the fact that Derbyshire has seven populous metropolitan districts adjoining its northern boundaries.

To what extent do the similarities that were evident in terms of overall in- and out-migration rates between the pairs of counties also extend to the origins and destinations of migrants? Derbyshire, and to a lesser extent Nottinghamshire, have experienced consistent and significant net inflows from the Yorkshire and Humberside and North West regions. Further analysis of figures for individual FPC areas within these regions indicates that Derbyshire's flows are predominantly from Sheffield, and from Stockport and to a lesser extent Manchester and Tameside respectively. In other words it seems likely that these are primarily short-distance housing-related moves from neighbouring areas, that happen to cross regional boundaries. Similar conclusions are reached in looking at Nottinghamshire's flows which, given its more easterly location, are less developed in relation to the North West, but certainly as strong with Sheffield and considerably stronger with Rotherham. Untypically, Nottinghamshire experienced net outflows to both Yorkshire and Humberside and the North West in 1988–89. The net inflow to Derbyshire, particularly from the North West, was also considerably reduced.

Extending this analysis further shows that in 1988–89 there were net inflows to Derbyshire from all the regions in the South (plus the West Midlands), and all at higher rates than the previous year. Indeed there was a net inflow from the South West region for the first time. By contrast, all the regions in the North (plus the rest of the East Midlands) experienced either lower net inflows or higher net outflows than the previous year. Again Nottinghamshire's experience is almost identical in every detail, the only significant exception being that it untypically received a substantial net inflow from the rest of the East Midlands.

The most significant development in recent years has been the very substantial increase in net inward migration to Derbyshire and Nottinghamshire from the rest of the South East region. In the case of Derbyshire, the current high rates of net gain are the product of a steady and almost continuous reversal since the early 1980s. Essex and Kent became the main FPC areas of origin from the South East for both counties, and indeed among the most important FPC areas of origin from any region. By the end of the 1980s net migration rates from the rest of the South East into Derbyshire and Nottinghamshire were higher than for any other region, although gross migration levels were considerably higher to and from other parts of the East Midlands.

By contrast the parallels between Lincolnshire and Northamptonshire are not as close when origins and destinations are explored, suggesting that their similar overall net migration rates and trends may simply be coincidence. This is perhaps not surprising given the different character of the two areas (for example in terms of their employment structure), echoing the fact that they were put into different 'families' in the Shaw classification of local authorities. However, one common pattern does emerge for these two counties and contrasts with the experience of Derbyshire and Nottinghamshire. 1988–89 saw reduced net inward migration or increased net outward migration rates for every region in the country, North or South. The only significant exception is that Lincolnshire's net rate of inflow from the West Midlands increased.

Both counties have consistently gained population from London and the rest of the South East, and until 1988–89, perhaps less expectedly, from the North West. Lincolnshire has gained consistently from both the West Midlands and the rest of the East Midlands, and until the last two years from Yorkshire and Humberside. After losing population to East Anglia in the late 1970s and early 1980s, Lincolnshire now gains, predominantly from neighbouring Cambridgeshire. In the mid-1970s, Northamptonshire gained heavily from Greater London, reflecting the planned migration associated with Northampton new town. By the early 1980s, this origin had become of much less importance for that county, and the second half of the 1980s saw a definite shift towards the Outer South East as the main area of origin. Northamptonshire has also tended to experience net inflows from Scotland, apart from around 1980–81, for reasons that will be discussed in more detail later.

Leicestershire has consistently experienced net losses to the most rapidly growing regions of East Anglia and the South West, and until the last two years, to Greater London and the South East. This recent net inflow, particularly from the Outer South East, again features Kent, Essex and Hertfordshire as the most important origins. Pre-dating this shift there has also been growing net outward movement from Leicestershire to other parts of the East Midlands, although there has recently been an inflow from Northamptonshire. The highest and most consistent rate of net inward movement has been from the West Midlands, and specifically from the neighbouring areas of Coventry and Warwickshire. As with Nottinghamshire and Derbyshire there have also tended to be net inflows from all the regions of the North, although in 1988–89 these consistently went down or reversed, while the flow pattern from the regions of the South became more favourable.

10.6 Factors behind the trends

Two sets of factors are particularly important in accounting for migration trends in the East Midlands. First, there is the impact of London house price trends on migration, and secondly, the role of factors associated with the local economy.

10.6.1 The impact of London house prices

There appears to be a link in the second half of the 1980s between the migration trends that have been described and regional house price relativities. Hamnett (1989, 1990) has calculated indices of regional house prices relative to those in London over the last two decades. The cyclical patterns and ripple effect that he identifies can be aligned with trends in migration.

Between around 1981 and 1986, the house price differential between London and the East Midlands steadily widened to levels on a par with the early 1970s. At the same time wage differentials remained relatively stable. Factors such as the 'Big Bang' drove income/price ratios to unsustainable levels in the capital. This coincided with, and appears partly at least to explain, the period of rapid migration into the East Midlands region and elsewhere. The house price differentials were such that they more than offset the increased commuting costs, while wage rates for those working in the South East continued to remain higher, affording them greater purchasing power.

This competition for houses inevitably forced up prices for second-hand property and builders seized the opportunity to respond to the market by raising prices for new property. The price differential subsequently began to narrow both as prices in the East Midlands began to rise more sharply, and as prices in the South East actually began to fall back to levels that could be more realistically sustained by the incomes available. Hamnett suggests that for the regions of southern England that turning point came in the third quarter of 1986, but that the effects took up to a further two years to diffuse through the rest of the country.

The turnaround affecting the southern counties of the East Midlands was apparent in the 1988–89 NHSCR figures, when the pressure was directed towards the more northerly counties, both in terms of knock-on effects of short-distance displacement, and more direct long-distance moves for the South East. Yet even here there were signs in 1988–89 of pressure for further northward movement – hence the first-time losses to Yorkshire and Humberside that had appeared.

Improvements in transport infrastructure and services are not in themselves reasons to move. They simply enable a wider range of options and potential destinations to be considered. Commuting is probably regarded as no more than a necessary evil to be tolerated until house price differentials narrow, when the relative costs of travelling longer distances to and from the capital on an overcrowded motorway or train appear more significant. The attractions of moving out diminish and the pressure to move eases. Indeed some households, having moved out, may even decide to return.

10.6.2 The importance of local economic factors

Local economic developments can affect migration at the FPC area level. Thus in order to interpret and understand the figures fully, one needs a detailed local knowledge. One example, relating to Corby in Northamptonshire, which lies within the author's experience, can be used to explore how sensitive the NHSCR statistics are to such effects.

Corby has been described as a 'company town' (Grieco, 1985, p. 9) whose growth was inextricably linked to the activities of the steel producers, Stewart and Lloyds (later nationalised into British Steel). It was also noted earlier how Corby was (and to some extent still remains) a 'Scottish enclave' (Grieco, 1985, p. 13) on account of its long history of migration through transfer and later recruitment to the steelworks from north of the border (Pocock, 1966; Grieco, 1985). The NHSCR data indicates that Northamptonshire as a whole had higher net inward migration rates from Scotland in the second half of the 1970s than the other counties in the region, although the trend was downwards (consistent with the general downturn in the fortunes of the steel industry). However, in 1980, a major redundancy programme at the town's steelworks resulted in around 6,000 redundancies. Unemployment locally rose to 24 per cent. NHSCR figures for 1980–81 indicate a dramatic shift to high levels of net outward migration to Scotland from Northamptonshire, which were continued to a lesser extent in the following year. This pattern was not evident in any other county.

Net inward migration from Scotland into Northamptonshire resumed in the early 1980s. Indeed during 1985–87, rates returned to the levels witnessed in the mid-1970s. However, at this time OPCS estimated that Corby's population was actually falling. Over the 1980s the town's unemployment steadily fell to below the national average following major efforts to attract new employment and to diversity the local economy. Has the long-term history of movement to the area re-emerged as chain migration no longer linked to the requirements of the local steel industry? Or are we simply witnessing a shift to more general migration to Northamptonshire as a whole, as a relatively prosperous southern county? Because the NHSCR as a source is restricted to the FPC area scale, it is not possible to explore such questions in detail.

Other similar analyses could be attempted to explore the relationship between the fortunes of key local industries and migration trends. For example, in Derbyshire, Nottinghamshire and Leicestershire, the coal industry has been an important source of employment. However, the industry witnessed a major pit rationalisation programme during the 1980s, particularly in the second half of the decade following the miners' strike. Local knowledge could be used to test whether the NHSCR figures are sensitive to the movement of miners and their families between FPC areas across the country in response to closures, towards the areas where the limited new colliery developments are taking place.

Much of this chapter has demonstrated that areas such as Nottinghamshire and Derbyshire that are similar in terms of their social, demographic and economic characteristics are also likely to have similar migration trends and patterns, particularly where their locations in relation to major centres of population are similar. Other areas, such as Northamptonshire and Lincolnshire, at first sight appear to have similar migration trends. However, these tend not to stand up to more detailed examination, reflecting the very different characteristics (and planning policies in relation to development) of the two counties.

10.7 The future?

What will be the major influences over future migration trends and patterns in the East Midlands? Will the primary underlying influence be the mapping of national economic trends onto the local economic structure? Will the state of the national, regional and local housing markets superimpose shorter-term fluctuations on to these long-term trends? Will neighbouring regions, such as the South East, be ensuring that adequate housing units are provided to accommodate their own populations? The answers to such questions are far from clear.

Hamnett (1990) suggests that from late 1989 the house price differential between London and the East Midlands (and most other regions) has again begun to widen. How long will it be before the cycle widens sufficiently for potential commuters to the capital to be driven towards the East Midlands again in search of affordable houses? Planning policy talks of the South East region 'consuming its own smoke' in housing terms. Why should the 1990s be any different to the 1980s? Or are we likely to see major changes from previous patterns in the future?

In looking ahead, even long-term planning documents tend to be constrained in their vision by recent trends. In the early 1980s, the East Midlands Forum of County Councils, for example, expected the 'lower levels of net migration which are currently being experienced . . . to continue'. As we have seen, they actually increased sharply across most of the region in the second half of the 1980s. Perhaps this period of growth should be seen as exceptional. However, the East Midlands Regional Planning Forum (1991) still comments that 'the impact of the major factors affecting migration trends . . . can reasonably be expected to be much the same in the future as in the last decade.'

So to what extent can and will planning policy influence the future scale and pattern of migration into and out of the region? Although figures and statements on migration levels tend to figure strongly in strategic planning documents, such as the county structure plans, the policies in such plans can only influence migration levels indirectly, largely through a constraining or permissive influence over housebuilding. Past experience also suggests that strategic plans have little significant control over the state of the local economy, which responds primarily to the changes in the national economic situation.

Authorities such as Northamptonshire County Council are planning for continued, but reducing net inward migration. By contrast, Lincolnshire has now adopted a 'planning for growth' approach, and has indicated that it intends to respond positively to the accelerating rates of migration evident in the late 1980s by seeking to accommodate as much of the demand for housing development as is 'reasonably' possible (East Midlands Regional Planning Forum, 1991).

What is certain is that the location of areas such as the East Midlands will not change and at the same time the 'real' distance between regions and major centres of employment is rapidly diminishing through rail electrification and the extension and upgrading of the motorway network. One anticipates that the results of the 1991 Census are likely to show that longer-distance commuting, for example into the capital from southern parts of the East Midlands, is now more common than it was a decade ago. In other words the area of search for migrants is likely to have become wider. However, this area of search is likely to ebb and flow as potential migrants seek trade-offs between fluctuating house prices (and other housing costs), income levels and job opportunities, and travel costs (both financial and temporal).

How can the NHSCR as a source develop to meet changing circumstances? Will 1992 and the Single European Market, for example, bring an increased international dimension to regional and local migration patterns? What light will the NHSCR as a source be able to throw on this and the other issues raised in this chapter? What is certain is that the value of the NHSCR will continue to grow as the time series to which it relates extends and some of the cyclical patterns that have been hypothesised can be tested. All those interested in understanding more about the dynamics of migration in growth regions such as the East Midlands eagerly await the release of statistics for future years.

Disclaimer
The views expressed in this chapter are those of the author and do not represent those of Northamptonshire County Council.

11 Migration trends for the South: the emergence of a Greater South East?

Tony Champion and Peter Congdon

11.1 Introduction

The South is the largest single region examined in this volume in terms of population size: 24.1 million in 1989, or 42 per cent of the UK's total. In fact, it comprises the three standard regions of the South East, East Anglia and the South West. An important distinction is made between Greater London (henceforth referred to merely as London) and the rest of the South East (ROSE). The separate treatment of London makes good sense in many contexts, most notably because with 6.76 million people it is larger than either East Anglia (2.04 million) or the South West (4.25 million) – and indeed than the two combined – but it is particularly important in the study of population change and migration, for London constitutes the South's only 'metropolitan county' with a history of population decline and migratory loss – in contrast to ROSE which has many features in common with East Anglia and the South West in its recent history of population change. Moreover, it is primarily because of the dominant influence of London that the whole of the South needs to be examined together, as we shall see later when we examine the evidence for the existence of a 'Greater South East'.

Already a great deal is known about the history of migration patterns affecting the South. This is not surprising given the area's size and its importance in UK migration. London itself provides the linchpin of the national migration system, with marked implications for the counties and regions surrounding it (Johnston et al., 1974; Flowerdew and Salt, 1979; Champion and Congdon, 1987, 1988; Cross, 1990; Coombes and Charlton in this volume). In net terms it draws people in from longer distances, especially for further education and labour market entry, and sends people out over shorter distances. The latter stream comprises a broad spectrum of ages apart from school-leavers and young adults. It includes families and their children (especially over shorter ranges) and people around retirement ages (to more peripheral sub-regions in the South). Housing and environmental factors provide the main reasons for movement among these categories (Gordon, 1987; Congdon and Champion, 1989a, 1989b). Besides this clear age pattern to the London-based migration system, it has also been shown that London functions as a social 'escalator', helping to promote young adults who are then dispatched as members of higher occupational groups to the rest of the South and beyond (Fielding, 1989; Chapter 13 in this volume).

It is, however, questionable as to how well this conventional wisdom fits present reality. Most of the research on this topic up to now has been based on the Population Censuses, most notably those of 1966 and 1971 but with some further analyses from the 1981 Census and the associated Longitudinal Study. Yet it is known that circumstances have changed in several important respects since the beginning of the 1980s. In the first place, London – after years in the economic doldrums – led the 'national' economic recovery of the mid-1980s and saw a significant reduction in its rate of migration loss. Secondly, many parts of ROSE saw strong employment growth in the 1980s, as earlier trends of residential decentralisation were complemented by employment decentralisation from London and by ROSE's increasing ability to generate jobs in its own right. It has been argued (Congdon and Champion, 1989b) that an increased proportion of migrants from London to ROSE have taken local jobs rather than opting for extended commuting. Moreover, the zone experiencing net migration loss has extended beyond London to the outer metropolitan area as house price differentials and environmental factors have made the more peripheral regions of the South potentially more attractive to families with children as well as to the older migrants that have traditionally dominated these longer-distance net outward flows.

It is the primary purpose of this chapter to discover the extent to which these developments have been associated with changes in population trends and migration patterns and to find out whether our established conceptions of the South's migration patterns need to be substantially revised. Of course, the majority of the earlier census-based analyses cannot be updated until the results of the 1991 Census are available, but in this chapter we get as far as we can by examining the NHSCR migration data. We can also use as context the official data on international migration and the series of annual population estimates made by the OPCS. These sources can provide an indication of the magnitude of the changes which took place in the 1980s and suggest the sorts of questions which data from the 1991 Census and other sources can be used to address.

The chapter begins with an examination of 1980s trends for the South as a single region. The next section explores the relative contribution which each of the four southern 'regions' has made to these trends. The third section looks at the patterns of overall and age-specific flows which have produced changes in net internal migration balances for the South. In the last two sections we deal respectively with the local impact of recent migration developments and with their underlying causes and implications for the future.

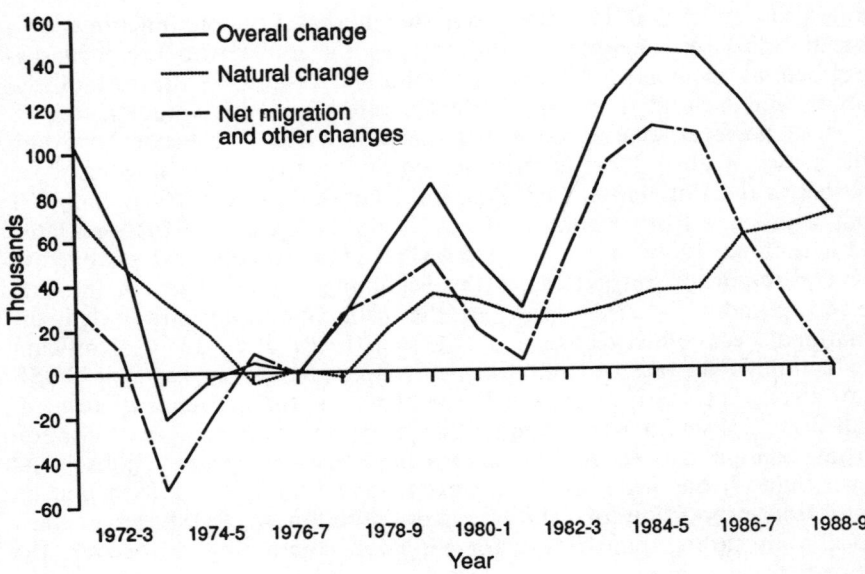

Figure 11.1   Annual trends in population change and its components, the
South, 1972–89

11.2 The South's recent population experience

The 1980s was the decade of the 'North–South divide' and, as such, was
the decade of the South. In economic terms it witnessed the effects of
the economic recession which bit more deeply in the North of the country and the subsequent recovery which began in London in 1983–84 and
disproportionately favoured the South through much of the remainder of
the decade. This period also saw a southward shift in the dividing line
itself to a position stretching between the Severn estuary and the Wash
and excluding most of the Midlands from the 'South'.

The population evidence behind the South's 1980s prosperity is shown
in Figure 11.1. A major upward shift in growth rate clearly took place
between the mid-1970s and the mid-1980s. Indeed the South registered
overall population loss and net out-migration in 1973–74, the year which
is now associated with the peak of 'counterurbanisation' and of growth
in the outer rural areas and more peripheral regions of the UK. The
annual trend actually reveals two cycles of demographic recovery for the
South, each involving a significant acceleration in population growth (in
1977–80 and 1982–85) followed by a marked retrenchment.

The South was responsible for the greater part of the UK's total
population growth in the 1980s, taking almost 90 per cent of the 885,000
national increase estimated for 1981–89 (Table 11.1). In fact, this share
was not much higher than for the previous decade (85 per cent), but the
overall 1981–89 figure disguises the South's very strong position during

Table 11.1 Population change in its national context, the South, 1971–89

	1971–81	1981–89	1981–85	1985–89
Change (000s)				
South	361	795	371	425
Rest of UK	63	90	– 103	193
UK	424	885	267	618
South's share of UK (%)	85.2	89.9	138.7	68.8

Source: Calculated from mid-year estimates, derived from *Population Trends*, 61, Tables 2 and 3.

the first half of the 1980s. At that time the South gained 370,000 people in four years while the rest of the UK declined by over 100,000. In the later 1980s the South's share of national growth averaged 69 per cent, as the population recovered elsewhere. Nevertheless, in terms of absolute increases in the South, it can be seen that both of the four-year periods in the 1980s added more people than the whole of the 1970s had.

The contribution of migration to these overall changes is presented in Figure 11.1. The migration component is clearly more volatile over time than is natural change and has been largely responsible for the short-term fluctuations on overall growth rate. The two cycles of population growth since the early 1970s are clearly the result of the surges in net migration gains recorded during the late 1970s and mid-1980s, while the natural change component variously reinforces the migration surge (as in most of the 1970s) or dampens down the effect of the migration cutback (as in the later 1980s).

Migration's role in overall population growth in the South is shown in Table 11.2. The volume of the South's net migration gains rose markedly between the 1970s and 1980s, running particularly strongly in 1981–85 at an average 65,000 a year. As a result, migration's share of the South's overall growth rose steeply from 30 to 70 per cent between the 1970s and early 1980s. At the same time, however, it is important to note the significant contribution made by the surplus of births over deaths, accounting for over half of the South's growth in 1985–89 and averaging over two-fifths for the decade as a whole.

The relative importance of internal as opposed to international migration is shown in the second panel of Table 11.2 and in Figure 11.2. It is important to be cautious about the precise figures for international migration, because they exclude exchanges with Eire and are based on very small samples obtained from the International Passenger Survey (IPS). Nevertheless, the data are probably robust enough to draw two major conclusions.

First, over half the upward shift in the South's migration balance between the 1970s and 1980s appears to have resulted from the switch in

Table 11.2 Population change and its components, the South, 1971–89

	1971–81	1981–89	1981–85	1985–89
		Annual averages		
Components (000s)				
Total change	36	99	93	106
Natural change	25	43	28	58
Migration/other changes	11	57	65	49
% total change due to migration	29.7	57.0	70.0	45.7
Recorded net migration (000s)				
International	−7	14	7	21
Internal (rest of UK)	19	38	48	29

Note: Recorded net migration data refer to calendar years 1971–80, 1981–88,
1981–84 and 1985–88, except for internal migration 1971–81. They exclude
exchanges with the Irish Republic, movements of the armed forces, and 'other
changes', and so are not directly comparable with 'migration/other changes'.
Sources: Calculated from data extracted from
    (i) OPCS, *Monitor*, PPI 90/1, Table 4;
    (ii) OPCS, *Key population and vital statistics*, VS 13/PP1.9, Table
        3.1, *Population Trends 55*, Table 18, and 61, Table 18;
    (iii) OPCS, *International Migration MN7*, Table 2.9, and *MN15*, Table
        2.9; and
    (iv) Unpublished data files on components of population change
        supplied by OPCS.

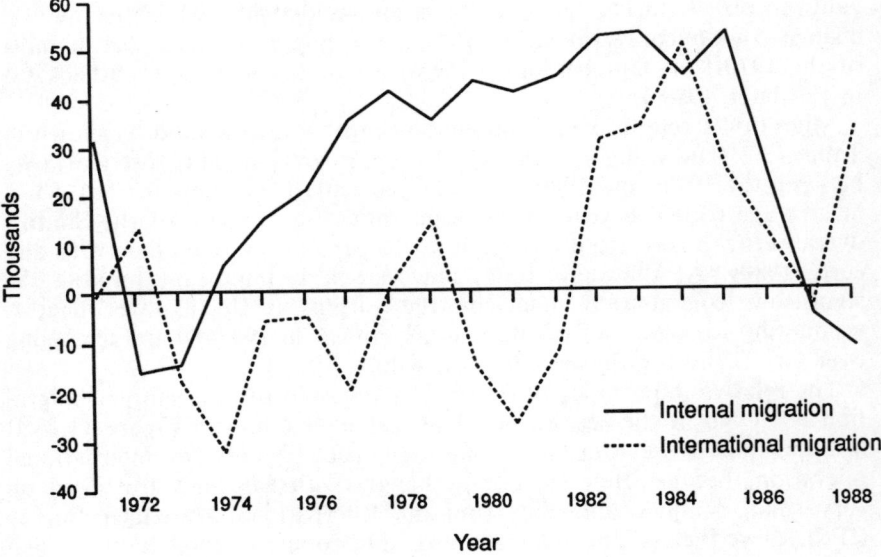

Figure 11.2 Annual trends in net international and internal migration, the
           South, 1971–88

international migration balance from net emigration to substantial net immigration. The internal migration balance had experienced its main upward shift between 1973 and 1977 and then remained remarkably stable for the next 10 years.

Secondly, Table 11.2 shows that, despite this, internal migration remained the major component of the South's migration gains in the 1980s, outnumbering the international migration gain by three to one. This dominance of internal migration gains, however, was far less marked in the latter half of the 1980s as a result of the marked acceleration of net international immigration alongside a significant reduction in net internal migration to the South.

The context for this study is therefore one of a significant upturn in rate of overall population growth for the South between the early 1970s and mid-1980s. Within-UK migration was clearly the largest single factor helping to produce this transformation, but it made its principal contribution to the altered trend during the 1970s, after which it was relatively stable until the late 1980s when it fell back to the level recorded in the early 1970s. By contrast, natural change emerged as the most important source of growth towards the end of the decade. It has also been seen that international migration was almost as important as internal migration in generating population growth for the South in the mid-1980s and, moreover, that it formed the principal influence on annual trends between the mid-1970s and mid-1980s.

11.3 Regional population changes within the South

This section examines the data on population change and migration for the four 'regions' of the South, recognising London as a separate region as mentioned earlier. It has two aims. One is to describe the part which each of the regions played in the South's relatively high population-growth rates during the 1980s. The other is to set the 1980s experience into a longer-term context to find the chief developments which initiated the resurgence of population growth and migration gains for the South during the 1970s.

The key ingredients of the South's population growth in the 1980s were the population gains recorded by the three 'non-metropolitan regions' (i.e. ROSE, East Anglia and the South West), which more than offset London's overall population decline (Table 11.3). In absolute terms, ROSE was responsible for as much growth as the other two regions combined, but taking into account their differences in base population East Anglia is found to have the highest growth rate, followed by the South West. These two outer regions appear very similar to each other in terms of internal migration rates, which at over 8.0 per 1,000 are more than twice the annual average rate for ROSE.

London's overall population decline of around one per 1,000 a year in the 1980s is the net result of much larger changes. The data show that London was running a rate of natural increase much higher than any of

Table 11.3 Population change and its components by region of the South, 1981–89

	South East	of which London	ROSE	East Anglia	South West	Total South
Absolute (000s)						
Total change	374	– 49	423	150	271	795
Natural change	329	175	153	22	– 9	342
Migration/other	45	– 225	270	128	280	454
International migration	118	126	– 8	– 6	– 4	108
Internal migration	– 107	– 387	279	128	283	304
Rate (per 1,000 per year)						
Total change	2.7	– 0.9	5.2	9.9	7.7	4.3
Natural change	2.4	3.2	1.9	1.4	– 0.3	1.8
Migration/other	0.3	– 4.1	3.3	8.5	8.0	2.4
International migration	0.9	2.3	– 0.1	– 0.4	– 0.1	0.6
Internal migration	– 0.8	– 7.2	3.4	8.4	8.1	1.6

Note: See Table 11.2 for notes and sources.

Table 11.4 Rates of population change, natural change and net migration by region of the South, 1971–89

	South East	of which London	ROSE	East Anglia	South West	Total South	UK
			Per 1,000 per year				
Overall change							
1971–76	– 1.7	– 11.7	6.1	14.9	8.2	1.3	1.0
1976–81	0.4	– 8.0	6.4	8.9	4.7	1.9	0.5
1981–85	2.7	– 1.4	5.4	9.2	6.8	4.0	1.2
1985–89	2.8	– 0.4	4.9	10.2	8.4	4.5	2.7
Natural change							
1971–76	1.8	1.3	2.2	2.5	– 0.2	1.5	1.7
1976–81	1.2	1.2	1.3	1.2	– 1.4	0.7	0.7
1981–85	1.8	2.4	1.3	1.0	– 0.9	1.2	1.2
1985–89	3.0	4.1	2.4	1.8	0.3	2.4	2.2
Net migration and other changes							
1971–76	– 3.5	– 13.0	3.9	12.4	8.4	– 0.2	– 0.7
1976–81	– 0.8	– 9.2	5.2	7.7	6.1	1.1	– 0.3
1981–85	0.9	– 3.8	4.1	8.3	7.7	2.8	0.0
1985–89	– 0.2	– 4.5	2.5	8.4	8.1	2.1	0.6

Sources: Calculated from data extracted from
   (i) OPCS, *Monitor*, PP1 90/1, Table 4;
   (ii) OPCS, *Key population and vital statistics*, VS 13/PP1.9, Table 3.1; and
   (iii) Unpublished data files on components of population change supplied by OPCS.

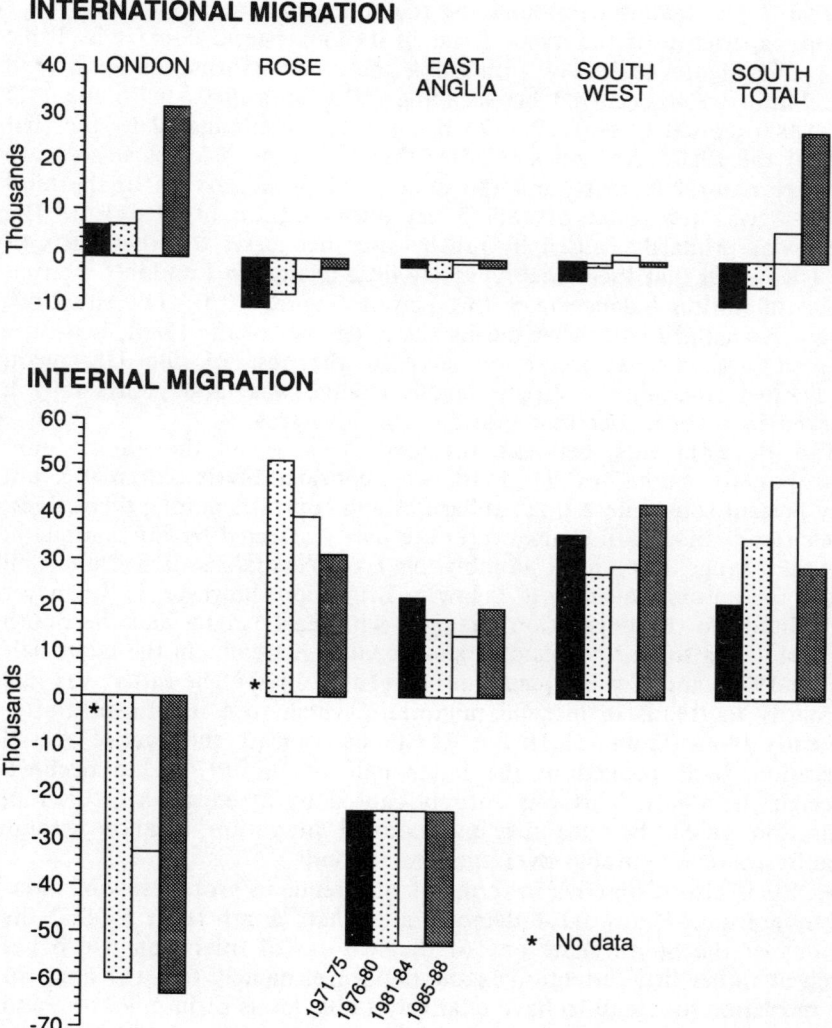

INTERNATIONAL MIGRATION

INTERNAL MIGRATION

Figure 11.3 Net volume of international and internal migration by region of the South, 1971–88

the other three regions in the South and nearly twice the national average. This has been attributed in part to London's large ethnic minority population (Champion and Congdon, 1988). It is also clear that, of all four regions, London was the only one to record net immigration from overseas and was therefore entirely responsible for the South's immigration gains over this period. At the same time, however, London was experiencing a high rate of net out-migration to other parts of the UK, averaging almost 50,000 a year and representing a population loss of 7 per cent if continued for the full decade.

The experience of the 1980s is set in its longer-term context in Table 11.4 and Figure 11.3. For London a major transformation in overall population trend occurred between the 1970s and 1980s, with the 11.7 per 1,000 annual loss of 1971–76 being virtually eliminated by the first half of the 1980s. Around a third of this reduction in losses was due to stronger natural increase, but the major part – at least up to the mid-1980s – was the result of falling net out-migration (Table 11.4). The latter was primarily caused by much lower net losses to other parts of the UK, given that there was relatively little change in London's international migration balance over this period (Figure 11.3). The situation, however, changed somewhat during the latter half of the 1980s, when the rate of net internal migration loss to the rest of the UK again accelerated, though the effect of this change was largely offset by a marked increase in net immigration from overseas.

The developments between the two decades in the three 'non-metropolitan regions' of the South were considerably less dramatic, but they present some interesting similarities and contrasts among themselves. Their trends in overall change rates are partly affected by fluctuations in natural change rate, most notably by East Anglia's switch from well above the national average to below it. Migration, however, is the major contributor to the population changes, with East Anglia and the South West showing similar trends of a slowdown in net gains in the latter half of the 1970s and a subsequent upturn (Table 11.4). The latter was due primarily to trends in internal migration, which rose significantly after the early 1980s (Figure 11.3). For ROSE, by contrast, the level of overall migration gains peaked in the latter half of the 1970s and declined through the 1980s. This was entirely caused by a reduction in internal migration gains, because the international migration balance became steadily more favourable over the four periods.

ROSE is also distinctive in terms of the trends in gross levels of internal migration. Figure 11.4 demonstrates that, apart from ROSE, the regions of the South share one of the features of migration which has received rather little attention in the literature, namely that the areas of net migration loss tend to have relatively stable levels of in-migration and fluctuating levels of out-migration while net gain areas are the opposite, with relatively stable levels of out-migration and fluctuating in-migration rates. East Anglia and the South West fall into this latter category as would be expected from their position as net gainers, while London represents the former category with a stable volume of inward movement, at least until the mid-1980s. By contrast, for ROSE the fluctuations in gross in- and out-migration tend to have paralleled each other pretty closely over most of this period until the mid-1980s when there was an upturn in out-migration outpacing that of inward movement. This is not the pattern to be expected of a migration-gaining region and reflects two important aspects of ROSE's situation: first, ROSE's dual roles as net gainer from London and net loser to the regions beyond and, second, the increasing importance of the latter role during the 1980s, to

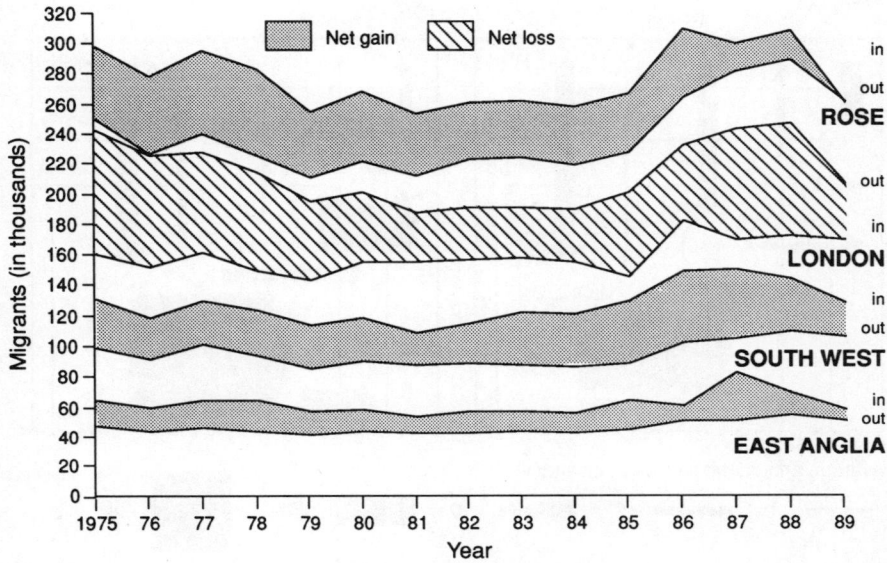

Figure 11.4   Gross internal migration flows by region of the South, 1975–89

the extent that in 1989 ROSE became a net loser of internal migrants for the first time since these records began.

11.4 Internal migration flows affecting the South

The above evidence indicates that the 1980s witnessed significant population developments in all four regions of the South, these being caused chiefly by changes in internal migration, occurring most notably in the latter part of the decade and having an especially remarkable effect on ROSE. They raise important questions which can be answered only by reference to data on migration flows between areas. First, which places (as migrant destinations) were most effected by the accelerated exodus from London in the latter half of the 1980s? Is the reduction in net in-migration to ROSE due to smaller numbers entering from London or to larger numbers leaving for other parts of the UK, and if the latter, where? Was the outward movement from ROSE, and perhaps from London too, accommodated largely in the counties lying immediately adjacent to the South East's official regional boundary, or has it been dispersed over a much wider zone? Finally, as well as overall numbers, it is important to know what types of people have been involved in these trends, in order to gauge better whether these developments are essentially quantitative in nature or perhaps signify some more fundamental change in migration behaviour.

The availability of the NHSCR data allows us to answer most of these

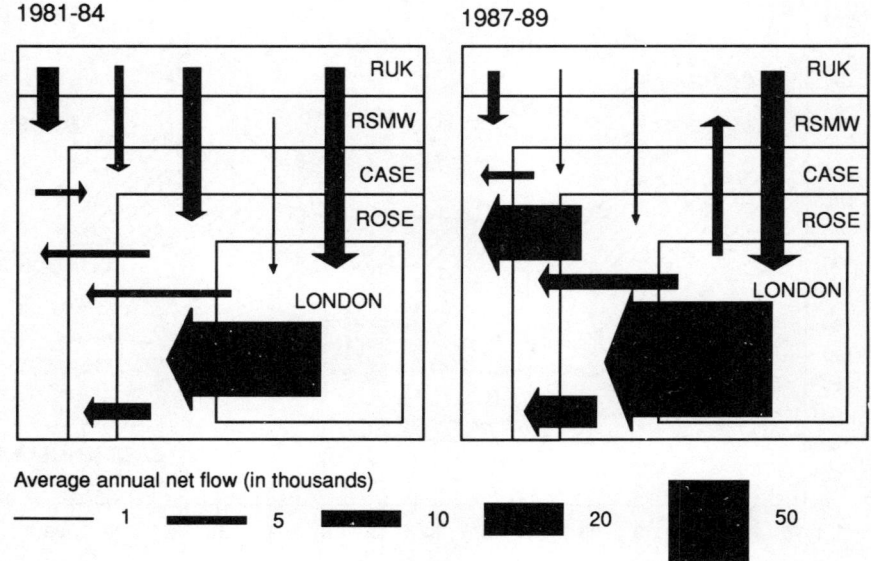

Figure 11.5 Net flows between five subdivisions of the UK, 1981–84 and 1987–89

questions. As outlined in Chapter 1, the NHSCR provides statistics on gross movements between FPC areas since 1975. For present purposes we will not make full use of the spatial detail, but instead recognise five groupings of areas, as follows:

1. London.
2. The rest of the South East (ROSE).
3. The seven counties lying adjacent to the South East region (CASE), i.e. Dorset, Wiltshire, Gloucestershire, Warwickshire, Northampton-shire, Cambridgeshire and Suffolk.
4. The remainder of the South, Midlands and Wales (RSMW), i.e. Cornwall, Devon, Somerset, Avon and Norfolk, plus the East Midlands bar Northamptonshire, the West Midlands bar Warwick-shire, and all of Wales.
5. The rest of the UK (RUK), comprising the three standard regions of northern England together with Scotland and Northern Ireland.

This framework enables us to do three things – to explore in more detail the flows directly affecting London and ROSE, to test the validity of a 'Greater South East' and to distinguish the relative importance of medium- and long-distance exchanges for the South East. As regards types of people, the NHSCR also furnishes data on the age of migrants, but information on their socio-economic and other characteristics needs

Table 11.5 Net migration by age for five subdivisions of the UK, 1981–84 and 1987–89

	0–14	15–24	25–44	Age group 45–59	60–74	75 +	Total
			Annual averages (000s)				
London							
1981–84	− 12.9	22.1	− 15.2	− 9.5	− 15.7	− 4.0	− 35.3
1987–89	− 21.9	20.0	− 33.2	− 15.0	− 18.6	− 6.9	− 75.5
Shift	− 9.0	− 2.1	− 18.0	− 5.5	− 2.8	− 2.9	− 40.3
ROSE							
1981–84	9.9	− 0.5	19.4	3.4	6.0	2.9	41.2
1987–89	0.8	5.6	18.1	− 3.6	− 4.1	1.9	18.8
Shift	− 9.1	6.1	− 1.3	− 7.0	− 10.1	− 1.0	− 22.4
CASE							
1981–84	4.8	− 0.9	8.3	4.1	5.2	1.3	22.7
1987–89	5.4	0.7	11.2	3.5	3.3	1.2	25.3
Shift	0.6	1.6	3.0	− 0.5	− 1.9	− 0.0	2.7
RSMW							
1981–84	4.5	− 6.0	1.7	4.8	6.1	1.2	12.3
1987–89	13.7	− 3.5	15.4	12.9	13.6	3.3	55.3
Shift	9.2	2.5	13.6	8.1	7.5	2.1	43.0
RUK							
1981–84	− 6.4	− 14.9	− 14.3	− 2.9	− 1.5	− 0.9	− 40.9
1987–89	2.0	− 22.7	− 11.5	2.1	5.8	0.5	− 23.9
Shift	8.4	− 7.8	2.9	5.0	7.3	1.3	17.0

Note: ROSE = Rest of the South East; CASE = Counties adjacent to the South East; RSMW = Rest of the South, Midlands and Wales; RUK = Rest of the UK.
Source: Calculated from NHSCR data.

to await the results of the 1991 Census and particularly their incorporation into the Longitudinal Study (see Chapter 13).

Figure 11.5 shows the annual average net flows between the five parts of the UK for 1981–84 and 1987–89. The basic pattern is the well-known one of influx towards London from the more distant parts of the UK and net outward movement from London to closer areas. On the other hand, while this pattern appears to have been fairly stable between the two periods (with only two changes in direction of net flow), some sizeable changes are evident in the volume of flows. In particular, London's annual supply of migrants to ROSE grew by 25,000 in net terms, its contribution to the adjacent counties (CASE) doubled to over 9,000, and its exchange with RSMW reversed direction to supply 6,000 in contrast to its earlier net gain of 2,500 from there. The single most noteworthy change, however, is the increase of 29,000 in the net migration from ROSE to RSMW. This compares with the much smaller contribution made by the seven adjacent counties to the South East's migration overspill. CASE took merely an extra 5,000 from London and only 10,000 more from ROSE, and this was made possible only because CASE itself switched to net loss to RSMW and received far fewer from RUK.

The overall effect of these changes is summarised in the 'Total' column of Table 11.5. This makes clear that the late 1980s was characterised by two major departures from the earlier situation. One was the upturn in outflow from London, and the other was the significant contraction of ROSE's net internal migration gain. The combined effect of these two changes was a marked increase in net migration from the South East. The latter appears to have impacted not so much on the immediately adjacent counties which saw only a very small increase in net in-migration, but leap-frogged over them into the rest of the South, Midlands and Wales.

Table 11.5 also provides information about the age structure changes resulting from these flows on the basis of six broad age groups. London has a distinctive net migration schedule, with net out-migration of all age groups except 15–24-year-olds. This has been noted by previous research, though the strength of net in-migration of 15-24-year-olds is a particular feature of the 1980s (it has been running at only around 5,000 a year in the mid-1970s, barely a quarter of its 1980s average). All age groups contributed to the acceleration in London's exodus between the early and late 1980s, but the upturn in decentralisation was primarily due to the 25–44 and 0–14 age groups, i.e. dominated by parents and their children. By contrast, ROSE experienced changes in the direction of net flows as well as in their size. Traditionally, ROSE has constituted the mirror image of London, with net gains of all age groups except 15–24-year-olds, as was still the situation in 1981–84. By the late 1980s, however, ROSE had begun to take on features more usually associated with London, comprising a switch to net losses of older working and retirement age groups, a downward shift in the positive balances for younger working age and children, and a major change for the 15–24-year-olds into substantial net inflow. This latter feature is also found for the seven adjacent counties (CASE), which by contrast also saw some acceleration in in-migration of the 25–44 age group at the expense of older people.

Basically, changes in migration in the later 1980s suggest an outward ripple to places more distant from London of the type of migration patterns traditionally associated with places closer to it; a corresponding change in the importance of job considerations in migration decisions is therefore implied. By 1987–89 the retirement and older working age groups were, in net terms, spilling not only out of London but also out of ROSE and were not being channelled into the adjacent counties (CASE) so much as to more distant areas including the northern half of the country (Table 11.5). The 25–44 and 0–14 age groups were being squeezed in like fashion, though less so for the former, suggesting that larger families were moving further away from London than those

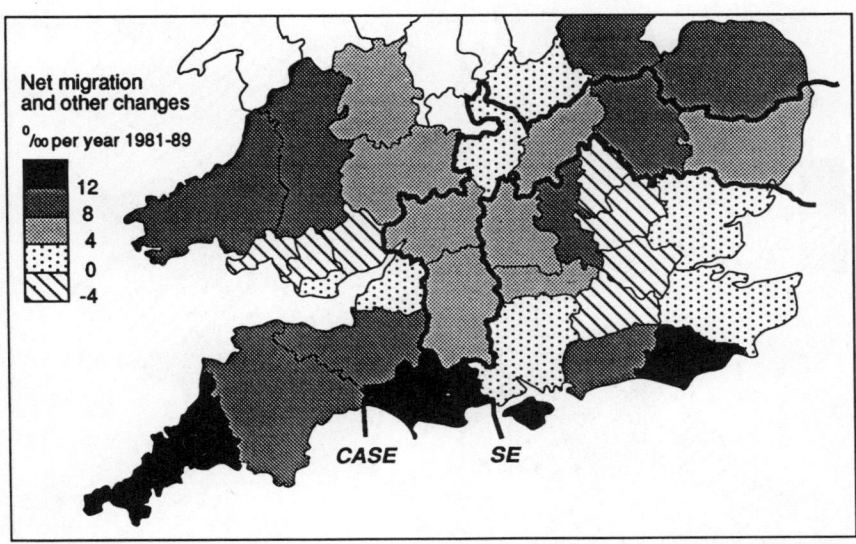

Figure 11.6   Net migration rates by county, 1981–89

25–44-year-olds who were childless or at an earlier stage of family building. These contrasts may in turn be related to house price differences: most important for retirees, least for childless adults of younger working age. Finally, the 15–24-year-olds – the age group most in need of access to employment opportunities and further education facilities and also least demanding in their choice of housing – were shifting away from the North in greater numbers at the end of the 1980s than previously, and were increasingly destined for ROSE (and, to a lesser extent, CASE) rather than for London.

11.5 The county dimension

An examination of migration patterns at the county scale can provide extra insight into the developments of the 1980s and, in particular, reveal how it was that the adjacent counties (CASE) failed to play a bigger role in accommodating pressures from London and ROSE. Figure 11.6 shows rates of population change due to 'net migration and other changes' calculated from the 1981–89 OPCS mid-year estimates for a rather broader area than the South as defined for this chapter.

Two points are most relevant to the present context. First is the fact that during the 1980s it was not only London that experienced overall migration loss, but also Bedfordshire, Hertfordshire and Surrey. This, along with the comparatively low migration gains recorded by Essex, Kent and Hampshire, helps to clarify why ROSE appears to have been able to receive the large volume of migration from London only by itself

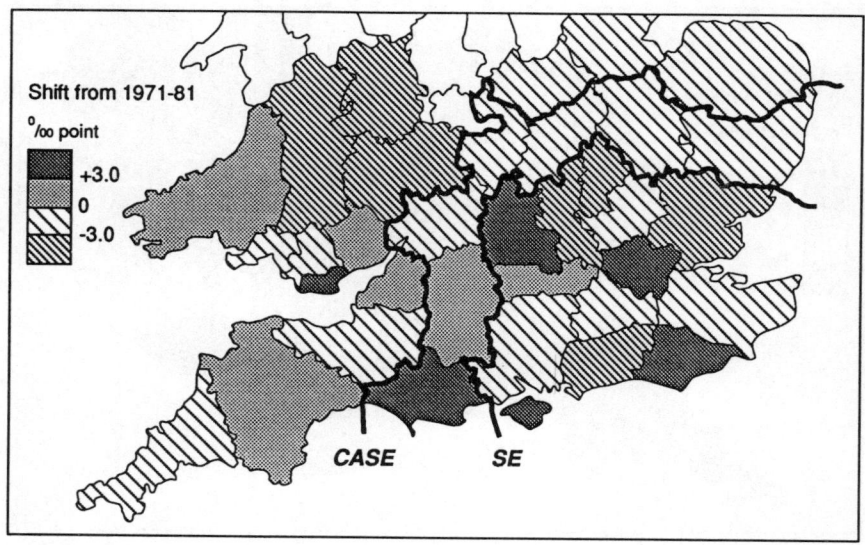

Figure 11.7　Net migration rate shifts by county, 1971–81 to 1981–89

sending large numbers elsewhere.

The other point is the low rate of growth achieved by most of the adjacent counties (CASE) compared with the majority of more distant ones in the South and surrounding regions. Of the seven, only Dorset and Cambridgeshire average net migration gains of more than 8 per 1,000 a year, whereas this rate was achieved by all other counties in the rest of the South bar Avon, as well as by Lincolnshire, Powys and Dyfed further out still.

Figure 11.7 shows the sizeable cutbacks in the rate of net migration inflow which this meant for many of the ROSE counties as compared with their overall performance in the previous decade. West Sussex, Buckinghamshire, Bedfordshire and Essex all saw their annual net in-migration rate move downwards by three per 1,000 or more between 1971–81 and 1981–89, while several other ROSE counties saw some diminution, as did five of the seven adjacent counties. Besides East Sussex and the Isle of Wight, the only counties in the South outside London that experienced an upward shift in net migration rate in the 1980s were located in a broad version of the 'M4 corridor' and in parts of the far west.

An even bigger contrast across the South, however, is evident in the trends during the 1980s, reflecting a shift in the main focus of net migration gains from ROSE in the early stages of the decade out into the more remote counties in the later years. Comparison of the NHSCR data for 1987–89 with 1981–84 reveals particularly large downward shifts in annual migration balance for Hertfordshire (− 5,760), West Sussex, Essex, Berkshire, Hampshire and Dorset (all − 2,500 or more). Meanwhile, three

Table 11.6 Annual averages of net migration between selected counties and five regional subdivisions of the UK, 1981–89

County	London	ROSE	CASE	RSMW	RUK	Total
			Annual averages			
Hertfordshire						
1981–84	6,217	− 3,037	− 1,535	− 753	720	1,612
1987–89	9,769	− 5,848	− 3,726	− 4,224	− 119	− 4,115
Shift	3,552	− 2,811	− 2,191	− 3,471	− 839	− 5,757
Hampshire						
1981–84	1,370	2,737	− 710	232	2,331	5,960
1987–89	3,093	4,662	− 1,161	− 3,430	32	3,196
Shift	1,723	1,925	− 451	− 3,198	− 2,299	− 2,764
Norfolk						
1981–84	1,276	1,836	− 70	740	917	4,699
1987–89	2,506	4,582	834	− 453	− 196	7,273
Shift	1,230	2,746	904	− 1,193	− 1,113	2,574
Devon						
1981–84	588	2,557	489	1,105	1,591	6,330
1987–89	2,209	6,513	934	1,189	561	11,406
Shift	1,621	3,956	445	84	− 1,030	5,076

Notes: (i) Counties are arranged in order of shift in total net migration.
  (ii) ROSE = Rest of the South East; CASE = Counties adjacent to the South East; RSMW = Rest of the South, Midlands and Wales; RUK = Rest of the UK.
Source: Calculated from NHSCR data.

of the largest upward shifts (+ 2,500 or more) took place in the most remote counties of the South (Devon, Cornwall and Norfolk), but five others were in even more distant locations – Derbyshire, Staffordshire, Lincolnshire, Nottinghamshire and Shropshire.

Part of this analysis is reproduced in Table 11.6, focusing on four counties which span the range between high downward and upward shifts in migration balance during the 1980s. All these counties were affected by the acceleration in the exodus from London and together provide evidence of the widespread impact which this had. Note the increased migration loss from Hertfordshire to other parts of ROSE and the greater intake by the other three counties of people migrating from ROSE. In their turn, Norfolk and Devon registered significant increases in net in-migration from CASE, while except in one case there were reductions in the net volume of inflows from RSMW and RUK, with some instances of a switch to a net exodus to these other parts of the country.

11.6 Implications for the 'Greater South East' concept

Clearly the impacts of the recent migration changes in the South East spread out far beyond the region as officially defined and raise important questions over the validity of the concept of the 'Greater South East'. Are flows within the entire UK being re-oriented in such a way as to support the notion of some more extensive metropolitan region focused on London and, if so, over what scale of area? What effects derive from the enhanced links between the peripheral counties of the standard South East and the adjoining counties of the other standard regions?

One approach to this issue is to undertake a cluster analysis of migration flows, using a hierarchical procedure (Masser and Brown, 1975). This procedure is used to group the 97 FPC areas in the NHSCR's entire UK data set into eight zones on the basis of the difference between the actual migration flows and the flows expected on the basis of statistical independence. These deviations are used to form zones in such a way that the proportion of total migration which takes place within the zones is maximised and the proportion between zones is minimised.

The results of three pairs of analyses are presented in Table 11.7 in so far as they relate to the South. These are for all migrants and for two specific age groups representing retirement migrants and younger working ages most likely to be in the main period of family-building, while each pair compares the situation in the early 1980s with that later in the decade. In all but one of the analyses it can be seen that the South, as defined for this chapter, divides into two, or at the most three, of the eight zones produced for the UK by the clustering procedure.

The all-ages analysis shows a significant swing in allegiance for central southern England over the decade and the incorporation of the far west into an essentially 'southern' migration system by the late 1980s (Table 11.7, first two columns). In 1981–84 the migration linkages of the main part of the South are clearly focused on London and the South East, with a northward extension into Northamptonshire and East Anglia, leaving the South East and the southern half of Wales as a separate zone (and the Isle of Wight as an isolated oddity). In the latter part of the decade, however, it is found that a split has appeared within the South East, with its north-eastern counties continuing to be grouped with East Anglia but with the South's migration patterns now being dominated by strong linkages welding together the remainder of ROSE, the South West and the southern half of Wales. This new division reflects the increase in the importance of ROSE in the South's migration patterns at the expense of London, as well as the way in which ROSE counties tend to orientate themselves in broad sectors out into the more remote counties.

The same is broadly true for the 25–44 age group, showing the important influence which this group exercises over the total migration picture. The only significant difference from the all-ages result is that the three East Anglian counties form their own migration zone at both dates used for this part of the analysis (1980–81 and 1985–86), suggesting lower

Table 11.7 Migration clusters for the South

County	All ages		25–44		60 +	
	81–84	87–89	80–81	85–86	80–81	85–86
Norfolk	1	1	1	3	1	1
Suffolk	1	1	1	3	1	1
Cambridgeshire	1	1	1	3	1	1
Essex	1	1	1	1	1	1
Hertfordshire	1	1	1	1	1	1
Bedfordshire	1	1	1	1	1	1
Northamptonshire	1	–	–	2	1	1
Buckinghamshire	1	2	1	2	1	1
Kent	1	2	1	1	2	2
East Sussex	1	2	1	2	2	2
West Sussex	1	2	1	2	2	2
Surrey	1	2	1	2	2	2
Hampshire	1	2	1	2	2	2
Berkshire	1	2	1	2	2	2
Oxfordshire	1	2	1	2	2	2
Isle of Wight	4	2	4	2	2	2
Dorset	2	2	2	2	2	2
Wiltshire	2	2	2	2	2	2
Cornwall	2	2	2	2	2	2
Devon	2	2	2	2	2	2
Somerset	2	2	2	2	2	2
Avon	2	2	2	2	2	2
Gloucestershire	2	2	2	2	5	2
South & Central Wales	2	2	2	2	–	2

Notes: (i)   See text for clustering methodology.
   (ii) Numbers refer to common membership of a cluster in each
         separate analysis: 1 = cluster which includes Essex/Herts/Beds;
         2 = cluster which includes most counties of the South West
         region; 3 = East Anglia (where separate); 4 = Isle of Wight
         (where separate); 5 = Gloucestershire (where separate); – =
         county not in a cluster represented in the South.
   (iii) South & Central Wales refers to Dyfed, Powys, Gwent, and West,
         Mid and South Glamorgan.
   (iv) The London FPCs were included in the analysis, but are not
         shown here.

levels of migration linkage from London and ROSE in this direction than
westwards from London.

Finally, it is interesting to see that the broad 'southern' migration zone
which the all-ages and 25–44 analyses produced for the later periods used
had been anticipated by the retirement age-group by the beginning of the
decade (Table 11.7, last two columns). In 1980–81 the retirement migration linkages already split the South into a smaller north-east zone and
a much larger zone across the south and west of the region, which

remained remarkably stable except for spreading even further to include Gloucestershire and much of Wales.

This analysis therefore largely confirms the observations derived from the county-level calculations in the previous section, showing the complex and very extensive nature of the migration systems which help to produce population change in the South. All the evidence points to an important change taking place during the 1980s, with the South East forming a fairly self-contained system early in the decade but with no clear image of a 'Greater South East' later, least of all in terms of a compact area embracing just the adjacent counties.

More research is merited on the South's migration patterns and their relationship to other aspects of regional structure. In particular, the robustness of the above results needs to be examined by reference to alternative methods of clustering. In this context the finding on the younger age groups following the patterns pioneered by retirement migrants is noteworthy, because it conforms to previous observations in the counterurbanisation literature (Champion, 1989a; Kontuly and Vogelsang, 1989). Further work should also study the extent to which the degree of change in the 1980s has been paralleled by previous experience and examine the full matrix of inter-county migration flows, including the analyses by other variables besides age using the 1991 Census results.

11.7 Explaining the migration trends of the 1980s

These analyses point to a dramatic reorientation of internal migration flows during the 1980s, with the principal elements being the increasing volume and geographical spreading of centrifugal movements from the heart of the South East. As regards explanations, several possible causal factors can be put forward and to some extent quantified, as follows:

1. Differential job growth, with higher growth in the 'sun-belt' counties, especially those on the M4 corridor. This particularly applies to growth-sector jobs such as financial services which have shown highest job growth in less urbanised labour markets (especially freestanding towns) in the South.
2. Access to cheaper housing and higher levels of development of new housing, especially in the private sector. (Public sector additions were still high in the early 1980s in some New Towns but have since dwindled to insignificance.)
3. Transport developments serving to widen the commuter catchment areas of the South East, and particularly London. These include road improvements such as the M40, M11 and A1(M), together with the electrification of the Liverpool Street rail-link to Kings Lynn via Cambridge and the upgrading of services on the East Coast main line and of the line from St Pancras to Bedford and beyond.
4. Amenity and environmental factors, including access to the countryside, which underpinned much of the intermediate-distance

migration associated with counterurbanisation in the 1970s and which in recent years have become more heavily weighted in favour of more remote parts of the South as development pressures on the South East counties increased.

Table 11.8 attempts a partial analysis of the 1980s migration re-orientation. It presents regression results linking NHSCR migration data in 1981–84 and 1984–87 to changes in total jobs, growth in financial services, house price differentials and new private housing supply. These variables do not directly measure explanatory factors (3) and (4) above, but are interconnected with them; for example, inclusion of a population density index (a crude index of a less urbanised environment) in addition to new housing, house prices, etc., tended to produce unexpected effects in the latter, pointing to collinearity. The regression is via a general linear approach with correction for extra-Poisson heterogeneity. It is applied to migration flows specific for both origin and destination and extends the gravity model to include housing and labour market variables (Congdon and Champion, 1989b). The analysis is for the 13 counties of the South East (with all London FPCs aggregated to form a single county) plus the seven adjacent counties.

The analysis for all persons in the upper panel of Table 11.8 shows constant gravity parameters (the effects of distance and population mass at origin and destination), showing there is no decline in 'distance deter-rence' *per se*. However, comparison of columns (A) and (B) for 1981–84 and 1984–87 respectively shows a marked increase in the impact of house price differentials – both the push effect of higher prices at origin and the pull effect of lower prices at destination. In the earlier period the push effect is only weakly significant and the pull effect not so, whereas in the latter period both are. This is evidence for the impact of the house price inflation of these years on migration. The enhancement of the house price effect would obviously increase the tendency for migration to be directed more to the peripheral counties.

The impact of new housing is relatively stable, with only the destina-tion effect being consistent with migration equilibration in the housing market. Effects of total job growth are relatively weak, though equilibra-tion in total job change seems to characterise the later 'boom' period as against the recession period of the early 1980s. If we consider the growth of the financial services sector, however, then a destination effect is significant – a sectoral impact which may be linked to the selectivity of migrants by income and skill group.

Regressions for different age groups are shown in the lower panel of Table 11.8. They suggest, first, the greater impact of house price differentials and new housing on family and retirement migrants as against young (15–24) and mostly single labour migrants; and, secondly, the most pronounced impact of house price differentials on the retired and pre-retirement age groups expecting or receiving lower incomes and making a capital gain on the retirement move. The growth sector effect of financial services is apparent for all labour market age groups, but as

Table 11.8 Regression analyses of inter-county migration flows for the South East and its seven adjacent counties in the 1980s

	(A) 1981–84		(B) 1984–87		(C) 1984–87		(D) 1984–87	
Variable	Parameter	T-ratio	Parameter	T-ratio	Parameter	T-ratio	Parameter	T-ratio
Constant	−6.849	2.45	−6.013	2.28	−4.095	1.47	−5.526	2.11
Distance	−1.294	24.37	−1.306	24.65	−1.305	24.53	−1.304	24.83
Population (origin)	0.9856	20.95	0.9698	21.00	0.9486	22.11	0.9720	21.60
Population (destination)	0.8859	18.85	0.8443	18.37	0.8490	19.87	0.8541	19.00
House prices (origin)	0.2958	1.59	0.4584	2.68	0.4542	2.50	0.4325	2.51
House prices (destination)	−0.1087	0.58	−0.3003	1.76	−0.4738	2.60	−0.3576	2.07
New private housing (origin)	0.08560	1.27	0.1470	1.75	0.07190	0.93		
New private housing (destination)	0.2306	3.43	0.2493	3.03	0.1788	2.37		
New total housing							0.1788	1.92
New total housing							0.3281	3.53
Growth total jobs (origin)	0.8385	1.16	−1.053	1.19			−1.018	1.21
Growth total jobs (destination)	0.6735	0.93	0.1287	0.15			0.1349	0.16
Growth financial services (origin)					0.2930	0.54		
Growth financial services (destination)					1.331	2.46		
Degrees of freedom (= generalised Chi square)	370		370		370		370	
Phi statistic	0.294		0.308		0.314		0.305	

Variable	Age groups, 1984–87							
	16–24		25–44		45–59		60 +	
	Parameter	T-ratio	Parameter	T-ratio	Parameter	T-ratio	Parameter	T-ratio
Constant	−12.23	3.98	−5.794	2.04	−4.923	1.30	−11.53	2.52
Distance	−1.268	21.60	−1.445	26.59	−1.325	18.35	−0.9753	11.16
Population (origin)	0.8534	17.58	1.045	23.04	0.9159	14.90	0.8251	11.48
Population (destination)	0.9891	20.25	0.9469	21.13	0.7559	12.64	0.6954	9.80
House prices (origin)	0.2885	1.44	0.2885	1.56	0.8324	3.38	1.238	4.14
House prices (destination)	0.1536	0.77	−0.4953	2.67	−0.9568	3.88	−0.7159	2.39
New private housing (origin)	0.08704	1.01	0.1785	2.22	−0.03621	0.34	−0.3146	2.45
New private housing (destination)	0.1160	1.37	0.3023	3.87	0.2957	2.85	0.3887	3.12
Growth financial services (origin)	0.3431	0.57	0.2827	0.51	0.1651	0.22	−0.02510	0.03
Growth financial services (destination)	1.435	2.40	1.310	2.37	1.436	1.96	−0.5470	0.62
Degrees of freedom (=generalised)	370		370		370		370	
Chi square	370		370		370		370	
Phi statistic	0.354		0.297		0.401		0.513	

would be expected, has no effect on retirement moves. It is notable that the least distance deterrence relates to retirement moves and the highest deterrence to moves assumed to be mostly by families (the 25–44 group).

Thus the migration realignments noted in Table 11.7, particularly for middle-age groups (25–59) can be linked both to housing and labour market factors. Further analysis by socio-economic group would be desirable to show the impact of income as well as age selectivity on these findings. The 1991 Census will also provide the opportunity of examining the precise relationship of these migration trends to change in commuting patterns; for instance, one can compare the workplaces of migrants and non-migrants to infer the extent to which migrants switch their workplace to their new area of residence (Congdon and Champion, 1989b).

11.8 Conclusions: looking back and looking forward

The 1980s brought some major developments in population and migration for the South. Most impressive in the early part of the decade was the recovery of London's population change rate from the massive levels of migration loss of the 1970s, brought about principally by a reduction in the exodus to other parts of the South during the recession but also by greater net inflows from the rest of the UK and overseas as the economy began to pick up again through the 1980s. By contrast, the mid–late 1980s were dominated by a resumption of centrifugal movement, deriving most notably from London but also featuring knock-on effects of outward flows from the rest of the South East and the surrounding counties. This 'ripple' pattern seems to have been closely associated with developments in housing and labour markets, involving the outward shift of people and firms in search of the cheaper housing and business premises and the less congested environment and operating conditions. Before the end of the decade, however, this process had ground to a halt, with the collapse of the South East's property boom and the onset of renewed economic recession induced partly by the government's attempt to put a brake on runaway inflation tendencies.

This last development of the 1980s serves a valuable purpose in reminding researchers to exercise caution in interpreting the patterns of the 1980s and in using them as a basis for projecting trends through the rest of the 1990s. In attempting the latter, the key question is whether or not the 1980s constituted a period of revolutionary change for London and the South. With the decade now over, the record provided by the migration data smacks – superficially, at least – of a degree of cyclic fluctuation overlying some powerful continuing trends, particularly when seen in its longer-term context. In particular, a parallel can be drawn between the South's experience since 1975 and that of the previous 15–20 years which were characterised initially by the 'drift to the South East' and then by massive centrifugal shifts. Even if this is so, however, fundamental differences do arise because each period begins with a new starting point in terms of the new patterns of people, housing, jobs, etc., put into place by the previous round of changes. The two most significant developments have been the fuller incorporation of much of the South East into London's metropolitan economy and the rapid growth of some major urban centres in the outer parts of the South East and in the adjacent regions. Their implications for future population trends in the South will become much better known, once the nature of these developments and their relationships to migration and commuting can be explored in more detail by reference to other sources, most notably the 1991 Census of Population.

Acknowledgements
This chapter draws heavily on the data provided by the Office of Population Censuses and Surveys, most notably the mid-year population estimates, estimates on the components of change, the National Health Service Central Register data on internal migration, and international migration data derived from the International Passenger Survey; these data are Crown Copyright. The regression analyses include variables calculated from the Census of Employment and from the Nationwide Anglia Building Society's mortgage-lending records. The authors are also grateful to Ann Rooke for the cartography.

PART III

SYSTEMATIC PERSPECTIVES

12 Migration and employment
David Owen

12.1 Introduction

Individuals are induced to migrate by a variety of events in their lives, and often as a result of a combination of changes in their circumstances. Among the most important of these events are changes in an individual's position in the labour market, into or out of employment, or from one type of employment into another. In the study of aggregate migration patterns, it is often implicitly or explicitly assumed that the movement of population from place to place is influenced by the changing spatial pattern of employment opportunities. This chapter is concerned with identifying the relationship between migration and employment in Great Britain, using recent data on migration and employment trends, and survey evidence on the nature of employment-related migration.

In the first substantive section of this chapter, the main dimensions of economic change in Britain during the 1980s are outlined in greater detail, with particular emphasis on regional differentials. The role of migration in labour market adjustment is explored in the second substantive section. Distinctions between different types of migration flows and economic status and occupational differentials in propensities to migrate are identified. In the third substantive section, data from three Labour Force Surveys (LFS) are used to explore inter-regional variations in propensities to migrate and spatial patterns of job-related flows. Finally, the key points emerging from the analysis are summarised and discussed in the conclusion.

12.2 Employment trends in Great Britain

Britain has experienced widely fluctuating economic fortunes during the last twenty years. The 1970s saw the ending of the post-war boom and then a series of increasingly severe recessions within overall conditions of 'stagflation', but relatively high levels of employment and manufacturing output. The decade ended amidst intense recession, marked by substantial declines in employment and output. The ensuing recovery was slow and painful at first, before the economy changed gear in the second half of the 1980s, with economic growth proceeding at breakneck speed and official levels of unemployment falling rapidly through the influence of

Table 12.1 Employment change by region, 1971-89

Region	1971 (000s)	Change 1971–81 (%)			1981 (000s)	Change 1981–89 (%)			1989 (000s)
		Total	Manufac-turing	Services		Total	Manufac-turing	Services	
South East	3,305	9.9	−12.5	24.5	3,632	11.8	−11.9	26.5	4,054
East Anglia	607	10.5	−4.6	25.8	670	14.0	−1.6	33.4	763
Gtr London	3,937	−10.4	−36.1	−0.2	3,528	−1.0	−34.6	9.1	3,488
South West	1,426	7.7	−11.5	21.3	1,536	11.7	−6.7	25.9	1,713
West Midlands	2,207	−8.8	−28.5	14.7	2,012	3.3	−12.8	20.2	2,077
East Midlands	1,413	2.7	−15.6	24.2	1,451	6.0	−6.9	26.5	1,536
Yorks & Humberside	1,916	−4.9	−26.9	14.8	1,823	3.6	−11.2	20.3	1,885
North West	2,656	−8.5	−29.3	8.8	2,430	−0.6	−16.6	11.1	2,413
North	1,206	−7.7	−26.4	11.5	1,114	−0.5	−16.6	14.5	1,107
Wales	962	−3.6	−26.6	17.1	927	4.3	2.2	16.2	966
Scotland	2,003	−1.7	−26.9	15.0	1,969	0.0	−18.7	10.6	1,967
Great Britain	21,638	−2.5	−24.3	13.5	21,092	4.3	−14.3	17.9	21,969

Source: Census of Employment (via NOMIS).

worldwide economic expansion, and a domestic consumer boom fuelled by an unprecedented expansion of credit. The macroeconomic measures then taken to dampen this boom were themselves largely responsible, in combination with deteriorating world economic conditions, for the emergence of another deep recession at the end of the 1980s and in the early 1990s.

Since the mid-1960s, there has been a continued shift in the industrial structure of employment from manufacturing to services, and in the occupational composition of employment from manual to non-manual occupations (notably those requiring high levels of skill) across all industries. Manufacturing industries have adopted increasingly capital-intensive production methods, which have dramatically raised labour productivity but resulted in job losses due to sluggish output growth, and have also tended to relocate routine production facilities to regions of the world with lower labour costs. Manual workers – notably the unskilled – have borne the brunt of the resulting job losses in Britain, whilst non-manual workers have gained from the increased importance of managerial, technical and knowledge-based occupations. Table 12.1 shows that manufacturing employment fell by nearly a quarter between 1971 and 1981, not quite made up for by the 13.5 per cent growth in employment in service industries. Increased demand in the mid- and late 1980s resulted in growth in manufacturing employment, and hence employment in this sector declined by only 14.3 per cent between 1981 and 1989, compared with a growth of nearly 18 per cent in service sector employment. The return of severe recession conditions in the early 1990s has once again resulted in job losses in manufacturing industry, which has followed the newer service industries whose growth was dependent upon rising real incomes, into recession.

Within this overall national context, in which aggregate employment was only 300 thousand greater in 1989 than 1971, there has been a marked inter-regional shift of employment. In general terms, the South (defined as London, the South East, East Anglia, the South West and East Midlands) has tended to suffer least from recession conditions and gain more from economic recoveries than the North (the remainder of Britain). With the exception of the decentralisation of employment from London to the rest of the South East, the southern regions displayed the strongest employment growth in both the 1970s and the 1980s, with the small regions of East Anglia and the South West growing fastest, but the South East containing the bulk of new employment growth. The highly industrialised West Midlands, North West and North suffered the greatest declines in the 1970s, with smaller declines in Wales, Yorkshire and Humberside and Scotland. The North West and North continued to perform worse than any other regions in the 1980s, but Wales, the West Midlands and Yorkshire and Humberside experienced notable recovery. Throughout the period 1971–89, the South experienced more favourable employment trends in both manufacturing and services, but employment growth in Yorkshire and Humberside and the West Midlands in the 1980s was underpinned by the strong growth of service employment in these regions, while the recovery of Wales resulted from an increase in manufacturing employment, in strong contrast the North West, North and Scotland, where manufacturing employment declined at the fastest rates and service sector employment growth was most sluggish.

Overall, employment opportunities contracted by 535 thousand between 1971 and 1989 in the North, and expanded by 866 thousand in the South, with the greatest contractions occurring in the West Midlands and North West. Hence, in the context of continuing population growth, the availability of employment opportunities became much more strongly biased towards the southern part of Britain during this period, leading to considerable concern about the emergence of a growing 'North–South divide', and debate about how this could be lessened (Champion and Green, 1988; Green, 1988; Martin, 1988). The combination of massive job losses and demographic pressure led unemployment to rise above three million in the early 1980s, with huge spatial variations in unemployment rates. This resulted in the awakening of political interest in the role of migration in reducing these differentials. At the 1981 Conservative Party Conference, Margaret Thatcher and Norman Tebbit argued that the prevailing economic circumstances demanded the movement of 'workers to the work'. Tebbit went on to make the notorious statement that even in the depths of recession, workers could still find work if they 'got on their bikes' and looked for it. His statement implied both the necessity of labour migration for labour market adjustment and the inadequacies of prevailing patterns of job search behaviour, with the failure of labour markets to clear the huge total of unemployed being interrupted as a clear indicator of the existence of rigidities (Department of Employment, 1985) such as minimum wage rates, employment protection policies, and excessive trade union power, the removal of which became adopted as Government policy. The remainder of the chapter will examine the role of migration in alleviating unemployment differentials, and the extent and characteristics of job-related migration in the 1980s.

12.3 Migration models and employment-related migration

Both this political response and academic attempts to explain patterns of migration have been powerfully influenced by neo-classical economic theory. Models of factor equalisation developed in this tradition assume that factors of production (labour and capital) will be attracted to the areas offering the highest returns. Thus, any spatial inequalities in wages or profits which emerge will eventually be ironed out over time by migration of labour and capital from areas of low returns to areas of high returns. Movement of labour from low-wage areas into areas of high wages serves to increase labour supply and force the wage rates down in the favoured areas and by reducing the availability of labour, increase competition for workers by employers and hence push wages up in the less-favoured areas. Models based on this theory have been used to account for net migration of population from less to more prosperous areas. However, in estimating such a model which related inter-regional net migration to differences in unemployment rates and wages in Britain, Pissarides and Wadsworth (1987) showed that the equilibrating effects of migration upon regional labour markets operated only in the very long run.

An alternative perspective on migration in response to labour market differentials is offered by human capital theory, which is concerned with the response of individuals to perceived differentials in spatial labour markets, in the context of their own circumstances. Sjaastad (1962) suggested that an individual or household migration is carried out in the expectation of being better off. Movement may increase the stock of human capital (measuring skills, experience and knowledge), representing the ability to generate an income stream over a lifetime, or it may produce an increase in 'utility', representing factors such as quality of life. The net gain from moving is a function of the difference between the expected utility or real income in origin and destination areas, minus the costs of moving adjusted by a discount factor, aggregated over remaining lifetime. An individual would choose that destination which maximised the net present value of movement.

Both neoclassical and human capital concepts of the response of individuals to labour market differentials have been articulated in studies of the role of 'push' and 'pull' factors in determining the level of migration between areas (and to a lesser extent intervening opportunities). Simple gravity models which relate migration between pairs of places to the product of the populations of the origin and destination and the intervening distance have been extended to incorporate independent variables measuring labour market conditions at the origin and destination. Within the context of the distance–decay effect, and the tendency for flows to vary in proportion to the respective masses of the areas involved, migrants tend to be repelled by high rates of unemployment and attracted to areas of high employment growth. However, empirical analyses of migration flows demonstrate that all areas experience both inflows and outflows, with gross migration rates having been found to be closely correlated in each of the last three British Censuses of Population. Levels of gross flows are found to be highest in the most prosperous areas and lowest in the most depressed areas, as shown by Owen and Green (1989). The success of 'push–pull' models has been therefore limited, due to the use of the same variables in each pair of areas to account for both in- and out-migration.

12.4 Aggregate migration patterns and labour market conditions in the 1980s

To provide a context for the remainder of the chapter, Figures 12.1 and 12.2 present the relationship of gross in- and out-migration to employment change at the county scale, using data from the National Health Service Central Register (NHSCR). Figure 12.1 depicts the relationship for 1980–81, at which time employment was falling rapidly in many areas (represented by the rate of employment change between 1978 and 1981). Both

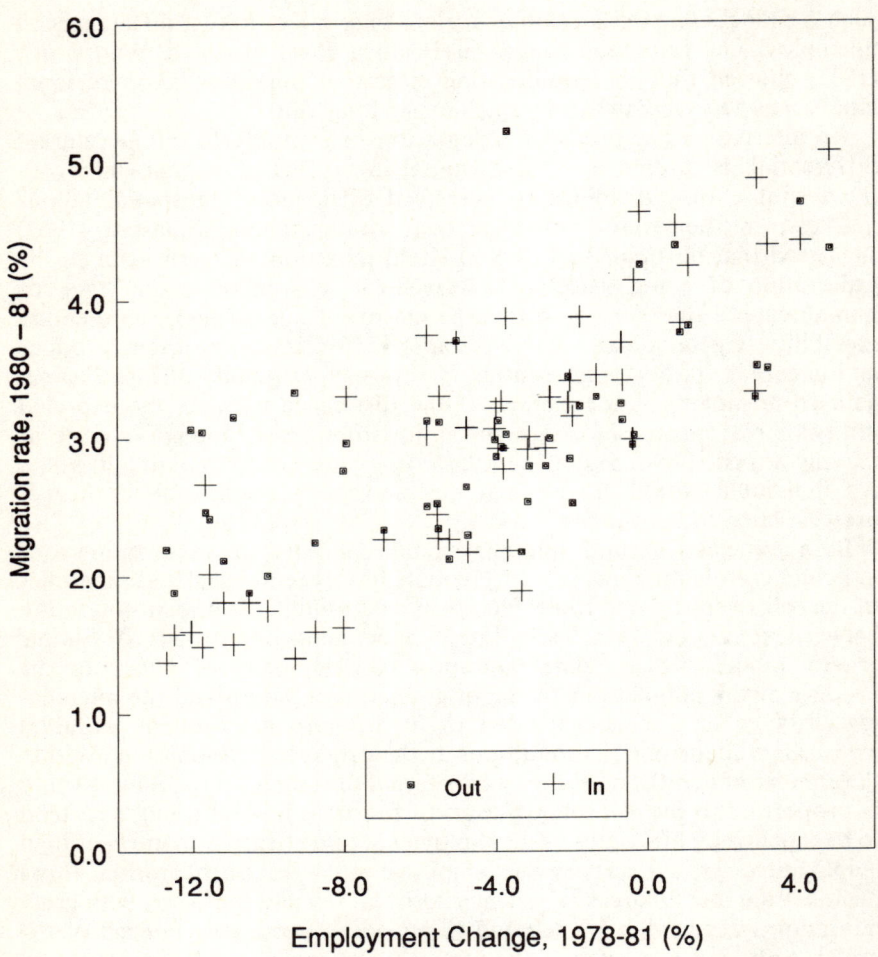

Figure 12.1   Gross in-migration and out-migration rates, 1980–81, and
                  employment change by county of England and Wales, 1978–81

Sources: Census of Employment and NHSCR.

in- and out-migration rates display a fairly close relationship with the
rate of employment change, both being lowest in the counties experiencing fastest employment decline, and highest in areas of employment
growth. By 1987–88, employment growth had resumed, but the relationship between employment change between 1987 and 1989 and gross
migration rates was less obvious; rates of both in- and out-migration
seemed to vary little with employment change, and the dispersion of
migration rates was greater than in 1980–81.

The relationship demonstrated for 1980–81 is consistent with the
results discussed above for Census of Population data. The least

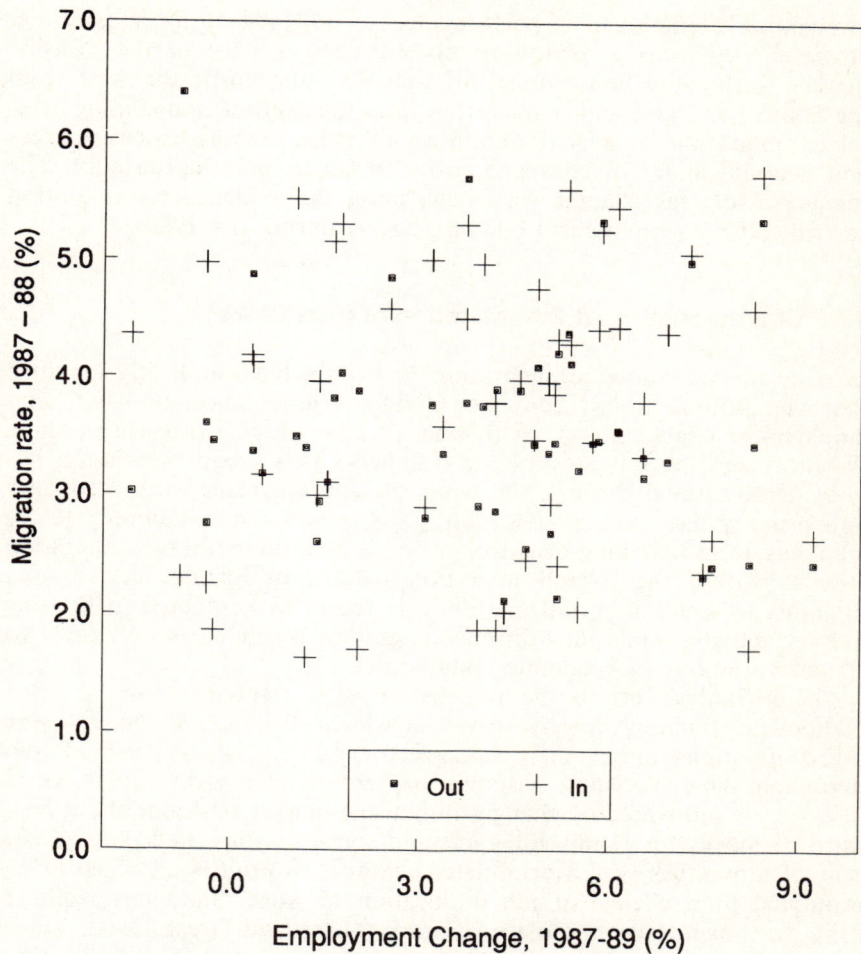

Figure 12.2   Gross in-migration and out-migration rates, 1987–88, and
                  employment change by county of England and Wales, 1987–89

Sources: Census of Employment and NHSCR.

prosperous areas display the lowest levels of mobility, while the more
prosperous areas exhibit high levels of mobility. The potential for
mobility is greatest in the areas of greater prosperity, due to higher levels
of income, the greater availability of employment to migrate to, and
greater activity in the housing market. The less prosperous areas exhibit
lower velocity of both job and housing markets, depressed by persistent
long-term unemployment (Green, 1986), while the high proportion of
council housing in these areas also depresses migration rates, since council tenants tend to be relatively immobile (Hughes and McCormick, 1981,
1987). The similarity of migration rates in areas of favourable and

unfavourable employment performance in 1987–88 is more puzzling. However, this was a period of considerable activity in the housing market, with rapid house price inflation diffusing north and west from the South East, and higher migration rates may reflect non-employment-related migration in order to obtain capital gains in more expensive areas and take advantage of cheaper housing within commuting distance. The remainder of this chapter will focus upon the evidence for migration carried out for employment-related reasons during the 1980s.

12.5 Characteristics of job-related migration flows

Most academic studies of migration in Britain have implicitly assumed that migration flows can be divided into housing-related and employment-related flows, with the former likely to be over short distances and the latter over long distances. This broad association has been demonstrated through the work of Gordon, using both secondary and primary data sources (Gordon, 1988; Gordon and Lamont, 1982), who has identified long-distance, regional and short-distance migration streams within the overall migration pattern in Britain, and among migrants to London. Local migration is found to be related to housing market activity, while long-distance migration is related more closely to spatial variations in economic conditions.

These findings are borne out by detailed responses from a 1981 Nationwide Building Society survey in which all house purchasers were asked questions about their reasons for moving, their personal and household characteristics, distance of moves, etc. Over one-third of moves were motivated by changes in housing market position, about one-third of moves for family life cycle and social reasons, and only 15 per cent of moves were for work-related reasons, two-thirds of which being prompted by a change of job or location of work, and the remainder being to move nearer the place of work (Owen and Green, 1992, Table 2.8). Two-thirds or more of all moves for housing market, family life cycle, social, neighbourhood, and other reasons were over a distance of up to five miles, compared with only one-eighth of job-related moves. By contrast, one-third of all job-related moves were over one hundred miles, compared with three per cent or less in any other category (Owen and Green, 1992, Table 2.1). Moves for work-related reasons accounted for nearly 80 per cent of moves over 100 miles, and for over half of all moves over 25 miles (Owen and Green, 1992, Table 2.2).

The influence of age and household structure factors upon employment-related migration can be investigated through the use of data from the 1987 Labour Force Survey. A clear tendency for job-related mobility rates to decline with age is evident in Table 12.2. Those aged between 16 and 34 years account for 70 per cent of job-related moves; there is little difference in the propensities of 16–24-year-olds and 25–34-year-olds to migrate, but there is a marked decline in employment-related mobility among the older age groups. Turning to the influence of

Table 12.2 Job-related moves by age group, 1986–87

Age group	Job-related moves (%)	Job-related mobility rate (%)
16–24	36.0	3.7
25–34	33.9	3.4
35–49	23.1	1.8
50–65	6.9	0.8

Source: 1987 Labour Force Survey.

Table 12.3 Job-related moves by household type, 1986–87

Household type	Job-related moves (%)	Job-related mobility rate (%)
One adult aged 16–59	12.4	5.6
Two adults aged 16–59	25.6	3.2
Small family	22.1	2.2
Large family	8.2	1.9
Large adult household	29.8	2.0
Two adults, 1 or 2 over 60	1.8	0.8
One adult aged over 60	0.1	0.7

Source: 1987 Labour Force Survey.

household structure, single adults display the greatest propensity to migrate for job-related reasons, followed by households comprising two adults, while households comprised solely of adults in late working age account for a very small proportion of all job-related moves (Table 12.3). Small families exhibit a higher job-related mobility rate than large families. Two-thirds of job-related moves are accounted for by individuals from households comprised solely of adults, suggesting that those with families have greater locational ties (for example, through ties to schools).

Changes in the characteristics of job-related migration as economic conditions changed in the 1980s can be identified by comparing results from the Labour Force Surveys for 1981, 1984 and 1987. Migration tends to take place from positions of economic strength; at each of the three dates, approximately two-thirds of job-related movers were in employment one year previously. The majority of job-related moves are made by people in employment rather than the unemployed, and just over half of those in employment at the time of the survey and one year previously remained in the same occupation and the same industry. This may point to the continued significance of internal labour markets (Salt, 1988) for the organisation of migration in Britain, despite the relative decline of large public and private sector employers (Fielding and Savage, 1987).

Table 12.4 shows the economic circumstances in 1986 of all those

Table 12.4 Economic circumstances one year ago of job-related movers, 1986–87

Economic circumstances, 1986	Job-related movers (%)	Job-related mobility rate (%)
Working	69.5	2.5
Laid off/short time	0.2	6.2
Unemployed	11.4	3.7
On Government scheme	0.8	3.6
Student	11.8	4.4
Retired	0.2	0.3
Looking after family	3.4	0.7
Sick/disabled	0.6	0.5
None of these	2.3	1.2

Source: 1987 Labour Force Survey.

reporting a move for job-related reasons in 1986–87 and associated mobility rates. After those in work, the next two largest groups contributing to job-related migration are students and the unemployed. Together these three groups account for 90 per cent of job-related moves. While the employed make up the bulk of job-related migrants, other groups have a greater likelihood to move for reasons of employment. The importance of geographical movements of students to take up employment in the overall volume of job-related migration is well illustrated, with students displaying a propensity to migrate well above the average for the entire working population. As might be expected, the unemployed, those laid off or on short-time, and those on Government schemes also display higher propensities to migrate in search of work than those in work.

12.5.1 Occupational factors in job-related migration

The occupation demand for labour may be perceived in terms of a hierarchy – with managerial and strategic functions at the apex and unskilled manual jobs at the base. In keeping with the tendency for migrants to move from positions of economic strength, it is to be expected that job-related migrants would be concentrated in higher-status occupational groups and in those occupations which display a propensity to operate in regional and national scale labour markets. By contrast, more 'open' occupational groups, characterised by more localised labour markets, would be expected to display lower job-related mobility rates.

Table 12.5 shows job-related mobility rates (expressed as a proportion of the total workforce) by the nine 'major groups' identified in the Standard Occupational Classification (SOC) devised for the 1991 Census of Population (Thomas and Elias, 1989). Managers and administrators, and those in professional, associate professional and technical, and personal

Table 12.5 Job-related mobility rates by SOC major group, 1980–87

SOC major group	1980–81 (%)	1983–84 (%)	1986–87 (%)
Managers & administrators	2.6	5.0	4.8
Professionals	1.9	4.6	4.9
Assoc. professional & technical	1.9	3.5	4.4
Clerical & secretarial	1.5	1.3	1.4
Craft & skilled manual	0.9	1.2	1.5
Personal & protective service	2.1	4.4	5.0
Sales occupations	1.7	1.8	1.3
Plant & machine operators	1.0	1.2	1.2
Other occupations	1.3	1.6	1.8

Source: 1981, 1984 and 1987 Labour Force Surveys.

Table 12.6 Proportion of job-related moves accounted for by each SOC major group, 1980–87

SOC major group	1980–81 (%)	1983–84 (%)	1986–87 (%)
Managers & administrators	18.8	11.9	22.1
Professionals	9.0	8.4	15.9
Assoc. professional & technical	9.7	8.8	15.3
Clerical & secretarial	17.6	16.9	9.2
Craft & skilled manual	10.4	16.9	9.4
Personal & protective service	8.6	6.9	13.3
Sales occupations	7.7	7.6	3.7
Plant & machine operators	8.2	11.2	4.5
Other occupations	9.9	11.4	6.6

Source: 1981, 1984 and 1987 Labour Force Surveys.

and protective service occupations (a group which includes the armed forces) consistently display above-average propensities to migrate for job-related reasons. By contrast, at the opposite end of the occupational hierarchy, plant and machine operators (corresponding to semi-skilled workers) exhibit among the lowest job-related mobility rates. Increases in job-related activity rates since 1980–81 are most marked for those groups displaying the highest propensities to migrate.

Table 12.6 reveals that the proportion of all job-related moves accounted for by managers and administrators, professionals and associated professional and technical workers rose from 38 per cent in 1980–81 to 53 per cent in 1986–87. These are also the occupational groups which have experienced the highest rates of employment growth over the period. In 1980–81, the craft and skilled manual workers displayed the lowest propensity to migrate of any occupational group, but there is evidence for increased job-related mobility since then. By contrast, there is no such evidence for workers in sales and clerical and secretarial occupations, and for plant and machine operators. Indeed, these three occupational groups accounted for only 17 per cent of all job-related moves in 1986–87, compared with 34 per cent in 1980–81 (Table 12.6).

12.5.2 Implications for spatial variations in job-related migration propensities

Introducing a spatial dimension, an association would be expected between inter-regional and inter-local labour market area job-related migration, on the one hand, and the structure of labour demand and supply on the other. The greater the extent to which employment is concentrated in growing industries and occupations, the greater the number of job opportunities, and hence the higher the level of turnover and vacancies – and the greater the propensity for in-migration. Higher levels of turnover will also result in higher levels of out-migration, as people in growing occupations move to other areas – a spatial expression of career progression.

The fact that managerial and professional workers exhibit among the greatest job-related migration propensities is related to the fact that such workers tend to move in national labour markets, or in internal labour markets with a clear regional or national expression. Their movements would be anticipated to involve both prosperous and depressed local labour market areas. It would be expected that it would usually be possible to fill vacancies in occupations lower down the occupational hierarchy more locally, thus reducing or negating the need for job-related migration in order to fill vacancies. This accounts for the positive association between rates of job-related mobility and position in the occupational pyramid demonstrated above. The occupational concentration of females and part-time workers (who are often tied to specific localities by wider household responsibilities and low rates of pay) in occupations close to the base of the pyramid will tend to further exaggerate the lower rates of mobility characteristic of workers at the base of the pyramid.

The corollary of inter-occupational variations in job-related migration propensities outlined above is that inter-local labour market area differentials in migration propensities will be related to the occupational structure of the local areas. Thus, the greater the volume of higher-status occupations, the higher the levels of gross in- and out-migration. Conversely, the greater the volume of lower-status occupations, the lower the gross migration rates anticipated. Moreover, it is expected that these static associations will have a temporal as well as a spatial expression. In theory, as growth of high-status occupations increases (as has been the case during the 1980s), so migration propensities would be anticipated to increase. Since the occupations forecast to grow fastest over the medium term are managers, professionals, scientists and technicians, while the employment opportunities for manual and low-skilled workers continue to contract, these differentials are likely to widen in the future, as the potential for obtaining an employment opportunity through migration will be even more strongly related to occupational status.

12.6 Temporal and spatial variations in propensities to migrate and patterns of job-related migration flows

12.6.1 Temporal variations

Analyses of Census of Population and NHSCR migration data have demonstrated that rising mobility of the 1950s and 1960s reached a peak in the early 1970s, after which the propensity of the British population to migrate declined as economic conditions worsened through the 1970s (Ogilvy, 1982). The 1981 Census revealed lower rates of mobility than recorded in the 1971 Census. As the economy began to recover through the 1980s, rates of mobility (as measured by the NHSCR data) increased, until the sudden collapse of the housing market in 1989, which resulted in a dramatic reduction in mobility, in advance of renewed recession conditions (Owen and Green, 1992, Figure 2.1).

It is difficult to identify employment-related migration from aggregate migration data, but one simple indicator of migration for employment reasons may be a tendency for migrants to move from higher to lower unemployment-rate areas. Figure 12.3 presents the trend in the proportion of all migration flows between counties in England and Wales accounted for by movements from counties with higher to counties with lower unemployment rates between 1975–76 and 1988–89. This proportion varies around 50 per cent, and tended to rise continuously to reach a peak in the later 1980s, afterwards falling. The relatively high figures for the mid-1980s perhaps indicate mobility in search of work at a time of high unemployment, while the decline in the late 1980s may have resulted from the prevailing rapid employment growth, in which employment could be found without the need for migration.

The LFS distinguishes job-related migration flows from all other migration flows taking place in the last year (in 1984 and 1987; in 1981 these were deduced from moves associated with job changes). As indicated above, it is well-established that the majority of flows – even by the economically active – are not related to changes in employment. LFS data reveal that job-related moves accounted for a mere 10–15 per cent of all changes of address in the 1980s. In the UK the gross number of job-related flows rose from 552 thousand in 1980–81, to 770 thousand in 1983–84 and 816 thousand in 1986–87 as economic circumstances improved. However, as Table 12.7 indicates, per head of the population the job-related mobility rates are low.

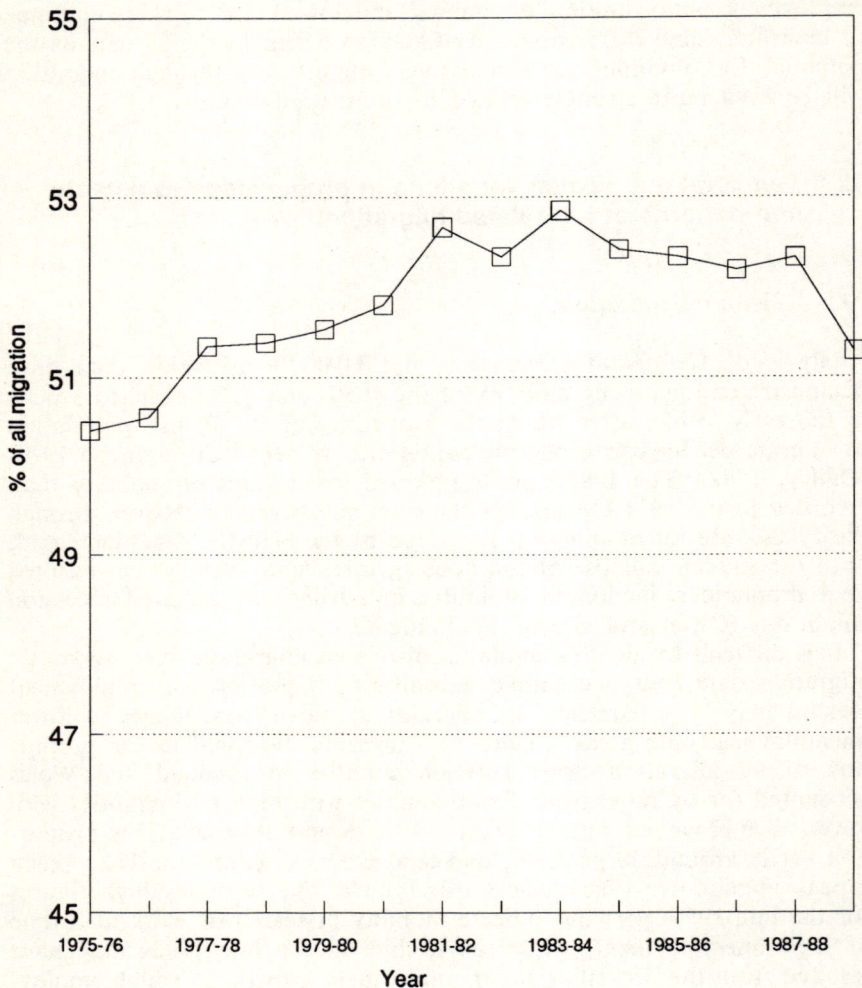

Figure 12.3   Migration from higher- to lower-unemployment counties in
England and Wales, 1975–89

Note: Proportion of all inter-county migrants moving from counties with
higher-unemployment rates to counties with lower-unemployment rates, 1975–
76 to 1988–89.
Source: OPCS NHSCR migration data.

Table 12.7   Job-related mobility rates by region, 1980–87

Region	1980–81 (%)	1983–84 (%)	1986–87 (%)
South East	1.0	1.4	2.0
East Anglia	1.0	1.9	2.5
South West	0.9	1.6	2.9
SOUTH	1.0	1.5	2.3
East Midlands	0.8	1.2	2.3
West Midlands	0.6	1.0	1.0
MIDLANDS	0.7	1.1	1.9
Yorkshire & Humberside	0.8	1.3	2.3
North West	0.6	1.1	2.0
INDUSTRIAL NORTH	0.7	1.1	2.2
North	0.8	0.9	1.9
Wales	0.6	1.0	2.0
Scotland	0.7	1.3	1.9
Northern Ireland	0.5	0.8	1.6
PERIPHERY	0.7	1.1	1.9

Source: 1981, 1984 and 1987 Labour Force Surveys.

12.6.2 Spatial variations in job-related migration propensities

Alongside the temporal variations in migration propensities, there are also significant inter-regional variations in line with theoretical expectations. Table 12.7 shows that all regions witnessed an increase in job-related mobility rates as economic fortunes improved during the 1980s, with the South (the most prosperous part of the UK) consistently recording the highest job-related mobility rates. However, it is interesting to note a marked convergence in the proportions of job-related in-migrants across regions between 1983–84 and 1986–87. Rates were typically two per cent or more in most regions, Northern Ireland and the West Midlands being the least attractive in 1986–87. The long-standing regions of migration gain, East Anglia, the South West and the East Midlands, maintained their attractiveness to job migrants, but Yorkshire and Humberside, and the 'periphery' in general (in particular Wales) greatly increased their attractiveness between 1983–84 and 1986–87. The relative attractiveness of the South East tended to decline during the 1980s.

Job-related net gains and losses at the regional scale are recorded in Table 12.8 and Figure 12.4. The South East, East Anglia and South West recorded net gains in 1980–81, 1983–84 and 1986–87, as the South received an increasing volume of net inflows from the Midlands, the 'industrial North' and the periphery. The East Midlands was a 'net loser' in 1980–81 but thereafter became a 'net gainer', whereas the West Midlands recorded net losses in all three years, with the greatest loss occurring in 1983–84. Figure 12.4 shows that in general the Midlands has

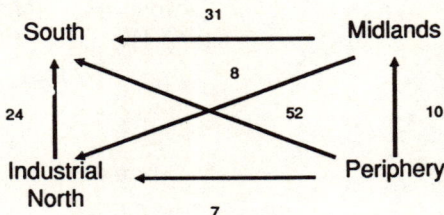

1980-81

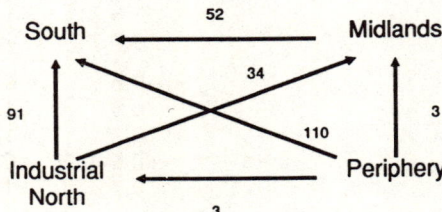

1983-84

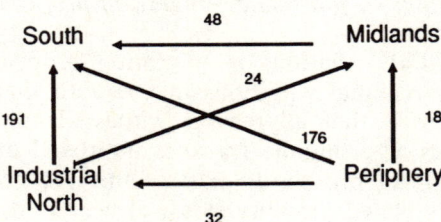

1986-7

South =	South East, East Anglia, South West
Midlands =	West Midlands, East Midlands
Industrial North =	Yorkshire & Humberside, North west
Periphery =	North, Wales, Scotland, N Ireland

Figure 12.4 Job-related net moves between four spatial divisions of the UK, 1980–87

Source: 1981, 1984 and 1987 Labour Force Surveys.

Table 12.8 Job-related net gains or losses by region, 1980–87

Region	1980–81 ('00s)	1983–84 ('00s)	1986–87 ('00s)
South East	+ 18	+ 204	+ 325
East Anglia	+ 56	+ 33	+ 32
South West	+ 15	+ 43	+ 39
East Midlands	– 8	+ 39	+ 10
West Midlands	– 18	– 46	– 16
Yorkshire & Humberside	– 11	– 105	– 141
North West	+ 4	– 13	– 43
North	– 29	– 10	– 48
Wales	– 17	– 42	– 30
Scotland	– 7	– 23	– 86
Northern Ireland	– 17	– 20	– 64

Source: 1981, 1984 and 1987 Labour Force Surveys.

acted as a net exporter of job-related migrants to the South while impor-
ting such migrants from the industrial North and the periphery. All
regions in the industrial North and the periphery recorded net losses in
1980–81, 1983–84 and 1986–87, with the exception of the North West in
1980–81. In general, these net losses have become greater in absolute
terms as national economic recovery has proceeded, reflecting higher
rates of job-related mobility. Net exports from the industrial North to
the South (the overwhelmingly most important destination for job-related
migrants) rose from 2.4 thousand in 1980–81 to 9.1 thousand in 1983–84
and to 19.1 thousand in 1986–87. The corresponding net exports from
the periphery were 5.2 thousand, 11.0 thousand and 17.6 thousand.
Obviously, these net figures disguise much larger gross flows.

Table 12.9 shows regional variations in job-related mobility rates for
those in work and the unemployed over the same period. The share of
job-related migrants accounted for by those in work one year ago ranges
from 61 per cent in Northern Ireland to 80 per cent in East Anglia. In
general, those in work one year ago form a smaller proportion of job-
related migrants in the periphery than in the Midlands, the industrial
North or the South. The propensity of those in work to migrate is
highest in the South and the lowest in the periphery. However, the West
Midlands records the lowest propensity for those in work to migrate than
any other region with the exception of Northern Ireland. The proportion
of job-related migrants accounted for by those unemployed one year ago
appears to be positively associated with the regional rate of unemployment: less than 10 per cent of job-related migrants in the South were
unemployed one year ago compared with 16 per cent in the periphery,
demonstrating that the unemployed in the less favoured regions have
used migration as a response to unemployment. However, the propensity
of the unemployed to migrate is highest in the low unemployment regions
of the South. This perhaps indicates the difficulties of moving over long

Table 12.9 Regional variations in economic circumstances one year ago of job-related migrants, 1986–87

| | Economic circumstances one year ago | | | |
| | Working | | Unemployed | |
Region	Job-related movers (%)	Job-related mobility rate (%)	Job-related movers (%)	Job-related mobility rate (%)
South East	67.3	2.7	9.5	5.1
East Anglia	80.0	4.1	7.1	5.2
South West	75.6	3.4	10.5	6.8
SOUTH	70.2	3.0	9.5	5.4
East Midlands	76.2	2.8	11.4	3.9
West Midlands	69.4	1.8	16.5	3.0
MIDLANDS	72.9	2.3	13.8	3.3
Yorkshire & Humberside	71.0	2.2	12.0	2.9
North West	71.1	2.2	11.8	2.4
INDUSTRIAL NORTH	71.0	2.2	11.9	2.6
North	68.7	1.9	16.3	3.3
Wales	60.8	2.1	17.6	3.7
Scotland	66.9	1.9	13.9	2.6
Northern Ireland	61.0	1.0	20.5	1.8
PERIPHERY	65.4	1.9	15.9	2.9
UK	69.5	2.4	11.4	3.7

Source: 1987 Labour Force Survey.

distances and of penetrating the housing market in the more prosperous parts of Britain.

Table 12.10 reveals that occupational differentials in job-related mobility rates are repeated at the regional scale. Regional variations in the propensity of the same occupational group to migrate indicate that the regional differentials in migration propensities are not due solely to variations in the occupational structures of the regions. For the managerial and professional occupations job-related mobility rates are highest in the South and lowest in the periphery – in keeping with regional variations in economic prosperity. However, for manual workers no such clear pattern of regional differentials emerges, with those in the North displaying a propensity to migrate for job-related reasons similar to the rates recorded for East Anglia and the East Midlands.

12.7 Conclusion

This chapter has demonstrated the significance of migration for work-related reasons in the overall pattern of migration within Britain during

Table 12.10 Regional variations in job-related mobility rates by occupation, 1986–87

Region	Managerial[i] and professional (%)	Manual[ii] (%)
South East	5.6	1.5
East Anglia	6.5	1.5
South West	5.3	2.1
SOUTH	5.3	1.6
East Midlands	5.3	2.0
West Midlands	4.0	0.9
MIDLANDS	4.5	1.4
Yorkshire & Humberside	4.2	2.0
North West	4.5	1.4
INDUSTRIAL NORTH	4.4	1.1
North	2.9	2.0
Wales	3.9	1.1
Scotland	3.4	1.3
Northern Ireland	1.5	0.8
PERIPHERY	3.2	1.4
UK	4.7	1.4

Notes: (i) Managers and administrators, professional staff, associate
professional and technical staff.
(ii) Craft and skilled manual workers, plant and machine operators.
Source: 1987 Labour Force Survey.

the 1980s. The proportion of all migration accounted for by job-related moves is quite small, but has increased during the 1980s. It is clear that migration for reasons of employment was severely depressed by the intense recession of the early 1980s, and that rates of mobility have been increased by growth in the number of employment opportunities since 1984. The long-established pattern of net regional migration is broadly reflected in the pattern of job-related migration, but with some interesting variations. Despite the employment revival in the periphery, notably the Northern region, the South East has increased in strength as a magnet for those moving for work, and the numbers being lost by the periphery have increased over the decade. One exception to this trend is Wales, where the number of job-related out-migrants fell between 1983–84 and 1986–87, probably reflecting the strong performance of manufacturing employment. While East Anglia, and the East Midlands have grown in employment most rapidly in the later 1980s, the number of job-related migrants has declined, perhaps because the rapid growth of the South East and West Midlands have provided more accessible employment opportunities for potential migrants.

The expected association between occupation and job-related mobility has been demonstrated. The increases in mobility at the top of the occupational hierarchy and the widening differential between occupations provides some confirmation of the hypothesis that migration will be related to the growing availability of different types of employment. With the service sector expected to continue to provide the main source of employment growth in all parts of the UK and a continued shift from manual to non-manual work within manufacturing, it is likely that this pattern of occupational migration rates will be maintained.

There was some evidence for unemployed persons migrating in search of work, in confirmation of the expectations of theoretical models. However, migration is a difficult and costly activity, and thus the bulk of migration was carried out by those moving from one job to another, in most cases before family responsibilities restrained the ability of a household to migrate. The analysis of aggregate flows from the NHSCR migration data indicated that migration conformed more closely to theoretical expectations in more depressed periods when mobility was more likely to be constrained by employment factors than in periods of prosperity where housing factors become more significant for migration.

13 Migration and social change
Tony Fielding

13.1 Introduction

This chapter uses migration data in conjunction with data from the OPCS's Longitudinal Study (LS) to address three aspects of the relationship between migration and social change in contemporary Britain. The first is the role of social change in shaping population redistribution patterns; the second is the association between social mobility and geographical mobility; and the third is the role of internal migration in promoting social change in British cities and regions.

These three aspects of the relationship between migration and social change raise interesting and important issues of fact and interpretation. In the case of the role of social change in determining migration patterns, the following kinds of question arise: to what extent do migration patterns reflect changes in the social class composition of the British population? One has in mind here the growth of the service class of professional, technical and managerial employees, the decline of the blue-collar working class, and the increase in the number of people who are unemployed. Alternatively, do these population redistribution trends relate to changes in modes of consumption? Such changes include the rapid expansion of home ownership and the further extension of the ownership and use of the private car. Or perhaps the migration patterns are manifestations of changes in the social relations of family life, and in the demographic structures of households? Such changes include an increase in the proportion of older people in the population and the relative absence of children, higher levels of divorce and separation and the growth in the proportion of people living in non-nuclear family households.

The association between social mobility and geographical mobility at the individual level also raises important issues. Are certain kinds of people more likely to migrate than others? If so, which kinds, and why? Is movement from one social class to another associated with a heightened propensity to migrate? If so, what interpretation do we place on this relationship, and what are its social and geographical implications? How does geographical mobility intersect with other factors in affecting upward social mobility into service-class employment? Can one identify specific 'social and geographical mobility regimes', that is, patterns of social change and migration which are characteristic of particular regions or groups of regions? Can the South East, for example, be accurately described as a 'social escalator' region as some recent commentators have suggested (see Fielding, 1989)?

Interesting questions are also raised by the suggestion that internal migration flows have been instrumental in bringing about significant changes in the class compositions and social relations of specific cities and regions in Britain during the recent period. To what extent, for example, have the social developments in inner city areas such as those characterised by the term 'gentrification', been influenced by changes in the composition and direction of inter-regional and intra-regional migration flows? Does the apparent lack of a social basis for high-technology investment in many northern and western regions reflect the low in-migration and high turnover of private sector service-class members in these regions? What role has migration from the South East played in the recent rapid social restructuring of the rural regions of southern England, and in the cultural and political evolutions of Wales and Scotland?

There are too many of these interesting and important questions to be dealt with satisfactorily in one short chapter. So the intention in this instance is to achieve a more modest objective. It is to show, by means of illustration, some of the ways in which the NHSCR migration data and the LS can be used to explore these relationships between migration and social change. The position adopted here is that while each of these data sets on its own has serious shortcomings for the analysis of migration and social change, in combination they form a powerful base upon which many fruitful lines of enquiry can be developed.

13.2 Data sources and definitions

The character of the NHSCR data and its strengths and weaknesses for migration research have been fully discussed elsewhere in this book (notably in Chapters 1 and 2). What needs to be emphasised here is how singularly unhelpful the NHSCR data are for analyses of the relationships between migration and social change. The NHSCR tells us very little about the migrants themselves, only their age and gender, and nothing at all about their social circumstances either before migration or after it. Such information is essential if we are to speculate meaningfully on the causes and consequences of migration, or, more specifically, to relate these migrations to processes of social change.

The strengths of the NHSCR data on the other hand lie in its spatial and temporal detail. This permits interpretation of causes and consequences through the spatial and temporal coincidence of certain migration patterns with specific social facts (for example the presence or absence of a university in a county, or the occurrence of a steep rise in house prices in a particular year – both of these examples are used below). Such interpretations, however, often have very weak foundations, and the statistical methods used to discover these spatial and temporal coincidences are subject to many criticisms. The best that can be hoped for is a theoretically consistent pattern of statistical association between migration variables on the one hand, and variables describing the social and economic contexts of migration on the other (for example, through multiple regression analysis).

The OPCS's Longitudinal Study is quite different in character. This time we do not know the exact age of the person at the point of migration, the year of migration within a 10-year period, or whether the migration took place in one or several steps. But we know an enormous amount about the social and economic characteristics of the migrant himself or herself, and about the social and economic contexts of that person's migration. Strictly speaking, the LS is not a true longitudinal study; rather it is a linked census record study, in which about 500,000 individuals (approximately 1 per cent of the population of England and Wales) have their census forms at one census (1971) linked to their census forms at the subsequent census (1981). OPCS (1988a, pp. v–xiii) provides a full description of the populations sampled in the LS. So we know about their migration between the censuses (locations of origin and destination), and we can associate this knowledge with all the information that the census provides us about the migrants and their households both at the time of the census before their migration, and at the time of the census after their migration. For example, it is possible in this way to connect changes in occupational class position (intra-generational social mobility) with changes in geographical location (such as inter-regional migration).

Writing in late 1990, however, the LS has one major drawback. The only LS data set available at this time is that which refers to the years 1971–81; the 1981–91 data will not be available until 1993 at the earliest. Two responses to this situation are possible. The first asserts that the changes brought about by the 'Thatcher revolution' are so profound and wide-ranging that the 1971–81 decade must now be regarded as part of history, and that the relationships linking migration and social change discovered through analyses of this LS data would have little relevance for the period since 1981. The alternative position would argue that, despite the significance of the 'new right' policies of the recent period, the basic facts of geography and of the political economy of the country have changed only slowly in the recent period. These changes may have introduced new relationships and modified previous ones, but they have been quite insufficient to bring about a total transformation of the connections between social class, region, and migration – connections observed for the first time in Britain through the use of this LS data for 1971–81. The author of this chapter subscribes to this second position, and believes, with some confidence, that many of the changes of the 1980s have served to augment rather than diminish the structures and relationships of the period 1971–81. A second disadvantage of the LS is that it is restricted to England and Wales; it was unfortunately decided that there was not enough research interest in the Scottish LS to justify seeing it carried through to completion.

It is inevitable that analysis of these two very large data sets should necessitate some difficult decisions about what constitutes migration and what constitutes social change. The NHSCR data has been analysed at the county and regional levels; flows within conurbation areas have been ignored. This results in inter-county migration flow matrices for England and Wales sized 54 by 54, and inter-regional migration flow matrices for the UK sized 11 by 11. The NHSCR migration flow data has been analysed for each year from 1975–76 to 1988–89, and the age-specific flow data has been analysed for 1985–86. The analyses of the LS data use the nine standard regions of England and Wales. In this case, as was pointed out above, the strength of the data lies not so much in its spatial detail as in its coverage of social variables. These are grouped into three sets of categories:

1. *Gender* (two categories).
2. *Housing tenure* (three categories – owner-occupiers, council tenants, and other (mostly private sector tenants)).
3. *Occupational class* (five categories – service class (professional, technical and managerial employees), petite bourgeoisie (self-employed and owners of small and medium-sized businesses), white-collar working class (for example, low-level workers in offices and shops), blue-collar working class (manual workers), and the unemployed).

For details of the SEG compositions of these social-class categories and a discussion of the problems of classifying occupations when using the LS, see Fielding, 1989.

13.3 Social change and migration

A sensible first step in considering the ways in which social change might have affected internal migration in the recent period is to identify what the most important social changes have been. This is not an uncontroversial task in itself. It is suggested here that these changes can be grouped under three headings: changes in social-class structure; changes in modes of consumption; and changes in household relations. First, Britain's social-class structure has been altered (a) by the decline both in numbers and in political influence of the manual 'blue-collar' working class (and the related increase in unemployment); (b) by the rapid growth of the 'service class' of professional, technical and managerial employees; and (c) by the reversal in the decline of the much smaller 'petite bourgeoisie' class made up of self-employed people and the owners of small and medium-sized businesses. Secondly, Britain has witnessed the development of important changes in the social relationships of consumption. In particular, as a result of a significant increase in the proportion of households in owner-occupation, a further extension of car ownership, and the growth of private sector health and education services, there has been a marked shift away from the consumption of publicly provided

goods and services (and away from the levelling-up of the living standards of the poorest sections of the population which a political commitment to this form of consumption implies). This shift coincided with
changes in political culture which allowed the 'sale' of nationalised
industries and the extension of individual share ownership. Thirdly,
related to these changes in the social relations of production and
consumption, there have been shifts in other bases of social stratification
such as gender, generation and ethnicity. Household social relations, for
example, have been altered by the changing demographic structure of the
British population (decline in the birth rate after the mid-1960s, increase
in the proportion of the very elderly), by the growing significance of
non-nuclear family households, and by the rapid increase in female
(often part-time) employment. Britain has also become more
multicultural (in fact if not in spirit); this is not just the result of the
growing presence of 'racial' minorities in British cities, it reflects a
marked differentiation in values and lifestyles within the majority 'white'
population (revealed, for example, in the increasing regional polarisation
of party electoral support).

The question at issue, then, is what impact have these changes had on
the pace and nature of population redistribution in Britain? This question is rather easier to pose than it is to answer, despite the wealth of
information provided by the NHSCR and the LS. What can be said,
however, is that certain expectations about the migration effects of these
social changes are not borne out by the facts.

One would have good reason, for example, for expecting the levels of
geographical mobility between cities and regions in Britain to have
increased over the last 20 years as a result of these social changes. First,
this is because the social classes which are geographically mobile have
grown while those which are immobile have declined. From the final
column of Table 13.1 it can be seen that the service class has an inter-
regional migration rate which is more than twice the average for England
and Wales, whereas the blue-collar working class has a rate which is only
about half the average. Secondly, the housing tenure which contains the
most geographically mobile people has grown while that which contains
the least mobile has declined. Table 13.1 shows that the inter-regional
migration rate for owner-occupiers is roughly three times that for council
tenants. Thirdly, demographic changes also favour higher levels of
geographical mobility. The peak birth-rate generation of the 1960s came
onto the labour market in the early mid-1980s at which time it would
have been in its maximum mobility age groups. Migration would also be
expected to be promoted by decreases in average household size and by
increases in family breakup and divorce.

The evidence from the NHSCR, however, shows that no such general
increase in migration has occurred. The slight increase in mobility in the
late 1980s after the low levels of migration in the late 1970s and early
1980s was insufficient to restore levels to those of the early mid-1970s.
There is some response on a year-by-year basis to the buoyancy or otherwise of the national labour and housing markets, but no underlying trend

Table 13.1 Inter-regional migration, social class and housing tenure, England and Wales, 1971–81

Social class/ housing tenure category	Class/ tenure in 1981	%	In labour market in 1981	In labour market in 1971–81	In same class/ tenure in 1971–81
Service class	45,988	21.1	194	188	222
Petite bourgeoisie	14,451	6.6	91	97	54
White collar	57,501	26.4	92	94	99
Blue collar	82,197	37.7	55	56	55
Unemployed	17,834	8.2	98	110	104
Total	217,971	100.0	100	100	100
Owner–occupiers	137,669	63.2	111	117	129
Council tenants	58,364	26.8	42	41	27
Other tenants	21,938	10.1	182	145	115
Total	217,971	100.0	100	100	100

Notes: (i) The data refer to people who were in England and Wales at both dates.
(ii) Inter-regional migration rates: England and Wales = 100. 1.096% sample.
Source: OPCS Longitudinal Study (Crown Copyright Reserved).

Table 13.2 Calculation of percentage increase in inter-regional migration expected on the basis of changes in the class composition of the population

Social class	A Pop. 71 millions	B Mig. rates	C A*B	D Pop. 81 millions	E D*B	F
Service class	3.81	222	846	4.86	1,079	
Petite bourgeoisie	1.50	54	81	1.49	80	
White collar	6.00	99	594	5.88	582	
Blue collar	10.00	55	550	8.37	460	
Unemployed	0.78	104	81	1.86	193	
Total	22.09	100	2,152	22.46	2,394	+ 11.25

Notes: (i) Column F = $(\Sigma \, E^*100/\Sigma C) - 100$.
(ii) Calculations exclude immigrants and emigrants.
Source: OPCS Longitudinal Study (Crown Copyright Reserved).

towards increased geographical mobility can be detected. On the basis of data in Table 13.2 it can be asserted that changes in the social class structure ought to have raised migration levels by about 11 per cent between 1971 and 1981, and therefore by more than 20 per cent in the period 1971–91 (since the social changes of the 1980s seem to have taken a similar form to those of the 1970s, and to have been at a rate which was at least equal, and probably greater, than that experienced in the previous decade). Because this increase did not occur, it follows (assuming that the levels are not determined by those who are outside the labour market) that class-specific migration rates must have fallen for some, probably most, and possibly all, social classes. It also follows that the usual research question, which is 'what social processes promote migration?', might usefully be turned on its head in this instance to take the form 'what are the factors which might have acted to reduce geographical mobility in the recent period?'

Reduced levels of class-specific geographical mobility could have arisen for a number of reasons in the recent period. But most lists will probably include the following:

1. The fact that some of the social changes which might be expected to raise levels of migration are double-edged in their migration effects. For example, the reduction in household size which might make migration easier, also implies that the number of people migrating per household-migration-decision is less.
2. Increasing female activity rates imply that a growing proportion of couples live in 'dual-career' households in which a migration is more difficult to effect because of the likely damage it will cause to one of the partners' job or career prospects.
3. Higher levels of car ownership and use, in conjunction with an extension of the motorway and trunk road network, may permit job changes to take place without a residential migration in cases where previously such a migration would have been unavoidable.
4. Major differences in house prices between regions may have reduced migration by making it difficult for those in the low-cost regions of northern and western Britain to migrate to the high-cost south and east, and by making it difficult for those in the south and east to move to the north and west because of the loss of capital gains that such a move would be likely to entail.
5. Changes in the internal labour markets of large organisations (including graduate entry and reduction in the range of in-house activities) seem to have led to lower levels of intra-organisational transfers between cities and regions (Savage, 1988). This is potentially highly significant since it is estimated that 58 per cent of inter-regional labour market migrants between 1980 and 1981 were intra-organisational transfers (Salt, 1990).

It may be the case that the general increase in mobility expected on the basis of changes in social class did not materialise, but the shorter-term effects of specific social and political events can be detected in the NHSCR data. Take, for example, the sudden rise in house prices which accompanied the politically inspired boom in consumer credit in the late 1980s. Assisted by a financial deregulation which increased the number of institutions lending for house purchase, supported by a very strong

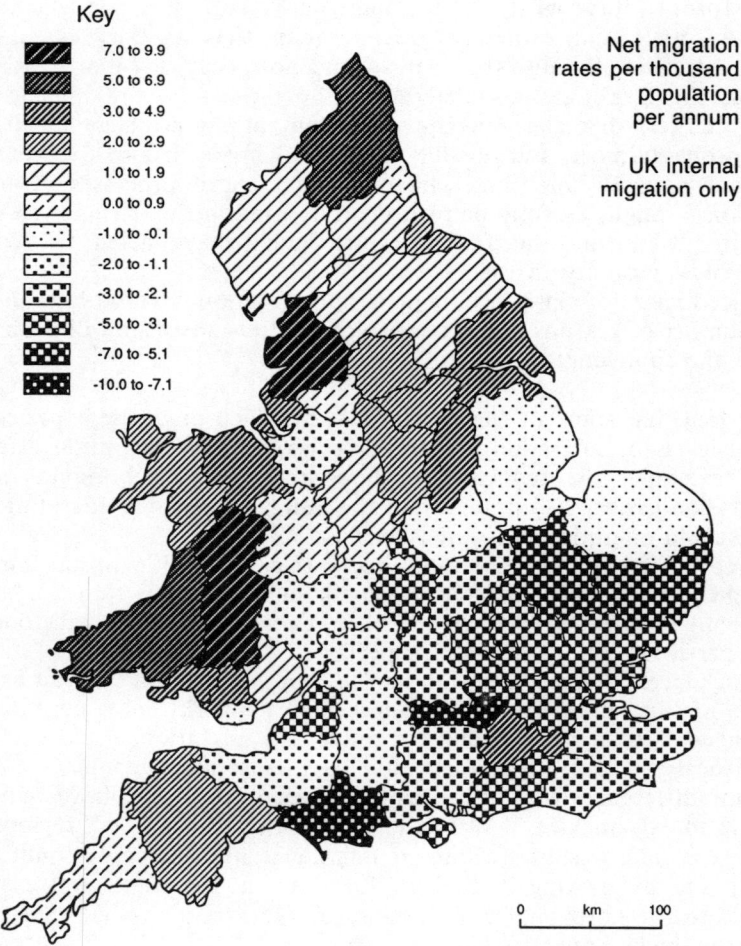

Key

7.0 to 9.9

5.0 to 6.9

3.0 to 4.9

2.0 to 2.9

1.0 to 1.9

0.0 to 0.9

-1.0 to -0.1

-2.0 to -1.1

-3.0 to -2.1

-5.0 to -3.1

-7.0 to -5.1

-10.0 to -7.1

Net migration
rates per thousand
population
per annum

UK internal
migration only

0   km   100

Figure 13.1 Differences between county annual net migration rates for
1988–89 and 1979–89

political commitment to home ownership, and further provoked by
changes in owner-occupier tax breaks announced well in advance which
led to some panic buying, house prices sharply increased first in the
booming South East region, then elsewhere in the South and East, then
elsewhere in the country (though at the end of the day the increases
elsewhere were never as high in absolute terms as in the South East).
This led for a time to massive differentials in house prices between the
South and East and the rest of the country. One can see the effect of
this on migration if one compares the net migration rates in 1988–89
with those for the 10-year period 1979–80 to 1988–89 (Figure 13.1). All
but one of the counties in the South and East of the country show

Table 13.3 Migration between counties grouped on the basis of male
unemployment rate, England and Wales, 1979–80 to 1988–89

			Destination county			
Origin county	Group	High unemp.	Medium unemp.	Low unemp.	Total	Net mig.
High	A	2,508	1,537	888	2,426	– 451
Medium	B	1,206	3,153	2,429	3,636	– 24
Low	C	769	2,074	1,903	2,842	+ 475
Total		1,975	3,611	3,318	8,904	0

Unemployment level in 1981	Group	Pop. in 1984	In-mig. rate	Out-mig. rate	Net mig. rate
High	A	18,025	10.96	13.46	– 2.50
Medium	B	17,921	20.15	20.29	– 0.14
Low	C	13,496	24.58	21.06	+ 3.52

Notes: (i) The migration and population figures are in 1,000s (rounded to the
nearest 1,000).
(ii) Rates are per thousand population in 1979, per annum.
(iii) Unemployment data are for 1981.
(iv) The 18 high unemployment counties have male unemployment
rates above 10.5%.
(v) The 18 medium unemployment counties have rates between 8.1%
and 10.5%.
(vi) The 18 low unemployment counties have rates below 8.1%.
Sources: NHSCR (OPCS Copyright Reserved); 1981 Census.

downward relative movements in their net migration rates while those of
northern and western Britain show upward relative movements (note in
particular the upward movements for Lancashire, Merseyside and
Humberside – three urban counties characterised by house prices which
are among the lowest in Britain).

One ought to be able to identify the effects of social structure and
social change on the spatial patterns of population redistribution as well
as in the temporal trends. Once again, however, the results of analyses
of the NHSCR and LS data sets do not always confirm expectations.
Take, for example, the data presented in Table 13.3. This shows the sum
of the annual inter-county migration flows 1979–80 to 1988–89 for counties grouped on the basis of their male unemployment rates in 1981. The
18 counties in England and Wales with the highest unemployment rates
form group A, the 18 with the next highest rates form group B, and the
18 with the lowest rates form group C. Unemployment rate was chosen
because it was at this time a highly efficient indicator of social class
structure; areas with high unemployment being very working-class in
character, those with low unemployment being very middle-class in
character. At first glance the figures seem to confirm an economic logic
to inter-county migration during this period. The net gains are in low

Table 13.4 Net migration and the importance of the three 'middle classes' by region

Standard region	Net mig. rate (UK)	Profess. LQ (EW)	Manag. LQ (EW)	Petit b. LQ (EW)
East Anglia	+ 8.07	0.98	0.96	1.29
South West	+ 7.53	1.02	0.96	1.53
East Midlands	+ 2.52	0.89	0.88	1.00
Wales	+ 2.33	0.97	0.73	1.15
South East	− 0.74	1.16	1.24	0.97
Yorkshire and Humberside	− 0.86	0.85	0.84	0.94
West Midlands	− 1.88	0.88	0.89	0.86
North	− 1.97	0.87	0.70	0.73
North West	− 2.85	0.91	0.91	0.91
Total	0.00	1.00	1.00	1.00

Notes: (i) Migration data for 1979/80 to 1988/89. Rates are per thousand population in 1979, per annum.
(ii) The social class data is for 1981 and is expressed in the form of location quotients where England and Wales = 1.00.
(iii) EW = England and Wales only; Profess = professionals; Manag = managers; Petit b = self-employed and owners of small and medium-sized businesses.

Sources: NHSCR (OPCS Copyright Reserved); LS (Crown Copyright Reserved).

unemployment counties and the net losses are in high unemployment counties. The gross rates tell a different story, however. While the in-migration rates conform to expectations, the out-migration rates are the opposite of what might be expected. The high unemployment counties have a low out-migration rate while the low unemployment counties have a high out-migration rate. It is the different social class structures which explain this finding. All but two of the counties in the low unemployment group are located in southern and eastern England in a continuous zone stretching from Suffolk and Cambridgeshire, around and to the west of Greater London as far as Gloucestershire, Somerset, and Dorset, and finishing up in Surrey, West Sussex and Kent. This is a zone of urbanised countryside, and of small and medium-sized towns; it has a high proportion of people with middle-class occupations and high levels of house and car ownership. It is an area inhabited by people who are in those groups which are most geographically mobile.

Another perspective on these associations is provided by data on UK regional net migration 1979–80 to 1988–89 (from the NHSCR) and regional social class structures for England and Wales in 1981 (from the LS) (Table 13.4). This shows that it was the regions with high concentrations of middle-class groups which experienced net gains while those with more working-class populations experienced net losses. However, two rather puzzling features can be detected in these data. The first is that the association between class and migration is much stronger for the petite bourgeoisie, who are geographically immobile, than for the service class, who are geographically highly mobile. The petite bourgeoisie accounts for only about 7 per cent of the labour force but it is most strongly represented in the South West and East Anglian regions, followed by the East Midlands and Wales; it is least represented in the industrial regions of the north of England. This is precisely the same distribution as the pattern of net migration gains and losses in the 1980s. Altogether, the regions with a petite bourgeoisie presence at or above the England and Wales average gained 650,000 people at the expense of regions (including the South East) which had lower than average proportions of the petite bourgeoisie. Since it clearly cannot be the petite bourgeoisie themselves who account for this net migration pattern, there must be something about regions that have high proportions of such people which attracts migrants, and something about regions that do not which makes them unattractive to migrants. The second puzzling feature is that the South East region, despite its booming economy in the mid-1980s based upon the growth of London as a financial centre, despite its character as the stereotypical 'service-class region', and despite its attractiveness as the region of maximum social promotion in Britain (see below), was a net loser to the tune of 130,000 people by internal migration during the 1980s (much of this loss was to the nearby regions of southern England).

It is when we focus down upon the migration trends for specific places undergoing rapid social change that the effect of such social change on migration seems to appear in its least equivocal form. Three such places have been selected in Figure 13.2: (a) Docklands, (b) Liverpool and (c) rural Wales. The Docklands area of East London was formerly a distinctively manual working-class district, but was transformed during the 1980s by the building of new offices and by the provision of new and converted housing for young upwardly mobile professional people. Liverpool's recent economic decline manifested itself in serious social and political unrest during the 1980s, including the Toxteth riot in 1981 and the local council's confrontation with the Conservative Government during 1983–85. Although culturally distinct, the rural areas of central and southwest Wales came to join much of lowland England in the recent period in becoming 'urbanised countryside'; in this process urban middle-class social relations tend to replace those of the local (usually declining) farm population. Figure 13.2 traces the migration effects of these local social changes. Each gross in-migration trend is recorded relative to the UK level of inter-FPC area mobility. The recent rapid increases in in-migration to the East End of London (City, Hackney, Newham and Tower Hamlets) and to rural Wales (Powys and Dyfed) are clearly visible, as are the sharp declines in migration to Liverpool.

To summarise, while it has been possible to demonstrate in specific instances the ways in which social change has impacted on migration, the relationships at a broader level are complex. Neither the temporal trends in migration, nor the spatial distributions of net migration balances can

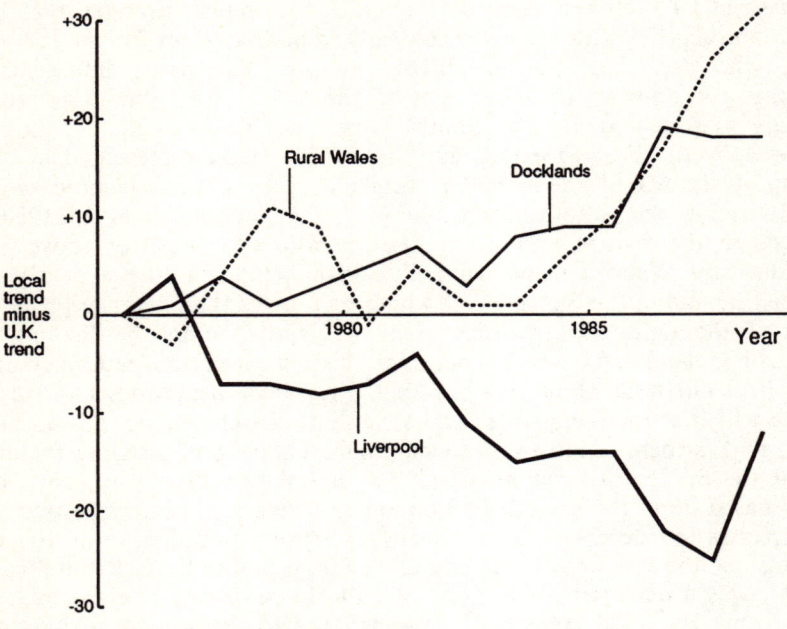

Index numbers: 1975/76 = 100

Figure 13.2 In-migration trend to selected places, 1975–89
Source: NHSCR (OPCS Copyright Reserved).

be predicted from a knowledge of social class structure or of changes in this structure over time.

13.4 Social and geographical mobility

Until now the relationship between social change and migration has been considered in aggregate terms, that is, in terms of social change at the national, regional or local levels, and of migration flows and balances. In this section we consider the association between social change and migration at the individual level. As individuals pass through their adult lives they describe social and geographical trajectories; for example, they change jobs, enter home ownership, marry and divorce, become unemployed, start their own business, and, similarly, they migrate to London, spend a year or two abroad, move to the suburbs, and migrate back to the region they came from, and so on. To understand the relationship between migration and social change we need to know if, in what ways, and to what degree, these two trajectories are connected.

It is sensible to begin on familiar ground. Table 13.1 showed that inter-regional migration rates varied in a systematic way with occupational class

Table 13.5 Association between inter-regional migration and changes in social class and housing tenure, England and Wales, 1971–81

Social class in 1971		Social class in 1981				
	Service class	Petite bourg.	White collar	Blue collar	Unemploy-ment	Total
Service class	103	117	89	73	115	100
Petite bourgeoisie	185	69	161	100	190	100
White collar	165	163	77	77	157	100
Blue collar	209	168	136	75	133	100
Unemployment	215	104	113	79	70	100

Housing tenure in 1971	Housing tenure in 1981			
	Owner-occup.	Council tenants	Other tenants	Total
Owner-occupiers	94	121	232	100
Council tenants	192	37	337	100
Other tenants	141	67	63	100

Notes: (i) The data refer to people who were in the labour market in England and Wales at both dates.
(ii) Inter-regional migration rates (England and Wales = 100) standardized by social class and housing tenure in 1971.
Source: OPCS Longitudinal Study (Crown Copyright Reserved).

and tenure. It also revealed, however, through the differences in the values between columns 3, 4 and 5, that the migration rates of the total labour force in 1981 (which includes entries 1971–81), and of those who were in the labour market in both 1971 and 1981 (which includes class and tenure 'movers') were not the same as those for the class and tenure 'stayers'. These differences are very significant. Take, for example, the petite bourgeoisie. The migration rate for the class movers plus the class stayers is about average at 97; but the migration rate for the class stayers alone is only 55. Clearly, the movers into the petite bourgeoisie are highly geographically mobile. A similar line of reasoning could be used to show that the private rented sector of the housing market is a tenure of transition, and that the well-known association between private renting and migration is capable of misinterpretation; it turns out that the 'stayer' private sector renters are only slightly more geographically mobile than the average.

The connections between social mobility and geographical mobility are much more directly confronted, however, in Table 13.5. Here, inter-regional migration rates have been calculated for all the possible transitions within the labour and housing markets. If there were no association between social mobility and geographical mobility all the values would be at or around 100. As it is, the values in the diagonals, representing the migration rates of the social class and housing tenure stayers, are, in all cases except one, less than 100, indicating low geographical mobility.

Table 13.6 Interactions between inter-regional migration, social class, housing tenure, gender and region, as they affect entry to the service class, England and Wales, 1971–81

			Total		Inter-regional migrants only	
			Total	Males only	Total	Males only
(a) In labour market in 1971						
	England	Total	11.4	12.3	23.1	26.0
Total	and Wales	Owner–occ. only	14.7	16.4	26.1	30.5
	South East	Total	13.5	15.1	28.2	32.0
	only	Owner–occ. only	17.4	20.0	33.9	39.9
	England	Total	18.8	31.7	31.1	45.6
White	and Wales	Owner–occ. only	21.7	35.6	32.6	48.0
collar	South East	Total	19.7	32.1	35.8	49.8
only	only	Owner–occ. only	22.9	36.0	40.6	55.4
(b) Entries from education 1971–81						
	England	Total	18.3	18.2	45.7	47.9
	and Wales	Owner–occ. only	24.0	24.2	49.0	50.5
	South East	Total	19.0	19.8	50.5	53.7
	only	Owner–occ. only	25.3	25.8	54.2	57.5

Notes: (i) The data refer to people in England and Wales at both dates.

(ii) A rate of entry into the service class is calculated by dividing the number of people entering the service class 1971–81 by the number of people in the category of origin in 1971. The rates of entry are therefore transition probabilities × 100.

(iii) Data for South East inter-regional migrants are for flows to the South East.

Source: OPCS Longitudinal Study (Crown Copyright Reserved).

(Incidentally, notice that the exception is the service class; this conforms to the notion that high geographical mobility is an inherent characteristic of this class). Conversely, the values in the off-diagonal cells are almost all above 100, indicating that social class and housing tenure movers are highly geographically mobile.

A very notable feature of Table 13.5 is the high migration rates of those who entered the service class. It needs to be recognised that these high rates could be produced both by the geographical mobility which accompanies entry into the service class, and by the higher mobility of the adopted class once entry has been effected. This association between migration and entry into the service class is explored in more detail in Table 13.6. The LS data has been used to isolate those who were not in the privileged service class of professional, technical and managerial occupations in 1971, but who were in that class in 1981. The top left-hand figure in Table 13.6 shows that the overall figure for England and Wales was 11.4 per cent, or about one chance in nine. As favoured groups are entered into the table, the proportion increases until it reaches

55.4 per cent, or more than one chance in two (for male inter-regional migrants to the South East originating from low-level white-collar jobs and owner-occupation households). Since the equivalent value for a blue-collar, female, non-migrant council tenant living outside the South East is about 3 per cent, one can see that there is a roughly twentyfold difference in rates of entry to the service class between these two extreme cases. This represents an extraordinary contrast in life chances, and means that Britain has a long way to go before the 'classless society' is realised. But for our purposes, the significance of Table 13.6 lies in the changes in value which accompany the introduction of inter-regional migration. In many cases the values are doubled! This is true not only for those already in the labour market in 1971, but also for those entering between 1971–1981. The message that one should draw from this, is that social promotion and geographical mobility are intimately connected.

One of the interesting features of Table 13.6 is the significance of the South East region in linking social and geographical mobility. This prompts the question as to whether or not it is appropriate to view the South East as a kind of 'social escalator region'. By 'escalator region' we mean three things. First, that the region attracts to itself young adults at the start of their working lives. Many of these young people will come from middle-class backgrounds, will be ambitious for social promotion, and will have already achieved good academic qualifications. Secondly, these in-migrants, together with young adults born and brought up in the escalator region will benefit from the accelerated social promotion that the 'region' provides (of course it is not the region 'itself', either as a physical entity or as a location, which promotes people but the conjunction there of a number of social processes favouring such promotion). Thirdly, many of these people, having benefited from promotion through the region's labour and housing markets, will 'cash in' these benefits in mid- or late career, or at retirement, by 'stepping off' the escalator as they migrate to an area of urbanised countryside outside the South East region.

Age-specific NHSCR data for 1985–86 has been analysed to see if the migration flow patterns to and from the South East conform to the escalator region concept. Figures 13.3 (a), (b) and (c) show the net flows to the South East for people aged 20–24, 40–49, and 60–69 respectively. The values used in the maps are migration velocities, calculated by dividing the size of the migration flow by the product of the populations at the origin and destination regions. The evidence of these maps is quite unequivocal. Figure 13.3 (a) shows that, at the age when young people are leaving universities and colleges and entering their first full-time jobs, there is a massive net migration gain to the South East region from almost every part of England and Wales but particularly from counties in the Midlands, the southwest peninsula, parts of west Wales, and much of northern and northeastern England. To check on the significance of higher education in this process the counties were grouped according to whether or not they contained a university, and on the basis of their net

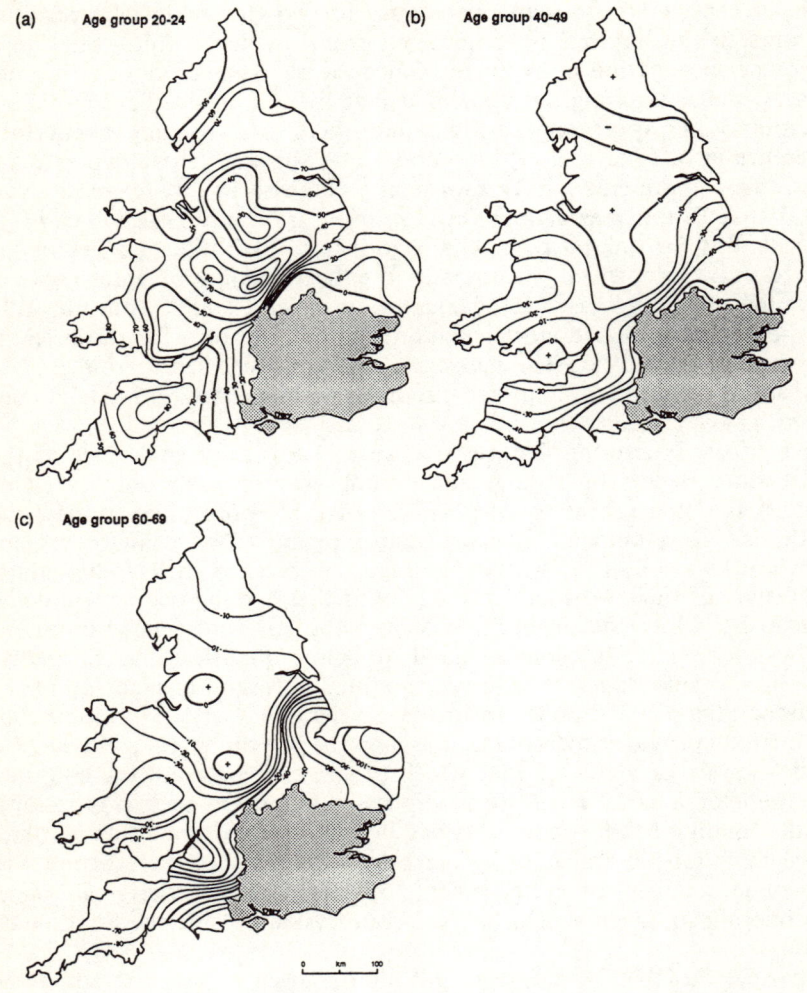

Figure 13.3 Net migration flows to the South East region by age group,
1985–86

Source: NHSCR (OPCS Copyright Reserved).

migration velocities. The results are given in Table 13.7, which shows
that there is a clear bias in favour of counties with universities.

Figure 13.3 (c) shows the pattern of retirement-aged migration; it
shows that the net flows are away from the South East region and
towards the South West and East Anglian regions. In this age group it
is only from the West Midlands conurbation and from Greater
Manchester that the South East makes net migration gains (presumably
from retirement migration to the south coast). What is perhaps much less
expected is the pattern of net migration gains and losses for those aged

Table 13.7 Young adult net migration to the South East and university location by county of England and Wales

Migration velocities	University location Present	University location Absent	Total
>50	17	6	23
<50	5	13	18
Total	22	19	41

Notes: (i) Migration velocities of people aged 20–24 in 1985–86.
(ii) Net migration velocity $= (N_{ij}{}^*K)/(P_i{}^*P_j)$

where:

N_{ij} = net migration flow from county i to county j;
K = constant = 10^{11};
P_i = population of county i (origin); and
P_j = population of county j (destination).

Source: Based on data from the NHSCR (OPCS Copyright Reserved).

40–49 (Figure 13.3 (b)). The South East does gain from some counties, but the rates of gain from the industrial midlands, north and northeast England and South Wales are very small, while the losses to counties in eastern England, the South West, and non-industrial Wales are very considerable, and losses are also registered to the more scenically attractive areas of northern England. So, long before the retirement age groups, there is a sizeable movement of people away from the South East region towards counties which are characterised by rural environments, small and medium-sized 'market' towns, and 'historic' freestanding cities.

The LS data can now be used to provide the social detail which is so strikingly missing from this NHSCR-based picture. First, we should consider those young people who migrate to the South East. The rate of net migration gain to the South East region for those making the transition from education in 1971 to professional occupations in 1981 is +46.0 per thousand, and the equivalent figure for managers is +16.7 per thousand. These represent highly significant net gains to the South East region. The LS also shows that while young adults always account for a large proportion of regional in-migrants, the proportion of in-migrants making the transition from education in 1971 to employment or unemployment in the South East in 1981 was 62.2 per cent, whereas the equivalent figure for England and Wales was only 50.2 per cent. Secondly, by examining the social promotion rates of non-migrants relative to the England and Wales average (location quotient = 1.0), it can be shown that the South East region is uniquely privileged, in that its rates of promotion from education and working-class origins to professional and managerial destinations are in all cases higher than

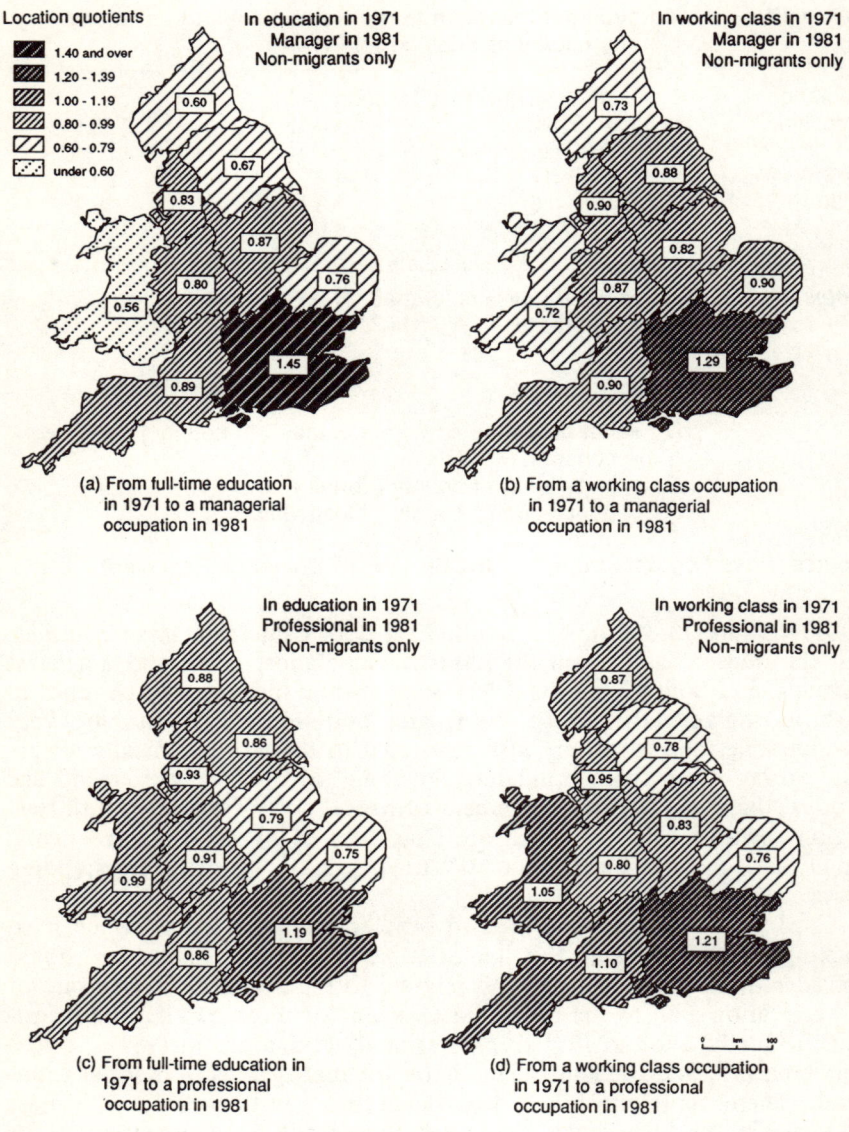

Location quotients

- 1.40 and over
- 1.20 - 1.39
- 1.00 - 1.19
- 0.80 - 0.99
- 0.60 - 0.79
- under 0.60

In education in 1971
Manager in 1981
Non-migrants only

0.60
0.67
0.83
0.87
0.80
0.76
0.56
1.45
0.89

(a) From full-time education
in 1971 to a managerial
occupation in 1981

In working class in 1971
Manager in 1981
Non-migrants only

0.73
0.88
0.90
0.82
0.87
0.90
0.72
1.29
0.90

(b) From a working class occupation
in 1971 to a managerial
occupation in 1981

In education in 1971
Professional in 1981
Non-migrants only

0.88
0.86
0.93
0.79
0.91
0.75
0.99
1.19
0.86

(c) From full-time education in
1971 to a professional
occupation in 1981

In working class in 1971
Professional in 1981
Non-migrants only

0.87
0.78
0.95
0.83
0.80
0.76
1.05
1.21
1.10

(d) From a working class occupation
in 1971 to a professional
occupation in 1981

Figure 13.4 Transitions to managerial and professional occupations by region, 1971–81

Source: OPCS Longitudinal Study, Crown Copyright Reserved.

those for other regions (Figure 13.4). The South East is indeed a region of accelerated social promotion (incidentally, this is also revealed in the data for the transition from education to unemployment where the South East's location quotient is the lowest in the country at 0.77). Finally, the LS provides a considerable amount of detail about those who are in mid-career or have reached the end of their working lives. The South East experienced a rate of net migration loss of -15.0 per thousand for those who were in professional occupations in both 1971 and 1981, and a loss of -10.5 per thousand for managers (virtually all of these people would have been over 25 in 1971 and under 65 in 1981). These figures would undoubtedly come as a surprise to those who are trapped in the popular image of the South East as a magnet for mid-career managers and professionals. An interesting aspect of the process whereby people who have achieved service-class jobs in the South East 'step off' the escalator by migrating elsewhere, is that a significant proportion of them transfer into self-employment or the ownership of small businesses when they migrate. Thus the LS tells us that about 47,000 people who were in the service class in the South East in 1971 were in the labour markets of East Anglia, and the South West and the East Midlands in 1981. Some 10.0 per cent of these were in the petite bourgeoisie at the latter date; the England and Wales average for this transition is 4.7 per cent. To complete the picture the LS shows that at retirement the South East is a net loser of professionals at a rate of -10.3 per thousand, and of managers at a rate of -13.0 per thousand.

For a fully rounded picture, however, one must also specify the ways in which the results of analyses of the NHSCR and LS data sets qualify the picture presented above. First, it needs to be said that the service class in the South East region is, to an extent which is remarkable when compared with other regions, recruited from outside the boundaries of England and Wales altogether (this is particularly true for professionals). Secondly, despite its 'escalator region' character, the South East does not experience a high rate of population turnover. It would be reasonable to suspect that this is related to the fact that the South East's labour and housing markets are uniquely large and complex. Finally, the relationship between social and geographical mobility is not always as simple as has been suggested above. It is clear from the LS that the South East region makes net migration gains at both ends of the social class structure (service class and unemployed). While most of the inter-regional migrants achieve upward social mobility, some of them clearly move downwards into unemployment (see below for a further discussion of this point).

To summarise, the data from the NHSCR and LS combine to support the view that the South East acts as a social 'escalator region' in the context of the British socio-demographic system. We have also seen that migration is social class-(and housing tenure)specific, that social and geographical mobility are closely but complexly related, that social promotion seems to be enhanced by geographical mobility, and that certain regions play a very special role in class formation and in the reproduction of the national class structure through their migration and social promotion regimes.

13.5 Migration and social change

In this final section we examine the way that the NHSCR and LS data sets can assist our understanding of the role that internal migration plays in shaping the social geography of the country. At the broadest scale, the level of internal migration not only constitutes one of the salient characteristics of a society (British society differs, for example, from that of the USA partly because its mobility levels are lower), but it also acts as a determinant of the pace of social change. Given the strong association between social mobility and geographical mobility discussed above, a country (or a region) which has low levels of population turnover due to internal migration is likely also to experience a low rate of social change. This thought raises an interesting question. We know from the NHSCR data that geographical mobility has not increased overall in Britain during the last 20 years, and that certain class-specific mobility rates must have decreased, and yet politically and socially it seems that this period has been one of turbulence and change. Could it be the case that in retrospect it will be decided that the picture presented by the migration rates was nearer the truth?

When attention is shifted to the urban and regional scale it can be seen that the relationship between migration and social change is an ambivalent one. While it is undoubtedly true that many of the most significant social changes in Britain's cities and regions in the recent period could not have taken place without internal migration, it is also the case that the social class structures of areas often depend on long-established migration patterns for their continued existence. For example, without a continuous flow of elderly migrants into the coastal retirement resorts, their social structures and 'ambience' change; several south coast resorts which at one time were regarded as havens of middle-class values, have become less genteel and more working-class in character as the well-off retired have chosen not to migrate at all or to migrate instead to inland villages and small towns.

However, as was seen from the LS data discussed earlier, inter-regional migration flows consist largely of young adults (about one half of them were within 10 years of being in full-time education), and of those who are already in the labour market, an overwhelming majority are owner-occupiers, and about 40 per cent belong to the middle classes. This means that in general the areas of high in-migration are areas which are already, or are in the process of becoming, more middle-class in character, while areas of low in-migration are more likely to remain as working-class districts. Given the connection between social change and population turnover mentioned above this generates a fourfold classification of areas:

1. Low turnover plus net migration-loss areas are likely to be working-class districts undergoing slow social change (many northern industrial towns and cities would fall into this category).
2. Low turnover plus net migration-gain areas are likely to experience maximum conflict since a stable population of locals is likely to feel socially and/or culturally threatened by the arrival of the newcomers (this category would include certain inner city areas undergoing 'gentrification', as well as remoter rural areas).
3. High turnover plus net migration-loss areas are likely to be places which are middle-class already, and are experiencing little social change (some counties in the South East region outside Greater London fall into this category).
4. Finally, areas of high turnover plus net migration gain. These areas are perhaps particularly interesting; they are becoming more middle-class in their social structures and in their lifestyles, but, in contrast to the low-turnover net-gain areas, this process is less likely to be contested (many of the high-growth areas or urbanised countryside in lowland England would be classified in this group).

The LS is currently being used in a major exercise to identify these kinds of regional differences, and to trace the social and geographical origins and destinations of all occupational groups and classes. One of the products of this research is a social-class 'balance sheet' for each of the standard regions. This balance sheet records all the sources of change in the social class composition of the region; it does not, of course, tell us why such changes occurred, only how they occurred. The significance of such data for studies of the relationship between migration and social change lies in the fact that it allows us to identify the specific contributions of in- and out-migration flows to the total change in the social structure of the region. This can be done for the South West region using the data supplied in Table 13.8. From this table it can be calculated that in-migrants represented 26 per cent of all the additions to the labour force over the period 1971–81 (3,067/11,797), and 16.5 per cent of the total labour force in 1981. This latter figure, however, differs markedly between classes with the service class out in front with 28 per cent, followed by the unemployed at 20.9 per cent and the petite bourgeoisie at 17.6 per cent. Dividing the individual migration flow figures by the average of the population figures for those classes in 1971 and 1981, produces class-specific migration rates. These show that while the average in-migration rate for social class stayers is 54.1 per thousand, that for the service class is 132.9! The out-migration rates are also interesting. While the average for social class stayers is 26 per thousand, that for the service class is 64, presumably many of them being intra-organisational transfers. One of the remarkable figures that this exercise produces, however, is that for in-migrant social class movers into the petite bourgeoisie. While the average in-migration rate is 47.3 per thousand, that for the movers into the petite bourgeoisie is 107.0 per thousand. The picture which emerges from this data, then, is of a region of significant

Table 13.8 A social class 'balance sheet' for the South West region

	SC	PB	Social class WC	BC	UE	TO
Total in class X in SW in 1971	2,917	1,779	4,681	6,985	541	16,903
Additions:						
Transfers into X within SW	856	548	643	772	476	3,295
Entries from education within SW	524	147	1,254	1,378	416	3,719
Other entries within SW	235	108	809	506	58	1,716
In-migrants from E&W	1,119	332	755	599	262	3,067
of which:						
in class X in 1971	459	65	219	208	9	960
in LM other than X in 1971	243	198	135	138	125	839
in education in 1971	339	31	246	173	102	891
in other in 1971	78	38	155	80	26	377
Total additions	2,734	1,135	3,461	3,255	1,212	11,797
Subtractions:						
Transfers out of X within SW	499	394	965	1,264	173	3,295
Deaths	205	171	304	625	56	1,361
Retirements within SW	397	269	503	1,051	107	2,327
Other exits within SW	203	124	1,043	547	81	1,998
Out-migrants to E&W	355	68	346	274	80	1,123
of which:						
in class X in 1981	221	13	102	120	6	462
in LM other than X in 1981	62	23	114	105	42	346
in retirement in 1981	32	18	24	21	9	104
in other in 1981	40	14	106	28	23	211
Total subtractions	1,659	1,026	3,161	3,761	497	10,104
Net change 1971–81	+ 1,075	+ 109	+ 300	− 506	+ 715	+ 1,693
Net migration 1971–81	+ 764	+ 264	+ 409	+ 325	+ 182	+ 1,944
Total in class X in SW in 1981	3,992	1,888	4,981	6,479	1,256	18,596

Notes: (i) The data include migration to and from the rest of England and Wales but not to and from the rest of the world. Untraced records are also excluded. 1.096% sample.

(ii) SC = Service class; PB = Petite bourgeoisie; WC = White-collar working class; BC = Blue-collar working class; UE = Unemployed; TO = Total; LM = Labour market.

Source: OPCS Longitudinal Study (Crown Copyright Reserved).

net migration gain, dominated by service-class in-migrants, but with other distinctive features, notably the transfer of many people into self-employment and the ownership of small businesses as they migrate into the South West region.

To summarise, migration can sometimes have a devastating effect on local social structures and relations; it can involve 'the appropriation of one class's history by that of another'. But more usually, migration slowly (sometimes almost imperceptibly) shapes the social geography of Britain. It gentrifies certain parts of the inner city and it urbanises whole sections of the countryside. With its ability to trace all the social class changes which accompany migration, the LS is ideally suited to this kind of research. Its potential usefulness in this respect has scarcely begun to be realised.

13.6 Conclusions

One general conclusion can be gleaned from this study. It is that the NHSCR and LS data sets show that the relationship between migration and social change is both intimate and reciprocal. It is intimate in the sense that our changing relationships with one another at work, in the home, and elsewhere, together with our relationships with the changing institutions and structures of our society, determine whether we migrate, where we migrate from and where we migrate to. It is reciprocal in the sense that while social change affects migration, migration also affects social change. When we migrate we influence the nature and pace of social change in both the places we leave and the places we join. One of the manifestations of the intimate and reciprocal nature of the relationship is the close association between intra-generational social mobility and inter-regional migration. Our data showed the class-specific character of migration, the clear relationship between change in class position and spatial relocation, and the distinctive role of migration in social promotion. All this supports the view that we are at an extremely exciting stage in the development of our understanding of the contemporary human geography of Britain. The connections between class and region, society and space, are increasingly visible, and as this happens, the centrality of migration in these relationships and processes is becoming fully revealed.

Acknowledgements
I wish to thank Nicole Commerçon and the *Revue de Géographie de Lyon* for permission to use material (notably Tables 13.1, 13.5 and 13.6) from the recent special issue of the journal (Volume 65, 3, 1990) entitled 'Regards sur la mobilité socio-spatiale'.

14 Temporal and spatial patterns of elderly migration

Tony Warnes

14.1 Introduction

This chapter examines aspects of the migration patterns of elderly people within the UK since 1975. The discussion is based on those features of the spatial and year-by-year variations that can be considered from the NHS patient re-registration data for Family Practitioner Committee areas. Where appropriate, comparisons with younger age groups are made. The FPC data are organised by five-year age groups up to an open-ended age category of 75+ years. This enables the examination of some age variations within the elderly age groups (but quinquennial groupings at older ages would be even more helpful).

The analysis has been guided by recent inductive generalisations concerning the spatial structure, motivations and social selectivity of migrants at successive stages of old age (Grundy, 1987a, 1987b; Rees, 1987; Rees and Warnes, 1988; Rogers, 1989, 1990; Rogers and Serow, 1988; Rogers and Watkins, 1987; Warnes, 1992a; Watkins, 1989). For example, previous work suggests that there are substantial differences between the migrations made around the normal ages of retirement and those undertaken in advanced old age (Cribier, 1982, 1989). Questions have been raised about the extent both to which the moves made by people in their late seventies or older are return migrations to areas of working-age residence and to which the migrants are impoverished, sick or frail (Bohland and Rowles, 1988). It is known that the average age of entry into Housing Association and private sector sheltered housing schemes is around 76 years, and that the great majority of people entering this rapidly growing housing sector are widows and that they move short distances (Warnes, 1987, 1988).

A second theme imported from previous studies is the distinctiveness of migrations from very large cities. How different are the late-age migrations of Londoners compared to people in the rest of the country? How widespread are the metropolitan effects? Do they apply in other large cities of the country?

Another theoretical component of this study reflects the repeated finding of recent gerontological studies that there are significant differences in the health and behaviour of successive birth cohorts

(Abrams, 1989; Svanborg, 1988; Uhlenberg, 1988; Willis, 1989). The experience, circumstances, expectations and actions of those born in the 1910s may be only a weak guide to those of the cohort born in the 1930s. For example, there have been considerable increases in the incomes and housing assets of elderly people in Britain since 1975 (Hamnett et al., 1991; Mackintosh et al., 1990). More speculatively, the entrance into old age of the first cohorts with mass experience of overseas holidays and even car ownership may alter their locational and residential decisions (Warnes, 1992b). An additional reason for studying change over time is the need to assess the impact of socio-economic and political changes in Britain during the 1980s. These range from major changes in state pensions entitlements and funding levels, wholesale revisions to the funding and organisation of residential care, and the first large-scale sales in England of housing specially designed for retirement (Williams, 1990). The locations of these new residential opportunities may be reflected in the changing spatial pattern of migrations.

Serendipity has also been allowed. The patient re-registration data, like the National Health Service from which it comes, are exceptionally comprehensive and sound but austere and impersonal. The migrants are described only by their age and sex. This severely limits the social meaning which can be extracted as Fielding emphasises in the previous chapter. On the other hand, the data's quantitative and locational richness yields a great deal of evidence about the spatial patterns of internal migration in Britain. The main harvest from this evidence are hypotheses concerning age- and sex-specific residential mobility. It will be seen, for example, that over the decade the greatest changes in the propensity and spatial patterning of elderly people's migrations have been in the oldest age group. The extent to which these changes can be attributed to socio-demographic, social administrative or housing market factors can however only be assessed to a limited degree.

14.2 Temporal trends in the number and rate of migrations

The total number of migrations between FPC areas within England and Wales (with identified origin and destination areas) declined during the late 1970s from 1.83 million in 1975–76 to 1.50 million in 1981–82. The early 1980s saw a steady growth in migrations to 1.96 million in 1987–88 but a decline in the following year to 1.86 million.

Expressed as a ratio of the 1980–81 rate, the range of the 14 annual totals of male migrations at all ages was from 0.94 to 1.23, i.e. through 29 points (Table 14.1). Least variation was found among teenagers, those in their early twenties and those in their early seventies. Possibly these are the ages where the decision to migrate or not is least influenced by exogenous economic and housing factors and most associated with 'inevitable' life transitions and events, such as the onset of sickness. The annual fluctuation in the number of migrations for other elderly age groups were among the most substantial. Among males, the total of

Table 14.1 Age/sex-specific rates of migration within England and Wales, 1975–76 to 1988–89 as ratios of 1980–81 rates

	Age group (years)												
	0–4	10–14	15–19	20–24	25–29	40–44	50–54	55–59	60–64	65–69	70–74	75+	All
Males													
1975–76	1.34	1.19	1.00	1.09	1.24	1.12	1.31	1.13	1.15	1.13	0.98	1.00	1.14
1988–89	1.03	0.85	0.80	1.22	1.34	1.63	1.37	1.20	1.18	1.08	0.95	1.50	1.17
Min.	0.91	0.85	0.80	0.93	0.90	0.94	1.00	0.96	0.90	0.93	0.86	0.93	0.94
Max.	1.34	1.20	1.04	1.22	1.34	1.73	1.44	1.34	1.38	1.33	1.19	1.68	1.23
Range	0.43	0.35	0.24	0.31	0.44	0.35	0.44	0.38	0.48	0.40	0.44	0.75	0.29
Min. year	81/84	88	88	81	81	79	81	81	79	83	79	79	81
Max. year	75	75/77	77	88	88	87	87	87	87	87	87	87	87
Females													
1975–76	1.35	1.21	1.09	1.07	1.24	1.15	1.40	1.13	1.19	1.20	1.02	1.03	1.15
1988–89	1.07	0.89	0.81	1.22	1.46	1.70	1.35	1.07	1.00	1.05	0.89	1.41	1.18
Min.	0.93	0.89	0.81	0.94	0.95	0.97	0.99	0.92	0.87	0.93	0.89	0.92	0.95
Max.	1.35	1.21	1.09	1.23	1.46	1.83	1.44	1.28	1.21	1.28	1.12	1.53	1.25
Range	0.42	0.32	0.28	0.29	0.51	0.20	0.45	0.36	0.34	0.35	0.23	0.61	0.30
Min. year	84	88	88	79/81	81	79	81	81	79	82	88	79	81
Max. year	75	75/77	75	87	88	87	87	77	87	87	87	87	87

Notes: (i) The data refer to migrations with identified origins and destinations.
(ii) Min. and Max. (year) indicate the values and years in which the lowest and highest age/sex-specific rates occurred.
(iii) The year figures indicate the 12 months extending from April in the quoted year to the following March, e.g. 87 means 1987–88.

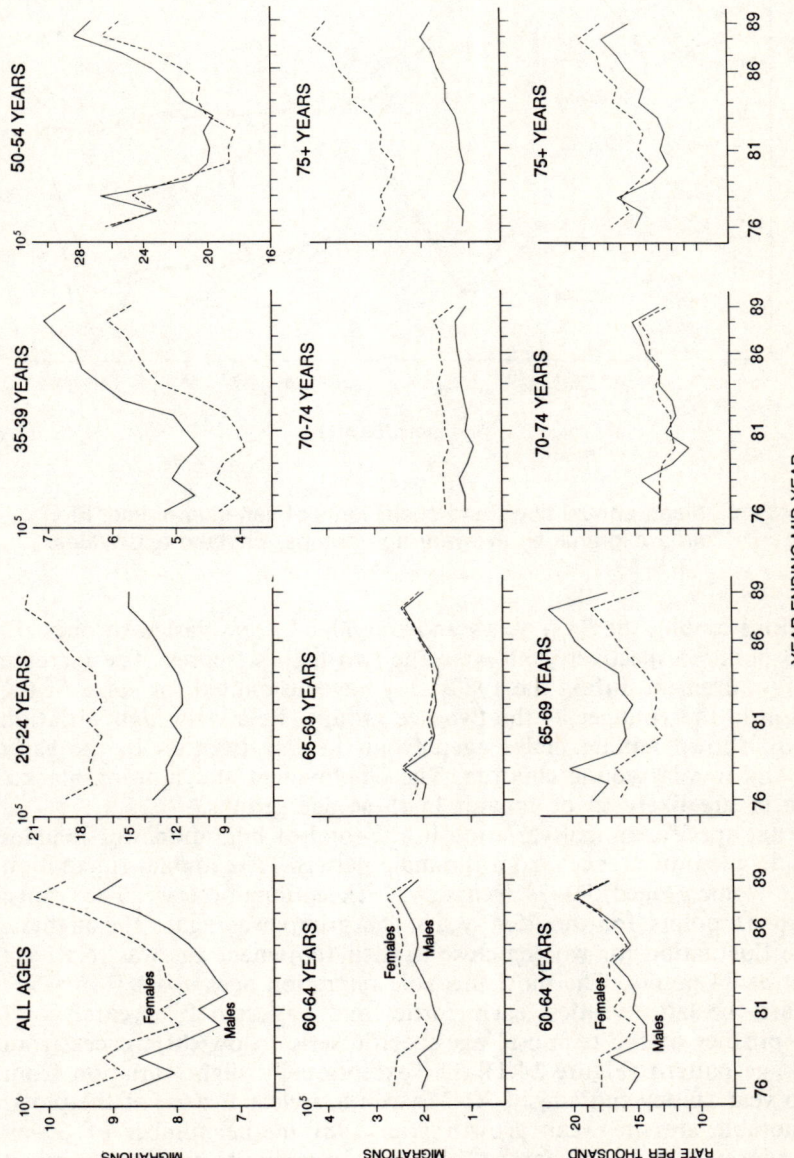

Figure 14.1 Migration between FPC areas in England and Wales by age group, 1975–89

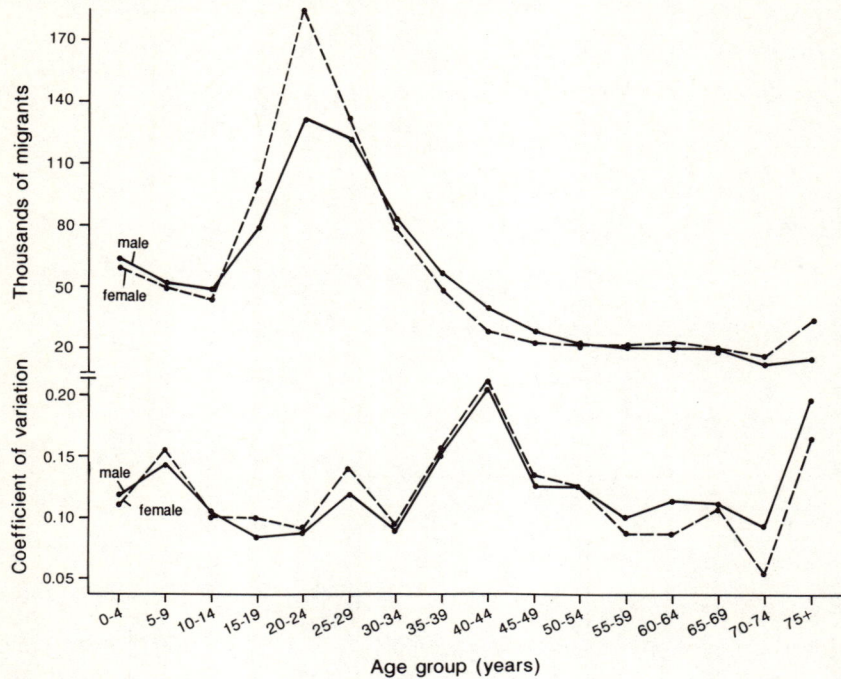

Figure 14.2   Mean annual flows and coefficients of variation of inter-FPC area migrants by five-year age groups, England and Wales, 1975–89

migrations among the 75+ years and the 60–64 years varied through 75 and 48 points respectively and were the two highest scores. The increase of early retirement during the 1980s may have accounted for some of the variation in the younger of the two age groups. Relatively high variation was also shown among males aged from the late twenties to the early fifties and in very young children. The employment and housing market influences are likely to be greater in these age groups.

The age-specific annual variation in the total of migrations for females shows detailed differences from the male pattern. The annual fluctuation among women aged 70–74 years was exceptionally low. The range through 61 points for the 75+ years age group was again the highest, but the fluctuation for women close to their retirement age was relatively modest at 34 points. The most unstable migration ages apart from 75+ years are the late twenties, early forties and less than five years.

The profiles of the temporal age-specific series show differences from the all-age pattern (Figure 14.1). The exceptionally slight variation from year to year among those aged 70–74 years is a clear feature of the plots. Also notable are the weak growth after 1981 in the number of 60–69 years migrants and, in marked contrast, exceptional increases among those aged 75+ years. These contrasts are shown by the ratios of the number of migrants in each year to the number in the Census migration year 1980–81 (Table 14.1), and the coefficients of variation of the annual age-specific totals (Figure 14.2).

Some part of the variation in the yearly number of elderly migrants can be attributed to changes in the populations at risk. The temporal series of age/sex-specific migration rates largely repeat the patterns of the absolute totals, at least among elderly people, and several discrepancies can indeed be attributed to the changing at-risk population (Figure 14.2). The rate of migration among people in their late sixties rose in parallel with the rise in all-age migrations during the 1980s, and it was the fall in the estimated population from 2.53 million in 1979–80 to 2.17 million in 1984–85 which accounted for the stability of the absolute number. Secondly, the strong rise in the number of 75+ year migrants was associated with the growth of this population from an estimated 2.86 million in 1980–81 to 3.42 million in 1988–89. The migration rates among this age group did increase but not to an exceptional degree.

14.3 Spatial patterns of gains and losses in England Wales

In- and out-migration rates have been calculated for the 94 FPC areas within England and Wales. For each area, the rates at the beginning and end of the study decade have been compared as a ratio. The number of male or female in-migrants and out-migrants to a FPC area in a five-year age group is normally no more than a few hundred. The total can change considerably from year to year. Partly to reduce this statistical 'noise', the mean rates of in-migration and out-migration among the 94 FPC areas in England and Wales have been calculated for the two five-year periods, 1975–76 to 1979–80 and 1984–85 to 1988–89. The at-risk populations have been calculated for the first period as the mean mid-year population estimates for the six years 1975 to 1980, and for the second period the mean for the five years 1984 to 1988. For most practical purposes, we are studying change over a decade, and for simplicity reference will be made to the situation at the beginning and end of the study 'decade'. Five-year age groups from 50–54 years to 70–74 and 75+ have been used, with additional comparative analysis of aggregated 60–69 years retirement and the 70+ years 'old old' age groups.

The age/sex specific rates of migration show the expected minor retirement peak (at 60–64 years among women and 65–69 years among men) and a rise from 70–74 years to the oldest age group in both sexes (Table 14.2). Male mean rates rose by around 13 per cent over the study decade and female rates by somewhat less although with a strong age differential: among women aged 60–64 years the migration rate hardly changed, while among those aged 75+ years there was a one-fifth increase.

Table 14.2 also shows the coefficients of variation of the in-migration rates by sex and by five-year age group among the 94 FPC areas in England and Wales. These indicate the spatial selectivity of migration

Table 14.2 Age- and sex-specific migration rates for the population aged 50+ years in England and Wales, 1975–80 and 1984–89

	Age group (years)					
	50–54	55–59	60–64	65–69	70–74	75+
Migration rate per 10,000 persons*						
Males 1975–79	160	151	153	176	127	144
Females 1975–79	151	160	170	153	128	153
Males 1984–89	190	167	173	194	138	157
Females 1984–89	175	166	174	164	133	176
Mean out-migration rate per 10,000 persons for 94 FPC areas						
Males 1975–79	162	148	150	170	120	136
Females 1975–79	149	153	164	146	120	143
Males 1984–89	192	167	169	190	135	153
Females 1984–89	176	165	170	160	130	173
Males 84–89:75–80	119	113	113	112	113	113
Females 84–89:75–80	118	108	104	110	108	121
Mean in-migration rate per 10,000 persons for 94 FPC areas						
Males 1975–80	160	149	149	164	120	134
Females 1975–80	149	154	163	144	120	147
Males 1984–89	193	169	170	185	134	154
Females 1984–89	176	165	168	158	130	174
Males 84–89:75–80	121	113	114	113	112	115
Females 84–89:75–80	118	107	103	110	108	118
Coefficients of variation of 94 FPC area out-migration rates						
Males 1975–79	0.46	0.48	0.53	0.57	0.49	0.40
Females 1975–79	0.48	0.52	0.55	0.49	0.47	0.35
Males 1984–89	0.41	0.44	0.50	0.53	0.44	0.36
Females 1984–89	0.41	0.47	0.52	0.47	0.40	0.33
Males 84–89:75–80	0.89	0.92	0.94	0.93	0.90	0.90
Females 84–89:75–80	0.85	0.90	0.95	0.96	0.85	0.94
Coefficients of variation of 94 FPC area in-migration rates						
Males 1975–79	0.43	0.51	0.63	0.61	0.47	0.41
Females 1975–79	0.50	0.58	0.61	0.54	0.45	0.46
Males 1984–89	0.39	0.48	0.62	0.58	0.43	0.38
Females 1984–89	0.43	0.55	0.58	0.48	0.41	0.41
Males 84–89:75–80	0.91	0.94	0.98	0.95	0.91	0.93
Females 84–89:75–80	0.86	0.95	0.95	0.89	0.91	0.89

Note: * Mean of the aggregate national rates of migration for the years 1975–76 to 1979–80 or 1984–85 to 1988–89.

gains and losses at various ages and bring out the distinctiveness of moves made by people in their sixties, with coefficients of around 60 per cent compared to 41–47 per cent for older migrants. As the migration rates have increased over the decade, some reduction in the variation of FPC area migration rates is shown, particularly for males and females aged 50–54 years, men over 70 years, and women over 65 years.

14.4 Over- and underrepresentation of elderly people among migrants

The number of migrants aged 60–69 years has been calculated as a percentage of all migrants and as a ratio of migrants aged 70+ years (Y:O). The total of older migrants has also been expressed as a percentage of the total. In the late 1970s the younger elderly formed 7 per cent or more of all male out-migrants from Middlesex, Redbridge and Waltham Forest and Cornwall and 6.4 per cent or more from the Isle of Wight, Surrey, Barking and Havering and Bromley. By the late 1980s, more than 8 per cent of the male out-migrants from Barking and Havering and Bromley and more than 7 per cent of those from Hertfordshire, Surrey and the Isle of Wight were young elderly people. Young elderly females tended to form much smaller shares of all out-migrants, but the areas where they were overrepresented were similar. In the late 1970s, 4 per cent or more female out-migrants were aged 60–69 years from East Sussex, the Isle of Wight, Redbridge and Waltham Forest, Middlesex and Dorset. By the late 1980s, only the Isle of Wight, Barking and Havering and Bromley generated young female elderly out-migrants at the same relative rate. The common characteristics of these generation areas, apart from being in southernmost England, are that they have good residential environments, and either a relatively strong local employment availability or a high share of affluent elderly people.

Areas with an exceptional generation of 'old old' out-migrants were all favoured destination areas for young elderly migrants. As many as 7.2 per cent of the Isle of Wight's male out-migrants in the late 1970s were aged 70+ years, and more than 5 per cent of those leaving East and West Sussex and Dorset. The situation was little changed in the late 1980s, for between 6.7 and 7.0 per cent of the male out-migrants from East Sussex, the Isle of Wight and Dorset were aged 70+ years. Among females, lower overrepresentations of 'old old' out-migrants were generated. In the late 1970s, 70+-year-old migrants formed 5.8 per cent of the females leaving East Sussex and more than 5 per cent of those leaving West Sussex and Dorset. By the late 1980s, 6.6 per cent of female out-migrants from East Sussex were 'old old', and at least 5.5 per cent from the Isle of Wight, West Sussex and Dorset.

The concentration of elderly migrants' destinations is even more pronounced. At the beginning of the study decade, one in eight of the male migrants entering the Isle of Wight (and the Isle of Man) were in their sixties and more than 1 in 10 of those going to East Sussex, Cornwall, Dorset and Norfolk. At least 9 per cent of those entering West Sussex, Devon, Somerset, Clwyd and Gwynedd were aged 60–69 years. The relative shares and the most favoured destination districts were little altered by the late 1980s except that the Sussex scores were reduced and Lincolnshire and Powys had joined the counties with more than 10 per cent of their male in-migrants aged 60–69 years. Female migrants showed a much lesser tendency to concentrate on these favoured retirement areas. During the late 1970s, 6.7 per cent of the female in-migrants to both East Sussex and the Isle of Wight were in their sixties, and the only other districts where young female elderly migrants exceeded 5 per cent of the total were West Sussex, Dorset and Clwyd. By the late 1980s, a slightly greater degree of concentration was evident with more than 1 in 20 of the female migrants entering Lincolnshire, the Isle of Wight, West Sussex, Cornwall, Dorset, Clwyd and Gwynedd being aged 60–69 years.

Migrants aged 70+ years have been increasingly attracted to the nation's 'classic' coastal retirement districts. At the beginning of the study decade, around 1 in 20 of the males entering East and West Sussex and Dorset were 'old old'. A decade later, 6.7 per cent of the males going to Sefton, and at least 6 per cent of those entering the Isle of Wight, West Sussex, Dorset and Powys were 70+ years old. More than 5 per cent of those going to Lincolnshire, East Sussex, Cornwall, Devon, Somerset, the Wirral, Clwyd and Gwynedd were of this age. Among women, West Sussex was the only district in the late 1970s to have more than 1 in 20 of its in-migrants of advanced old age, and the share exceeded 4 per cent only to East Sussex, Dorset and Sefton. The late 1980s saw this last district succeed to a remarkable extent in attracting women aged 70+ years. They formed 7.3 per cent of all female in-migrants by the late 1980s. The only other districts were 'old old' women exceeded 1 in 20 of all in-migrants were East and West Sussex, the Isle of Wight, Dorset, the Wirral and Powys.

Sefton also had the distinction in the late 1970s of being the only FPC area to attract more 'old old' than young elderly male migrants. Close behind, with ratios of 1.0, were Newcastle, Sheffield, Wolverhampton, Wigan and Croydon, although with the possible exception of Croydon these cities were unattractive to elderly migrants whatever their age and the numbers involved were low. At the end of the study decade, Hertfordshire had joined Sefton in attracting more 70+ years than 60–69 years males, and ratios of 1.0 were calculated for Berkshire, Surrey, Richmond and Kingston, Merton, Sutton and Wandsworth, and Bromley. Although these affluent London and Home Counties districts now have very high departure rates of people at retirement age, simultaneously they attract relatively high numbers of people aged 70 or more.

Reflecting the greater longevity of women, a large number of districts attract more female migrants aged 70+ years than in their sixties. The Y:O ratio was as low as 0.5 in the late 1970s in South Tyneside and Wolverhampton and was 0.6 in Croydon and South Glamorgan. By the late 1980s, Surrey and Croydon had joined Sefton with scores of 0.5, and 13 districts had ratios of 0.6 (Bradford, Herts, Berks, Richmond, Merton, Bromley, Middlesex, Birmingham, Bury, Oldham, Trafford, Liverpool, Wirral).

14.5 The spatial patterns of elderly migration

Migration data of the British Censuses from 1961 have established the now well-known features of the origins and destinations of elderly people's migrations (Law and Warnes, 1982; Warnes and Vergoossen, 1989). The main findings are confirmed by the present data. During the last 15 years approximately 1.5 per cent of people aged 60+ years have moved between FPC areas each year (Table 14.2). The male and female 60+ rates were virtually the same in the late 1970s although a slight female lead emerged by the late 1980s. The highest age-specific (in- and out-) migration rates at both the beginning and end of the study period among males were in the 65–69 years age group, the 1.9 per cent out-migration rate for the late 1980s being the highest elderly age/sex rate. Among females, however, there was a change over the study period, with both the in-migration and out-migration rates among those aged 70+ years overtaking those for the 60–64 years retirement peak. In the late 1970s, the 'old old' and 'retirement' rates of out-migration were 1.43 and 1.64 per cent and of in-migration 1.47 and 1.63 per cent, but by the late 1980s the respective rates of out-migration were 1.73 and 1.70 per cent and of in-migration 1.74 and 1.68 per cent.

14.5.1 Out-migration rates at retirement age and in extreme old age

The spatial patterns of high and low out-migration rates are similar for the retirement and the 'old old' age groups. The greatest variation among the FPC area out-migration rates for males was in the 65–69 years age group and for females in the 60–64 years age group. In both the late 1970s and the late 1980s, the coefficients of variation of the area rates at the retirement ages for both sexes exceeded 50 per cent and the distributions had strong positive skewness. The variation was greater for males than females. The means and standard deviations of the 94 FPC-area rates for each age/sex-specific group have been calculated. Exceptionally high and low migration rates are identified as greater than one or two standard deviations (s) above or below the mean (represented as $> +2s$, $> +1s$ and $< -1s$).

The highest retirement-age out-migration rates are in a contiguous belt of districts in London and the outer metropolitan area counties of Surrey, Berkshire, Hertfordshire and Buckinghamshire (Figure 14.3). Male rates of out-migration from several districts in this core approach 5 per cent each year (Table 14.3). This level is consistent with survey evidence that of the order of a fifth or a quarter of the populations reaching retirement leave the Greater London County area (Stuart, 1987; Warnes and Condon, 1990). This 'export area' consolidated and deepened during the study period, with the male 65–69 years rates for the last two counties mentioned and for Barking and Havering rising above two standard deviations from the mean by the late 1980s ($\overline{X} + 2s = 2.96\%$). Bedfordshire had also joined the male cluster with a rate exceeding 1s. The London core of

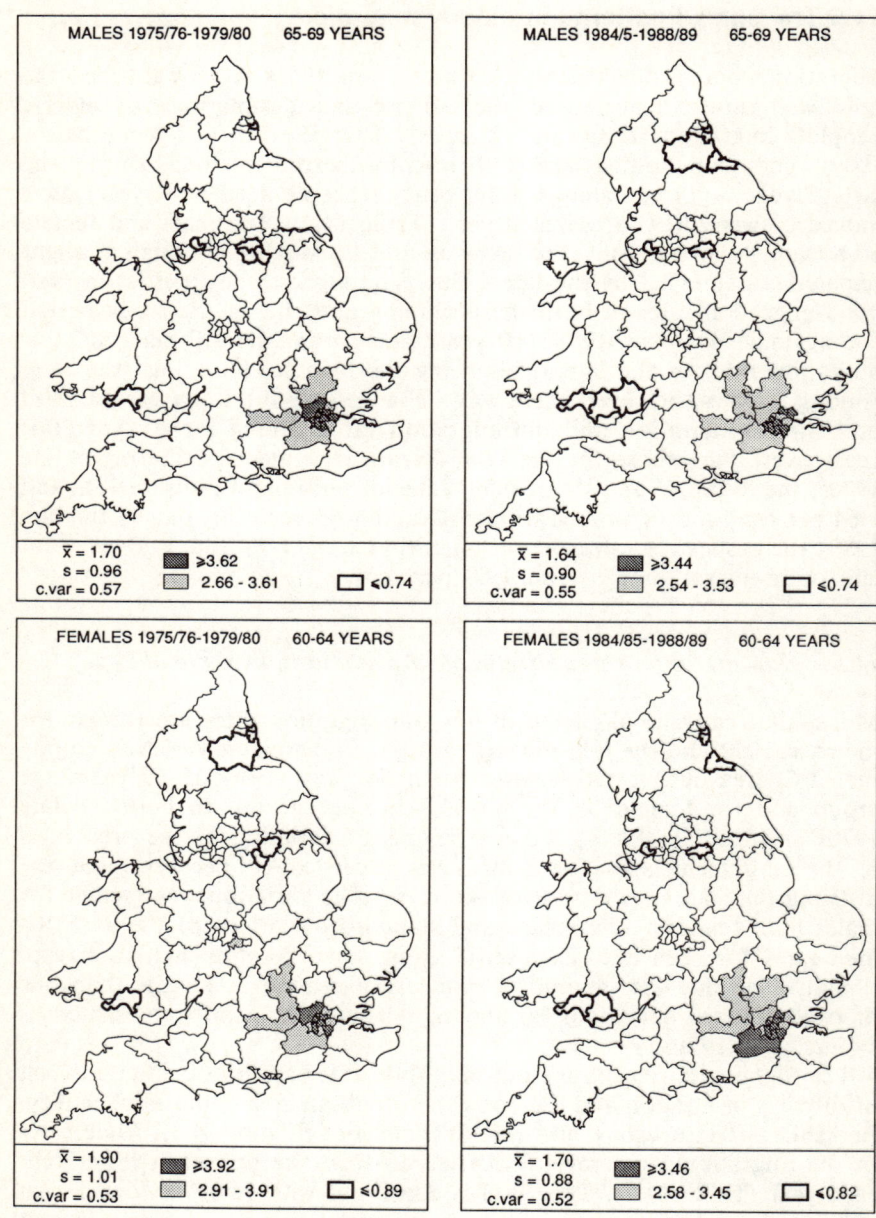

Figure 14.3 Out-migration rates from FPC areas of England and Wales at retirement age, 1975–80 and 1984–89

Table 14.3 FPC areas of exceptional rates of out-migration of elderly people, 1975–80 and 1984–89

Origin FPC area	Males 65–69 years		Females 60–64 years	
	1975–80	1984–89	1975–80	1984–89
Camden & Islington	4.98(1)	3.67(11)	3.85(4)	3.16(11)
Kensington, C. & W.	4.76(2)	4.52(2)	4.60(1)	4.14(1)
Lambeth, S. & L.	4.14(3)	4.51(3)	4.42(2)	3.90(3)
Merton, S. & W.	3.81(4)	4.18(4)	3.46(6=)	3.59(5)
Croydon	3.74(5)	4.80(1)	3.33(8)	4.06(2)
City, H., N. & TH.	3.73(6)	3.91(8=)	3.93(3)	3.47(8)
Middlesex	3.66(7)	3.84(10)	3.46(6=)	3.41(9)
Redbridge & WF.	3.53(8)	4.13(6)	3.30(9)	3.56(6)
Bromley	3.35(9=)	4.16(5)	3.63(5)	3.71(4)
Surrey	3.35(9=)	3.91(8=)	2.93(12)	3.49(7)
Doncaster	0.98(72=)	1.02(82)	0.68(92)	1.02(74)
Sunderland	0.91(78)	0.92(84)	0.58(94)	0.74(90)
Durham	0.80(84)	0.86(86)	0.69(90=)	0.85(85=)
Cleveland	0.79(85)	0.85(87)	0.86(81=)	0.73(91)
Gwent	0.76(87)	0.80(90=)	0.77(88)	0.83(87)
Mid Glamorgan	0.75(88)	0.72(93)	0.82(84=)	0.68(93)
Rotherham	0.70(90)	0.91(85)	0.69(90=)	0.94(81)
Wigan	0.69(91)	0.83(88)	0.82(84=)	0.78(89)
South Tyneside	0.64(92)	0.69(94)	0.67(93)	0.69(92)
West Glamorgan	0.51(93)	0.73(92)	0.71(89)	0.62(94)
Barnsley	0.46(94)	0.80(90=)	0.88(78)	0.81(88)
	Males 75+ years		Females 75+ years	
	1975–80	1984–89	1975–80	1984–89
Camden & Islington	2.82(1=)	2.52(6=)	2.75(2)	2.76(8=)
Kensington, C. & W.	2.82(1=)	3.37(1)	3.37(1)	3.25(1)
Lambeth, S. & L.	2.73(3)	3.04(2)	2.61(3)	3.11(2=)
City, H., N. & TH.	2.51(4)	2.67(4)	2.35(7)	2.94(4=)
Bromley	2.46(5)	2.47(9)	2.53(5)	2.74(10)
Surrey	2.43(6)	2.53(5)	2.36(6)	2.70(11)
Richmond & Kingston	2.23(7)	2.49(8)	2.14(10)	2.87(6)
Merton, S. & W.	2.18(8)	2.52(6=)	2.05(12)	2.76(8=)
Isle of Wight	2.10(9)	1.69(26)	1.43(34)	1.75(34=)
Croydon	2.08(11=)	2.74(3)	2.25(8=)	3.11(2=)
Solihull	2.08(11=)	2.24(13)	2.57(4)	2.94(4=)
Middlesex	1.89(17)	2.42(10)	2.25(8=)	2.60(13)
Manchester	1.83(18)	2.15(15)	1.67(23)	2.77(7)

Note: Values in parentheses are ranks.

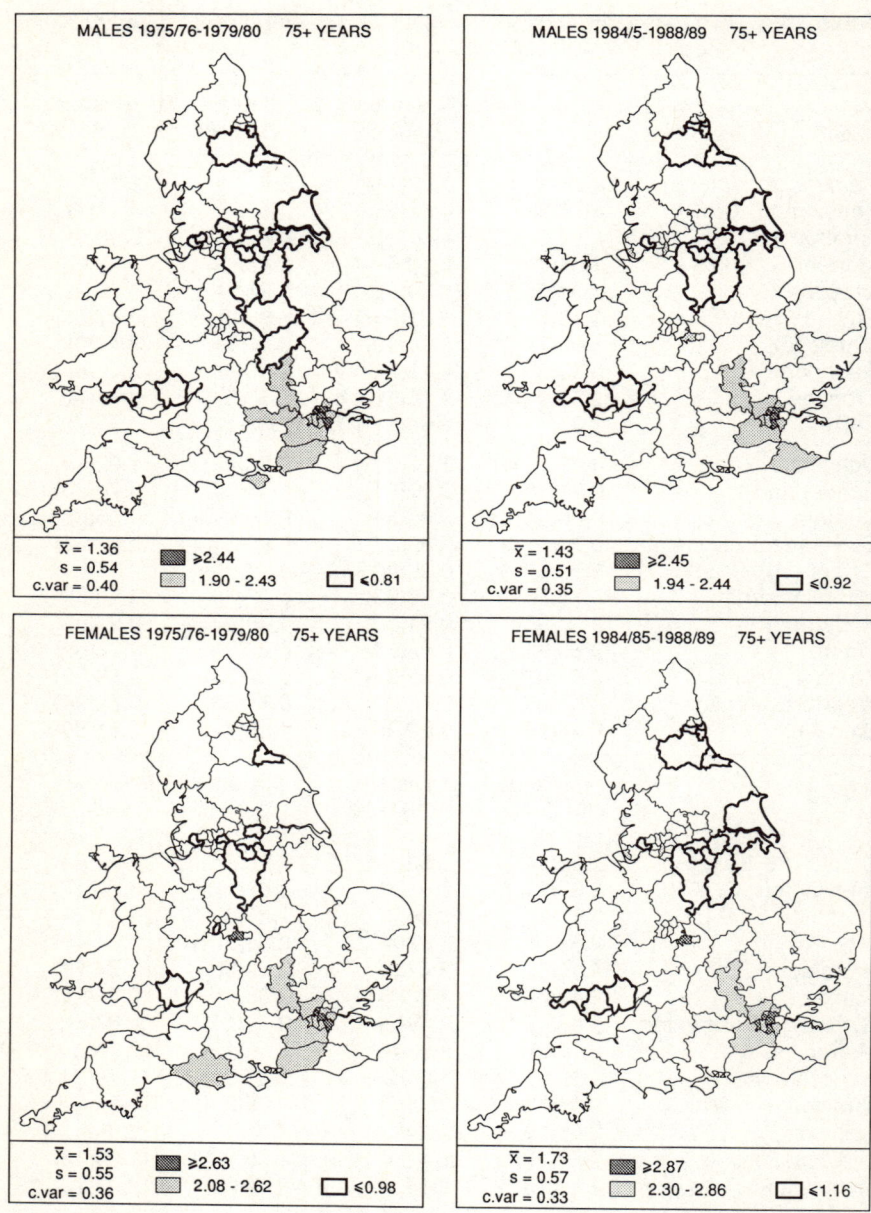

Figure 14.4 Out-migration rates from FPC areas of England and Wales in later life, 1975–80 and 1984–89

female retirement out-migration was less extensive and showed more confusing trends with, for example, Surrey joining but Middlesex leaving the $> +2s$ category over the study period. The extensive reach of the area around London which exports a high proportion of its retiring population, and which includes districts of the highest quality residential environments, is still not widely appreciated. The only FPC areas outside London with out-migration rates exceeding $+1s$ were in central districts of the West Midlands and Greater Manchester, with long-established, affluent suburbs areas like Solihull and Trafford tending to have very high rates.

The areas with high out-migration rates of people aged $75 +$ years are similar, being dominated by London and neighbouring districts (Figure 14.4). Over the study decade, the out-migration rate from Croydon moved to very high levels, while the surprisingly high male out-migration rate from the Isle of Wight in the late 1970s fell to near the national mean.

Exceptionally low male out-migration rates for retirement peak and post-74 years migration (i.e. $< -1s$) were found widely in the Midlands and northern England and South Wales. Many mining and heavy industrial areas are included, such as Tyneside, Teesside, South Yorkshire and Glamorgan, and also a few rural or variegated areas including districts favoured for retirement such as Cumbria, Clwyd, Shropshire and Norfolk. The few areas with exceptionally low female rates of retirement peak out-migration replicate the core distribution of the male pattern.

The most substantial increases in the retirement-age out-migration rate over the study decade occurred in a number of industrial cities and conurbation areas that had had low departure rates at the beginning of the study period, such as Sheffield and Wolverhampton (Table 14.4). Similar areas also experienced unusual increases in the rate of out-migration of $75 +$ years people. Calderdale had the second highest ratio of increase for both men and women. Large increases in the out-migration rate were also found in the contrasting deeply rural areas of Powys and Dyfed which, as they have become more popular districts for retirement, have been drawn into a system of higher migration turnover.

Exceptional reductions in the retirement-age out-migration rate over the study decade were experienced by a few London districts and several adjacent outer metropolitan area counties, such as Essex and Surrey. The set of districts with the greatest reductions in their rate of loss of the 'old old' comprise inner London districts and a few northern industrial districts. It is striking that from the late 1970s to the late 1980s, Sheffield experienced the highest increase of the male retirement-age out-migration rate and the second highest reduction in the 'old old' out-migration rate. It is suggested that this clear alteration in the age of a life course transition is associated with the collapse of male employment in the steel and metal fabrication industries. Oldham shows the opposite switch among women: departures at retirement age have substantially fallen while departures among the $75 +$ years age group have increased markedly.

Table 14.4 FPC areas with the highest and lowest ratios of the late 1980s to the late 1970s age/sex-specific in-migration and out-migration rates

Males 65–69 years	Females 60–65 years	Males 75 + years	Females 75 + years
Out-migration			
2.05 Sheffield	2.17 Wolverhampton	1.86 South Tyneside	1.88 Oldham
1.62 Sandwell	1.42 Bolton	1.79 Calderdale	1.48 Calderdale
1.56 Powys	1.34 Doncaster	1.55 Durham	1.43 Sefton
1.50 Salford	1.29 Dudley	1.53 Shropshire	1.41 Walsall
1.50 Rotherham	1.28 Dyfed	1.51 Powys	1.38 Bradford
1.50 Kirklees	1.25 S. Glamorgan	1.48 Wakefield	1.35 Sunderland
0.70 Merton	0.62 Surrey	0.66 Avon*	0.71 St Helens
0.66 Surrey	0.62 Berkshire	0.64 Hertfordshire	0.71 Kensington
0.64 Essex	0.59 Essex	0.62 Trafford	0.69 Middlesex
0.64 Bromley	0.57 West Sussex	0.60 Barking	0.69 S. Tyneside
0.63 Bedfordshire	0.50 Hertfordshire	0.58 Sheffield	0.68 Lambeth
0.52 Barking	0.46 Barking	0.54 Kensington	0.62 City

In-migration

1.47 Barnsley	1.25 Doncaster	2.13 Wakefield	1.74 Wigan
1.46 Calderdale	1.23 Shropshire	1.51 Tameside	1.55 Dudley
1.24 Sheffield	1.17 Cambridgeshire	1.50 Northants	1.49 St Helens
1.21 Powys	1.14 Gwynedd	1.48 Wigan	1.47 Wakefield
1.20 West Glamorgan	1.12 Bury	1.31 Calderdale	1.44 Oldham
1.19 Avon	1.10 Northants	1.30 Salford	1.37 Manchester
1.19 Wolverhampton	1.09 Bradford	1.28 Kirklees	1.34 Leeds
0.77 Solihull	0.71 Cleveland	0.66 Norfolk	0.83 Camden
0.74 Walsall	0.70 Wirral	0.66 Sandwell	0.82 Hampshire
0.71 Stockport	0.69 Mid Glamorgan	0.67 Oldham	0.81 Kensington
0.71 Sandwell	0.68 S. Glamorgan	0.66 Rochdale	0.73 S. Glamorgan
0.66 Bury	0.66 Somerset	0.65 Isle of Wight	0.71 Northumberland
0.62 Camden & Islington	0.66 Sefton	0.65 Gateshead	0.68 Gateshead
0.61 Gateshead	0.58 Solihull	0.58 Mid Glamorgan	0.61 S. Tyneside

Note: * Also Lambeth, Southwark & Lewisham, and Rochdale.

Given the intricacies of the age/sex profile of employees in cotton spinning up to the 1970s, the vicissitudes that have affected this industry and Oldham's engineering trades, and the complexities of the area's marriage rates and ages, an explanation of this change requires detailed local investigation.

14.5.2 Rates of in-migration around the retirement ages

The areas of the country which attract an unusually high rate of in-migration of those around retirement age are sufficiently distinctive from the areas attracting older in-migrants for the two distributions to be dealt with separately. The study decade also witnessed greater changes in the patterns of in- than out-migration. At the beginning of the study period, very high ($> +2s$) male and female in-movement retirement-age rates were experienced by Dorset, the Isle of Wight and Sussex, as had been the case since the late 1950s (Allon-Smith, 1982; Karn, 1977) (Figure 14.5). There was a high male in-movement rate to Somerset. Also common to the male and female patterns were $> +1s$ rates of in-migration to the whole of East Anglia, Lincolnshire, North Wales, Buckinghamshire and Cornwall. By the late 1980s, however, for both sexes West Sussex had dropped from the highest category and four counties had joined: Lincolnshire, Powys (central Wales), Somerset and Cornwall (Table 14.5). Buckinghamshire had lost its special attractiveness, the consolidation of a high net in-migration area in central and North Wales had occurred, and North Yorkshire had emerged as a prominent destination for female retirement-age migrations. In other words, there was a clear trend for the most popular retirement-age destinations to shift from the traditional south coast counties towards the periphery of the densely settled urban–industrial core of southern England.

The areas with unusually low rates of in-migration were similar for men and women around their retirement ages but this distribution showed little change over the study period. The FPC areas of Sheffield, Liverpool and Birmingham appear frequently in the various age/sex tabulations, and South Tyneside generates strong female out-migration. These districts represent core areas of low losses and they are surrounded inconsistently by various neighbouring districts. No London district has an exceptionally low rate of in-migration at either date.

14.5.3 Rates of in-migration in advanced old age

The pattern of FPC areas with unusually high rates of in-migration of the 75+ years at the beginning of the study decade was focused on the western arc of home counties from Hertfordshire through Buckinghamshire, Berkshire and Surrey to West Sussex (Figure 14.6). Four London districts, including Kensington & Chelsea and the southern middle-class boroughs of Richmond, Kingston, Croydon and Bromley were also

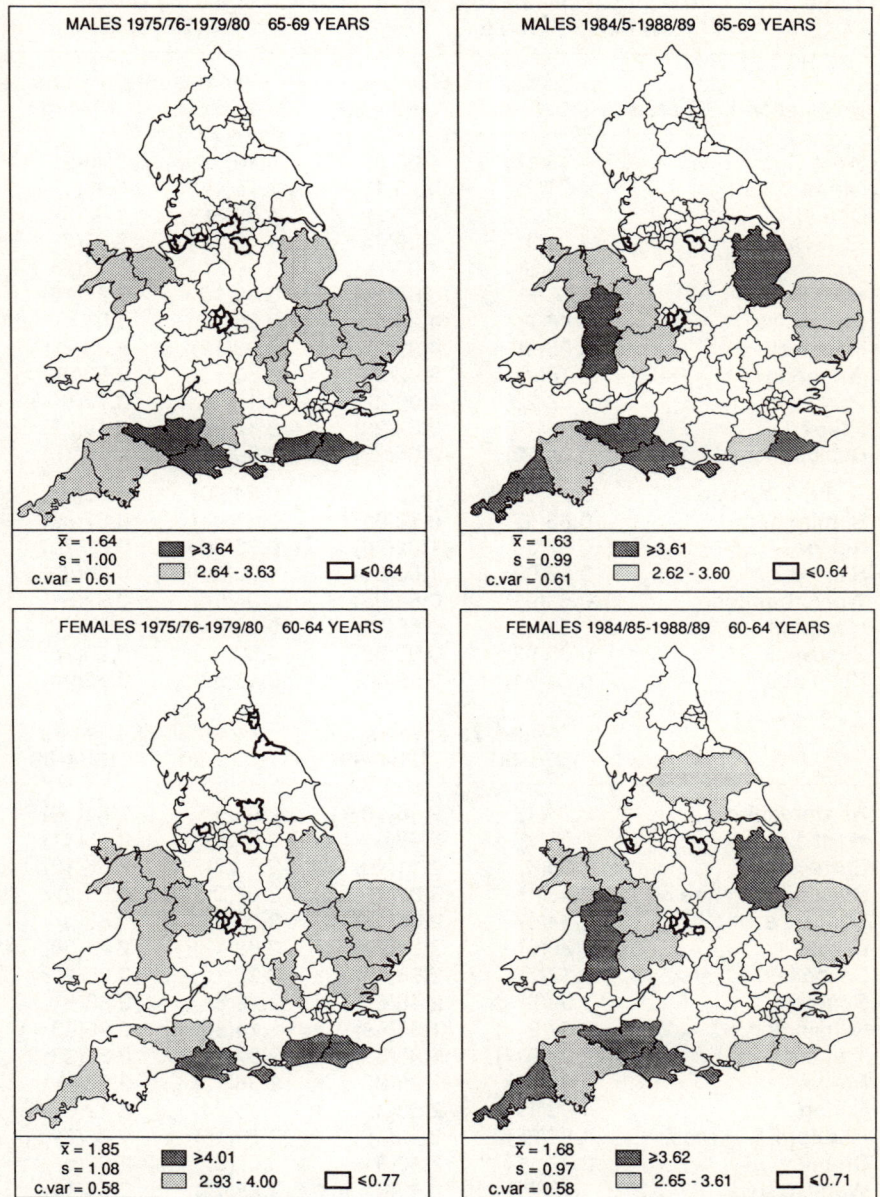

MALES 1975/76-1979/80   65-69 YEARS

$\bar{x}$ = 1.64
s = 1.00
c.var = 0.61
■ ≥3.64
▨ 2.64 - 3.63
□ ≤0.64

MALES 1984/5-1988/89   65-69 YEARS

$\bar{x}$ = 1.63
s = 0.99
c.var = 0.61
■ ≥3.61
▨ 2.62 - 3.60
□ ≤0.64

FEMALES 1975/76-1979/80   60-64 YEARS

$\bar{x}$ = 1.85
s = 1.08
c.var = 0.58
■ ≥4.01
▨ 2.93 - 4.00
□ ≤0.77

FEMALES 1984/85-1988/89   60-64 YEARS

$\bar{x}$ = 1.68
s = 0.97
c.var = 0.58
■ ≥3.62
▨ 2.65 - 3.61
□ ≤0.71

Figure 14.5   In-migration rates to FPC areas of England and Wales at retirement age, 1975–80 and 1984–89

Table 14.5 Areas of exceptional rates of in-migration of elderly people, 1975–80 and 1984–89

Destination FPC area	Males 65–69 years		Females 60–64 years	
	1975–80	1984–89	1975–80	1984–89
West Sussex	4.48(1)	4.00(8)	5.10(1)	3.48(9)
Isle of Wight	4.21(2)	5.16(1)	3.75(4)	4.43(1)
Dorset	4.16(3)	4.73(3)	4.09(3)	4.32(3)
East Sussex	4.07(4)	4.09(6)	4.13(2)	3.61(7)
Somerset	3.68(5)	4.05(7)	3.59(5)	3.72(5=)
Norfolk	3.55(6)	3.59(11)	3.00(10=)	3.28(10)
Cornwall	3.46(7)	4.23(5)	3.33(6)	3.96(4)
Lincolnshire	3.25(8)	4.89(2)	2.93(12)	4.33(2)
Gwynedd	3.18(9)	3.93(9)	2.86(13)	3.50(8)
Powys	2.28(23)	4.29(4)	3.17(7)	3.72(5=)
Essex	2.96(14)	2.34(23)	3.14(8)	2.19(22)
Buckinghamshire	3.04(12)	2.65(20)	3.09(9)	2.59(19)
South Tyneside	0.70(83=)	0.79(89=)	0.54(90)	0.63(91)
Birmingham	0.63(87)	0.73(91)	0.51(91)	0.67(89)
Kirklees	0.57(89)	1.02(76)	0.75(80=)	0.99(70)
Salford	0.56(90)	1.00(81)	1.00(63)	0.86(82)
Wolverhampton	0.50(91)	0.84(88)	0.34(94)	0.87(81)
Liverpool	0.43(92)	0.68(93)	0.65(84=)	0.57(93)
Sandwell	0.36(93)	0.66(92)	0.50(92)	0.66(92)
Sheffield	0.24(94)	0.59(94)	0.43(93)	0.52(94)

	Males 75+ years		Females 75+ years	
	1975–80	1984–89	1975–80	1984–89
Hertfordshire	2.74(1)	2.16(16=)	2.94(5)	2.61(13)
West Sussex	2.69(2)	2.58(4=)	2.67(6)	2.76(11)
Surrey	2.56(3)	2.11(20)	2.60(7)	2.66(12)
Buckinghamshire	2.46(4)	3.03(1)	3.05(3)	3.50(2)
Berkshire	2.44(5)	2.34(10)	3.00(4)	2.88(6)
Dorset	2.29(6)	2.04(24)	2.08(17)	2.21(28)
Solihull	2.17(7)	2.58(4=)	3.23(1)	3.00(4)
Somerset	2.08(8)	2.46(6)	2.49(8)	2.83(8=)
Kensington, C. & W.	2.07(9=)	1.35(48)	1.14(53=)	0.96(83=)
Trafford	2.07(9=)	1.65(39)	2.07(18)	2.30(22)
Powys	1.62(27)	2.95(2)	2.36(10)	3.53(1)
Sefton	1.96(14)	2.93(3)	1.98(24)	3.42(3)
Hereford & Worcs.	1.66(26)	2.42(7)	2.09(16)	2.86(7)
Bromley	2.05(11)	2.40(8=)	3.07(2)	2.96(5)
Warwickshire	1.78(21)	2.40(8=)	2.25(12)	2.81(10)
Croydon	2.00(12)	2.07(21)	2.38(9)	2.83(8=)

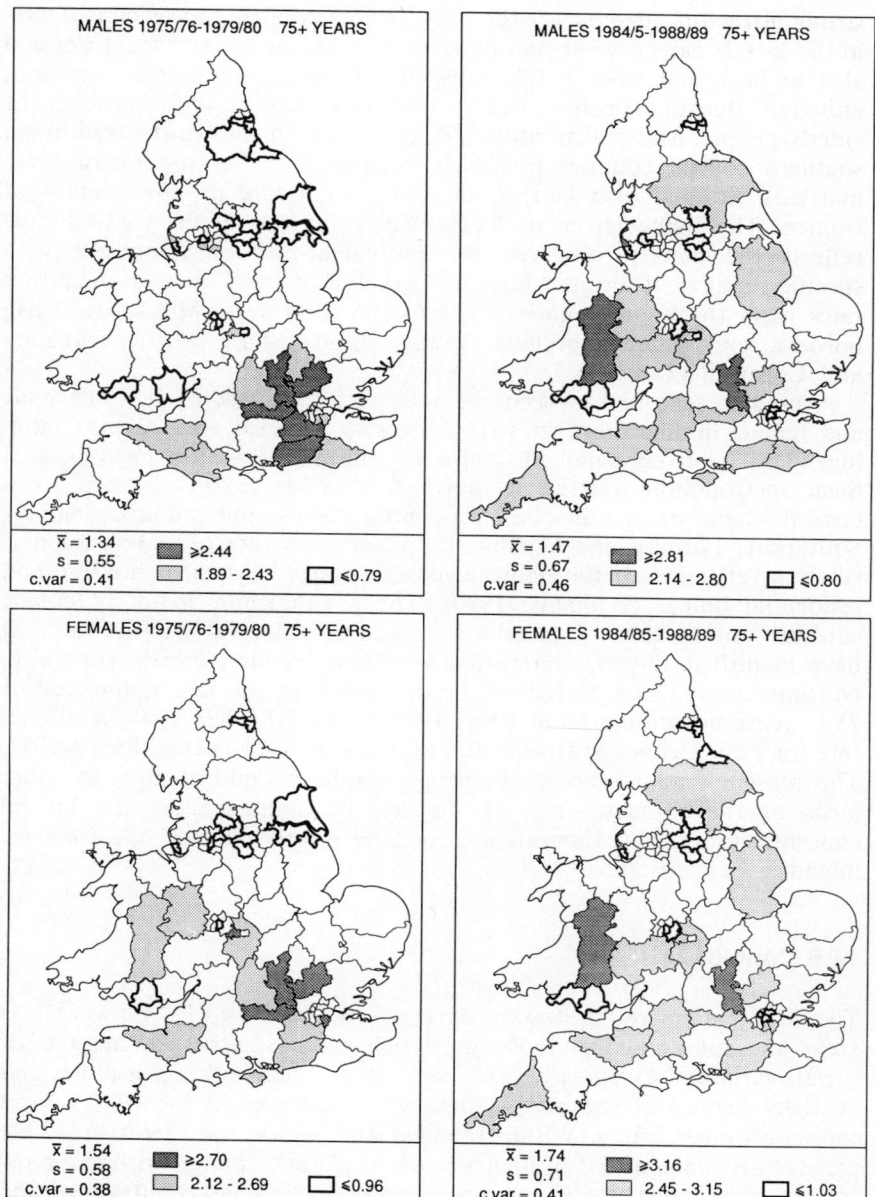

Figure 14.6 In-migration rates to FPC areas in England and Wales in later life, 1975–80 and 1984–89

strong attractors. Bromley is the only FPC district to appear consistently
in the $> +2s$ category for out-migrations of people of retirement age and
also to be found with $> +2s$ rates of female 75+ years in-migration,
although Buckinghamshire nearly replicates such a high turnover of
elderly people. Males were more attracted than females to the traditional
southern coastal counties (probably because a higher proportion were
married). Solihull also had an unusually high rate of in-migration of
women. The change from the beginning to the end of the study decade
reflects the pattern observed for retirement-age migration but with
specific features. There has been a dispersion of the highest in-migration
rates from the home counties towards the rural West Midlands, Welsh
borders, mid-Wales (especially Powys), Lincolnshire, North Yorkshire
and Cornwall (Table 14.5).

A notable feature has been the substantial increase of Sefton's male
and female in-migration rates (to at least 3 per cent and to third ranking). This relatively small FPC area is coterminous with a local government metropolitan district in north Merseyside and is formed by a
coastal chain of middle-class residential towns and suburbs, namely
Southport, Formby and Crosby. Its newly high rate of in-migration is
surely a reflection of the boom in private sector retirement housing and
residential homes (Williams, 1990). The phenomenon is not of course
confined to the south Lancashire coast. Stillwell et al. (1991, Table 8)
have identified Powys, Hereford and Worcestershire, North Yorkshire,
Northumberland and Dyfed as the districts with the fastest increase of
75+ years net in-migration from 1980–81 to 1988–89. The net annual
rate for Powys changed from -0.3 to $+1.9$ per cent in this short period.
The present data set no doubt masks similarly rapid changes in other
areas of the country, such as Torbay, by amalgamating the littoral
concentrations of accommodation for frail elderly people with extensive
inland shire districts.

14.6 Conclusions

The NHS patient re-registration data, as organised by FPC (now FHSA)
areas and for annual periods, are a rich source despite the absence of
social variables except age and sex. One potentially misleading and
artificial feature of the present data set is however its inconsistent and
capricious areal frame. Within England and Wales, the FHSA areas are
particularly unhelpful for analyses of migration change within metropolitan areas. The districts are also generally too large outside of the
metropolitan counties to detect exceptional rates of in- and out-migration
to distinctive social or environmental settlements. The data set's strongest
feature is the continuous monitoring through time of the population's
mobility. It clearly will permit further analyses of the changing distances
of internal migrations.

Another desirable technical improvement would be the extension of
quinquennial age groups up to 85–89 years. Some of the most interesting

results reported here, from the perspectives of both migration studies and applied social welfare, concern the population of advanced old age. The data have provided more detail on their residential mobility than any previous source with the exception of the OPCS Longitudinal Study, which is handicapped by its 1 per cent sample basis. A special merit of the re-registration data is its ability to yield, within months, information on changing migration patterns. This facility is particularly apposite to the changing destinations of 'old old' migrants and useful for estimating the resulting trends in health and social service demands. The additional coding and tabulation would give valuable management data for public service planners.

The data permit several new insights into the temporal and spatial patterns of elderly migration. Since 1975, the low number of migrations by those aged 70–74 years has varied very little from year to year. On the other hand, migrations around retirement age and by those aged 75 + years have been among the most dynamic. There was particularly rapid growth among the oldest age group during the middle of the 1980s. For all age groups except children, the last census migration year, 1980–81, had the lowest or near-lowest migration rates of the last 15 years. The decrease in the migration rate since 1988 must be associated with the collapse of the private housing market in Britain. A recovery may occur by 1992. One suggests that the 1991 Census will again report untypically low migration rates.

As to the spatial pattern of the origins and destinations of elderly migrations, the NHS patient re-registration data confirms the principal features that have been described using census data. Compared to the patterns of other age groups, elderly migration origins concentrate in the London metropolitan area – not by any means confined to the poorer, higher-density, inner London boroughs. There are strands of evidence that during the last decade, high out-migration rates have consolidated from the largest provincial conurbations, particularly Birmingham and Manchester. Sometimes it is the core area and sometimes a neighbouring middle-class suburban district which generates the greatest relative outflow.

The destination areas are also concentrated in a few favoured districts although the last decade has seen significant dispersion of these away from the home counties and traditional south coast coastal counties to more peripheral and environmentally attractive rural areas, notably Lincolnshire, Powys and North Yorkshire. Various districts in the rural West Midlands have also had growing popularity. The greatest change of all during the period since 1975 has been the much greater dispersal of destination areas favoured by 75 + years migrants. The quantitative and distributional changes have been relatively greater for males than females, as might be expected from their smaller total of migrations. Changes in the availability of private, voluntary and public sector accommodation for frail and solitary elderly people are probably the cause of the most pronounced changes in the migration pattern, such as the strongly increasing 'old old' flows into Sefton and to a lesser extent into the prosperous boroughs of south London.

The results presented here support the view that there are significant differences between the migrations undertaken by people around retirement age and those which occur very late in life. Previous research indicated differences in migration propensity and distances, e.g. the relatively high prevalence of long-distance migrations in the retirement peak. The FPC data show additionally that there are three distinctive elements in the spatial patterns of 'old old' migrations. First, there is a high rate of departure from the most popular retirement-age destination areas. Second, there is a strong in-movement to middle-class metropolitan suburbs and, third, high rates of in-migration are attracted to the districts which are gaining a disproportionate supply of special housing and care homes for elderly people. These results are all consistent with evidence from social surveys and housing organisations which shows that migrants in advanced old age commonly move alone and over short distances, their moves being triggered by bereavement or the onset of frailty or sickness. These migrations deserve more attention, for to a greater extent than the residential moves engaged in by any other age group, the success or otherwise of the change of address will have a direct influence on the quality of the migrant's life and on their need for informal and formal support.

15 Move on up: the mobility of Britain's Afro-Caribbean and Asian populations

Vaughan Robinson

15.1 Introduction

There are now almost 2.58 million non-whites in Britain, where they form 4.7 per cent of the total population (Haskey, 1990). They are highly unevenly distributed across the country (Jones, 1978; Robinson, 1986, 1989a) and are therefore simultaneously unimportant to the demographic make-up of large tracts of the country, yet crucial to that of others. Particularly in the inner areas of the largest metropolitan centres non-white may well be the dominant element in demographic change. In Bradford, for example, no less than 62 per cent of the town's Asian voters lived in Asian-dominated 250m^2 cells in 1976 (Cater and Jones, 1979), and in Blackburn, several streets have entirely Asian populations. Consequently, an understanding of the mobility of Britain's blacks and Asians is not only important to any analyst wishing to construct a complete picture of British mobility patterns but is also vital to those studying the demographic transformation currently taking place within our towns and cities. In addition, when groups such as Pakistanis and Bangladeshis are some of the most rapidly growing sectors of the British population, it is clear that the salience of their mobility is likely to increase over time, rather than diminish. Nor is Asian and Afro-Caribbean mobility simply of interest to the academic demographer. The importance of black labour to particular sectors of the economy (e.g. London Transport or the textiles industry of Lancashire and Yorkshire), their growing political significance as voters (Anwar, 1986) and the vocal claims of some groups (e.g. Muslims) for separate facilities and services all suggest that patterns of black and Asian distribution and redistribution will become more important to public and private decision-makers during the coming decade.

Data on the internal migration of Britain's ethnic minorities are extremely limited. The major source of data is the national Census but this has two major flaws. It relies upon place of birth as a way of defining ethnicity and it is only undertaken decennially. As a result, although this chapter is being written at the beginning of the 1990s, the most recent data that are available on ethnic migration relate to 1981 and 1971. This chapter is therefore based primarily upon these two sources.

Table 15.1 Selected demographic measures for Britain's West Indian and Asian populations, 1971–83

Year	West Indians	Indians	Pakistanis
		Population (000s)	
1971	553	307(i)	171
1976	604	390	246
1981	528	563	336(ii)
		Immigration (000s)	
1971	+5	+24	
1976	+4	+15	+12
1983	+5	+13	+12
		Total period fertility rate (children per woman)	
1971	3.4	4.3	9.3(ii)
1983	1.8	2.9	5.6
		Live births (000s)	
1971	12.5	13.4	8.5
1983	5.3	11.5	17.3(ii)

Notes: (i) The Indian ethnic group excludes East African Asians.
      (ii) Including Bangladeshis.
Sources: (i) 1971 and 1975 population figures from *Population Trends*, 9 (1977).
       (ii) 1981 population figures from Labour Force Survey.
      (iii) Immigration figures from Diamond and Clarke (1989).
      (iv) Birth and fertility data from OPCS *Monitor*, FMI 84/9.

15.2 The context

It would be impossible to discuss the spatial mobility of Britain's blacks and Asians without first outlining the basic demographics of these groups. Table 15.1 contains selected demographic statistics for West Indians, Indians and Pakistanis for the period 1971–83. Because data have to be drawn from a variety of different sources, definitions are not always identical and therefore temporal comparisons rarely compare like with like. Nevertheless, Table 15.1 does make it clear that Asian groups grew at a far more rapid rate during the 1970s than did the West Indian population. Moreover, this growth was a result of both higher net migration to the UK and higher fertility levels among those already resident here. In contrast, the West Indian population appeared static in numbers due to its earlier arrival in Britain, low net immigration, and declining fertility rates and number of births.

Table 15.2 provides information on the social mobility of the three groups over the same decade (from Robinson, 1990a). It reveals the way in which members of the West Indian sample were relatively immune to unemployment, but equally how they were gaining little real upward

Table 15.2 Class mobility by ethnic group, 1971–81

	Indians %	Pakistanis %	West Indians %	UK origins %
Stable	42	37	54	57
Mobile	59	64	46	43
of which:				
rapid upwards	15	13	11	12
slow upwards	15	17	12	11
rapid downwards	15	17	11	10
slow downwards	14	17	12	10
Mobility into unemployment	14	19	8	5

Note: 'Rapid' mobility is defined as movement of two social classes or more.
Source: Robinson (1990a).

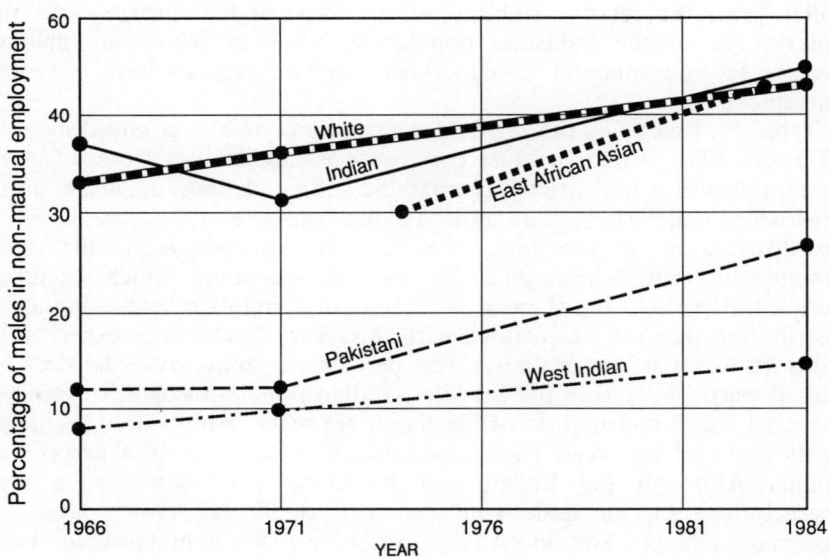

Figure 15.1 Population subgroups employed in white-collar work, males, 1966–84

social mobility. It shows how Pakistani downward social mobility (especially into unemployment) exceeded upward mobility. And it indicates that Indians appeared to be gaining upward mobility, some of which was rapid (i.e. movement of two or more social classes). Figure 15.1 shows the aggregate impact of individual social mobility on the proportion of each group employed in white-collar work. It confirms the steady progress made by Indians, who are now overrepresented in white-

Table 15.3   Regional distribution of West Indians and Asians, 1971–81

	West Indians		Indians		Pakistanis	
	1971 %	1981 %	1971 %	1981 %	1971 %	1981 %
North	0.3	0.2	0.8	1.3	2.0	2.2
Yorkshire & Humberside	5.0	4.9	5.9	6.5	19.7	21.1
North West	4.6	4.8	6.6	8.3	14.6	15.7
East Midlands	4.9	5.2	7.4	9.4	3.5	4.2
West Midlands	15.2	15.6	20.9	20.8	20.9	21.7
East Anglia	1.1	1.0	1.0	1.2	1.2	1.4
South East	65.3	64.9	53.8	48.4	35.6	31.1
South West	3.0	2.7	3.3	3.0	1.4	1.6
Wales	0.6	0.6	0.4	1.0	1.1	1.1

Source: Robinson (1989a).

collar jobs, the relative stability of the West Indian profile, and the polarisation of the Pakistani population, some of whom are gaining access to non-manual occupations whilst others have become unemployed.

Table 15.3 contains the regional distributions of blacks and Asians in 1971 and 1981. Again, because the two years are derived from different sources they are not strictly comparable, although they do allow us to draw some conclusions. The most striking feature about the data is that the distributions of the three ethnic groups remained essentially static despite the radical reshaping of the space-economy which occurred during this period, and the major changes in Britain's overall population distribution that were associated with this. Very few regions experienced gains or losses of more than a few percentage points over the decade. This is particularly true for the West Indian population which exhibited the most stable distribution of the three. No region experienced a change in its share of the West Indian population greater than 0.4 percentage points. Although the Indian and Pakistani distributions were also characterised by an underlying stability, there were some signs of systematic change. The South East lost some of its dominance for both groups whilst the industrial regions of the North attracted a greater share, as to a lesser extent did the East Midlands.

15.3 Inter-regional migration

15.3.1 Data availability

Whilst all geographers researching the internal migration of Britain's population face problems of inadequate data (Champion and Fielding, 1992), for those interested in the distribution and redistribution of Britain's ethnic minorities, the problems are almost insurmountable.

There are no regularly updated statistics on the spatial distribution of a nationally representative sample of ethnic minorities that could be disaggregated to a sufficiently fine scale to provide meaningful analysis. Instead, those researching the changing ethnic geography of the nation are forced to rely upon the 1981 Census (now 10 years out of date) or the Labour Force Survey which contains no information on the process of migration, is published only at the coarse regional scale and relies upon samples which can be as small as 200. Given the inadequacies of official statistics, it is hardly surprising that the field is so underdeveloped and that our knowledge is so sparse. Until ethnic origin is appended to NHSCR records or academics generate their own bespoke data sets from comprehensive research programmes of the type proposed by Robinson (1992), we will be able to provide only a skeletal, outdated and absurdly spatially undiscriminating sketch of how Britain's ethnic population is reshaping its own distribution across the country.

One data set which is of particular value to those studying black migration is the Office of Population Censuses and Surveys' (OPCS) Longitudinal Study (LS). This forms the basic data set for the analysis presented here. The LS involved linking anonymised records from the 1971 and 1981 Censuses for a 1 per cent sample of Britain's population (Brown and Fox, 1984). Within the resulting national sample of circa 400,000 individuals, approximately 20,000 recorded places of birth which were overseas. Retabulation of records allowed four samples to be extracted for analysis, defined according to father's place of birth. These samples contained approximately 4,600 Indians, 3,600 West Indians, 1,500 Pakistanis and 371,000 individuals of UK origins. Samples are defined by father's place of birth not by the place of birth of the individual. 'Black Britons' are therefore incorporated in the ethnic samples. This allows a much more sensitive analysis than is usual from published census data. The group with fathers born in the UK is therefore overwhelmingly, but not exclusively, white. They are variously described in the following text as the UK sample, those with UK origins, and the UK population. Because of the relatively small ethnic sample sizes, data could not satisfactorily be disaggregated into smaller spatial units than the nine standard regions of England and Wales. This chapter cannot therefore do other than focus upon long-distance migration. Equally, because the LS links 1971 and 1981 Census returns, only the 1970s can be discussed. Analysis of developments in the 1980s will have to await the addition of 1991 Census material to the LS sample.

15.3.2 Propensities to migrate

The first finding to be revealed by analysis of the LS data is the relative propensity of the various groups to undertake inter-regional migration. West Indians proved to be the least mobile, with a decennial gross migration rate of only 49.4 per thousand, barely 62 per cent of the figure recorded by those in the LS or UK origins (80.7 per thousand). West

Indians are above all, an immobile population. In contrast, Indians proved far more mobile, with a decennial rate of 111.8 per thousand. Pakistanis recorded exceptionally high rates of migration at 150.1 per thousand.

15.3.3 Currents of gross migration

Patterns of gross mobility for the UK population were overwhelmingly focused on the South East of the country. Some 56 per cent of all moves either originated or terminated there, and the five largest inter-regional exchanges of population involved the South East and the South West, East Anglia, the East Midlands, the North West and the West Midlands in declining order of volume. Commentators such as Salt and Flowerdew (1980) do not therefore exaggerate when they claim that the South East plays a pivotal role in the migration patterns of the entire country. The same is also true to differing degrees for the Asian and West Indian populations. West Indians in particular exhibit a pattern of gross migration akin to the spokes of a wheel converging on a hub in the South East. Fully three-quarters of that group's limited gross migration either begins or ends in that particular region, as do their six largest inter-regional flows. The South East is also the key to an understanding of Indian gross migration patterns. Sixty-eight per cent of all mobility is associated with the region and six of the seven main exchanges of inter-regional migrants involve that part of the country. The other important current of mobility is between the West and East Midlands, a movement which has no real parallel among the West Indian population. Patterns of mobility among the Pakistani population are less easily accounted for by reference to the South East. Just over half the group's gross circulation begins or ends there, against 40 per cent for the West Midlands, 39 per cent for Yorkshire and Humberside and 37 per cent for the North West. (Percentages total to 200 since each migration involves both a source and a destination). In fact the second, fifth and sixth largest exchanges of Pakistanis between regions do not involve the South East at all, being between Yorkshire and the North West, Yorkshire and the West Midlands, and the North West and the West Midlands.

15.3.4 Spatial redistribution: net migration

Whilst the South East is clearly an important stimulator of migration in its own right, some commentators argue that it should not be seen in isolation but rather needs to be placed within the broader framework of a North–South divide. One of the major debates that surfaced at the close of the 1980s was whether Government policy, and the restructuring of the British economy, had accentuated regional imbalance to the extent that a structural schism had developed, effectively dividing the country into two (Green, 1988; Champion et al., 1987). Those who felt that this

Table 15.4 Summary of net migration between the North and the South by population subgroup, 1971–81

	% retention rate in North (i)	Ratio of N–S to S–N move	% of population in net transfer South (ii)
UK origins	95.5	17:1	0.53
Indian	90.0	9:1	1.19
Pakistani	90.8	6:1	2.41
West Indian	93.2	10:1	1.33

Notes: (i) Retention rate equals the proportion of the 1971 population still resident in the same region in 1981.
(ii) Number of net N–S migrants divided by sample size.
Source: Extracted from unpublished LS tables.

was the case, argued not only that the quality of life and opportunities on offer in the North were demonstrably inferior to those in the South, but also that the dividing line between the two halves of the country had shifted South during the decade. Indeed, most re-allocated the previously affluent and dynamic West Midlands into the North, leaving only the South West, South East, East Anglia and East Midlands to make up the favoured South. Given the credence lent to such a division of the country by public, press and policy-maker alike, it is important that net migration be discussed at this scale prior to more detailed analysis.

Table 15.4 contains a range of summary indices of net migration from the North to the South. The data reveal that the North has a better record of retaining its population of UK origin than its black or Asian populations. However, those of UK origins who do leave the North are rarely replaced by migrants moving in the opposite direction, as witnessed by the flow ratios of 17:1. Furthermore, the net flow of UK population to the South only involved 1 in 190 of the population over the decade, 1971–81. Figures for the West Indian respondents reveal a somewhat different picture. Again the North tends to retain a high proportion of its existing West Indian residents, but in their case, out-migrants by no means as heavily outnumber in-migrants from the South. In addition, the drift to the South is a more significant feature of West Indian demography since it involved 1 in 75 adult respondents. The Indian figures reveal a third pattern. Those already resident in the North are less likely to remain there, whilst conversely the North is able to attract in-migrants from the South. Again the net drift to the South involves around 1 in 85 of the Indian population. Finally, because of the heavy concentration of Pakistanis in the North, and the relative inability of that part of the country to retain its Pakistani population, the North–South drift represents a very significant demographic force for that group, involving some 1 in 40 of the total population. Despite this, Pakistanis also record the strongest flows from South to North.

Lastly, Table 15.5 allows an examination of which specific regions in the North are losing to the South. It reveals that migration to the South

Table 15.5 Regional losses of population to the South by subgroup, 1971–81

| | North–South transfers per thousand population from: | | | | |
	North	Yks & Humbs	North West	West Midlands	Wales
UK origins	– 10.6	– 9.4	– 16.1	– 13.6	+ 1.8
Indian	0	– 17.4	– 43.6	– 36.2	+ 60.0
Pakistani	– 29.4	– 24.1	– 100.4	– 18.9	0
West Indian	+ 133.3	– 72.4	– 40.6	– 45.8	+ 28.6

Source: Extracted from unpublished LS tables.

is characteristic of West Indians and Indians in Yorkshire and Humberside, the North West and the West Midlands. Pakistanis record net losses from all parts of the North but they are particularly acute from the North West where approximately 1 in 10 residents left for the South between 1971 and 1981. All these data indicate that the drift to the South, which has been such a prominent feature of the redistribution of the British population as a whole, is even more pronounced for the Asian and Afro-Caribbean populations. What is also true is that the rate of loss has not been even across the North, since it has been the industrial heartland that appears to be losing population more than the periphery.

Figure 15.2 portrays the data at regional level and demonstrates the likelihood that individuals will not have changed their region of residence between 1971 and 1981. West Indians are shown to have a high propensity to remain within the same region, whereas Pakistanis are much more mobile. Turning to individual regions, there seems to be one similarity across all ethnic groups. East Anglia has a particularly footloose population, no doubt due to its proximity to the South East and its acknowledged role as an 'escalator region', temporarily housing those who are upwardly mobile in the South East. Beyond this one similarity, the patterns for the black and Asian populations diverge considerably from those with UK origins. Whereas the UK populations of the North and Wales are particularly rooted, the same cannot be said of their West Indian and Asian residents. The converse is true of the South East, West Midlands and East Midlands, all of which are more effective at retaining Afro-Caribbeans and Asians than those of UK origins. The other regions display varied powers of attraction. Yorkshire and Humberside is able to retain its UK and Asian populations but not its West Indians, the North West does not hold its Pakistani and West Indian populations as well as its Indians or UK population and the South West exhibits a unique attraction to blacks.

Net population change is not simply determined by a region's ability to retain its existing population, but also by its ability to attract migrants from others. Table 15.6 therefore contains net transfer rates per thousand resident population. These indicate whether an area is gaining through net migration, and the scale of that gain (or loss) relative to its

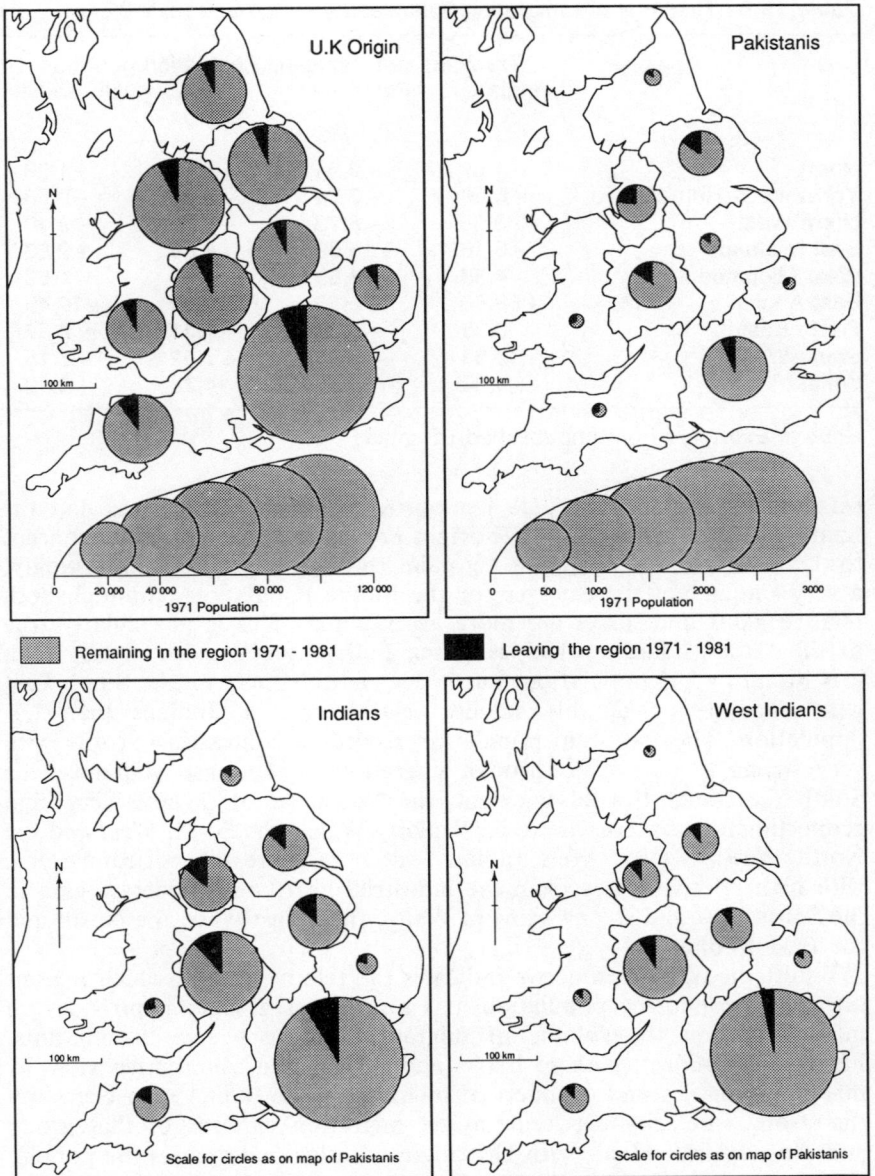

Figure 15.2 Non-movers and movers of subgroup populations by region, 1971–81

Table 15.6 Regional net migration balances by subgroup, 1971–81

| | Transfers per thousand population per year | | | |
	Indians	Pakistanis	West Indians	UK origins
North	− 1.67	+ 2.94	+ 6.67	− 1.28
Yorkshire & Humberside	− 0.69	− 3.79	− 5.88	− 0.68
North West	− 3.39	− 8.73	− 6.60	− 2.40
East Midlands	+ 6.18	+ 15.09	+ 6.56	+ 2.88
West Midlands	− 4.35	− 1.89	− 4.94	− 1.62
East Anglia	+ 53.50	− 5.56	− 4.54	+ 10.43
South East	− 0.35	+ 6.50	+ 1.31	− 2.37
South West	+ 12.08	− 15.38	+ 7.02	+ 8.15
Wales	+ 4.00	− 18.51	+ 14.28	+ 2.42

Source: Extracted from unpublished LS tables.

existing population. The data demonstrate that northern areas and the South East are losing their UK-origin populations, whilst areas adjacent to the latter record the largest net gains through migration. Interestingly, a very similar pattern emerges for the Indian population, although both relative gains and losses are more accentuated. This is particularly true of the West Midlands which is losing Indians much more rapidly than it is losing its UK population, but it does not characterise the South East which has a considerably smaller relative loss of Indians than UK population. The Pakistani population records a contrasting profile with very strong relative gain through migration in the East Midlands, the South East and, to a lesser extent, the North, set off against very high proportional losses elsewhere, particularly Wales, the South West and the North West. Finally, West Indians exhibit a more diversified pattern, with high relative losses from the industrial heartland, moderate gain in the South East and strong gains in Wales, the South West, the North and the East Midlands.

Whilst the discussion above indicates the relative rate at which regions are gaining or losing population it is a little unreal since it provides no information on the volume of migration or the source of migrants. Figure 15.3 addresses these issues and provides an alternative view by mapping volumes and channels of migration. The Indian map bears out the strong similarity between the net migration patterns of that group and those of individuals with UK origins. It also underscores the population haemorrhage to the South East from the industrial areas of the North West and West Midlands, as well as the counterurbanisation tendency from the South East into East Anglia, the South West and the East Midlands. In addition, it highlights the plight of the West Midlands, and the relatively strong gains made by the South West, East Midlands and East Anglia. Finally, it also makes clear the scale of Indian migration, with six or seven major flows of population. The Pakistani map shows how migrants from that group are abandoning the traditional

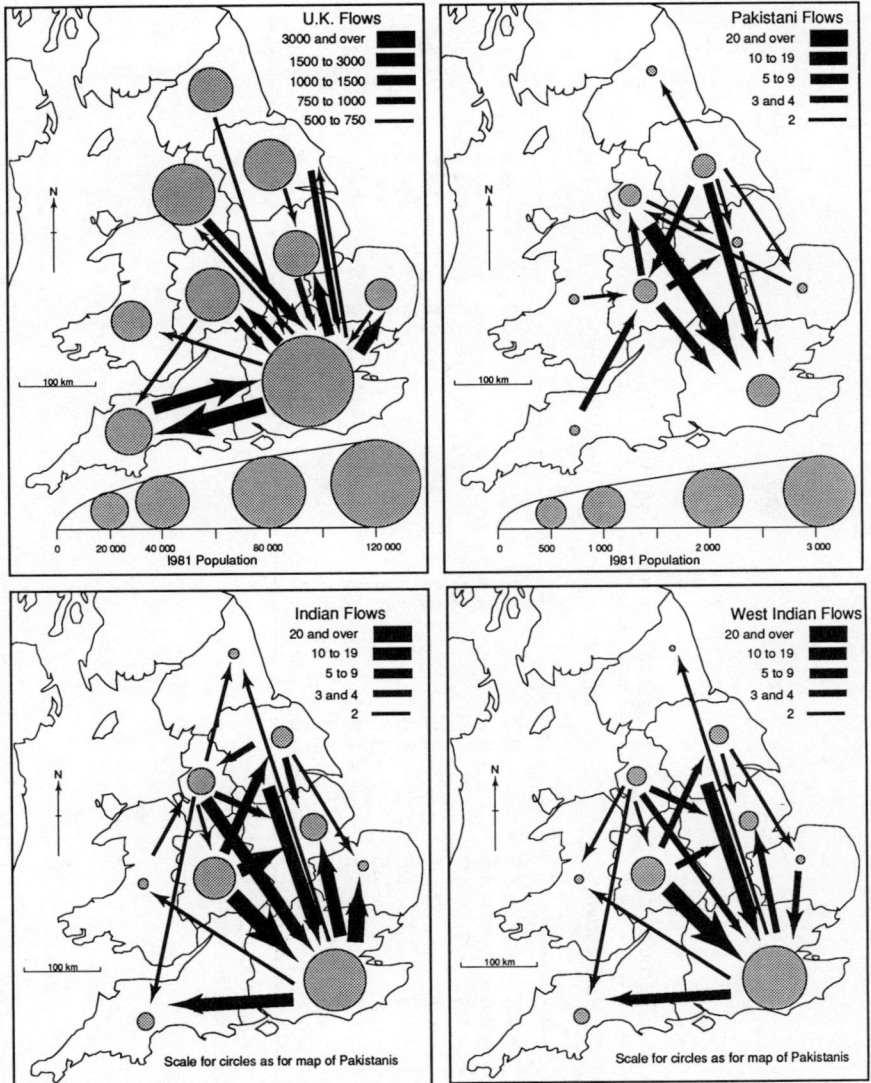

Figure 15.3 Net migration flows of subgroup populations by region, 1971–81

industrial areas of the North West, Yorkshire and Humberside and the West Midlands, in favour of the South East and to a lesser extent the East Midlands. It also demonstrates the withdrawal of Pakistanis from the western margin of the country into the Midlands. Finally, the West Indian map shows two major streams of migration. Both of these involve movement to the South East from, in order of magnitude, the West

Table 15.7 Regional change in subgroup populations as a result of net migration, 1971–81

	Pakistanis		Indians		West Indians		UK origins	
	No's	%	No's	%	No's	%	No's	%
North	+0.2	+2.9	-0.2	-1.7	+0.1	+6.7	-49.6	-1.3
Yorkshire & Humberside	-2.4	-3.8	-0.3	-0.7	-1.9	-5.9	-39.5	-0.7
North West	-4.3	-8.7	-2.2	-3.4	-1.9	-6.6	-184.9	-2.4
East Midlands	+1.7	+15.1	+3.8	+6.2	+1.9	+6.6	+123.9	+2.9
West Midlands	-1.3	-1.9	-6.6	-4.3	-4.1	-4.9	-95.5	-1.6
East Anglia	-0.2	-5.5	+3.6	+53.4	-0.3	-4.5	+205.0	+10.4
South East	+7.7	+6.5	-1.3	-0.35	+4.2	+1.3	-424.1	-2.4
South West	-0.9	-15.4	+2.8	+12.1	+1.2	+7.0	+386.0	+8.2
Wales	-0.4	-7.4	+0.3	+4.0	+0.7	+14.3	+78.8	+2.4

Note: Numbers in thousands grossed up from sample.
Source: Extracted from unpublished LS tables.

Midlands and Yorkshire and Humberside. There is, in addition, some outflow from the South East into adjoining regions including the East Midlands, which appears to be the second centre of growth.

Lastly, Table 15.7 provides some information on the likely impact of these net transfers upon resident populations. The Indian data again closely parallel those for the UK sample, albeit in a more accentuated form and with more moderate losses from the South East. The patterns of Pakistani and West Indian gain and loss show similarities: both exhibit growth in the South East and the East Midlands at the expense of the traditional industrial areas. The former group also records losses in most peripheral areas, whereas the latter are seen to be migrating west.

15.4 Selectivity of migration

Having ascertained that the different ethnic groups have their own spatial patterns of migration it is also important to consider whether those migrations are selective, and if so, whether that selectivity operates in a different way for each group. Four socio-demographic variables were selected as possible axes of selectivity and each of these was cross-tabulated against whether individuals were movers (i.e. inter-regional migrants) or stayers (non-migrants). The four variables were age, social class, highest qualification and housing tenure.

The first issue to be addressed was whether inter-regional migration was indeed selective for all of the ethnic groups. Analysis demonstrated that Indian movers and movers with UK origins were statistically different in all aspects of their socio-demographic profile from their counterparts who were stayers. West Indian migration was selective on all criteria but housing tenure, and Pakistani mobility was selective on all but social class and housing tenure.

Given that the migrations did appear to be selective, it became necessary to enquire whether migration selected the same type of people from each ethnic group as it did from those with UK origins. This proved not to be the case. West Indian movers were statistically different from UK movers on all counts. Pakistani and Indian migrants were also different from the UK control group. Table 15.8 investigates this issue further by presenting migration propensities for population subgroups defined by ethnicity and the four socio-demographic variables. It suggests several conclusions.

Whilst all groups experience peak mobility among their 16–29-year-olds (ignoring the suspect Pakistani figure of 111), and thereafter a progressive decline in migration propensities, the form of this relationship is not the same for all groups. For Pakistanis, higher levels of mobility are maintained into the 30–44-year-old age band but then drop more sharply in later working life. For West Indians, mobility is never very high but drops precipitately after the age of 30 and is non-existent for the retired. And for Indians peak propensities are lower than those for whites but are sustained more effectively during working life.

Table 15.8 Migration propensities of different population subgroups

Characteristic	UK origins	Pakistani	Indian	West Indian
Age:				
0–15 years	82	90	81	35
16–29 years	117	106	95	54
30–44 years	57	76	62	19
45–65 years	37	25	46	19
65 years +	17	111	7	0
Social class:				
I	118	175	87	45
II	99	33	112	69
IIIN	74	17	77	34
IIIM	35	86	60	21
IV	38	103	76	16
V	23	83	39	14
Unemployed	68	88	72	57
Qualifications:				
Higher degree	160	0	161	0
Degree	156	154	120	100
Beyond A level	123	33	85	66
No qualifications	61	85	73	31
Tenure:				
Owner–occupation	72	85	65	24
Council rented	34	54	86	32
Private rented	60	78	85	31
Furnished rented	234	95	112	40

Note: All entries are decennial mobility rates per 1,000 individuals.
Source: Extracted from unpublished LS tables.

Among those with UK origins, it is the white-collar workers and the unemployed who are the most mobile. For those in work there is an almost linear relationship between social class and migration propensity. The semi-skilled form a partial exception to this, since they are more likely to migrate than their skilled counterparts. A similar general relationship is apparent for Indians, albeit with two significant deviations: the professional workers are not the most mobile group, and the migration propensities of Indian manual workers are considerably higher than those of their white counterparts. The converse is true for West Indians who largely follow the pattern established by the UK sample, but at a much lower level of mobility, and without the secondary peak of mobility for the semi-skilled. Pakistanis record very different figures, with a mobile group of professionals, very immobile employers, managers and junior white-collar workers, and blue-collar workers who are much more mobile than their white counterparts.

Qualifications and migration are again linked in almost linear fashion within the population of UK origins, such that the most educated are the

Table 15.9 Socio-demographic characteristics of West Indian and Asian LS respondents, 1971

Characteristic	West Indians %	Indians %	Pakistanis %
Age:			
0–15 years	44	30	30
16–29 years	17	30	29
30–44 years	32	27	33
45–65 years	11	10	7
65 years +	1	2	0
Social class:			
I	1	7	3
II	12	10	4
IIIN	7	14	4
IIIM	28	25	25
IV	34	28	38
V	12	10	20
Unemployed	6	5	6
Qualifications:			
Higher degree	*	0.6	0.2
Degree	0.5	4.0	1.4
Beyond A level	2.7	2.6	1.1
No qualifications	96.7	92.9	97.2
Tenure:			
Owner–occupier	51	74	75
Council rented	26	6	7
Private rented	10	6	7
Furnished rented	13	13	10

Source: Extracted from unpublished LS tables.

most likely to engage in long distance mobility. This is also true of West Indian and Indian respondents. What is worthy of comment is that the uneducated within both Asian groups record migration propensities which are greater than those for the uneducated members of the UK sample.

Furnished renters stand out as the most mobile tenure group within the UK sample, and council renters as the least. Owner-occupiers are the second most likely group to participate in long-distance migration. This is also true of Pakistanis, although the propensity of furnished renters to move is much lower within this group than it is for those of UK origins. For Indians, the positions are almost reversed with council renters and private renters being relatively mobile, and owner-occupiers being relatively immobile. All tenure categories record low West Indian inter-regional migration but here again it is the owner-occupiers who are the least mobile and the council tenants who are some of the most mobile.

Taken together the LS data presented above suggest two paradoxes associated with black and Asian migration. First, the immobility of West Indians appears an anomaly. Why when their Asian counterparts are so mobile are West Indians so static, regardless of whether one looks at the whole group or particular age groups or tenure groups? Indeed why are West Indians so immobile when compared against the UK population? Secondly, why when Asians are so mobile do their spatial distributions change so little over time?

Closer scrutiny of the data, and in particular the socio-demographic profile of West Indian respondents presented in Table 15.9, demolishes the anomaly of West Indian immobility. West Indians were predominantly a working-class population in 1971–81, housed in council accommodation, mainly settled in the South East and employed in manual occupations. Such a group would be the very kind of people that writers on UK migration would expect not to move; they were already located in the most economically buoyant part of the country; they were in a tenure category renowned for stifling long-distance mobility; and they worked in labour markets which are highly localised in nature and within which personal contacts are more important in gaining vacancies than formal channels of information dissemination. In short, West Indian immobility is exactly what would be expected given their social-class profile and their pre-existing spatial distribution.

If West Indian immobility is what might be expected given that group's social and economic characteristics, then the high levels of Asian mobility begin to appear anomalous. Table 15.9 also contains comparable socio-economic profiles for Indian and Pakistani respondents of the LS. It demonstrates that they too were working-class populations (in 1971–81), largely without higher qualifications, employed in manual work, and housed in a combination of owner-occupied and privately rented accommodation. Both groups also had significant concentrations in areas renowned for relatively immobile indigenous populations (e.g. the North West), and in the ranks of the unemployed, a group which is often mobile but only over short distance (Hughes and McCormick, 1985). Again, the expectation would therefore be of immobility, whereas the reality is of considerable long-distance mobility. What makes the Indian and Pakistani cases more of an anomaly is that the most mobile members of these groups (relative to their counterparts with UK origins) are those individuals who would be expected to be least mobile, i.e. the unemployed, manual workers, the unqualified and those in council housing. Clearly, therefore, whilst West Indians might be said to be following the mobility trajectories and propensities of comparable sectors of the UK population, this is not the case for Asians, who have developed distinctive long-distance migration propensities of their own.

15.5 Migration and social mobility

Although the LS does not allow any behavioural analysis of migration, it is possible to investigate whether long-distance mobility was associated with various measures of upward social mobility. Given the fact that the LS contains information on individuals for only two of the decade's 10 years it is, however, impossible to know whether migration and upward social mobility were simultaneous (and therefore possibly causally related) or were separated by as much as eight years. Equally, we are unable to ascertain whether individuals decided to migrate in the hope of locating better opportunities, and then subsequently found them, or whether they located better opportunities and then had to migrate in order to take advantage of them. Despite these problems, the LS does reveal some interesting conclusions about migration and social mobility (as measured by changes in social class, housing tenure and qualifications).

For white-collar workers with UK origins, long-distance migration has little impact upon social mobility between classes. There may be an improvement in the likelihood of gaining entry to a higher social class, but it would only be slight. UK manual workers, however, improve their prospects of social mobility into white-collar work considerably by migrating, and in particular long-distance mobility is often linked to entry into social class II (employers and managers). This broad pattern is also true for Indians, with the manual and unemployed workers gaining most from migration and the white-collar workers least. Pakistanis record a different pattern altogether. White-collar workers do benefit from migration but only in the sense that it reduces the risk of downward mobility. It is thus a survival strategy rather than a strategy oriented towards long-term gain. Conversely, migration appears to be of little benefit to manual workers since it rarely improves their chances of penetrating the middle classes and often increases their exposure to unemployment. For both Pakistani and West Indian workers migration appears to be somewhat of a risk. Some individuals gain limited class mobility from it whilst others become unemployed or slip down the occupational hierarchy. The fact that people are willing to take this risk perhaps suggests that migration is being undertaken because of the deteriorating economic conditions in the source region rather than because of the lure of opportunities in the destination region. It might also begin to explain why so few West Indians engage in long-distance migration.

Whilst long-distance migration within the UK sample is most associated with a shift from other tenure categories into owner-occupation, the exact opposite is true for Pakistanis. Migration reduces the probability of Pakistanis gaining access to owner-occupation, or remaining within it, and instead increases the likelihood of council renters going into furnished property, and of unfurnished renters going into council housing. Those in the furnished sector are likely to remain there. Indians follow the UK pattern with migration increasing the likelihood of movement out of council housing into owner-occupation and sharply reducing the likelihood of gaining access to, or remaining within, the public sector. This latter point is also true for West Indians within or seeking access to council housing. Those who are already owner-occupiers are likely to be forced into other tenure categories as a result of long-distance migration, whilst conversely those in the furnished and unfurnished rented sectors have their chances of gaining entry to owner-occupation considerably enhanced by mobility.

Gains in educational qualifications are frequently associated with inter-regional migration for the UK sample regardless of whether the individual was initially unqualified or highly qualified. The linkage between educational and spatial mobility also exists in the Indian sample. But the same cannot be said of Pakistanis and West Indians. Few of the former had any qualifications in 1971 or 1981, but there appears to be no association between spatial mobility and gains in qualifications. This equally true of West Indians. This suggests that whilst long-distance migration might well be associated with career development for many of the UK sample and Indians, Pakistanis – and the few West Indians who do move – are moving either in search of similar work or of any work.

Thus, overall, Indians are gaining similar benefits from long-distance migration to those gained by their UK counterparts: namely increasing penetration of owner-occupation, better educational qualifications and upward social mobility out of manual work. Whether these changes in status were the cause of migration or concomitants of migration is unknown. Pakistanis on the other hand seem to have an entirely different form of involvement in migration. It is often the unemployed and the uneducated who migrate and they seem to gain little in terms of housing or educational qualifications from the move. One suspects that the group is not necessarily moving out of choice to further their existing ambitions but, rather, is moving to escape unemployment, underemployment and the progressive collapse of regional and sectoral economies. West Indian patterns are harder to typify, perhaps because so few West Indian LS respondents had actually engaged in long-distance migration. For those which had, migration often brought an improvement in housing but rarely enhanced qualifications and frequently increased exposure to downward occupational mobility.

15.6 Conclusions

This chapter has described and quantified the inter-regional migration of some of Britain's ethnic groups. It has indicated that the main Asian and Afro-Caribbean groups exhibit migration propensities and patterns which are not only different from those of the UK population, but also different from each other. Disparities have also been shown to exist between the groups in both the selectivity of their migration and the social concomitants of mobility.

Several significant findings have come out of the research. First, it is clear that, at the regional scale, the West Indian population is very immobile, whilst Indians and Pakistanis record net rates well in excess of those of the sample with UK origins. Superficially, West Indian immobility appears an anomaly, but when the social-class profile of that group is taken into account, their immobility is on a par with comparable members of the UK population. The reasons which may well be restricting the mobility of both West Indian members of the working class and their UK counterparts have been described by Green et al. (1986). They include low pay, lack of skills, inadequate access to information about vacancies, uncertainty about future job security, the desire not to lose a spouse's income and reluctance to break family and community ties. What must also be added to this list for West Indians is their current reliance upon council housing, a sector which is notorious for stifling long-distance mobility (Hughes and McCormick, 1981). If all these factors are successful in reducing West Indian long-distance migration, why do they not also apply to the Asian groups under study? Superficially, one might expect them to, but closer analysis reveals several reasons why this is not necessarily the case. In particular, the broader geographical spread of Indians and Pakistanis throughout the country ensures wider access to information about employment opportunities. *Biraderi* and kin networks ensure not only that this information is transmitted efficiently and speedily, but also that workers may well be able to secure a job through personal contacts prior to making the decision to move, and that they have an initial point of contact on arrival in a new area. Muslim families do not need to consider the loss of the wife's wage since she is unlikely to be working outside the house. The literature suggests that some Asian groups are imbued with a strong entrepreneurial instinct and might therefore be more willing to take economic risks. And finally, Asians are much more likely to be owner-occupiers, and therefore able to organise their own housing exchanges. As a result, although West Indians and Asians ostensibly occupy similar positions within British society and economy, they record very different volumes of mobility.

The second major finding is that patterns of Indian migration parallel those of the UK population, albeit in exaggerated form. This perhaps reflects the changing social-class profile of the Indian population, which is increasingly moving into white-collar employment on the back of educational qualifications. Commentators have already noted significant social mobility within the existing adult population (Robinson, 1990a) and this is likely to be accentuated in the future as British-born Indians enter the labour market, and we are able to assess intergenerational social mobility, as well. Whether this new Indian middle class (Robinson, 1988, 1990b) is adopting the macro-level spatial distribution of its UK counterparts because of the spatial concentration of new economic opportunities or the adoption of broader aspirations from the UK middle class is not yet clear.

The third finding is that West Indians and Pakistanis exhibit similar spatial patterns of migration, albeit of a different numerical order. Both groups are abandoning the traditional industrial areas of the North West, Yorkshire and Humberside, and the West Midlands. This presumably reflects the loss of manual employment opportunities experienced by these areas as a result of recession and the restructuring of the British economy. Support is lent to this view by the profile of those areas which are attracting West Indians and Pakistanis. The South East and East Midlands have both retained a higher share of their manufacturing employment than other regions and it appears to be this which is attracting black and Pakistani migrants. In the case of the former group, there are also signs of nascent migration streams to the South West and Wales, both areas of strong manufacturing growth as a result of the 'M4 effect' and inward international investment. It could thus be argued that the migration patterns of these two groups are still being determined by the availability of manufacturing and manual employment.

Fourthly, an attempt has been made to link net migration with changes in the overall distribution of West Indians, Indians and Pakistanis. Because of the former's low rates of regional mobility, their pattern of distribution remained largely unchanged over the decade 1971–81. In contrast, at first sight the data for Indians and Pakistanis appear paradoxical. There are relatively high rates of net inter-regional migration but the regional distributions of the two groups appear to have changed little. Clearly, the factor which explains this apparent paradox is fertility. Although net migration might have been drawing people out of some existing centres of concentration, this has been compensated for, or even overshadowed by, the fertility of the people who remain in those agglomerations. This would be particularly true of the Muslim Pakistanis and Muslim Indians of Lancashire and Yorkshire.

Fifthly, the issue of whether migration is selective in the same way for all groups has been addressed. This proved not to be the case. Pakistanis and Indians continue to migrate longer into their working lives and the key group of movers within the Pakistani population are the manual workers and the less well educated. West Indian and Indian council tenants are more mobile than their UK counterparts, whilst West Indian mobility effectively ceases beyond the age of 30.

Finally the links between social mobility and spatial mobility were explored. The Indians again appeared to follow the patterns established by those with UK origins, with social and spatial mobility going hand in hand. For West Indians and Pakistanis, migration appeared to be more of a response to economic threat than a search for superior opportunities. Migration was thus having little appreciable impact upon social mobility.

All of the analysis above suggests that it is possible to typify ethnic spatial mobility during the 1970s. Indians appear to have adopted the migration strategies and patterns of their white middle-class counterparts. They are mobile, they migrated both to the South East and out from that area. Their migration was often associated with a gain in qualifications, housing status, and access to white-collar employment. And it was the white-collar members of that group who were the most mobile. All of this is very much in line with their increasing penetration of the middle class (Robinson, 1988) and the new stereotype of that group as successes (Robinson, 1989b). The Pakistani population, too, were highly mobile, but the motivation behind their migration was economic survival not social enhancement. As the economies of the industrial heartlands began to crumble under the weight of recession and restructuring, Pakistanis abandoned these areas in search of manual work in the South East and, to a lesser extent, the Midlands. Their status as economic transients was borne out by their socio-demographic characteristics: blue collar or unemployed, uneducated, older than the norm for UK migrants and gaining little social mobility from their move. They were a replacement labour force desperately searching for someone to replace, a group economically disenfranchised by wider changes in the space-economy (Robinson, 1990b). Finally, West Indians conformed to the mobility propensities of working-class members of the UK sample. They were immobile, blocked in the South East by the dead-hand of the council housing system and by a lack of transferable skills appropriate to the post-industrial economy. For those West Indians who moved, migration was a retreat from the margins of the economy not the beginnings of upward social mobility.

The 1991 Census should shortly allow us to investigate whether the position of West Indians and Pakistanis was a temporary response to transient economic circumstances, or whether their mobility patterns have also started to converge with those of the white population. Few of the signs encourage any degree of optimism, and it seems likely that West Indians will remain blocked in the inner city, increasingly alienated from decentralising economic opportunities and spatially divorced from the real growth sectors of the British economy (Cross, 1989). The future for Pakistanis appears no brighter. They seem likely to remain in constant circulation searching out the surviving remnants of labour-intensive manufacturing, only to be discarded again as successive employers succumb to the demands of the world economy and substitute capital for low-grade labour.

Acknowledgements
I would like to thank Guy Lewis for drawing the maps which accompany this chapter, Angus Stuart, Rosemary Creeser and Brian Dodgeon for extracting the LS data I requested, and OPCS for allowing me to use the Longitudinal Study. All LS data remain Crown Copyright and the author, alone, is responsible for their interpretation.

Bibliography

OPCS = Office of Population Censuses and Surveys, London
GRO(S) = General Register Office Scotland, Edinburgh

Abrams, M., 1989, Third age lives in the next generation: changing attitudes and expectations, in Warnes, A.M. (ed.), *Human ageing and later life*, Arnold, London, pp. 163–77.

Adams, D., 1980, Migration from Scotland to the rest of the UK, *ESU Discussion Paper 10*, Scottish Economic Planning Department, Edinburgh.

Allon-Smith, R., 1982, The evolving geography of the elderly in England and Wales, in Warnes, A.M. (ed.), *Geographical perspectives on the elderly*, Wiley, Chichester, pp. 35–52.

Anwar, M., 1986, *Race and politics*, Tavistock, London.

Armitage, R., 1989, Population in health areas, *Population Trends*, 56, 31–40.

Bates, J.J., Bracken, I., 1987, Migration age profiles for local authority areas in England, 1971–81, *Environment and Planning A*, 19, 521–35.

Bell, D., Kirwan, F., 1979, Return migration in a Scottish context, *Regional Studies*, 13, 101–11.

Boden, P., 1989, The analysis of internal migration the United Kingdom using Census and National Health Service Central Register data, *Unpublished PhD Thesis*, School of Geography, University of Leeds, Leeds.

Boden, P., Stillwell, J.C.H., Rees, P.H., 1987a, Migration data from the National Health Service Central Register and the 1981 Census: further comparative analysis of aggregate inter-zonal information, paper presented at IBG Population Geography Study Group Conference, Oxford (7 September).

Boden, P., Stillwell, J.C.H., Rees, P.H., 1987b, Migration data from the National Health Service Central Register and the 1981 Census: further comparative analysis, *Working Paper 495*, School of Geography, University of Leeds.

Boden, P., Stillwell, J.C.H., Rees, P.H., 1988, Linking Census and NHSCR migration data, *Working Paper 511*, School of Geography, University of Leeds.

Boden, P., Stillwell, J.C.H., Rees, P.H., 1991, Internal migration projection in England: the OPCS/DOE model examined, chapter 14 in Stillwell, J.C.H., Congdon, P.D. (eds), *Migration models: macro and micro approaches*. Belhaven Press, London.

Bohland, J.R., Rowles, G.D., 1988, The significance of elderly migration to changes in elderly population concentration in the United States, 1960–80, *Journal of Gerontology*, 43, 5, 145–52.

Bolton, N., 1988, The rural population turnaround: a case study of North Devon, *Unpublished PhD Thesis*, Polytechnic South West, Plymouth.

BP, 1990, *Statistical Review of World Energy*, June.

Bracken, I., Bates, J.J., 1983, Analysis of gross migration profiles in England

and Wales: some developments in classification, *Environment and Planning A*, 15, 343–55.

Britton, M., Birch, F., 1985, *1981 post-enumeration survey*, HMSO, London.

Brown, A., Fox, J., 1984, Longitudinal Study: ten years on, *Population Trends*, 37, 20–22.

Bulusu, L., 1988, The use of NHSCR data in migration statistics, paper presented at the Institute of British Geographers Population Geography Study Group Workshop on 'Problems and solutions of working with the NHSCR data', University of Birmingham.

Bulusu, L., 1989, Migration in 1988, *Population Trends*, 58, 33–39.

Bulusu, L., 1990, Internal migration in the United Kingdom, 1989, *Population Trends*, 62, 33–36.

Byron, R., MacFarlane, G., 1982, Pilots and pastures: social change in Dunrossness, Shetland, in Jones, H. (ed.), *Recent migration in northern Scotland*, SSRC North Sea Oil Panel Occasional Paper 13, Redhill, pp. 105–20.

Cambridge Econometrics and Northern Ireland Economic Research Centre, 1990, *Regional economic prospects: analysis and forecasts to the year 2000*, Cambridge Econometrics, Cambridge.

Cater, J., Jones, T.P., 1979, Ethnic residential space: the case of Asians in Bradford, *Tijdschrift voor Economische en Sociale Geografie*, LXX, 86–98.

Central Statistical Office, 1990, *Regional Trends*, 25, 1990 Edition, HMSO, London.

Champion, A.G., 1989a, United Kingdom: population deconcentration as a cyclic phenomenon, in Champion, A.G. (ed.), *Counterurbanisation: the changing pace and nature of population deconcentration*, Edward Arnold, London, pp. 83–102.

Champion, A.G., 1989b, Internal migration and the spatial distribution of population, chapter 8 in Joshi, H. (ed.), *The changing population of Britain*, Blackwell, Oxford, pp. 110–32.

Champion, A.G., Congdon, P.D., 1987, An analysis of the recovery of London's population change rate, *Built Environment*, 13, 4, 193–211.

Champion, A.G., Congdon, P.D., 1988, Recent population trends for Greater London, *Population Trends*, 53, 11–17.

Champion, A.G., Fielding, A.J., 1992, Introduction, in Champion, A.G., Fielding, A.J. (eds), *Migration processes and patterns: Volume I: Research progress and prospects*, Belhaven, London.

Champion, A.G., Green, A.E., 1988, *Local prosperity and the North–South divide: a report on winners and losers in 1980s Britain*, Booming Towns, Coventry and Newcastle-upon-Tyne.

Champion, A.G., Green, A.E., 1990, *The spread of prosperity and the North–South divide: local economic performance in Britain during the late eighties*, Booming Towns, Gosforth and Kenilworth.

Champion, A.G., Green, A.E., Owen, D.W., Ellin, D.J., Coombes, M.G., 1987, *Changing places: Britain's demographic, economic and social complexion*, Edward Arnold, London.

Champion, A.G., Townsend, A.R., 1990, *Contemporary Britain: a geographical perspective*, Edward Arnold, London.

Cole, K., Squires, S., 1987, The special migration statistics from the 1981 Census: the data and their implications, paper presented at the IBG Population Geography Study Group Conference on Information systems for population, Mansfield College, University of Oxford (7–8 September).

Compton, P.A., Power, J., 1991, Migration from Northern Ireland: a survey of New Year travellers as a means of identifying emigrants, *Regional Studies*, 25, 1, 1–11.

Congdon, P., 1989, Modelling migration flows between areas: an analysis for London using the Census and OPCS Longitudinal Study, *Regional Studies*, 23, 2, 87–103.

Congdon, P.D., Champion, A.G., 1989a, Recent population shifts in South East England and their relevance to the counter-urbanisation debate, in Breheny, M., Congdon, P.D. (eds), *Growth and change in a core region: the case of South East England*, Pion, London, pp. 106–29.

Congdon, P., Champion, A., 1989b, Trends and structure in London's migration and their relation to employment and housing markets, in Congdon, P., Batey, P. (eds), *Advances in regional demography: information, forecasts, models*, Belhaven, London, pp. 180–204.

Congdon, P., Shepherd, J., 1986, Modelling population changes in small English urban areas, *Environment and Planning A*, 18, 1297–322.

Coombes, M.G., Raybould, S., 1991, Local trends in house price inflation, *Housing Research Findings 30*, Joseph Rowntree Foundation, York.

Coombes, M.G., Dalla Longa, R., Raybould, S., 1989, Counterurbanisation in Britain and Italy: a comparative critique of the concept, causation and evidence, *Progress in Planning*, 32, 1, 1–70.

Coombes, M.G., Dixon, J.S., Goddard, J.B., Openshaw, S., Taylor, P.J., 1982, Functional regions for the population census of Great Britain, in Herbert, P.T., Johnston, R.J. (eds), *Geography and the Urban environment 5*, Wiley, London.

Cribier, F., 1981, Aspects of retirement migration from Paris, in Warnes, A.M. (ed.), *Geographical perspectives on the elderly*, Wiley, Chichester, pp. 111–37.

Cribier, F., 1989, Change in the life course and retirement: the example of two cohorts of Parisians, in Johnson, P., Conrad, C., Thomson, D. (eds), *Workers versus pensioners*, Manchester University Press, Manchester, pp. 181–201.

Cross, D.F.W., 1990, *Counterurbanisation in England and Wales*, Avebury, Aldershot.

Cross, M., 1989, The black economy, *New Society*, 24 July, 16–19.

CSO (1989), *Regional Trends*, 24, HMSO, London.

Department of Employment, 1985, *Employment: the challenge for the nation*, Cmnd 9474, HMSO, London.

Department of Employment, 1991, Revised employment estimates for September 1987 to September 1990, *Employment Gazette*, April, 197–205.

Department of Health and Social Services, Registrar General Northern Ireland, 1983, *The Northern Ireland Census 1981 Summary Report, Table 7, 41*, HMSO.

Department of Trade and Industry, 1983, Regional industrial development, Cmnd 9111, HMSO, London.

Devis, T., 1984, Population movements measured by the NHSCR, *Population Trends*, 36, 15–20.

Devis, T., Mills, I., 1986, A comparison of migration data from the National Health Service Central Register and the 1981 Census, *OPCS Occasional Paper 35*, OPCS, London.

Diamond, I., Clarke, S., 1989, Demographic patterns among Britain's ethnic groups, in Joshi, H. (ed.), *The changing population of Britain*, Blackwell, Oxford.

Duley, C., 1989, A model for updating census-based household and population information for inter-censal years, *Unpublished PhD Thesis*, School of Geography, University of Leeds, Leeds.

Duley, C., Rees, P.H., 1991, Incorporating migration into simulation models, chapter 13 in Stillwell, J.C.H., Congdon, P.D. (eds), *Migration models: macro and micro approaches*, Belhaven Press, London.

East Midlands Forum of County Councils, no date, *East Midlands in focus*.

East Midlands Regional Planning Forum, 1990, *East Midlands regional planning guidance: issues paper*.

East Midlands Regional Planning Forum, 1991, *Regional strategy for the East Midlands: consultation draft*.

Fielding, A.J., 1982, Counterurbanisation in Western Europe, *Progress in Planning*, 17, Pergamon Press, London, pp. 1–52.

Fielding, A.J., 1989, Inter-regional migration and social change: a study of south east England based upon data from the Longitudinal Study, *Institute of British Geographers Transactions*, 14, 1, 24–36.

Fielding, A.J., 1990, A search for the 'missing link' between social and geographical mobility, *Revue de Géographie de Lyon*, 65, 3, 165–70.

Fielding, A.J., Savage, M., 1987, Social mobility and the changing class composition of South East England, *Urban and Regional Studies Working Paper 60*, University of Sussex.

Findlay, A., 1988, From settlers to skilled transients, *Geoforum*, 199, 401–10.

Findlay, A., Garrick, L., 1989, A migration channels approach to the study of skilled international migration: Scottish emigration in the 1980s, *APRU Discussion Paper 89/1*, Department of Geography, Glasgow University.

Findlay, A.M., Garrick L., 1990, Scottish emigration in the 1980s: a migration channels approach to the study of skilled international migration, *Institute of British Geographers Transactions NS*, 15, 2, 177–92.

Findlay, A., Gould, W.T.S., 1989, Skilled international migration: a research agenda, *Area*, 21, 1, 3–11.

Flowerdew, R., Aitkin, M., 1982, A method of fitting the gravity model based on the Poisson distribution, *Journal of Regional Science*, 22, 2, 191–202.

Flowerdew, R., Salt, J., 1979, Migration between labour market areas in Great Britain, 1970–71, *Regional Studies*, 13, 211–31.

Forsythe, D., 1980, Urban incomers and rural change: the impact of migrants from the city on life in an Orkney community, *Sociologia Ruralis*, 20, 287–307.

Fothergill, S., Gudgin, G., 1982, *Unequal growth: urban and regional employment change in the U.K.*, Heinemann, London.

Fox, A.J., 1990, The work of the National Health Service Central Register, *Population Trends*, 62, 29–32.

General Register Office (Scotland), 1990, *Annual report 1989, No. 135*, HMSO, Edinburgh.

Gleave, D., Cordey-Hayes, M., 1977, Migration dynamics and labour market turnover, *Progress in Planning*, 8, 1, 1–95.

Gordon, I.R., 1982, The analysis of motivation-specific migration streams, *Environment and Planning A*, 14, 5–20.

Gordon, I.R., 1987, Resurrecting counter-urbanisation: housing market influences on migration fluctuations from London, *Built Environment*, 13, 4, 212–22.

Gordon, I.R., 1988, Interdistrict migration in Great Britain 1980–81: a multistream model with a commuting option, *Environment and Planning A*, 20, 907–24.

Gordon, I.R., Lamont, D.W., 1982, A model of labour market interdependencies in the London region, *Environment and Planning A*, 14, 237–64.

Government of Northern Ireland, 1988, *Annual report 1987*, HMSO, Belfast.

Green, A.E., 1986, The likelihood of becoming and remaining unemployed in Great Britain, *Institute of British Geographers Transactions NS*, 11, 37–56.

Green, A.E., 1988, The North–South divide in Great Britain: an examination of the evidence, *Institute of British Geographers Transactions NS*, 13, 179–98.

Green, A.E., Owen, D.W., 1990, *Matching local labour supply and demand in Britain during the 1980s*, paper presented at the 22nd BSRSA Annual Conference, University of Liverpool (September).

Green, A.E., Owen, D.W., Champion, A.G., Goddard, J.B., Coombes, M.G., 1986, What contribution can labour migration make to reducing unemployment?, in Hart, P.E. (ed.), *Unemployment and labour market policies*, JSPP 12, Gower, Aldershot.

Gregg, P.A., Worswick, G.D.N., 1988, Recession and recovery in Britain: the 1930s and the 1980s, *National Institute Economic Review*, 126, 44–50.

Gregory, D., 1977, Green belt policy and the conurbation, in Joyce, F.E. (ed.), *Metropolitan development and change*, Teakfield, Farnborough, pp. 231–52.

Grieco, M.S., 1985, Corby: new town planning and imbalanced development, *Regional Studies*, 19, 1, 9–18.

Grundy, E., 1987a, Retirement migration and its consequences in England and Wales, *Ageing and Society*, 7, 1, 57–82.

Grundy, E., 1987b, Household change and migration among the elderly in England and Wales, *Espace Populations Sociétés*, 1987/1, 109–23.

Gwynedd County Council, 1988, *Language, planning and housing in Gwynedd: a memorandum to the Secretary of State for Wales*, Gwynedd County Council, Caernarfon.

Hamnett, C., 1989, Cycling across the gap, *Housing Review*, 38, 3, 83–5.

Hamnett, C., 1990, Back to the future? Regional house price changes in the U.K., *Housing Review*, 39, 5, 116–17.

Hamnett, C., 1991, Labour markets, housing markets and social restructuring in global city: the city of London, in Allen, J., Hamnett, C. (eds), *Housing and labour markets: building the connections*, Unwin Hyman, London.

Hamnett, C., Harmer, M., Williams, P., 1991, *Safe as houses: housing inheritance in Britain*, Paul Chapman, London.

Haskey, J., 1990, The ethnic minority populations of Great Britain, *Population Trends*, 60, 35–8.

Heath, T., 1989, Silence hinders police hunt for Welsh arsonists, *The Independent* (11 December).

Heath, T., 1990, Learning language of dissension, *The Guardian* (31 July).

Hirst, A., Mansley, M., Rhodes, J., 1990, Economic prospects for the counties and conurbations, in Cameron, G., Moore, B., Nicholls, D., Rhodes, J., Tyler, P. (eds), *Cambridge regional economic review*, PA Cambridge Economic Consultants and Department of Land Economy, University of Cambridge, Cambridge.

Hollingsworth, T.H., 1970, Migration: a study based on Scottish experience between 1939 and 1964, *University of Glasgow Social and Economic Studies Occasional Papers 12*, Oliver and Boyd, Edinburgh.

Hughes, G., McCormick, B., 1981, Do council housing policies reduce migration between regions?, *Economic Journal*, 19, 919–37.

Hughes, G., McCormick, B., 1985, Migration intentions in the UK: which households want to migrate and which succeed?, *Economic Journal*, 95, Supplement, 113–23.

Hughes, G., McCormick, B., 1987, Housing markets, unemployment and labour market flexibility in the UK, *European Economic Review*, 615–45.

Immigrant Statistics Unit, 1977, New Commonwealth and Pakistani population estimates, *Population Trends*, 9, 4–7.

Institute for Employment Research, 1988, *Review of the economy and employment*, IER, University of Warwick.

Institute of Welsh Affairs, 1988, *Rural Wales: population changes and current attitudes*, Institute of Welsh Affairs, Cardiff.

Johnson, J.H., Salt, J., Wood, P.A., 1974, *Housing and the migration of labour in England and Wales*, Saxon House, Farnborough.

Jones, H., 1970, Migration to and from Scotland since 1961, *Transactions of Institute of British Geographers*, 49, 145–59.

Jones, H., 1988, The human resource, in Selman, P. (ed.), *Countryside planning in practice: the Scottish experience*, Stirling University Press, pp. 31–48.

Jones, P., 1978, The distribution and diffusion of the coloured population in England and Wales, 1961–71, *Transactions, Institute of British Geographers*, 3, 515–33.

Jones, C., Armitage, R., 1990, Population change within area types: England and Wales, 1971–88, *Population Trends*, 60, 25–32.

Jones, H., Caird, J., Berry, W., Dewhurst, J., 1986, Peripheral counterurbanisation; findings from an integration of census and survey data in northern Scotland, *Regional Studies*, 20, 15–26.

Karn, V., 1977, *Retiring to the seaside*, Routledge, London.

Kennett, S., 1983, Migration within and between labour markets, in Goddard, J.B., Champion, A.G. (eds), *The urban and regional transformation of Britain*, Methuen, London.

Kontuly, T., Vogelsang, R., 1989, Federal Republic of Germany: the intensification of the migration turnaround, in Champion, A.G. (ed.), *Counterurbanisation: the changing pace and nature of population deconcentration*, Edward Arnold, London, pp. 141–61.

Law, C., Warnes, A.M., 1982, The destination decision in retirement migration, in Warnes, A.M. (ed.), *Geographical perspectives on the elderly*, Wiley, Chichester, pp. 53–81.

Liggins, D., 1977, The changing role of the West Midlands region in the national economy, in Joyce, F.E. (ed.), *Metropolitan development and change*, Teakfield, Farnborough, pp. 75–96.

Linton, M., 1989, Welsh passions fuel firebombing campaign, *The Guardian* (23 August).

Long, L.H., Boertlein, C.G., 1975, *The geographical mobility of Americans: an international comparison*, Current Population Reports, Special Studies, Series P-23, No. 64, US Department of Commerce, Bureau of the Census, Washington DC.

Lumb, R., 1980, Migration in the Highlands and Islands of Scotland, *ISSPA Research Report 3*, Aberdeen University, Aberdeen.

Mackintosh, S., Means, R., Leather, P., 1990, *Housing in later life: the housing finance implications of an ageing society*, School for Advanced Urban Studies, Bristol.

McCormick, B., 1991, Migration and regional policy, in Bowen, A., Mayhew, K. (eds), *Reducing regional inequalities*, Kogan Page, London.

McVittie, E., Birse, G., 1989, Offshore employment in the northern North Sea in 1988, *Statistical Bulletin E1.5*, Industry Department for Scotland, Edinburgh.

Markland, J., 1975, Some theoretical and empirical considerations of Scottish population migration 1961–71, *Unpublished PhD Thesis*, Dundee University, Dundee.

Martin, R., 1988, The political economy of Britain's north–south divide, *Institute of British Geographers Transactions NS*, 13, 389–418.

Martin and Voorhees Associates, John Bates Services, 1981, *Developing the migration component of the official sub-national population projections*, Final report prepared for DPRP3, DoE, London.

Masser, I., Brown, P., 1975, Hierarchical aggregation procedures for interaction data, *Environment and Planning A*, 7, 5, 509–24.

Molho, I., 1987, The migration decisions of young men in Great Britain, *Applied Economics*, 19, 221–43.

Morris, J., Wilkinson, B., 1989, *Divided Wales: local prosperity in the 1980s*, Cardiff Business School, Cardiff.

Moseley, M., 1984, The revival of rural areas in advanced economies: a review of some causes and consequences, *Geoforum*, 15, 447–56.

Munro, M., 1991, Housing and labour market mobility, paper presented at Housing Studies Association Conference, University of York (April).

Newton, M.P., Jeffery, J.R., 1951, Internal migration: some aspects of population movements within England and Wales, *SMPS No. 5*, HMSO, London.

Ogilvy, A.A., 1979, Migration – the influence of economic change, *Futures*, 11, 5, 383–94.

Ogilvy, A.A., 1980, Inter-regional migration since 1971: an appraisal of data from the National Health Service Central Register and Labour Force Surveys, *OPCS Occasional Paper 16*, OPCS, London.

Ogilvy, A.A., 1982, Population movements between the regions of Great Britain, *Regional Studies*, 16, 1, 65–73.

OPCS, 1981, *General household survey 1980*, HMSO, London.

OPCS, 1983a, *Census 1981, regional migration: Wales, Part 1* (100% tables), CEN81 RM9, HMSO, London.

OPCS, 1983b, *Census 1981, regional migration: East Midlands, Part 1* (100% tables), HMSO, London.

OPCS, 1984, Final mid-1981 and revised mid-1971 to mid-1980 population estimates for the local government and health authority areas of England and Wales, *OPCS Monitor*, PP1 84/2.

OPCS, 1988a, *Census 1971–1981 the Longitudinal Study linked census data, England and Wales*, CEN81 LS, HMSO, London.

OPCS, 1988b, *International migration, MN15*, HMSO, London.

OPCS, 1988c, *Labour force survey 1987*, HMSO, London.

OPCS, 1989, *Labour force survey 1987*, HMSO, London.

OPCS and GRO(S), 1990, *Census 1991, user consultation, topic statistics (including special migration and special workplace statistics), outline proposals*, Paper TS1, OPCS, London.

OPCS, 1990a, Population estimates for districts and health authorities (areas, England), *OPCS Monitor PP3/*, OPCS, London.

OPCS, 1990b, *General household survey, 1989*, HMSO, London.

OPCS, 1990c, *Population Trends*, 62, HMSO, London.

OPCS, 1990d, *Key population and vital statistics: local and health authority areas, England and Wales, 1988*, Series VS no. 15, PP1 no. 11, HMSO, London.

OPCS, 1990e, Mid-1989 population estimates for England and Wales, *OPCS Monitor*, PP1 90/1.

OPCS, SSRU, 1990, Using the LS for work on migration, *Longitudinal Study Newsletter*, 3, 3–6.

Openshaw, S., Charlton, M., Brunsden, C., Coombes, M., 1988, Modelling the North–South divide, *North East RRL Research Report 88/8*, CURDS, University of Newcastle-upon-Tyne, Newcastle.

Owen, D.W., Green, A.E., 1989, Spatial aspects of labour mobility in the 1980s, *Geoforum*, 20, 107–26.

Owen, D., Green, A., 1990, Migration differentials, *Working Paper D2*, IBG/Rowntree/ESRC Limited Life Working Party on Internal Migration in Britain.

Owen, D.W., Green, A.E., 1992, Migration patterns and trends, chapter 2 in Champion, A.G., Fielding, A. (eds), *Migration processes and patterns: Volume I: Research progress and prospects*, Belhaven, London.

Patten, J., 1973, Rural-urban migration in pre-industrial England, *School of Geography Research Paper 6*, University of Oxford.

Perry, R., Dean, K., Brown, B., 1986, *Counterurbanisation*, Geo Books, Norwich.

Peter, L.J., 1985, *Why things go wrong, or, the Peter principle revisited*, Allen and Unwin, London.

Philip G., Taylor, P., Hutton, A., 1982., Oil-related construction workers: travelling and migration, in Jones, H. (ed.), *Recent migration in northern Scotland*, SSRC North Sea Oil Panel Occasional Paper 13, Redhill, pp. 27–60.

Pissarides, C.A., Wadsworth, J., 1987, Unemployment and the inter-regional mobility of labour, *Discussion Paper 296*, Centre for Labour Economics, London School of Economics.

Pocock, D.S.D., 1966, The migration of Scottish labour to Corby new town, *Scottish Geographical Magazine*, 76, 169–71.

Population Statistics Division, OPCS, 1987, Migration in 1987, *Population Trends*, 54, 32–9.

Rees, G., Rees, P.H., 1990, Projection methods, Section N in the Programmer's documentation for SWIS: the Swansea ward population projection and information system, GMAP Ltd, University of Leeds, Leeds.

Rees, P.H., 1977, The measurement of migration from census and other sources, *Environment and Planning A*, 9, 65–73.

Rees, P.H., 1985, Does it really matter which migration data you use in a population model?, chapter 5 in White, P., Van der Knapp, B. (eds), *Contemporary studies in migration*, Geo Books, Norwich.

Rees, P.H., 1987, How many old people will there be in the United Kingdom and where will they live?, *Espace Populations Sociétés*, 1987/1, 57–72.

Rees, P.H., 1989a, Research policy and review 30. How to add value to migration data from the 1991 Census, *Environment and Planning A*, 21, 1363–79.

Rees, P.H., 1989b, *Britain's population: a geographical analysis*, draft of unpublished book.

Rees, P.H., Stillwell, J.C.H., 1984, A framework for modelling population change and migration in the UK, in Boyce, A.J. (ed.), *Migration and mobility: biosocial aspects of human movement*, Taylor and Francis, London, pp. 317–53.

Rees, P.H., Stillwell, J.C.H., 1990, The United Kingdom, chapter 20 in Nam, C.B., Serow, W.J., Sly, D.F. (eds), *International handbook on internal migration*, Greenwood Press, London, pp. 371–89.

Rees, P.H., and Warnes, A.M., 1988, Migration of the elderly in the United Kingdom, in Rogers, A., Serow, W. (eds), *Elderly migration: an international comparative study*, Institute of Behavioral Science, University of Colorado, Boulder.

Rich, D.C., 1980, *Potential models in human geography*, CATMOG 26, Geo Books, Norwich.

Robinson, V., 1986, *Transients, settlers and refugees: Asians in Britain*, Clarendon Press, Oxford.

Robinson, V., 1988, The new Indian middle class in Britain, *Ethnic and Racial Studies*, 4, 456–73.

Robinson, V., 1989a, Economic restructuring, the urban crisis and Britain's black population, in Herbert, D., Smith, D. (eds), *Social problems and the city*, Oxford University Press, Oxford.

Robinson, V., 1989b, Changing stereotypes of Indians in Britain, *Indo-British Review*, 16, 79–97.

Robinson, V., 1990a, Roots to mobility: the social mobility of Britain's black population, 1971–87, *Ethnic and Racial Studies*, 13, 274–86.

Robinson, V., 1990b, Boom and gloom: the success and failure of Britain's South Asians, in Clarke, C., et al. (eds), *South Asian communities overseas*, Cambridge University Press, Cambridge.

Robinson, V., 1992, Not a lot of people know that: research into the internal migration of Britain's ethnic population, in Champion, A.G., Fielding, A.J. (eds), *Migration processes and patterns: Volume I: Research progress and prospects*, Belhaven, London.

Roe, N., 1989, Latest battle in Wales's war, *The Independent* (10 April).

Rogers, A., 1989, The elderly mobility transition: growth, concentration and tempo, *Research on Ageing*, 11, 1, 3–32.

Rogers, A., 1990a, Requiem for the net migrant, *Geographical Analysis*, 22, 4, 283–300.

Rogers, A., 1990b, Return migration to region of birth among retirement age persons in the United States, *Journal of Gerontology*, 45, 3, 128–34.

Rogers, A., Belanger, A., 1990, The importance of place of birth in migration and population redistribution analysis, *Environment and Planning A*, 22, 193–210.

Rogers, A., Castro, L.J., 1981, Model migration schedules, *RR-81-30*, International Institute of Applied Systems Analysis, Laxenburg.

Rogers, A., Castro, L.J., 1986, Migration, chapter 5 in Rogers, A., Willekens, F.J. (eds), *Migration and settlement – a multi-regional comparative study*, Reidel, Dordrecht, pp. 157–208.

Rogers, A., Planck, F., 1984, MODEL: a general program for estimating parameterized model schedules of fertility, mortality, migration and marital status and labour force status transitions, *Working Paper 83–102*, International Institute of Applied Systems Analysis, Laxenburg.

Rogers, A., Raquillet, R., Castro, L., 1978, Model migration schedules and their applications, *Environment and Planning A*, 10, 475–502.

Rogers, A., Serow, W. (eds), 1988, *Elderly migration: an international comparative study*, Institute of Behavioral Science, University of Colorado, Boulder.

Rogers, A., Watkins, J.F., 1987, General versus elderly interstate migration and population redistribution in the United States, *Research on Ageing*, 9, 4, 483–529.

Rowntree, J.A., 1957, Internal migration: a study of the frequency of the movement of migrants, *SMPS No. 11*, HMSO, London.

Rowntree, J.A., 1990, Population estimates and projections, *Population Trends*, 60, 33–4.

Salt, J., 1988, Highly-skilled international migrants, careers and internal labour markets, *Geoforum*, 19, 387–399.

Salt, J., 1990, Organisational labour migration: theory and practice in the United Kingdom, in Johnson, J.H. Salt, J. (eds), *Labour migration*, David Fulton, London.

Salt, J., Flowerdew, R., 1980, Labour migration from London, *The London Journal*, 6, 36–50.

Salt, J., Kitching, R., 1990, Foreign workers and the UK labour market, *Employment Gazette*, 98, 538–46.

Savage, M., 1988, The missing link: the relationship between social and geographical mobility, *British Journal of Sociology*, 39, 4, 554–77.

Scholten, H.J., van der Velde, R., 1989, Internal migration: the Netherlands, chapter 4.2 in Stillwell, J.C.H., Scholten, H.J. (eds), *Contemporary research in population geography – a comparison of the United Kingdom and the Netherlands*, Kluwer, Dordrecht, pp. 75–86.

Scottish Economic Planning Board, 1970, *Migration to and from Scotland*, Edinburgh.

Scottish Office (1989), *Scottish Abstract of Statistics*, HMSO, Edinburgh.

Scottish Office Regional Development Division, 1969, *North east Scotland a survey of its development potential*, HMSO, Edinburgh.

Silvers, A.L., 1977, Probabilistic income maximising behaviour in regional migration, *International Regional Science Review*, 2, 29–40.

Simpson, D., 1988, How blue is my valley, *The Observer* (10 April).

Sjaastad, L.A. 1962, The costs and returns of human migration, *The Journal of Political Economy*, 70, 80–93.

Stewart, J.Q., 1947, Empirical mathematical rules concerning the distribution and equilibrium of population, *Geographical Review*, 37, 461–85.

Stillwell, J.C.H., 1984, IMP: a program for inter-area migration analysis and projection: user's manual (revised), *Computer Manual 12*, School of Geography, University of Leeds, Leeds.

Stillwell, J.C.H., 1985, Migration between metropolitan and non-metropolitan regions in the UK, chapter 2 in White, P.E., van der Knaap, B. (eds), *Contemporary studies in migration*, Geo Books, Norwich, pp. 7–25.

Stillwell, J.C.H., 1990a, Migration analysis based on National Health Service Central Register data: trends and models, *Working Paper 537*, School of Geography, University of Leeds, Leeds.

Stillwell, J.C.H., 1990b, Yorkshire and Humberside net migration turns positive, *The Regional Review*, 1, 0, 4.

Stillwell, J.C.H., and Boden, P., 1986, Internal migration in the United Kingdom: characteristics and trends, *Working Paper 470*, School of Geography, University of Leeds, Leeds.

Stillwell, J.C.H., Boden, P., 1989, Internal migration: the United Kingdom, chapter 4.1 in Stillwell, J.C.H., Scholten, H.J. (eds), *Contemporary research in population geography – a comparison of the United Kingdom and the Netherlands*, Kluwer, Dordrecht, pp. 64–75.

Stillwell, J.C.H., Boden, P., Rees, P.H., 1987, Migration schedule construction using MODEL and GIMMS, *Computer Manual 29*, School of Geography, University of Leeds, Leeds.

Stillwell, J., Boden, P., Rees, P., 1988, Internal migration change in the UK: trends based on NHSCR movement data, 1975–76 and 1985–86, *Working*

Paper 510, School of Geography, University of Leeds, Leeds.

Stillwell, J.C.H., Boden, P., Rees, P.H., 1990, Trends in internal net migration in the UK: 1975 to 1986, *Area*, 22, 1, 57–65.

Stillwell, J., Rees, P.H., Boden, P., 1991, Geographical patterns of migration, paper presented at the Annual Conference of the Institute of British Geographers, Sheffield (2–5 January).

Stuart, A., 1987, Migration and population turnover in a London borough: the incidence and implications of retirement out-migration, *Espace Populations Sociétés*, 1987/1, 137–51.

Sutcliffe, A., Smith, R., 1974, *Birmingham 1939–1970*, History of Birmingham 3, Oxford University Press, London.

Svanborg, A., 1988, The health of the elderly population: results from longitudinal studies with age-cohort comparisons, in Evered, D., Whelan J. (eds), *Research and the ageing population*, Ciba Foundation Symposium 134, Wiley, Chichester, pp. 3–16.

Taylor, J., 1990, Regional economic disparities: causes and consequences, *Discussion Paper EC1/90*, The Management School, Lancaster University, Lancaster.

Thomas, R., Elias, P., 1989, The development of the Standard Occupational Classification, *Population Trends*, 53, 16–21.

Townsend, A.R., Blakemore, M.J., Nelson, R., 1987, The NOMIS data base: availability and uses for geographers, *Area*, 19, 1, 43–50.

Uhlenberg, P., 1988, Ageing and the societal significance of cohorts, in Birren, J.E., Bengston, V.L. (eds), *Emergent theories of ageing*, Springer, New York, pp. 405–25.

Ullman, E.L., 1956, The role of transportation and the bases for interaction, in Thomas, W.L. (ed.), *Man's role in changing the face of the earth*, University of Chicago Press, Chicago, pp. 862–80.

Warnes, A.M., 1987, The ageing of housing schemes and their residents, *Age Concern Institute of Gerontology Working Paper 3*, King's College London.

Warnes, A.M., 1988, Areally defined and special elderly populations: projection methods and outputs, in Diamond, I. (ed.), *Local area demography in business and government*, Proceedings, British Society of Population Studies 1988 Annual Conference, Southampton, pp. 178–93.

Warnes, A.M., 1989, The ageing of populations, in Warnes, A.M. (ed.), *Human ageing and later life*, Arnold, London, pp. 47–66.

Warnes, A.M., 1992a, Migration and the life course, in Champion, A.G., Fielding, A.J. (eds), *Migration processes and patterns: Volume 1: Research progress and prospects*, Belhaven, London.

Warnes, A.M., 1992b, Elderly people driving cars: issues and prospects, in Morgan, J. (ed.), *Gerontology: responding to an ageing society*, Jessica Kingsley, London.

Warnes, A.M., Condon, S., 1990, Residential strategies for retirement among Londoners, paper presented to the CILOG Conference on Housing and Planning, Paris (July).

Warnes, A.M., Vergoossen, W.T.H., 1989, Mobility of the elderly in the Netherlands and Great Britain, in Stillwell, J.C.H., Scholten, H.J. (eds), *Contemporary research in population geography: a comparison of the Netherlands and the United Kingdom*, Kluwer, Dordrecht, pp. 129–46.

Watkins, J., 1989, Gender and race differentials in elderly migration, *Research on Ageing*, 11, 1, 33–52.

Weekley, I., 1988, Rural depopulation and counterurbanisation: a paradox, *Area*, 20, 3, 127–34.

Welsh Office, 1989, *1987 based population projections for the counties of Wales*, Welsh Office, Cardiff.

Welsh Office/Y Swydffa Gymreig, 1990, *Digest of Welsh statistics, No. 36*, HMSO, Cardiff.

White, P., 1990, Labour migration and counter-urbanisation in France, in Johnson, J.H., Salt, J. (eds), *Labour migration*, David Fulton, London.

Willekens, F., Baydar, N., 1986. Forecasting place-to-place migration with generalised linear models, chapter 9 in Woods, R., Rees, P.H. (eds), *Population structures and models*, Allen and Unwin, London, pp. 203–44.

Williams, G., 1990, *The experience of housing in retirement*, Avebury, Aldershot.

Willis, S.L., 1989, Cohort differences in cognitive ageing, in Schaie, K.W., Schooler, C. (eds), *Social Structure and ageing*, Erlbaum, Hillsdale, NJ, pp. 95–112.

Wilson, A.G., 1974, *Urban and regional models in geography and planning*, Wiley, London.

Index